Evidence and the Adversarial Process

The Modern Law

SECOND EDITION

Jenny McEwan

Professor of Law, Keele University

·HART·
PUBLISHING

HART PUBLISHING – OXFORD
1998

Hart Publishing
Oxford
UK

Distributed in the United States by
Northwestern University Press
625 Colfax
Evanston
Illinois
60208-4210 USA

Distributed in Australia and New Zealand by
Federation Press Pty Ltd
PO Box 45
Annandale, NSW 2038
Australia

Distributed in Netherlands, Belgium and Luxembourg by
Intersentia, Churchillaan 108
B2900 Schoten
Antwerpen
Belgium

Hart Publishing is a specialist legal publisher based in Oxford, England. To order further
copies of this book or to request a list of other publications please write to:

Hart Publishing, 19 Whitehouse Road, Oxford, OX1 4PA
Telephone: +44 (0)1865 434459 Fax: +44 (0) 1865 794882
email: hartpub@janep.demon.co.uk

British Library Cataloguing in Publication Data
Data Available

ISBN 1-901362-18-3

Typeset in Minion
by John Saunders Design & Production, Reading
Printed in Great Britain on acid-free paper
by Biddles Ltd, Guildford and King's Lynn

To John

Preface

Many students of evidence find it hard to see any system or coherence in the mass of apparently arbitrary and inconsistent rules. In this second edition of *Evidence and the Adversarial Process* I have included more explanatory material than in the first, for the benefit of readers unfamiliar with the exclusionary rules of evidence. But the book remains an attempt to show that the rules are to some extent a natural development of the trial procedures adopted in this country and exported to the United States and the Commonwealth. If those trial procedures should be at a critical evolutionary stage at this moment, and be found to be moving further away from the adversarial paradigm, as argued here, there is a pressing need to re-examine the necessity of retaining those rules. This, then, is an appropriate time to evaluate and examine critically the nature of our laws of evidence, asking why such laws, which frequently operate to exclude probative information, must exist. Also, if we must have rules of evidence, are those operated in the Anglo-American[1] systems of trial rules which rational persons would adopt as the best possible means to achieve justice?

It will be argued that many of these rules evolved to strike a balance between competing private interests which characterise the adversarial system of trial. There are, admittedly, other factors which have contributed to the content of the law of evidence, for example, the function of the jury and the traditional emphasis upon the taking of evidence on oath. But it is adversarial systems which develop laws of evidence, those familiar and intricate mazes upon which books are written and students sit examinations. The complexity of the law can lead to injustice, in that mistakes during trials can lead to "technical" appeals; we find that reliable and relevant evidence may be excluded. The complicated mysteries of this area of law may be a source of fascination or dread, according to one's lights. The Gothic structure of often eccentric or obscure prohibitions, each with its accompanying set of exceptions, its rigid dichotomies between issue, fact, credibility, guilt, weight, may have for some a quaint charm of its own. Whether or not these devices have much to do with the discovery of the truth is another matter. And the way in which lay participants in criminal cases are treated gives little cause for pride.

---

[1] Many Commonwealth countries still retain exclusionary rules of evidence very close to the English ones; the United States and surprisingly, Scotland, have not departed significantly from the traditional common law structure.

Contents

Table of Cases

Table of Legislation

1

The Adversarial Trial

Some in their Discourse, desire rather than commendation of
Wit, being able to hold all Arguments, than of Judgement in
discerning what is true.

"Of discourse", *Essays*, 32. *Bacon*

The Adversarial Tradition

"A litigation is in essence a trial of skill between opposing parties, conducted
under recognized rules, and the prize is the judge's decision. We have rejected
inquisitorial methods and prefer to regard our judges as entirely independent."[1]

The traditional distinctions drawn between adversarial and traditional
procedures of trial are frequently described as trite, simplistic, or as a cliché.
Certainly it is difficult to find any legal system which adheres strictly to all
the features of the classic models. The English legal system[2], often regarded
as the paradigm of the adversarial tradition, is not a perfect example by any
means; on close examination it is found even in criminal courts to allow
deviations from the proper adversarial structure, more significantly in recent
times. And some tribunals dealing with some kinds of case have very little in
common with it at all.[3]

Damaska, in a highly-regarded critique, defined the adversarial trial as
follows; the proceedings should be structured as a dispute between two sides
in a position of theoretical equality before a court which must decide the
outcome of the contest. The model depends upon the parties to establish the
existence of a contest and to delineate its borders through pleadings and
stipulations drafted by them. Evidence is adduced by the parties and is exclusive to the party bringing it. The balance of advantages depends on the
parties' own use of informational sources.[4] The adjudicator is an umpire

---

[1] *Thomson* v. *Glasgow Corporation*, 1961 SLT 237, *per* Lord Justice-Clerk Thompson at 246.

[2] Although I refer throughout to "England" and the English legal system, I am referring to the
system that operates in England and Wales unless the context clearly suggests otherwise. The systems
in Scotland and Ireland differ, although they are heavily based on the adversarial model.

[3] See text to nn. 159–175 below, e.g. family cases such as wardship, coroners' inquiries, etc.

[4] M.R. Damaska, "Evidentiary Barriers to Conviction and Two Models of Criminal Procedure: A
Comparative Study" (1973) 121 *U Penn. LR* 506.

whose role is to ensure that the parties abide by the rules, but is passive even in that regard; he intervenes only if there is an objection from one side against the conduct of the other. On this analysis, the procedures themselves are merely a facility provided by the state for persons in dispute. Only the parties themselves have any interest in the initiation of proceedings, in their subject-matter or in the outcome.

The Anglo-American criminal trial is not a pure example of this form since the state *is* interested in the bringing of proceedings[5] and in the outcome. The person aggrieved by a crime has no direct interest in such proceedings, nor in the outcome, apart from the possibility of compensation (more effectively dealt with by bringing civil proceedings in many cases). He or she certainly has no control over the conduct of the case for the prosecution.[6] Clearly the criminal justice system is in place today not to right private wrongs, but to protect the public as a whole. Yet many features of the adversarial model are retained. Acknowledged departures include the provision of information by the prosecution to the defence.[7] The key characteristics which remain are sufficient to make the Anglo-American criminal trial the most adversarial of all judicial proceedings:

1. The role of the judge as umpire. Not only must judges be impartial, but they are not involved with the preparation of the case or the content of the evidence. The verdict is not their concern as long as the trial is conducted fairly. They are there to keep the parties to the rules. Although Damaska points out that in the pure model it is for each party to object to the manner in which the other side conducts its case, it is not clear that in reality judges regard themselves as so constrained. For example, it has been said by distinguished judges that pressure for legal representation for rape complainants would not exist if trial judges (not prosecution counsel) did their jobs properly.[8] Also, many lawyers' experience is that unrepresented defendants will receive a great deal of assistance from trial judges, even though one view would be that if they have chosen not to avail themselves of the services of a lawyer, they should be assumed to be willing to accept full responsibility themselves. The theoretically limited judicial role reflects historical "distrust of public officials and the complementary demand for safeguards against abuse".[9] Damaska argues that, in

---

[5] Although, incredibly, England introduced a public prosecutions system only as recently as 1985, when the Prosecution of Offences Act set up the Crown Prosecution Service.

[6] This was the case in England even before the Crown Prosecution Service was set up, since the state, through the police service, was making the initial decision and footing the bill.

[7] See the text to nn. 90–114 below. Even the right of the parties to determine the issues in the case has to be controlled to prevent abuse: A. Zuckerman, *The Principles of Criminal Evidence* (Oxford University Press, Oxford, 1989), 15.

[8] Lords Hailsham and Morris, HL, Deb. vol. 375, col. 1773, 1785 (22 Oct. 1976).

[9] Damaska, n. 4 above, 583. However, the non-interventionist judge may be a myth See below, Ch. 3

England, we are prepared to tolerate the evidentiary barriers accompanying this model for fear of the greater horror of the abuse of power.

2. Judgment by one's peers is not an essential characteristic of adversarial trial,[10] but naturally emerges as a workable system. Rationally an independent, randomly-selected jury would be the choice of a society which was afraid of its own officials. Trial by magistrates is not quite so inevitable a development, nor is that of the civil trial becoming almost exclusively the domain of the judge as the trier of fact.[11]

3. The principle of orality is again, Damaska argues, not an essential of the adversarial model, but a natural consequence of the judges' umpireal role and the evidence-gathering functions of the parties. Each party will be anxious to attack the evidence of the other, and this is easier if the emphasis is on oral testimony.

4. The role of the advocate[12]—he must present the evidence in the manner most advantageous to his client: "an advocate, in the discharge of his duty, knows but one person in the world, and that person is his client",[13] although the modern view is that counsel is required to behave with "absolute probity".[14] Advocates have duties towards the court; they must not knowingly or recklessly mislead, and, in some cases, must reveal evidence in their possession even if unfavourable to their client,[15] but they have no duty to seek out unfavourable evidence. Some advocates have consequently become skilled at avoiding contact with evidence which they suspect could prejudice their client's interests. Since the judge is not entitled to demand that further evidence be produced, no participant in the courtroom process has an immediate obligation towards the truth. "The advocate in the trial . . . is not engaged much more than half the time—and then only coincidentally—in the search for truth".[16]

The essence of inquisitorial proceedings, on the other hand, is that the state *is* interested in the outcome and wishes an investigator to discover as many relevant facts as possible. Rather than a dispute, as such, there is an official inquiry triggered by the belief that a crime has been committed. Society has much less interest in the outcome of a civil dispute and therefore these proceedings remain inevitably party-dependent in terms of the gathering of

---

[10] *Ibid.* 564.

[11] Presumably, the risk of bias in the civil case is thought to be less probable.

[12] Usually cases are prepared by teams of lawyers rather than one. Solicitors and barristers have been grouped together for the purpose of the following discussion.

[13] Lord Brougham, quoted in J. Nightingale (ed.), *Trial of Queen Caroline*, (Robins, London, 1821). This seems to be construed by some barristers merely as an obligation to act in accordance with instructions from solicitors. In Baldwin's study, few prosecution counsel thought it appropriate to advise the Crown Prosecution Service to drop weak cases: J. Baldwin, "Understanding Judge Ordered and Directed Acquittals" [1997] *Crim. LR* 536.

[14] *Abse* v. *Smith* [1986] QB 536, 545, *per* Donaldson MR.

[15] See the text to nn. 121–122 below.

[16] M.E. Frankel, "The Search for Truth: An Umpireal View" (1975) 123 *U Penn. LR* 1031, 1035.

evidence. Although far from the pure inquisitorial model, Continental civil proceedings are closer than the English, in that judges are fully cognisant of the evidence from copious dossiers presented at the outset, and therefore their questioning of witnesses at the trial is designed to supplement or test what they have already read in the paperwork. The position of the parties is weaker in this model; they cannot limit the tribunal's field of inquiry through pleadings or by consent. The court itself will pursue facts, and avail itself of any sources, including the interrogation of the defendant. The increased importance of the judicial role correspondingly diminishes the power and function of the advocate.

Since one system has its fact-finder (jury, magistrate or trial judge) operating in a factual vacuum, and the other has the tribunal of fact prepared in advance with summarised records of all testimony taken during the preliminary investigation, evidential styles are inevitably distinct. In theory, the adversarial system gives the fact-finder the advantage of utter impartiality arising from ignorance of the case. Although it is not the responsibility of a party to present the tribunal with the *truth*, only with *his or her case*, it is argued that the vigorous pursuit of evidence to serve the same interests, when added to that of the opponent, is an effective means of discovering the truth, particularly since the tribunal witnesses the attack by each side upon the evidence of the other.

> "The English say that the best way of getting at the truth is to have each party dig for the facts that help it; between them they will bring all to light . . . Two prejudiced searchers starting from opposite ends of the field will between them be less likely to miss anything than the impartial searcher starting in the middle".[17]

The problem is that an interested party who has dug for, and discovered, relevant facts may not feel that it would help him or her to present them before the court. The other side, of course, is entitled to make the same discovery and produce those facts, but it may be that the facts advantage neither side. Thus a key witness may be omitted altogether from an adversarial trial if both sides fear what he or she might do to their case.[18] Supporters of this state of affairs argue that lawyers are not in a position to set themselves up as the ultimate arbiters of truth, and therefore should confine themselves to producing as effective a case as possible on behalf of the client. The client's interests would not be best served by finding his or her representatives turning judgmental, and there is a substantial risk that citizens would be actively prejudiced, if for example, a lawyer was sufficiently

---

[17] P. Devlin, *The Judge* (Oxford University Press, Oxford, 1979), 61.

[18] In a study carried out on behalf of the Royal Commission chaired by Lord Runciman, trial judges were aware that neither side had called a material witness in 19 % of cases: M. Zander and P. Henderson, *Crown Court Study*, Royal Commission on Criminal Justice Research Study 19 (HMSO, London, 1993).

convinced of his or her client's guilt to refuse to act on a plea of not guilty. It may well be that lawyers should not set themselves up as judge and jury when those bodies exist independently; but there seems to be no good reason that, if it appears to the independent tribunal of fact that a particular item of evidence should be produced in order to enlighten the court, the parties should be entitled to block it. That is, of course, unless the proceedings in court are seen only as an instrument for the parties to employ as they choose, rather than an important institution within society and an essential element in the enforcement and development of the law. This view of the adversarial mode of trial is to some extent tenable in the civil sphere, where the state is not directly interested in the outcome but provides the litigants with the necessary apparatus.[19] It may be that the underlying rationale of the adversarial trial is indeed an assumption that establishing the objective truth is not the purpose of the inquiry. Eggleston, for example, suggests that even when acting as the tribunal of fact, the judicial function is not to ascertain the truth in any real sense. The judge makes a decision that appears to be justifiable on the material presented in court.[20]

Jackson takes the plea of guilty as an example; "adversary procedure is not concerned with the truth of the material facts but only the truth of facts put in issue by the accused. As a result pleas of guilty, if considered voluntary, are not investigated".[21] Yet in criminal cases, the state is a party; the defendant is far less able to influence matters than the defendant in a civil case—a fact recognised in many ways by the rules of evidence. Witnesses for the prosecution are not in the position of the plaintiff; they may not choose whether or not to proceed, and they cannot select the charge. However, since the prosecution carries the burden of proof and the accused is presumed innocent until proved otherwise, they are "fair game" to the defence, and may emerge from court with their reputations in shreds or private lives the subject of public debate. Why should the court behave as if the "parties" are on equal terms and the state only an interested bystander, despite initiating, organising, and funding the criminal trial, and, where appropriate, exacting punishment upon the defendant?

The Alternative: The Inquisitorial Tradition

In contrast to the umpireal British judge, Continental judges are expected to arrive at the truth by their own exertions.[22] The Criminal Law Revision

---

[19] But this image of the civil case, born of the traditional common law actions, is no longer representative of every kind of civil case. There are cases involving individual welfare rights against the state, cases concerning the welfare of children, where the two-handed contest is not in fact involved, causing considerable problems to courts which have to proceed as if it were. See Ch. 7.

[20] R. Eggleston, *Evidence, Proof and Probability* (Weidenfeld and Nicolson, London, 1983), 32.

[21] J. Jackson, "Two Methods of Proof in Criminal Procedure" (1988) 51 *MLR* 249.

[22] G. Williams, *The Proof of Guilt* (Stevens, London, 1968), 28.

Committee seemed to regard as the hallmark of the inquisitorial system that there is full judicial investigation of the whole case, including that for the defence, before the trial.[23] In France this is done by the *juge d'instruction*, half magistrate, half policeman. He can demand that more evidence be produced; it is not within the power of the parties to prevent him from seeing it. It is his decision whether or not the case should proceed to full trial. At the trial, which is seen as an investigation rather than a dispute, the President questions the defendant and the other witnesses from the report he has been given. It has been argued that the preparatory stage is inquisitorial and the procedure at trial accusatorial,[24] but in any event the proceedings are very different from English trials, where, in theory, the judge has a passive role. In France, the President allows witnesses to tell their own story; the Code insists that they should not be interrupted.[25] Since all the evidence has been presented at the *instruction* stage, they have had time to prepare their stories. This they should relate in the most spontaneous way possible, without prompting, and free from objections to hearsay. Questions may then be put by the President, and the parties may then question only through him.[26] A formal, structured cross-examination by counsel for either side is therefore out of the question. "We are not unaware of the advantages of the English "cross-examination", but in our opinion it does not ensure free and frank testimony from the witness".[27] However, the questioning by the President can be fairly aggressive, and, in some cases, the defendant may appear to be receiving considerably harsher treatment than the other witnesses.

The role of counsel is necessarily very different in France, tending to concentrate on objecting to questions rather than devising lines of questioning, as in England. The more active the court itself, the less important the role of legal counsel The inactivity of the prosecutor, compared with the judge's interventionist role, may avoid jury hostility towards the prosecution case. But the unstructured process of taking evidence does not appeal to British advocates. A.C. Wright was appalled. He wrote of French trials[28]:

> "The art of cross-examination has but a spark of life . . . No one seems to know how to dissect a statement into its component parts, find out hidden contradic-

---

[23] *Evidence (General)*, Eleventh Report of the Criminal Law Revision Committee, Cmnd. 4991 (1972).

[24] R. Vouin, "The Protection of the Accused in French Criminal Procedure" (1956) 5 *ICLQ* 1 and 157 (two parts); doubted, C. van den Wyngaert, "Belgium", in van den Wyngaert (ed.), *Criminal Procedure Systems in the European Community* (Butterworths, London, 1993).

[25] A.C. Wright, "French Criminal Procedure" (1929) 45 *LQR* 98.

[26] Art. 319 of the Criminal Code provides that after a witness has given his spontaneous statement the accused or counsel may question him or her *par l'organe du président*.

[27] Vouin, n. 24 above, 168. See also Glanville Williams' description, n. 22 above, of French horror at the manner of cross-examination by the British at Nuremberg, where defendants were required to interpret and explain detailed items in documents selected from crateloads of papers.

[28] N. 25 above, 99.

tions, and cut through equivocations, generalizations or hearsay to the essence of facts within the witness's own knowledge. Nor does the national temperament seem to envisage counsel quietly pressing a point, asking for precise answers, demanding explanations or particulars—in short, testing his evidence.[29]

In contrast, Damaska refers to the "natural legato of testimony" in Continental proceedings, where a witness is questioned only at the conclusion of the uninterrupted account.[30]

Honoré[31] doubts whether any system, including the French criminal procedure, is a perfect example of the inquisitorial process. It may be that many of the identified shortcomings of that system result from its hybrid nature.[32] However, one marked contrast between the English system of trial and the French depends on the French view that documentary evidence is intrinsically more reliable than oral. Honoré quotes Dalloz, noting, "the primacy of written proof and the mistrust which is prima facie inspired by oral testimony". The reasoning is that oral evidence can be tailored to fit the witness's purpose at the trial, whereas what was said and done at the time is far more revealing.[33] The reliability of contemporary oral statements is taken to depend on their nature and circumstances.[34] Jury trial exists within some inquisitorial systems,[35] although Continental juries may be composed very differently from ours. Despite the apparent imperfections of the French version of jury trial, many French lawyers feel that considerable safeguards are provided at the *instruction* stage, not being of the view that "the guilt or innocence of the accused should be allowed finally to depend on what may seem to the French to be, and what in France might be, the extremely fortuitous outcome of that markedly gladiatorial, and in any event highly peculiar, enterprise which in England we call a trial"[36] The concentration in England

---

[29] One must wonder how many examples of such cross-examinations are found nowadays in our courts, and one has only to look at the cross-examination of the subnormal Derek Bentley in the 1950's to wonder whether the description given by A.C. Wright in the 1920's would have been somewhat romantic even then. See D. Yallop, *To Encourage the Others* (Corgi, London, 1990) and discussion of cross-examination below.

[30] M.R. Damaska, *Evidence Law Adrift* (Yale University Press, New Haven, Conn., London, 1997), 93.

[31] A. Honoré, "The Primacy of Oral Evidence" in C. Tapper (ed.), *Crime Proof and Punishment: Essays in Memory of Sir Rupert Cross* (Butterworths, London, 1981), 172; see also ch. 7.

[32] J.J. Hamson, "The Prosecution of the Accused—English and French Legal Methods" [1955] *Crim. LR* 272.

[33] Previous inconsistent statements in criminal trials, if admitted at all, are relevant only to credibility, and we shall see in Ch. 3, text to nn. 75–89, both the destructive effects of the blinkered opposition of the legal establishment in this country to reform of the hearsay rule and the doubtful methods of assessing the credibility of witnesses giving oral evidence.

[34] Honoré, n. 31 above 191.

[35] E.g., in France, Belgium and Portugal (van den Wyngaert (ed.), n. 24 above). The perception of jury trial as a beacon of democracy and freedom may account for the recent interest in introducing jury trial in countries such as Spain and Japan; see R. Munday, "Jury Trial Continental Style" (1993) 13 *LS* 202; also R. Munday, "What Do the French Think of Their Juries?' (1995) 15 *LS* 65.

[36] Hamson, n. 32 above, 280.

on the trial itself is regarded as an over-emphasis on the tip of the iceberg. In contrast, during *instruction*, questions may be asked and there may even be a confrontation between the victim and the accused, the outcome of which will be in the documentation available before the trial President. Clearly, such a system of justice is heavily dependent upon true impartiality from the officials able to influence it—here the investigating judge and the police. In 1988, the Italians responded to the perceived problems of corruption and intimidation of judges by introducing a much more adversarial system of criminal justice, allowing parties to control their cases.[37] Formerly, the secret, written pre-trial proceedings had meant that the trial itself was a mere verification of evidence obtained earlier. The *dossier* is no longer the basis of the trial, which now depends on witnesses giving oral evidence and being questioned by the parties. But the victims of crimes still have rights of partic</i>ipation at the trial and judges may call witnesses of their own choosing.[38] In France, political wrangling led the Socialist Government in 1992 to curtail the powers of the examining magistrate, giving the defence greater access to the *dossier* and more influence over the investigation. This was extremely unpopular with the *judges*, and was reversed by the new Government in 1993.[39] But justice will not be achieved in the adversarial model, given the enormous influence of the parties through their lawyers, without strictly ethical behaviour by those lawyers; Frankel has suggested that it works better in England, with a small and specialist Bar, than it does in the United States, where trials are four times as long.[40]

The emphasis in Anglo-American systems on the outcome of the "day in court" may seem curious to foreign observers; pre-trial inquiry allows more elements of evidence to be considered, and avoids the common catastrophe here of cases collapsing at trial because witnesses fail to "come up to proof"[41]:

> "Surprise is not felt to be a substantial danger. Accordingly the lawyer's initial preparation can be less than vigorous, and no pressure is created for out-of-court discovery. As the lawyer's out-of-court investigation is narrow in scope, and what is known to the lawyer is passed on to the court in detailed writings, there is little awkwardness in having the judge take over the chief burden of interrogating witnesses—especially so, as the judge need not conclude the matter in one session but can inform himself step by step over a period of time".[42]

---

[37] Code of Criminal Procedure 1988.

[38] P. Corso, "Italy" in van den Wyngaert (ed.), n. 24 above.

[39] H. Trouille, "A Look at French Criminal Procedure" [1994] *Crim. LR* 735.

[40] Frankel, n. 16 above, 1035

[41] In Baldwin's study, witnesses failed to attend court, or changed their minds about participating in the trial, or failed to come up to proof, or proved untrustworthy in the majority of cases where acquittal was ordered or directed by the judge (Baldwin, n. 13 above. About 56% of all Crown Court acquittals ordered or directed by trial judges, and outnumber jury acquittals: *Judicial Statistics: Annual Report* (HMSO, London, 1995), Cm 3290.

[42] A.T. Von Mehren and R. Schaefer, "Phases of German Civil Procedure" 71 *Harv. LR* 1193, 1471.

In the Netherlands, key witnesses, such as the complainant in a rape case, are questioned during the pre-trial phase by the examining magistrate in chambers. This phase can be lengthy and as hostile as adversarial cross-examination. Defence lawyers are present. Since the *dossier* evidence is admissible at the trial itself, there is no need for her to attend, and the trial is unlikely to last more than an hour and a half. A murder trial lasts, on average, about half a day.[43] The Scandinavian "mixed" version of trial has few rules of evidence; there is no hearsay rule. The parties produce their own evidence as in England, but the judge has a responsibility to see to it that the case is satisfactorily clarified, and may ask for supplementary evidence. The Codes of Procedure state that a witness shall have the opportunity to give a coherent account before more specific questions are asked.[44]

Reality of the Adversarial Trial

Scientific Inquiry or Theatrical Spectacle?

A dialectic system of proof, consisting of two sides conducting a dispute, could conceivably be an effective way of discovering the truth. But in the English system, the risk remains that the most effective advocate, rather than the truth, will win the day. Jackson[45] has argued that a more effective model would involve *more* dialectic, that is, more disclosure before trial, with defendants in criminal cases being asked to account for themselves early on. This would bring the English system closer to the Continental ones; in France, it is regarded as essential that defendants should be involved in the pre-trial inquiry.[46] It is seen as their right, rather than as an imposition. Both systems follow, inevitably, an inductive method of proof. The weakness of employing inductive reasoning is that there are other possible explanations

---

[43] M. Groenhijsen, "The Dutch Criminal Justice System in Comparative Perspective", Seminar, Thames Valley Police Headquarters, Apr. 1996.

[44] J. Andenaes "The Scandinavian Countries" in J.R. Spencer, G. Nicholson, R. Flin and R. Bull, (eds.) *Children's Evidence in Legal Proceedings*, (Faculty of Law, University of Cambridge, Cambridge, 1990).

[45] N. 21 above.

[46] But not in Belgium, where the defendant does not become a party until the trial stage, and therefore may not consult the *dossier*, nor be present at the interrogation of witnesses: van den Wyngaert, n. 24 above. Even in France, it seems that defendants may encounter obstacles in gaining access to the *dossier*. Trouille, although examining magistrates claim that they always co-operate, L.H. Leigh and L. Zedner, *A Report on the Administration of Criminal Justice in the Pre-Trial Phase in France and Germany*, Royal Commission Research Study No 1 (HMSO, London, 1992).

of events than the one selected by the trial process. Yet no alternative appears to be available, as syllogistic reasoning depends on the correctness of those initial premises which logically proceed to the conclusion. Jackson argues that all systems of proof are based on classic scientific method, but the French particularly so. After the French Revolution the increased powers of examining magistrates allowed them to collect what evidence they could, and to evaluate it according to their experience. The Anglo-American procedure is more schizophrenic. There is in England a movement towards greater disclosure of information by both sides in criminal cases, but it is a matter of great controversy, as will be seen below.[47] The reforms proposed for civil proceedings in the Woolf Report,[48] which would make them less adversarial and more "managed" by trial judges, are also the subject of heated debate.[49] The exclusionary rules of evidence sometimes embody and sometimes reject scientific principles. For, even if the hearsay rule can be regarded as designed to exclude evidence which cannot properly be tested for reliability, other rules acknowledged to prevent the admission of evidence which is relevant but excessively prejudicial[50] limit the amount of valuable information available to the court, detracting from the principle of completeness. Also, the parties control what facts are to be determined.

Bennett and Feldman[51] point out that the jury is not presented with a scientifically organised collection of facts to each of which it can attach statistical links to various variables and possibilities directing the proper verdict. Instead, an incoherent mass of data must be organised by the jurors themselves into a story which they can understand, and the cognitive techniques they employ are those they would use in reading a detective story or watching a thriller—identifying the central action and relating other evidence to it. For individual witnesses can testify only to matters of which they have direct knowledge, and therefore can rarely describe the event(s) in issue from start to finish. Thus, the more complex the facts in the case, the more organisational work the jury have to do. The passivity of the jury as fact-finders within an adversarial stucture is seen as a weakness by Damaska. Being excluded from the questioning process is unnatural: "would any professional judge want to decide a case without being able to question witnesses"?[52]

---

[47] Ch. 8.

[48] *Access to Justice: final report by Lord Woolf MR, to the Lord Chancellor on the civil justice system in England and Wales* (HMSO, London, 1996) 12.59.

[49] Ch. 8.

[50] E.g., similar fact evidence: see ch. 2.

[51] W.L. Bennett and M. Feldman, *Reconstructing Reality in the Courtroom* (Tavistock, London, 1981).

[52] Damaska, n. 30 above, 96.

Advocates in adversarial trials, unless the witness is given the right to speak uninterrupted, as in the Scandinavian "mixed" system, not only control what the issues are to be and which witnesses and other evidence are to be produced, but also limit what is said by those witnesses, over whom they have strict editorial control. Thus the material available to the tribunal of fact is selected by the advocates, who can then in court control the narration. Witnesses are not entitled to add material which has not been asked for to their account, and so counsel can manipulate them to obtain the (for counsel) most favourable or least damaging version of the facts. The authors observe that a common tactic is to ask questions that require precise and concrete answers; this produces the account that fits counsel's version best.[53] Once the narrow version has been achieved, counsel will interrupt the witness with another question, to prevent any damaging elaboration or explanation. Expert witnesses are regarded in the United States as being especially good at playing this game with counsel and are frequently hired for that particular skill.[54] Both sides, therefore, may miss or choose to ignore a potentially important aspect of the incident in question, leading Bennett and Feldman to conclude that trials probably are little more than highly stylised dramatisations of reality. Clearly, some theatrical gestures by advocates and even some brilliant lines of questioning have little to do with the development of a coherent story. The authors describe some fairly indefensible practices in the Washington court they studied; the use of objections to make the jury think the evidence must be suspect in some way; "fishing" cross-examinations to make witnesses explain how they know what they know, hoping something might emerge which will discredit the witness. Techniques to make fools of the jury are described, and the authors quote instances of lawyers' admiration for "gladiator-style" advocates. There is no reason for this country to feel superior; all young lawyers are brought up on tales of Marshall Hall and his tricks. There seems to be a large measure of agreement that lawyers are there to present highly selective versions of the case.[55]

The theatricality of the British criminal trial might be regarded as one of its most attractive features by those who do not find themselves unwilling participants in it. The traditional dress of the advocates is designed to impress witnesses with the solemnity of the occasion on the assumption that they are more likely to be truthful in such a setting. There is, however, no evidence that different settings affect the reliability of witnesses,[56] and from a lay point of view it might be difficult to see how witnesses can do themselves justice if utterly intimidated. They are required to stand in a special witness-box and asked to speak up so that the jury can hear them.

[53] Defended by M. Stone, *Proof of Fact in Criminal Trials* (W. Green and Sons, Edinburgh, 1984).

[54] Bennett and Feldman, n. 51 above, 124.

[55] M.J. Saks and R. Hastie, *Social Psychology in Court* (Van Nostrand, Reinhold, New York, 1978).

[56] K.H. Marquis, "Testamentary Validity as a Function of Form, Atmosphere and Item Difficulty", (1972) 2 *Journal of Applied Social Psychology* 167. See also Saks and Hastie, n. 55 above.

The accused is placed dramatically in a separate cage, the dock, whereas in some jurisdictions, such as Sweden, the defendant sits at a desk. The ordeal of particularly vulnerable witnesses is discussed in Chapter 4, but the experience is harrowing for most. Even practised expert witnesses find the ability of counsel to control, interrupt and ridicule their testimony difficult to handle. Experience gained over some years of court appearances does not make it significantly easier, since the basically subordinate position of witnesses is constant. The lack of courtesy and, in some cases, the bitter attacks on distinguished experts may make them reluctant to participate in the trial process at all.[57] Even Sheriff Stone, a well-known defender of the adversarial trial, concedes that expert witnesses can be shoddily treated.[58]

Impartial Umpire?

The passive, disinterested role of the judge in the trial process is a sine qua non of the adversarial theory. Yet it is doubtful that this is a reality. In the civil case and the magistrates' courts we find this "umpire" entering the arena as the trier of fact. This causes obvious problems when issues of the admissibility of evidence are discussed, since, if evidence is excluded, it must be disregarded. It is frequently difficult for an adjudication on admissibility to proceed without the nature of the disputed evidence becoming obvious. These problems are especially acute in the magistrates' courts, where a *voir dire* has to be held in certain circumstances, for instance, where the admissibility of a confession is challenged.[59] Prosecutors are still struggling to devise a system where this procedure can meaningfully be employed. It is not appropriate for magistrates who feel that they would be unduly prejudiced by having heard the disputed evidence to dismiss themselves from the case and refer the matter to another Bench. A later Bench would not be bound by the earlier adjudication on admissibility, and so the matter would have to be dealt with all over again. It is ironic, in view of the fact that magistrates are presumed capable of trying the case having dismissed the excluded evidence from their minds, that the professional judges who sit without jury in the "Diplock Courts" of Northern Ireland,[60] and similarly have to decide questions of both law and fact, may withdraw from the case if they feel that having rejected evidence but heard it makes the preservation of neutrality impossible. The decision on admissibility does bind the judge who subsequently deals with the case.[61]

[57] See Ch. 4.

[58] N. 53 above, 273.

[59] *R. v. Liverpool Juvenile Court, ex p. R* [1987] Crim. LR 572,. In a *voir dire*, or "trial within a trial" in the Crown Court, the jury are asked to leave and therefore do not hear the disputed evidence.

[60] Introduced in 1973. See J. Jackson and S. Doran, *Judge Without Jury: Diplock Trials and the Adversary System* (Clarendon, Oxford, 1995).

[61] Northern Ireland (Emergency Provisions) Act 1991, s. 11(2)(iii).

The passive umpire is a creature of theory rather than practice, although American judges appear to be closer to the ideal than their English counterparts, in that they interrupt less. Here, in the average criminal trial you will be interrupted far more often by the judge than by your opponent:

> "It has become the rule, now, for the English judge to come down into the arena and to take part to quite a surprising degree. The licence that he thinks entitles him to do this is to be found in the principle that all evidence should be relevant, and it is now the rule rather than the exception to hear judges breaking in on counsel with the question, 'What is the relevance of that?'"[62]

Judges may thus protect witnesses against some of the worst abuses of cross-examination discussed above, and are often especially sympathetic with expert witnesses. But Evans points out that explaining in advance the relevance of questions put in cross-examination gives witnesses early warning that may defeat the object. He also accuses judges of pro-prosecution bias to an extent that acting for the defence is like riding a bicycle uphill. The exclusive dominion of counsel over the evidence in the case means that any judge, who has no file of evidence, is completely in the dark, his or her interventions are frequently unhelpful[63] except insofar as he (quite properly) asks for clarification for the benefit of the jury. Judicial neutrality is the cornerstone of the adversarial system; without that, there seems to be little to be said for it.[64]

Examination and Cross-Examination

Strict rules govern the nature of the trial itself in terms both of the order of events and questions of admissibility. In a criminal trial, the prosecution must open its case and then call its witnesses. Each witness is taken through his evidence-in-chief, the purpose of which is to draw from him those facts which support the prosecution case. He may not be asked leading questions (suggesting the desired answer or putting contentious matters to him in a form requiring only the answer Yes or No). After the witness's examination-in-chief, the defence has the right to cross-examine all the witnesses for the prosecution and may in fact be obliged to do so given the nature of the defence case. For in any civil or criminal trial, any statement of fact made by a witness during his evidence-in-chief which is not contradicted through

---

[62] K. Evans, *Advocacy in Court: A Beginner's Guide* (Blackstone, London, 1995), 91; cf. Jackson and Doran, n. 60 above, Ch. 3.

[63] Frankel, n. 16 above, 1035, whose experience of the Bench leads him to conclude that the judges ought to have sight of the evidence before the trial begins, as a Continental judge would. He would also introduce an obligation on counsel to disclose adverse facts as well as law (see Disclosure, below). For the particular problems for the defence posed by judicial "clarification" interventions see Jackson and Doran, n. 60 above, and below, Ch. 3.

[64] For further discussion of the opportunity for trial judges to comment on matters such as the failure of the accused to give evidence and the strength of the case, see Chs. 3 and 5.

cross-examination is taken to be accepted. In *Bircham*,[65] it was in defence counsel's closing speech that he first suggested that the crime was committed by a prosecution witness and a co-defendant. He was stopped from doing this since neither allegation had been put during their cross-examinations.[66] The technique is called "putting your case"; it is regarded as unfair not to challenge a witness on his statement if it is to be contradicted later. Thus in many trials counsel is obliged to ask questions knowing that the witness will not be shaken, and mystifying the jury.

A complex statement from a witness containing numerous allegations all of which need to be challenged by the defence therefore requires an elaborate cross-examination dealing with each point. But, in any event, cross-examination is a necessary counterbalance to the way evidence in chief is elicited. Given the way witnesses are guided through their evidence in chief (albeit without leading questions as such) the right to cross-examine is essential to the other party. For the questions put in chief may omit, consciously or unconsciously, significant areas of fact which could be to the advantage of the other side. There may have been qualifications or explanations which the witness did not have the opportunity to add to his or her in chief testimony, and which subsequently can be uncovered only by cross-examination.

Cross-examination of witnesses is regarded by many Commonwealth lawyers as the perfect method of establishing the truth, hence the reluctance to abolish the hearsay rule. But it is frequently used to confuse witnesses, to get them to contradict themselves, showing their unreliability. Where there are many documents in a case, this is easily done, as the witness is taken through the papers and asked to explain entries in them about which he or she can remember nothing. It is clear from a growing body of research[67] that cross-examination of rape complainants is often used simply to humiliate them and therefore undermine the confidence with which they describe the alleged events. Yet the goodwill of witnesses is necessary for the protection of society. Fear of humiliation in cross-examination could affect their willingness to come forward or to report crimes. If a genuine victim suffers a stinging attack from the defence during a trial, it looks as if he or she is being punished for objecting to the crime, and that is surely not the object of the exercise. We have seen cases where, in the traditional obsessive pursuit of and concern for the interests of the client, valuable witnesses have been relentlessly grilled on matters which by no stretch of the imagination had any useful part to play in the proceedings.[68]

---

[65] [1972] Crim. LR 430.

[66] This rule does not, strictly, apply in the magistrates' court, *O'Connell* v. *Adams* [1973] Crim. LR 113, but its observance is regarded as good practice.

[67] See Ch. 4.

[68] E.g. *Hutchinson* (1985) 81 Cr. App. R 51. where the highly unconvincing defence of consent was run by a known Broadmoor escapee, who accused a journalist in court during the trial; consent was put at interminable length to the chief prosecution witness, who was required by the state to testify not only to her own rape, but to the murders of several of her family on the same occasion. And see below, Chs. 4 and 8.

In cross-examination, an advocate may ask leading or suggestive questions. The witness's credibility may be attacked on virtually any front.[69] Although many advocates appear not to have noticed, questions put in cross-examination should be as to fact. They should not invite the witness to explain the evidence of others, nor to enter into argument. The testimony of other witnesses should not be quoted to them.[70] The extensive use of leading questions in cross-examination is assumed by lawyers to provide them with a scalpel with which they can clinically and remorselessly lay bare the truth. Eggleston, however, is not convinced[71]; the assumption underlying lawyers' faith in cross-examination is that all honest witnesses are equally capable of holding their own against this barrage. But people are not uniformly articulate, confident and emotionally balanced. Defendants in criminal cases, however, are unlikely to score high in these departments:

"I have known a number of defendants who have really been quite psychologically disturbed and have been quite wrongly put into the witness box . . . against advice, and it has really been cutting up salami as far as the cross-examination is concerned and served up for the jury to eat. Sometimes, thankfully, juries, without any sort of caution, can see what is going on".[72]

Questions apparently designed to undermine a witness's credibility move so far from the matter to which he has deposed[73] that observers find the result highly inconclusive. McBarnett,[74] however, concedes that, given the nature of examination in chief, cross-examination is indispensable. This presents a major problem for the unrepresented defendant who has not the technique to do it.

Research by psychologists casts considerable doubt on the value of leading questions. Lawyers appear to regard it as significant if witnesses are led to contradict themselves, but work on suggestibility shows how ready witnesses are to adopt "planted" information contained in the question.[75] Yuille tested witnesses who already had an accurate memory of the event, and they were harder to mislead.[76] But if the questioner demonstrates an apparent level of knowledge, the suggestibility of the witness increases.[77] The language used by the questioner can be enough to affect the memory, as in Loftus and Palmer's

---

[69] Below, Ch. 3.

[70] *Baldwin* (1925) 18 Cr. App. R 175.

[71] R. Eggleston, "What is Wrong with the Adversarial System?" (1975) 49 *ALJ* 428.

[72] Dr Silverman, in discussion following G.H. Gudjonsson, "The Psychology of False Confessions" (1989) 57 *Medico-Legal Journal*, 93. See Right to Silence, Ch. 5.

[73] D. McBarnett, *Conviction* (Macmillan,. London, 1983).

[74] *Ibid.*

[75] E.F. Loftus, "Leading Questions and the Eyewitness Report", *Cognitive Psychology* , 7 (1975) 560.

[76] J.C. Yuille, "A Critical Examination of the Psychology and Practical Implications of Eyewitness Research", *Law and Human Behaviour*, 4 (1980), 335.

[77] V.L. Smith and P.C. Ellsworth, "The Social Psychology of Eyewitness Accuracy: Misleading Questions and Communicator Expertise", *Journal of Applied Psychology*, 72 (1987), 294.

famous question, "About how fast were the cars going when they smashed into/collided with/bumped into/hit each other?" The choice of verb had dramatic effect on the witness's estimation of the speed of cars in an accident he had been shown on film.[78] Gudjonsson's research into acquiescent, suggestible and compliant personalities' tendency to be misled by leading questions[79] suggests even more grounds for anxiety. The personality of the subject combined with the circumstance in which he is questioned dramatically affects suggestibility. People may not declare their actual uncertainty because they believe that they must provide an answer, or that it is expected of them that they know the answer and are capable of giving it.[80] Courts of law, by accident or design, are ideally suited to effect such an interpretation by a witness. It should be noted at this point that the doubts engendered by research into suggestibility have been carried over into the controversy surrounding techniques used in "disclosure" interviews with children suspected of having suffered abuse.[81] That anxiety should also affect the extent to which confession evidence can be considered to be reliable. In court, if, by use of suggestion, leading, hypothesis and demand for detail, counsel succeeds in shaking the confidence of a witness who consequently begins to look nervous and unsure, is this an indicator of unreliability? Köhnken,[82] who found lawyers just another group of people who overestimate their ability to recognise dishonesty, shows that skilful liars respond well to tough questions, indicative of suspicion. They are capable of adjusting their behaviour to conform to stereotypes of honesty, whereas an honest witness may, when nervous, appear decidedly unconvincing. Confident witnesses are more likely to be believed,[83] but research finds no consistent relationship between eyewitness confidence and accuracy.[84]

Damaska argues[85] that the Continental trial is more attuned to the fact that individuals have different cognitive needs. All lay assessors exercise the right to ask questions of their own, although not as frequently as one might expect.[86] Jurors in English criminal courts are extraordinarily passive, given

[78] E.F. Loftus and J.C. Palmer, "Reconstruction of Automobile Destruction: An Example of the Interaction Between Language and Memory", *Journal of Verbal Learning and Verbal Behaviour*, 17 (1974), 585.

[79] G.H. Gudjonnson and N.K. Clark, "Suggestibility in Police Interrogation; A Social Psychological Model", *Social Behaviour*, 1 (1986), 83; see Ch. 6.

[80] *Ibid.*, 92.

[81] See Ch. 4.

[82] "Psychological Approaches to the Assessment of the Credibility of Child Witness Statements" in Spencer, Nicholson, Flin and Bull (eds.), n. 44 above.

[83] K.A. Daffebaker and E.F. Loftus, "Do Jurors Share a Common Understanding Concerning Eyewitness Behaviour?" *Law and Human Behaviour*, 6 (1982) 15.

[84] A.D. Yarmey and H.P.T. Jones, "Is the Study of Eyewitness Identification a Matter of Common Sense?' in S. Lloyd-Bostock and B. Clifford (eds.), *Evaluating Witness Evidence*, (Wiley, Chichester, 1983).

[85] N. 4 above, 545.

[86] G. Casper and H. Zeisel, "Lay Judges in the German Courts" (1972) 1 JL *Stud.* 135.

the importance of their decisions. Although in theory jurors may ask questions of a witness, the system presents them with a variety of practical problems should they wish to do so. In the Crown Court study it was found that of the 44 per cent of jurors who would have liked to ask a question, only 18 per cent actually had.[87] Without the operation of the burden of proof, the task of adjudicating on the facts might be perplexing; if two versions of the story are presented, each in the most favourable light possible, it must be difficult to be sure that one of them is the accurate account (remembering that to lawyers, it may be that the object of the exercise is *not* to arrive at the truth, only to achieve a "just settlement of the dispute").[88] And, we shall see, the rules of evidence may be seen to suppose that the object of a criminal trial is not to ascertain the objectively accurate picture of the facts, but to adjudge how effectively or otherwise the prosecution has proved its case.[89]

Disclosure of Evidence

If the trial were an entirely adversarial proceeding, it would be the responsibility of the parties to furnish their own evidence in support of their case. Yet we find that in criminal cases defendants may expect help from the prosecution in supplying some information which otherwise they might find it difficult or impossible to uncover. There seems no reason in theory why one adversary should be required to do this; the principle that the prosecutor should supply information to the defence would appear to have more to do with obligation to the truth or with the presumption of innocence than with the idea of opponents researching for and adducing material for themselves. Merely exchanging details as to what evidence a party proposes to call is not, *prima facie*, inconsistent with the adversarial ideal. The task of investigation remains the party's own. But, as we shall see below, such a practice establishes a foundation for a shift towards more inquisitorial procedures involving less emphasis on oral evidence and argument. Emphasis on the trial itself is reduced; advance notice of the evidence to be presented by the other side, together with details of the legal basis of its case, enables each party to adjust his case in advance of the proceedings. This reduces the surprise element which can result in some unmeritorious triumphs.

At present, in the criminal case, the prosecution must supply witness statements in the committal bundle for offences triable either way or on indictment,[90] so that the accused will know precisely the nature of the case against him. This does not apply in summary cases, so the defence advocate has to

---

[87] Zander and Henderson, n. 18 above; cf. Jackson and Doran, n. 60 above.
[88] Damaska, n. 4 above, 580.
[89] See ch. 2.
[90] Magistrates' Courts (Advance Information) Rules 1985 (SI 1985 No. 601).

persuade a prosecutor who is unwilling to show him the statements.[91] Until very recently, the only defence duties to inform the prosecution were to give advance notice of any alibi witness to be called[92] and, like the prosecution, to give advance notice of any expert evidence to be relied upon in the Crown Court.[93] The presumption of innocence is thought to explain why for so long the defendant generally did not have to inform the prosecution of the nature of its case before the day of trial. But, as Jackson has shown,[94] there is nothing inconsistent with that presumption in providing parties with relevant information so that proceedings operate in a well-informed and scientific fashion.[95] Nor does it follow directly from the presumption of innocence that the prosecution should have to disclose its case to the defence. Indirectly, however, the presumption is at least consistent with prosecution disclosure. Since the burden of proof is on the prosecution, the issue at a criminal trial is whether the prosecution can prove its case in the light of any answer by the defendant.[96] Disclosure by the prosecution enables defendants to be ready with evidence in rebuttal, if they have it. This leaves less to chance, as far as the defence is concerned, and thus brings the court nearer to the truth. But some police officers and prosecutors have queried the wisdom of not allowing the situation in reverse, although one reply would be that knowing the defence case in advance would allow prosecution witnesses to tailor their evidence accordingly. Since the accused is at risk of conviction, unlike any other participant in the trial, that situation must be avoided.

Much harder to reconcile with adversarial theory is the duty at common law[97] of the prosecutor to disclose "unused material" to the defence. The explanation for the obligation upon police and prosecutor to hand over to the defence information which might undermine the prosecution's own case, which is not a process consistent with adversarial theory with its emphasis on the parties making their own efforts, is essentially pragmatic. The reality is that convictions based on suppression of exonerating information of which the prosecution was aware are morally unacceptable and damaging to public confidence. The Royal Commission chaired by Lord Runciman was itself set up as a response to the public criticism of the criminal justice system which centred primarily on the convictions of the Guildford Four, who served 14 years in prison; the Maguire Family, who served 15 years; and

---

[91] See J.S. Williams, *Civil and Criminal Procedure* (Sweet and Maxwell, London, 1997), 424.

[92] Criminal Justice Act 1967, s. 11.

[93] Police and Criminal Evidence Act 1984, s. 81; Crown Court (Advance Notice of Expert Evidence) Rules 1987 (SI 1987 No. 716).

[94] Jackson, n. 21 above.

[95] But see M. Zander, "Note of Dissent", Royal Commission on Criminal Justice, *Report* (HMSO London, 1993), Cm 2263.

[96] R. Leng, "Defence Strategies for Information Deficit: Negotiating the CPIA" (1997) 1 *E & P* 215.

[97] *Attorney-General's Guidelines* [1982] 1 All ER 734.

the Birmingham Six, who served 16.[98] It is clear from the strength of feeling engendered by these cases that verdicts in criminal matters are not generally regarded as a private affair between two opposing sides. It is also clear that where the state is funding and organising prosecution, the adversarial principle of "equality of arms" is violated. Unless the defence is to be provided with resources on the scale of those available to the other side, it appears easier and more economic to achieve a rough restoration of the balance by allowing the defence to take advantage of the information in the hands of the prosecutor:

"Inequality of resources is ameliorated by the obligation on the part of the prosecution to make available all material which may prove helpful to the defence".[99]

The defence should also be told of any material inconsistency between the evidence given by a prosecution witness and a previous statement in the possession of the prosecution, any known previous convictions of prosecution witnesses, and any previous convictions of the defendant, since the defence must know about these before deciding whether to put his character in issue.[100] If the prosecution elects not to call a witness who could give material evidence, his name and address must be supplied to the defence. At one time it was thought that there was no duty to hand over any statement such a witness might have made, as long as he or she was so "tendered". This assumption led to the wrongful conviction of Gerard Conlon of the Guildford Four; although the name and last known address of a potential alibi witness had been provided to his defence team, the significance of his statement, which they did not see, was not appreciated, and they did not interview him before the trial.[101] Recognition of the contribution of non-disclosure of this kind to miscarriages of justice like the Conlon case and that of Judith Ward[102] led the Court of Appeal to develop wider duties of disclosure of unused prosecution material. The cases culminated in the test of

---

[98] These convictions were eventually overturned, after many years of controversy, in *Richardson, Conlon, Armstrong and Hill, The Times*, 20 Oct. 1989; *Maguire and others* [1992] 2 All ER 433; *McIlkenny* [1992] 2 All ER 417. For an account of these cases, see I. Dennis, "Miscarriages of Justice and the Law of Confessions: Evidential Issues and Solutions" [1993] *PL* 291.

[99] *McIlkenny* [1992] 2 All ER 417 at 426, *per* Lloyd, Mustill and Farquarson LJJ.

[100] *Brown (Winston)* [1997] 3 All ER 769. The House of Lords could see no reason, however, why the prosecution should disclose previous inconsistent statements by potential defence witnesses; see ch. 8.

[101] Sir John May, *Return to an Address of the Honourable the House of Commons Dated 30 June 1994 for a Report of the Inquiry into the Circumstances Surrounding the Convictions arising out of the Bomb Attacks on Guildford and Woolwich in 1974: Final Report* (HMSO, London, 1994).

[102] *Ward* [1993] 2 All ER 577. In Ward's case, and that of the Birmingham Six, Government scientists suppressed information showing that some of their forensic testing produced results adverse to the prosecution. See Sir John May, n. 101 above, and Interim Report (HMSO, London, 1990). Also see below, Ch. 4.

materiality laid down by the Lord Chief Justice in *Keane*,[103] that is, anything which can be seen on a sensible appraisal by the prosecution to be relevant or possibly relevant to an issue in the case; to raise or possibly raise a new issue the existence of which is not apparent from the evidence the prosecution proposes to use; or to hold out a realistic prospect of providing a lead on evidence which goes to either of the above categories. In *Mills and Poole*,[104] the House of Lords confirmed that prosecutors have no discretion to withhold a material statement, even if the name and address are supplied. Although this test was in some respects rather narrower than that in *Ward*, which was thought to restrict the prosecution's ability to impose its judgment about the bearing unused material might have on the case, there was considerable opposition to the burden which, it was considered by some police officers and prosecutors, the prosecution was having to bear. It was argued that, in wide-ranging inquiries, such as police investigations door-to-door, in which large numbers of statements are taken but discarded, the effort of collating and delivering the material presented major practical difficulty. The defence, it was alleged, could require the police and prosecution to "comb through large masses of material in the hope of either causing delay or of chancing upon something that will induce the prosecution to drop the case rather than have to disclose the material concerned".[105]

The Royal Commission on Criminal Justice (the Runciman Commission) duly recommended that prosecution duties of disclosure should be cut back again. Further, the defence should have the obligation to inform the prosecution in advance of the trial of the nature of the defence, "to encourage earlier and better preparation of cases", which in turn might cause more cases to be settled without need for trial. It would assist with accurate planning of court lists, and prevent "ambush defences".[106] The seriousness of the problem presented by ambush defences is a matter of contention. It is difficult to see why the tactical advantage achieved by wrong-footing a prosecutor should ever be allowed to determine the outcome of a prosecution. However, it seems that surprise is rarely a factor affecting the verdict reached at a criminal trial. In the Crown Court study,[107] ambush defences were raised in only 7–10 per cent of cases, and in half of those the defendants were convicted. In Leng's study, also carried out on behalf of the Runciman Commission, such defences were raised in between 2 and 5 per cent of trials, and in all those cases the defendant was convicted.[108] The answer from the police and prosecution lobby to this point[109] is that there is no reason for surprise ever to play a part in achieving an unwarranted acquittal.

---

[103] (1994) 99 Cr. App. R 1.   [104] [1997] 3 All ER 780.

[105] Royal Commission on Criminal Justice, n. 95 above, 6.42.   [106] *Ibid.*, 6.57.

[107] Zander and Henderson, n. 18 above.

[108] R. Leng, *The Right to Silence in Police Interrogations: A Study of Some of the Issues Underlying the Debate*, Royal Commission on Criminal Justice Research Study 10 (HMSO, London, 1992).

[109] R. Leng, "Losing Sight of the Defendant" [1995] *Crim. LR* 704.

Since April 1997, prosecutors have had a duty to disclose by way of a two-stage process. Under the Criminal Procedure and Investigations Act 1996,[110] in all cases primary disclosure must be made of unused material "if in the prosecutor's opinion it might undermine the case for the prosecution".[111] In Crown Court cases, the defence must then inform the prosecution in general terms of the case it intends to present at trial.[112] This obligation is satisfied by completion of a fairly straightforward printed form which asks for brief summaries of the defence, matters with which the defence takes issue with the prosecution, and any alibi.[113] The defence is also invited to list any material the prosecution should disclose as being reasonably likely to assist the defence as disclosed, or to undermine the prosecution case. This material should be handed over at the stage of secondary disclosure by the prosecution. If there is no material of that kind, the defence must be supplied with a statement to that effect. The prosecutor is under a continuing duty to review questions of disclosure.[114]

For non-disclosure by the defence, one sanction is that unless it returns the statement, there is no trigger for secondary disclosure by the prosecution. But also, under section 11 of the 1996 Act, if the defence fails to make disclosure, or if it is done late, or if it sets out inconsistent defences, or if the defendant at trial puts forward a different defence, the court or jury may "draw such inferences as appear proper". That decision should take account, if a new defence is offered at trial, of the extent of the difference and whether there is any justification for it. The defendant cannot be convicted solely on the basis of an inference drawn under section 11.[115] These provisions were brought into force amidst a storm of protest from defence lawyers, particularly solicitors, who felt they would be blamed for any future miscarriages of justice,[116] whilst being asked to demonstrate clairvoyant powers insofar as they could demand material from the prosecution only if they knew it existed and could show it was relevant.[117] Otherwise they must rely on the police to anticipate the defence, which is not a matter to which police officers generally pay a great deal of attention.[118] Murray suggests that the alleged difficulties caused by the common law duties of disclosure for prosecutors were much exaggerated,[119]

---

[110] N. 1–7

[111] Sensitive material is excluded from these provisions: s. 3(6).

[112] For summary trials defence disclosure is voluntary (s. 6), but necessary to trigger secondary disclosure by the prosecution. But see J. Sprack, "The Criminal Procedure and Investigations Act: The Duty of Disclosure" [1997] *Crim. LR* 308.

[113] S. 5(7), replacing s.11 of the Criminal Justice Act 1967.

[114] S. 9.

[115] S.11(5). See Ch. 1, n. 115 above.

[116] Jim Nicol (solicitor to the Bridgewater Three), *The Times*, 28 Mar. 1997.

[117] The defence can make application to the court for disclosure if it has reasonable cause to believe there is undisclosed prosecution material which might reasonably be expected to assist the defence as disclosed: s. 8.

[118] Roger Ede. *The Times*, 1 Apr. 1997.

[119] C. Murray, "Fair is Foul and Foul is Fair" [1996] *NLJ* 1288.

and that to replace them with Crown Prosecution Service judgements of relevance is dangerous; this is not a reflection on their *bona fides*, but a lesson learnt from the miscarriage of justice cases.[120]

In civil cases, again, there are obligations on the parties to assist each other in their search for relevant material. At the close of pleadings, each party must present a list of documents in its possession, whether adverse to its case or not.[121] This process is traditionally known as the discovery of documents.[122] The pleadings have not provided a list of witnesses, nor proofs of their evidence, but the practice, which developed first in the Commercial Court, of providing these is now embodied in Court of Appeal Practice Directions.[123] Although in no civil case has a party a duty to point out the existence of non-documentary evidence which may assist the other side, professional ethics demand that counsel does not mislead the court. This means that a case may not be pleaded which is inconsistent with evidence of which counsel is aware, without drawing it to the attention of the judge. These procedures may at first sight appear to be inconsistent with the adversarial tradition, which suggests that the parties should be turning up information entirely by their own efforts, but they acknowledge reality, in that otherwise it would be impossible to predict what, if any, relevant documentary material the other side might have in its hands. The duty not to mislead the court shows that although some rules create the impression that all that it represents is a neutral facility, it is recognised that courts must never be associated in the public consciousness with underhandedness or injustice.

In the civil jurisdiction in England and Wales, recent years have seen a striking and radical departure in the procedural approach to litigation. The Commercial Court practice of exchanging written witness statements prior to the trial became, from 1986, an optional direction by the Master in the Chancery Division,[124] and since then has been the subject of considerable expansion. It now applies to all civil jurisdictions of the High Court. It is a standard requirement that a party intending to produce factual evidence at

---

[120] It is clear that the Runciman Commission was to a considerable extent influenced by police concerns that defence lawyers were on occasion demanding access to police documents which might reveal the identity of informers. Any claim to public interest immunity to protect informants' anonymity is likely to fail: *Turner* [1995] 3 All ER 432; and consequently, police witnesses to the Commission argued, many cases had to be abandoned even where the true value of that information to the defence was questionable n. 95 above, 6.59).

[121] RSC Ord. 24; CCR, Ord. 17rr. 11(3)(a) and 11(5)(a); the court may order the production of the documents in question if the party holding them does not make an appointment to inspect at the request of the other side.

[122] The rules on disclosure (as it is now to be described) of documents will now be the province of a new Civil Procedure Rules Committee, set up under the Civil Procedure Act 1997 as a step toward implementation of the Woolf Report.

[123] *Civil Litigation Practice Direction* [1995] 1 WLR 262; cf. for the Family Division [1995] 1 WLR 332.

[124] RSC, Ord. 38, r. 2A.

trial must provide the other parties with a written statement of the evidence which the witness is expected to give.[125] However, it was also stipulated that these statements should generally stand as the witness's evidence in chief. This led lawyers to attach great significance to them and, as Lord Woolf MR observes, resulted in massive overdrafting, which is expensive and time-consuming, in the effort to anticipate all eventualities. The answer, he suggests, is to allow witnesses to amplify their statement orally at the trial itself, so that the statement need not be definitive, but couched in the witness's own words.[126] These innovations were part of a cultural movement which inspired the review of civil procedure conducted by Lord Woolf MR, whose Final Report[127] contained recommendations designed to expedite and reduce the cost of proceedings, eliminate the element of surprise, identify the issues prior to trial and encourage settlement.[128]

In *Comfort Hotels* v. *Wembley Stadium*,[129] Hoffman J quoted Master Jacob, then editor of the Supreme Court Practice on the subject of exchange of witness statements:

"This significant rule . . . removes some of the defective factors and the more confrontational aspects of the adversary system of civil procedure. Above all it greatly improves the pre-trial process by providing the machinery for enabling parties to know before the trial precisely what facts are intended to be proved at the trial, and by whom, and thereby it reduces delay, costs and the opportunity for procedural technicalities and obstruction towards the trial".

The increased openness to which these observations refer has been accompanied by the announcement that judges would exert greater control over the conduct of civil cases. Failure by the parties to conduct cases economically would be visited by appropriate orders for costs. The House of Lords has made it plain that it will be more difficult in future to reopen the decisions made by judges in their capacity as case managers. In *Ashmore* v *Corporation of Lloyds*,[130] it was held that a trial judge is perfectly entitled to decide as a preliminary matter whether the defendants owed a duty of care to the plaintiffs. Appellate courts should be reluctant to entertain complaints about a judge who controls the conduct or proceedings and limits the time and scope of evidence and argument. "Litigants are not entitled to the uncontrolled use of a trial judge's time".[131] The philosophy of the Practice Directions and of the Woolf Report is that civil courts will have discretion to limit discovery, the length of oral submissions, the time allowed for the examination of witnesses and of reading aloud from documents and legal authorities, and the issues on which they wish to be addressed. Before trial, a "trial

---

[125] N. 123 above.   [126] N. 48 above, 12.59.   [127] *Ibid.*
[128] Sir Richard Scott V-C (ed.), *Supreme Court Practice* (Sweet and Maxwell, London, 1997), vol. 1, 38/2A/2.
[129] [1988] 1 WLR 872.   [130] [1992] 2 All ER 486.   [131] *Ibid., per* Lord Roskill at 488.

bundle"[132] of witness statements, expert reports, and summary of the issues and authorities—"skeleton arguments", must be handed to the court, giving time for the judge to read them in advance. Even the pagination, indexing and binding[133] of the documentation is specified in the Directions. In cases expected to take more than ten days, application must be made for pre-trial review. The parties should use their best endeavours to agree a timetable. They must be ready to tell the judge whether they have tried alternative dispute resolution to avoid coming to court. These developments have shown beyond doubt that the framework of the modern civil trial is becoming more "paper-oriented" and, with pre-trial exchange of witness proofs, the significance and impact of the trial itself—even with its adversarial features intact—becomes greatly reduced. In this way, the English and European models are moving closer together.

Movement in the direction of a less adversarial culture may be observed in cases such as *Chapman* v. *Chief Constable of South Yorkshire*,[134] where Steyn J held that in complex multi-party litigation, the "sporting theory of justice" had no place. The concept of a party being in control of litigation ought, as far as possible, to be subordinated to case management techniques in the control of the court. In the Family Division, Wall J[135] commended the advocates involved for the use of time-table templates which had greatly assisted the conduct of the case. Not only had it defined the length of the case, but it imposed a continuous intellectual discipline and helped to concentrate the minds of the advocates on the continuing need to structure the evidence as it emerged within the estimated timescale of the case. Through the 1980s the provision of skeleton arguments had become an established practice, and at the same time the judiciary began to express resentment at the protracted nature of proceedings still predominantly oral. In *Banque Keyser Ullman SA* v. *Skandia (UK) Insurance Co.*,[136] Lord Templeman condemned the opportunities for timewasting which reliance on the "day in court" affords:

> "Proceedings in which all or some of the litigants indulge in over-elaboration cause difficulties to judges at all levels in the achievement of a just result. Such proceedings obstruct the hearing of other litigation . . . The costs must be formidable . . . The present practice is to allow every litigant unlimited time and unlimited scope so that the litigant and his advisers are able to conduct their case in all respects in the way which seems best to them. The results not infrequently are torrents of words, written and oral, which are oppressive and which the judge

---

[132] Called in the rules the "Court bundle", but better known as the "trial bundle" according to Scott V-C n. 128 above, vol. 1, 34/10/1.

[133] Ring-binder or lever-arch file.

[134] *The Times* 230 Mar. 1990.

[135] Unreported at first instance, but in the Court of Appeal as *Re C (A Minor: Care Proceedings: Disclosure)*, *The Times* 22 Oct. 1996.

[136] [1990] 3 WLR 364.

must examine in an attempt to eliminate everything which is not relevant, helpful and persuasive. The remedy lies in the judge taking time to read in advance pleadings, documents certified by counsel to be necessary, and short skeleton arguments of counsel, and for the judge then, after a short discussion in open court, to limit the time and scope of oral evidence and the time and scope of oral argument. The appellate courts should be unwilling to entertain complaints concerning the results of this practice."[137]

In 1995, the Court of Appeal announced that in order to reduce the backlog of unheard civil appeals, oral argument would be limited to the amount of time which the skeleton arguments suggested was appropriate to the case. Oral argument in support of applications for leave to appeal were to be confined to a maximum of twenty minutes.[138]

This shifting of power from the parties, through their advocates, to the judges clearly heralded a new era in civil litigation in England and Wales. Nevertheless, it was still considered too elaborate and costly.[139] The conclusions of the Woolf inquiry proclaimed a "new landscape" for civil justice. The adversarial system is to work in a more disciplined way, so that parties cannot use control of their case to grind down opponents, by failing to meet deadlines (which would be dealt with severely[140] by striking out or punitive orders for costs) or excessive demands for information. Courts, with the assistance of litigants, will be responsible for the management of cases, setting timetables, establishing which procedures are appropriate, setting a budget so that costs are predictable and deciding what evidence will be necessary to try the issues. Greater openness and co-operation between the parties should encourage timely settlement of disputes. The principles of equality, economy, proportionality and expedition according to the Report constitute the requirements of procedural justice, and, "operating in the traditional adversarial context, will give effect to a system which is substantially just in the results it delivers as well as the way in which it does".[141] Barring the appearance of an Advocate-General, the system of civil trial which is apparently evolving is highly reminiscent of proceedings in the European Court of Justice at Luxembourg. The European Court of Human Rights at Strasbourg also relies heavily on written submissions provided in advance, but more significantly, given its role in a predominantly adversarial structure, so does the United States Supreme Court, where counsel's oral argument must occupy no more than

---

[137] *Ibid.,* at 380.

[138] *Practice Statement (Court of Appeal: Procedural Changes), The Times 27* July 1995.

[139] Though the system had many supporters within the legal profession: D. Greenslade, "Objections to Woolf" [1996] *NLJ* 1147.

[140] See Woolf MR living up to his principles in *Beachley Property* v. *Edgar, The Times,* 18 July 1996, in refusing to allow late service of witness statements, where there was no reasonable explanation for the failure to comply. See C. Passmore, "Whither Discovery?" [1996] *NLJ* 1321.

[141] N. 48 above, 1.8.

an hour. Whether or not the new structure will reduce costs, or merely transfer the major financial outlay to a different stage of the proceedings, remains to be seen.[142]

Development of Exclusionary Rules

The developments on disclosure in criminal trials, and the radical proposals for judicial management of cases proposed for civil trials in the Woolf Report may be thought to mark a gradual evolution away from the adversarial model in England and Wales. As the system's adversarial character is lost, the fate of the exclusionary rules of evidence becomes increasingly uncertain. Although adversarial structures clearly encourage the development of such rules, it has long been thought that the British tradition of trial by jury has played a substantial part in their evolution. Phipson argues that the law of evidence assumes jury trial. "It is of importance that they should not have before them matters which it is not proper for them to take into account when arriving at a verdict".[143] Thus, it is supposed that in civil trials, where in most cases there is no jury, the rules are considerably less rigid. The rules excluding hearsay evidence were considerably relaxed, first in the Civil Evidence Act 1968, and, more recently, in the Civil Evidence Act 1995.[144] Civil courts have in any event been cavalier about the hearsay rules. In reality, civil cases would have collapsed under the weight of time and expense if the hearsay provisions of the Civil Evidence Act had been complied with. Thayer and Wigmore[145] regarded the survival of the jury as highly important to the historical origin and continuance of the exclusionary rules, although the latter also attributed some of these to the limitations imposed by the trial having to be held at a fixed time and place (which applies equally to civil cases). Yet the exclusionary rules are retained in Singapore despite the abolition of trial by jury in non-capital criminal cases.[146] Professor Morgan[147] doubted whether the jury's presence had significant impact on the manner in which criminal trials are conducted. The first juries were expected to inquire locally into the disputed events, and therefore were likely to rely heavily on second-hand information. Doubts as to the capacity of jurors realistically to assess the proper weight of hearsay evidence were first expressed comparatively recently in *Wright* v.

---

[142] See ch. 8.

[143] M.N. Howard, P. Crane and D.A. Hochberg (eds.), *Phipson on Evidence*, (14th ed., Sweet and Maxwell, London, 1990), 1.02.

[144] The Act came into force on 31 Jan. 1997. See below, Ch. 7.

[145] J.B. Thayer. *A Preliminary Treatise on Evidence at Common Law* (Little, Brown, Boston, Mass., 1898) and J.H. Wigmore, *The Principles of Judicial Proof* (Little, Brown, Boston, Mass., 1940).See W. Twining, *Theories of Evidence: Bentham and Wigmore* (Weidenfeld and Nicolson, London, 1985).

[146] Criminal Procedure Code (Amendment) Act 1969.

[147] E.M. Morgan, *Some Problems of Proof under the Anglo-American System of Litigation* (University of North Carolina, New York, 1956).

Tatham,[148] by which time the hearsay rule had been operating for a 100 years at least. Earlier cases had also reflected concern about the inability to cross-examine the maker of the original statement. Cross acknowledges that the presence of lay jurors does not entirely account for the development of exclusionary rules, suggesting that a second factor is the common law adversarial system of procedure.[149]

Support for the theory that the jury is not the principal begetter of the adversarial trial may be found in the work of Jackson and Doran[150] on the "Diplock Courts" in Northern Ireland. In certain categories of case which feature crimes which may be terrorist-related, the trial judge sits without a jury, and is the tribunal of fact as well as arbiter of legal issues.[151] The procedures remain the same as those in traditional jury trials, except that the judge must deliver a written judgment to accompany the verdict.[152] One of the purposes of the study was to discover if and to what extent judges in Diplock Courts departed from rigid adversarial practices to develop a more inquisitorial style. The authors found that although some procedures inevitably were adapted to the absence of a jury, for example, the relationship between the *voir dire* and the full trial. Also, the formal closing speeches inevitably delivered for the benefit of juries had relaxed into debates between counsel and the judge. However, in most respects judges were found not to operate very differently in Diplock Courts, although some judges tended to be more informal than others, some intervened more than others and some demanded a higher degree of technical compliance with the rules than others; these behaviours appeared to have more to do with the personality of individual judges (and whether they got on with particular advocates) than whether they were sitting in a conventional or a Diplock Court.[153] The authors concluded that although the trial without jury was less adversarial, and featured more of the polite inter-lawyer discussion which may be found in appellate courts, it was not inquisitorial.

A further, closely related and still highly influential factor in the development and dominance of exclusionary rules, it is submitted, is that of the presumption of innocence.[154] It governs the order of events in criminal trials, the exclusion, in general, of the accused's bad character although that

---

[148] (1834) 7 A. & E. 313.

[149] C. Tapper, *Cross on Evidence* (Butterworths, London, 1995), 1. A third factor is said to be the importance attached to the oath.

[150] N. 60 above.

[151] In much the same way as is a stipendiary magistrate, who is a professional lawyer, as opposed to the lay magistrates, who do adjudicate on issues of law and fact, but have the assistance of the clerk on matters of law.

[152] Northern Ireland (Emergency Provisions) Act 1991, s. 10.

[153] The behaviour of advocates appeared to be affected by the presence of the jury; e.g., defence lawyers were more likely to provoke a quarrel with the judge, apparently a tactic designed to induce the judge into a reaction which could alienate the jury.

[154] Under attack, see Ch. 5.

of all other witnesses is admissible,[155] and the operation of the right to silence.[156] Furthermore, although the inability to cross-examine absent witnesses is one of the objections to hearsay evidence, we find that since 1988 the disadvantage is regarded as significant, and therefore a justification for excluding the evidence, only where it affects the defence.[157] Many defenders of the adversarial trial in fact argue that it is the most effective means of preserving the right of the unconnected to be presumed innocent until proved guilty.[158]

There are examples within our own jurisdiction of non-adversarial proceedings. Some of them use juries, but, whether or not they do, it has proved difficult to justify the application of the rules of evidence to something which is essentially an inquiry. Coroners' courts require a jury relatively infrequently these days, but still do so for inquests into deaths in prison, deaths from notifiable accidents or diseases, and cases where there is a risk of prejudice to public health or safety.[159] Inquests are non-accusatorial proceedings which are not circumscribed by the usual procedural and evidential restrictions; an inquest "is an inquisitorial process, a process of investigation, quite unlike a trial where the prosecutor accuses and the accused defends, the judge holding the balance".[160] Consequently, it is for coroners to decide which witnesses are to be summoned to attend.[161] Yet, it is interesting to note, the leading textbook on inquests, while acknowledging that they are not bound by the rules of evidence, nevertheless reproduces a basic outline of them "to reduce as far as possible the number of occasions upon which it is necessary to depart from them".[162] Similarly, efforts have been made to make arbitrations more informal than court proceedings. County court arbitrations are specifically so described, and it is stated that the strict rules of evidence shall not apply.[163] The Arbitration Act 1996 seeks to introduce a complete flexibility in terms of procedure; section 34 states that it shall be for the tribunal to decide all procedural and evidential matters, subject to the right of the parties to agree any matter. This tribunal hence may use its discretion in relation to disclosure of documents, the manner of any questions to be put to witnesses and whether the rules of

---

[155] See Ch. 5.

[156] See below, Ch. 5.

[157] Criminal Justice Act 1988, ss. 25, 26; see Ch. 7.

[158] Eg. Wright, n. 25 above, whose observations of French criminal trials led him to conclude that the defendant appeared to be presumed guilty from the start. However, he gave insufficient weight to the preparatory stage, *instruction*, which, the French believe, ensures that there is a strong case for the prosecution which the defendant should be required to answer. This explains the admittedly hostile attacks by some Presidents in the opening examination of the accused.

[159] Coroners (Amendment) Act 1926, s. 13(2).

[160] *R. v. South London Coroner, ex p. Thompson* (1982) 126 SJ 625.

[161] *McKerr v. Armagh Coroner* [1990] 1 All ER 865.

[162] P. Matthews and J.C. Foreman, *Jervis on Coroners* (Sweet and Maxwell, London, 1986), 15.24–5.

[163] CCR, Ord. 19.17(3).

evidence should apply. Since arbitrators may be selected from outside the legal profession it is unlikely that many will opt voluntarily to submerge themselves in the murky waters of the law of evidence.[164]

There has recently been considerable confusion about the nature of proceedings concerned with child welfare. It had been supposed until recently that care proceedings were "essentially non-adversarial",[165] and that therefore the strict rules of evidence did not apply. This belief was weakened by the Court of Appeal decision in *Re H and Re K*,[166] where it was held that only the High Court exercising the wardship jurisdiction was exempt; however much other courts might feel that the purpose of the proceedings is simply to protect the welfare of the child in question, the normal rules, including the hearsay rule, apply.[167] *In Bradford City Metropolitan Council v. K*[168] the doubts expressed in *Re H and Re K* were resolved in a categorical assertion that the hearsay rule applied in care proceedings.[169] The nature of cases brought under the 1989 Act has been thrown into question when parties have claimed legal professional privilege in relation to their communications with lawyers concerning the legal proceedings. Judges considering the issue have acknowledged that legal professional privilege is essentially a product of the adversarial system of justice. Parties operating within such a system must be able to trust their own legal advisers and communicate with them freely. It was said of wardship that the proceedings were non-adversarial, and that therefore the operation of the privilege was inappropriate.[170] Once care proceedings effectively became the only forum where intervention to protect a child was possible, the applicability of legal professional privilege in that context was clearly questionable. Judges appeared to take differing views on the nature of care proceedings. Douglas Brown J held that they were "not paternal, they are not administrative, and they are not in reality non-adversarial, although they should be conducted in a non-adversarial spirit".[171] An exactly opposite view was taken by the Court of Appeal,[172] which held that care proceedings had many features incompatible with adversarial litigation. The paramount consideration is the welfare of the child; the judge may make orders which neither party to the proceedings has sought; the judge may require the guardian *ad litem* to obtain further

---

[164] F. Miller, "A Reason Why Arbitrators should get *Cross*" [1994] *NLJ* 1381.

[165] Lord Widgery CJ, *Humberside County Council v. DPR (an Infant)* [1977] 3 All ER 964.

[166] [1989] FLR 356.

[167] *In Re W (Minors)*, *The Times* 10 Nov. 1989.

[168] *The Times*, 18 Aug. 1989.

[169] Hence the need for specific provision that in child-centred civil proceedings evidence given in connection with the upbringing, maintenance or welfare of a child shall be admissible notwithstanding any rule of law relating to hearsay: Children (Admissibility of Hearsay Evidence) Order 1993; now see the Civil Evidence Act 1995, below, Ch. 7.

[170] *Re A (Minors: Disclosure of Material)* [1991] 2 FLR 473.

[171] *Barking and Dagenham London Borough Council v. O* [1994] 4 All ER 59, 63.

[172] *Oxfordshire County Council v. M* [1994] 2 All ER 269.

evidence on behalf of the court, including experts' reports. "The proceedings under the Children Act are not adversarial, although an adversarial approach is frequently adopted by various of the parties".[173] Although the House of Lords agreed that care proceedings are not adversarial, legal professional privilege was held to be necessary even in that context to protect confidences between lawyer and client.[174] But the related privilege, more firmly rooted in adversarial procedures, known as "litigation privilege", which normally attaches to reports commissioned by a lawyer on behalf of a client, does not apply to care proceedings. The same reasoning was adopted by Hale J in relation to issue estoppel, which she held to be an inappropriate doctrine in the non-adversarial setting of care proceedings.[175]

When we find bands of lawyers joining together to defend exclusionary rules and extol the virtues of the adversarial trial,[176] the issue of self-interest inevitably arises. A common criticism of the structure of the Anglo-American trial is that it is a device to protect the interests of lawyers. The minefields of technical requirements in evidence and procedure are a fertile source of appeals, many of which have no intrinsic merit. But it is not central to the theory of adversarial trial that these rules should be rigid. The same object could be achieved by leaving it to the discretion of the trial judges whether particular items of evidence should be admitted. Appeals would then succeed only where the discretion had been improperly exercised. The idea that judicial discretion should replace the current law of evidence is highly controversial. In Canada, for example, the legal profession mounted strong resistance to the suggestions of the Law Reform Commission of Canada, whose Draft Evidence Code would provide a more flexible system with a greater role for judicial discretion. And yet it can be argued that the rules of evidence themselves were originally merely illustrations of the exercise of judicial common sense. Guidance which was developed to help judges use their discretion wisely has ossified into unhelpful and sometimes lunatic rigidity.[177]. At the same time, there is already in reality considerable discretion behind the technical distinctions, and leading writers have identified the advantages of this.[178] For instance, Pattenden suggests that it may be impossible to formulate a rule in some contexts. Discretion also avoids bad results in hard cases, and enables the court to strike the right balance between conflicting interests.[179] There is a certain amount of intellectual

---

[173] *Ibid.*, 278.

[174] *Re L (A Minor: Police Investigation: Privilege)* [1996] 2 All ER 78.

[175] *Re B and Another (Minors: Care Proceedings: Evidence)* [1997] 2 All ER 29.

[176] As in the House of Lords debates on the hearsay provisions of the Criminal Evidence Act 1988; see Ch. 7.

[177] R. Delisle, "Judicial Discretion and the Law of Evidence", Paper presented to Conference of Society for the Reform of the Criminal Law, London, 1987.

[178] E.g., Zuckerman, n. 7 above, 12; R. Pattenden, *The Judge, Discretion and the Criminal Trial* (Oxford University Press, Oxford, 1982).

[179] *Ibid.*, 35–9.

dishonesty in objecting to discretion determining the admissibility of evidence and at the same time defending the current system, where so much has been shown already to exist.[180] The Law Commission recently argued that to replace the existing hearsay exceptions with a general judicial discretion to admit any hearsay evidence which appears reliable and probative would lead to unacceptable levels of uncertainty. Yet the Commission concedes that the mostly carefully-defined categories of admissibility would probably not cover every item of hearsay deserving of admission. Therefore it proposes a "safety-valve" inclusionary discretion so that particularly probative hearsay, which ought to be admitted in the interests of justice but which falls outside the recommended new exceptions, may yet be admitted.[181]

The same contradiction may be observed in the provisions governing the manner in which children may give evidence in criminal courts. The Pigot Committee[182] appeared more reluctant than the Scottish Law Commission to allow judges a discretion to select the means by which vulnerable witnesses give evidence.[183] Yet judges have complete discretion to refuse to allow a child to use the closed circuit television facility without even having to give reasons.[184] The New Zealand Law Commission appears more sanguine and more straightforward than English law reform bodies as far as judicial discretion is concerned. A recent report suggests the extension of the measures currently available in the New Zealand court to ease the process of giving evidence for juvenile and mentally handicapped complainants in sexual cases[185] to all witnesses who appear to the court to be in need of special assistance. This would provide complete flexibility for a judge who wishes to select the most appropriate mechanism to counter the difficulties faced by a particular witness including the defendant. It is curious that the English law reform bodies appear so unenthusiastic about judicial discretion when it is clear that a measure of it is inevitable within a system of exclusionary rules of evidence. But at the same time, as Zuckerman points out, there is little guidance on its proper exercise developed in a climate where the prevailing fiction is that it does not exist; and the reality is that the more familiar with the current rules judges are, the more they can manipulate them to achieve the result they want. It is quite clear that in practice many judges and advocates virtually ignore such matters as the exceptions to the hearsay rule because they do not understand them. If all participants in the trial are of the same mind, these unwelcome complications effectively cease to exist.

---

[180] Delisle, n. 177 above; Pattenden, n. 178 above; Zuckerman. n. 7 above.

[181] Law Commission, *Evidence in Criminal Proceedings: Hearsay and Related Topics* (HMSO, London, 1997) Cm 3670. See also ch. 7.

[182] *Report of the Advisory Group on Video Evidence* (Home Office, London, 1980).

[183] Although the Scottish legislation, as implemented, is no more flexible than the English: see Ch. 4.

[184] *The Evidence of Children and other Vulnerable Witnesses: A Discussion Paper*, New Zealand Law Commission Preliminary Paper 26 (Wellington, New Zealand, 1996).

[185] Screens, audio and television links, videotaped interviews.

It is difficult, therefore, to be convinced by those who say that to extend judicial discretion would create great uncertainty, since it would be impossible to predict in advance what evidence would be used. Yet the legal profession is often found to be resistant to moves intended substantially to reform the law of evidence, whether by extending discretion, altering procedure or introducing new exceptions. Is the hostility to change a manifestation of pure self-interest? A cynic might say that the rules are there to enable lawyers to pull technical tricks and manipulate the participants. They can score points or whole victories which are nothing to do with the real merits of the case. But it is probably more realistic to accept that many lawyers are deeply committed to the adversarial trial and the presumption of innocence. The fact that from these foundations springs an eccentric Gothic edifice composed of extraordinary rules, presumptions, exceptions and confusion has its own charm. The seductive appeal of this structure in itself breeds a sentimental attachment, so that one might feel that preservation of the traditional form of trial, with all its historic characteristics, is indeed worthwhile to protect our heritage, just as we conserve ancient monuments.

2

Proving Facts in Court

Relevance

Relevance in the Law

In *R. v. Blastland*,[1] B was charged with the murder of a boy, K. He suggested that the murderer was another man, M, who had been in the vicinity while B was with the boy. M was investigated by the police but not charged. There was evidence that M had arrived home mudstained and told certain witnesses that a boy had been killed in the woods. This was correct, but he said it before K's body had officially been found. In his defence at his trial, B wished to call these witnesses in order to suggest that M's knowledge had not been innocently come by, and could be explained by the conclusion that M had committed the murder himself. The House of Lords upheld the trial judge's decision to disallow this evidence; apart from possible conflict with the rule against hearsay,[2] the evidence of these witnesses should be excluded on the ground that it was irrelevant.

What then, is the legal perception of relevance? Clearly, evidence which is not relevant is not admissible. There are numerous definitions of relevance, but it is doubtful whether they express its meaning any more clearly than Rule 401 of the Federal Rules of Evidence of the United States which defines relevant evidence as:

> "Evidence having any tendency to make the existence of any fact that is of conse-
> quence to the determination of the action more probable or less probable than it
> would be without the evidence".

Unfortunately, the effect of disputed evidence, in terms of whether it does indeed make the fact in issue more probable, is frequently the subject of heated arguments which it may be difficult to resolve. And relevance as an instrument of logical reasoning is not the same thing as relevance as judges see it.[3] Logical relevance is a *sine qua non* of admissibility; but it cannot

---

[1] [1985] 2 All ER 1095.   [2] See Ch. 7.
[3] E.g., Coleridge J, referring to the "fallacy that whatever is morally convincing and whatever reasonable beings will form their judgments and act upon, may be submitted to the jury": *Wright* v. *Tatham* (1838) 7 Ad. & E 5.

guarantee that the evidence will be admitted; in fact, on its own it is far from sufficient.[4] Case law has developed a legal refinement upon the concept of relevance and, whether or not one adopts the complicated distinctions in leading textbooks between relevance (in the judicial sense), materiality and admissibility, it seems that the ultimate fate of evidence which can be seen to be *logically* relevant depends upon the nature and purpose of the trial. Judges talk of "probative force", as opposed to relevance. Some writers consider that relevance is absolute (either the fact is a relevant fact or it is not), whereas facts can have varying degrees of probative significance.[5] For instance, if a rape was committed by a man who throughout sang "Land of Hope and Glory" is it relevant that in his flat he has a copy of the sheet music of that patriotic song? It is relevant in that he would find it difficult to deny that he knows it. If it were the only music in the flat it might have some probative value in suggesting that it is a particular favourite. But if he has many shelves of sheet music the probative value diminishes, and may reach the point where it has insuffient significance and is inadmissible. To say that it is irrelevant overstates the situation—he *does* know "Land of Hope and Glory". But, since many other people also know it, his knowlege on its own may not be of sufficient probative value to interest the court. If relevance is a variable quality, then it is not suffiently relevant to be admissible.

There are many exclusionary rules affecting the admissibility of what at first sight appears to be relevant evidence. These rules provide meat and drink to lawyers, whether they write books, teach students or participate in trials. Laymen have heard of some of them, like the hearsay rule (which appears even in Dickens[6]) and have a vague idea that the criminal record is excluded. Judges have shown a new vigour in excluding relevant evidence if they disapprove of police conduct. These matters have been said to be instances of judicial concern with the reliability of evidence, but will be dealt with in more detail in later chapters. Courts rely heavily on inductive or empirical reasoning: "[t]he law furnishes no test of relevancy. For this, it tacitly refers to logic and experience".[7] Thayer was quite clear that he meant here the inductive logic of knowledge or science.[8] Any attempt such as Stephen's to construct a logical syllogism where a specific premise combined with a general one inevitably leads to a conclusion to illustrate the way findings of fact are made[9] is frustrated by the impossibility of identifying the

---

[4] R.W. Baker, *The Hearsay Rule* (Pitman, London, 1950).

[5] J. Michael and M. Adler, *The Nature of Judicial Proof* (privately printed, 1931); M. Trautman, "Logical or Legal Relevancy—a Conflict in Theory" (1952) 5 *Vand. LR* 385.

[6] As Sam Weller gives evidence in *Bardell* v. *Pickwick*: "You must not tell us what the soldier said, sir", interposed the judge; "it's not evidence": C. Dickens, *The Pickwick Papers*.

[7] J.B. Thayer, *Preliminary Treatise on Evidence at the Common Law* (Sweet and Maxwell, London, 1893), 265.

[8] J.B. Thayer, "Law and Logic" (1900) 14 *Harv. L Rev.* 139.

[9] J.F. Stephen, *General View of the Criminal Law* (1st. edn., Sweet & Maxwell, London, 1898), 236

contents of the initial premise without adopting everyday assumptions about human behaviour or commonplace experiences.

There are inevitably divergent views on these matters, whether the supposition is "[t]hose who have a motive to kill are more likely to do so than those with none" or "[a] man with an elegant and intelligent wife is unlikely to seek the services of a prostitute, or to hand over large sums of money to a prostitute he has never met".[10] Findings of fact, say Binder and Bergman, are based upon conventional wisdom about how people and objects function in everyday life. All of us, through our own personal experience, through hearing about the personal experience of others and through knowledge gained from books, films, newspapers and television, have accumulated vast storehouses of commonly-held notions about how people and objects generally behave in our society. From this storehouse one formulates a generalisation about typical behaviour. This generalisation, in turn, becomes the premise which enables specific evidence to be linked with an element to be proven.[11] The development of presumptions illustrates how the law itself attempts to save time and argument by adopting some of these common-sense assumptions, processing them into conveniently snappy formulations. Circumstantial evidence also relies on such inferences. The law has got itself into difficulty whenever it has insisted on proof in the strict logical sense, failure to admit the inductive nature of its own reasoning having led to unrealistic restrictions being imposed. Bentham asked what were the realistic possibilities of documents produced being forgeries—yet rules to eliminate this insubstantial risk prevented vast numbers of perfectly genuine documents being used. How likely is it that someone will set out deliberately to manufacture evidence, for instance by making remarks that will be overheard by bystanders, and then disappearing, all to incriminate someone else? Yet the hearsay rule strives to protect us from these remarkable possibilities. Thus the baby is thrown out with the bathwater; it may be that the odd forgery or concoction is preferable to the loss of so much valuable evidence.

It has been known since the time in the eighteenth century that David Hume demonstrated them that inductive reasoning has logical weaknesses. But one of the law's strengths is that it reflects the common experience and embodies the layman's understanding of common sense. The cases on similar fact evidence, discussed below, are full of references to everyday experience, and observations about what consitutes "normal" criminal behaviour. Yet, as Zuckerman has pointed out,[12] the rules of inductive logic have nothing to say about what standard of proof is desirable in criminal trials, nor whether there is a moral objection to punishing the accused twice for the same offence, but these are major concerns throughout that same case law on evidence of disposition. Hence these judicial decisions cannot be

---

[10] *Archer* v. *Daily Star*, July 1987.

[11] D. Binder and P. Bergman, *Fact Investigation* (West, St Paul, Minn., 1984), 274.

[12] A. Zuckerman, "Similar Fact Evidence: The Unobservable Rule" (1987) 103 *LQR* 187, n. 45.

seen entirely as an application of inductive reasoning, the objective being to minimise the risk of unreliable evidence being given too much weight. As Zuckerman has shown, the common law attempts to place inductive notions of relevance in the balance against what is actually a concept redolent of moral issues, namely, the risk of prejudice. The width of the considerable discretion left to trial judges as a consequence has been defended on the basis that, by this means, justice is given due attention.[13] Generally, judicial discretion is acceptable where it is operated on a rational basis which can be perceived. Unfortunately, here it seems that judges are condemned to an exercise in irrationality; it is therefore entirely to be expected that the Court of Appeal, in reviewing the exercise of this discretion, has produced surprising results from time to time.

Since it is for the parties to determine which are the issues to be decided in any case, we can see that the relevance of an evidential fact to the matter in dispute depends upon which issues each party chooses to introduce. For instance, if A is accused of murder, is it relevant to his guilt that his wife was having an affair? If the allegation is that he stabbed a supporter of a rival football team in a public house, that fact appears to be irrelevant. But if A pleads that as a result of his wife's affair he suffered severe depressive illness to an extent affecting his responsibility for his action and seeks therefore to rely on the defence of diminished responsibility,[14] the affair is a material fact. A more obvious example is where the wife was herself the victim of the killing, in which case her affair would suggest that he might rely on the defence of provocation,[15] but it is entirely up to A to decide upon what defence (if any) he will rely. That decision can then make a fact which hitherto appeared to be irrelevant an important matter in the case. Some lawyers use the word "materiality" here, by which they mean the relationship between the evidential fact and the issues in the trial. Whether or not a particular item of evidence is material depends upon whether the party who seeks to adduce it has successfully raised the issue on which it depends, and also on the substantive law. In the example just given, A would not be able to raise the defences of either provocation or diminished responsibility if he were charged with any offence other than murder. In a grievous bodily harm case his wife's affair would be irrelevant on the issue of guilt, although it might have some bearing at the sentencing stage.

Zuckerman has argued that "materiality" is an unnecessary concept; whether or not a certain fact can affect a legal result is not a question of evidence but of interpreting the substantive law.[16] Zuckerman is right to

---

[13] *R. v. Davis* [1980] 1 NZLR 257: "The price . . . is some uncertainty in borderline cases, but some uncertainty is inevitable with the questions of relevance or degrees of relevance. In criminal law it is more important to have a just and fair trial than a certain one."

[14] Homicide Act 1957, s. 2.

[15] Homicide Act 1957, s. 3.

[16] Zuckerman, "Relevance in Legal Proceedings" in W. Twining (ed.), *Facts in Law* (Steiner, Wiesbaden, 1983).

point out that the trier of fact is concerned only with those facts which the substantive law allows to have legal effect.[17] But it is still within the power of the parties to exclude elements of the substantive law altogether by choosing not to rely on them. It is for the parties to decide upon which planks (depending on the evidence and the law) to rest their case. They may find that they lose the opportunity to introduce an item of evidence if they fail to raise the issue which would render it material, either because they have not satisfied the required procedures[18] or because the evidential burden has not been discharged.[19] Thus the concept of materiality does exist independent of the effect of the substantive law; it is a creature of adversarial theory. Objective facts and operation of law are far from being the only influences on the conduct and outcome of trials; choices made by individuals have an important part to play too.

How then, should we explain the view of the House of Lords in *Blastland* that M's knowledge of the boy's death before it was officially known was irrelevant? Lord Bridge explained that it might have been relevant if the prosecution could show that M came by this knowledge by committing the crime himself, but the evidence did not amount to that. M could have acquired it in various other ways, for instance, by witnessing the murder. Given that Blastland would not have been able to use a confession by M if he had made one,[20] the evidence here had an even weaker case for admissibility. It is difficult to follow Lord Bridge's reasoning. An out of court confession by a third person is certainly inadmissible under the hearsay rule, but that does not affect the potential relevance of the behaviour of M. The significance of that was the justifiable inference from it that he knew a boy had been killed because he had killed him himself. Lord Bridge suggested that if an eye-witness had seen M do it, that would have been relevant because it would have been direct evidence against M, rather than a possible interpretation of the evidence, as here. Thus it seems that a defendant may not make out a circumstantial case against another person, but may accuse another of the crime if he has direct evidence against him—and then not if it is a confession, since that is hearsay.

The Court of Appeal in an earlier case, however, seem to have gone even further than the House of Lords. In *Steel*,[21] the defence wished to put to a police witness during cross-examination questions concerning the interrogation by police of one R. R had given the police an alibi which Steel wished to

---

[17] A. Zuckerman, *Principles of Criminal Evidence* (Oxford University Press, Oxford, 1989), 52.

[18] E.g., in civil cases, pleadings must contain the necessary particulars of any claim, defence or matter pleaded: RSC, Ord. 18, r 12. This limits the generality of issues at the subsequent trial.

[19] If D's defence above had been automatism, for example, he would have had to raise it by introducing evidence of involuntariness. If he had not done this, the evidence of medical experts on the likely effect of epilepsy or diabetes would have been immaterial. D would have had to make the issue "live" by adducing evidence of his own condition. See Ch. 3, text to nn. 20–32 below.

[20] Because it would be hearsay, *Turner* (1975) 61 Cr.App.R 67: see Ch.7.

[21] (1981) 73 Cr.App.R 17.

contradict. The trial judge refused to allow such questions on the ground that R's statements to the officer were hearsay, In the Court of Appeal Lord Lane CJ agreed that it probably was hearsay, but added that it "is absolutely certain that what Mr R may or may not have been doing as related by the police or anyone else at this particular time was an irrelevance, and on that basis the evidence was rightly rejected". This view of the Court of Appeal is not limited to the narrower ground given in *Blastland* (that what M knew or did not know had nothing to do with the case), since here the claim is that what R did was nothing to do with the case. The allegation that someone other than the accused was responsible for the crime is most frequently made where several persons are jointly charged, but is seen often enough in other cases to show the remarks in *Steel* to be a misleading exaggeration. In his judgment, Milmo J referred to a case cited by the defence in which the out-of-court confession of a third person was admitted, but dismissed it on the ground that the hearsay rule was never mentioned. This case, *Cooper*,[22] is of some interest. A group of youths were harassing a girl whose friend walked off in embarrassment. The friend realised help was needed and turned back, only to be punched in the face by one of the youths. The others she did not see. She selected Cooper at an identification parade, but other evidence undermined the significance of this. A member of the gang accused another member, B, of being the assailant. A friend, D, gave evidence that B admitted to him that he had hit the girl. From photographs, which the jury saw, the physical resemblance between Cooper and B was "really quite striking". Lord Widgery CJ was not in the least disturbed by all this evidence going before the jury; on the contrary, he commented that they had "every advantage" and that "every issue was before" them.[23] Despite the natural reluctance of the court to interfere with the verdict of a jury which was aware of the risk of wrongful identification, and which had had the opportunity (not available in the Court of Appeal) to observe the demeanour of the witnesses, the court was sufficiently worried about the reliability of the conviction to overturn it. Granted Lord Widgery CJ did not refer to the hearsay rule once throughout his judgment on behalf of the court, which may be regarded as a triumph for common sense. It should also be noted that not only did he not dismiss all the evidence against B as irrelevant, he clearly thought it so important that his only concern was whether the jury had underestimated its significance.

It is impossible to reconcile the remarks in *Blastland*, indicating that it was the wholly circumstantial nature of the evidence against M which made it objectionable, with those in *Steel*. But it is not difficult to identify some areas of concern which may underlie these judgments. There are three candidates: the first is that judges fear that trials would be too time-consuming if they examined the likelihood of persons other than the accused having committed the crime. This could not seriously be maintained as a proper

[22] [1969] 1 QB 267.   [23] *Ibid.*, at 270.

principle. Innocent men cannot justifiably be convicted because we will not go to the trouble and expense of listening to their defence. However, there must be limits to the probative value of the evidence against the third party; the court is not to be involved in chasing hares. The judgment in *Blastland* seemed concerned to draw that line, but *Steel* is a much less convincing example of this. The second concern may be that it is unfair to persons not present in court to accuse them. But this would not explain the assertion in *Blastland* that the defence could have called an eyewitness (had there been one) to establish M's guilt. Are the judges worried that any defendant could escape justice by establishing a vague circumstantial case against someone else, who, if charged, would promptly rely on the evidence incriminating the other to cast doubt on the evidence against him? There is a short answer to that, which is that in any case the prosecution must have sufficient evidence to prove guilt beyond a reasonable doubt. Thirdly, and this seems to be the only remaining possible rationale of *Steel*, is that judges may be thinking that the purpose of the trial is to test the strength of the prosecution case, and that if the disputed evidence is nothing to do with that case as pleaded, it has nothing to do with the trial. In other words, the prosecution must be met on its own terms. Thus the jury are not there to determine what actually happened. They are there to decide who won.

Remoteness: Credibility a Collateral Issue?

The law imposes artificial limits on evidence which may be both relevant and material, by demanding that other conditions are met. For there are limits to the amount of time and energy which courts are prepared to expend on cases in court. The exigencies of time and place inevitably restrict courts of law in their assessment of the relevance of evidence. They cannot afford the sort of thoroughness which a scientist would employ before reaching a conclusion. Hence Phipson's assessment: "[e]vidence is not a matter of mere logic. It is a question of ascertaining the truth as to facts that are in dispute. Such an inquiry must be reasonable, practical and fair".[24] The problem is that although restricting the scope of the inquiry may be necessary for practical reasons, it may impede the establishing of the truth. If this is the case, then it is not fair.

The need to impose limits on the scope of the oral inquiry has resulted in a distinction being drawn in many contexts[25] between evidence which has relevance to the issue at trial and evidence which relates simply to the credibility (in terms of either reliability or veracity) of a witness. The former is regarded as a matter of central importance to the case, the latter as one

---

[24] M.N. Howard, P. Crane and D.A. Hochberg, *Phipson on Evidence* (Sweet and Maxwell, London, 1990), 7.03.

[25] See, e.g., the problems which flow from the distinction with regard to the defendant's criminal record: Ch. 5.

which is only peripheral (or collateral or subordinate) to the main issue. This perspective involves two assumptions; one is that there is a logical difference between the issue at trial and matters of credibility, and the second is that credibility is never the central issue. Both are open to challenge on logical grounds. Nevertheless, the law operates as if this rigid divide can be supported. Hence, a party may not lead[26] evidence of the good or bad character of a witness,[27] since that is not a central issue, and may not form part of the case pleaded.[28] There is a little-known and barely comprehensible exception where it can be established that a witness has a reputation for untruthfulness. In *Richards and Longman*,[29] it was acknowledged by the Court of Appeal that there is a curious rule at common law to say that, although credibility is a collateral issue on which evidence may not be led, it is possible to call a witness, X, to say of another witness, Y, that he has such a reputation for untruthfulness that he should not be believed on his oath. The Court of Appeal noted that this is never done.[30]

Issues of character are collateral to the main issue, and therefore are the province of cross-examination. Further, to prevent the court being drawn into a protracted and complicated debate on the matter of the witness's good or bad character, there is a rule that the answer a witness gives to a question put in cross-examination on a matter relating to his or her credibility is final. This means that on that matter the witness may not be challenged by evidence contradictory to the answers he or she gave,[31] even if the cross-examiner has rebutting evidence to hand and could easily disprove it. Although the rule keeps the scope of the inquiry within reasonable practical limits, its interpretation is not without difficulty. Whether a question is directed at matters of credibility alone, or the issue itself—for example, the guilt of the defendant in a criminal trial—is not always apparent. The test is that if the party cross-examining could have raised the matter in evidence in chief, then the issue is central and not collateral.[32] The apparent circularity of this reasoning was noted in *Funderburke*,[33] where Henry J suggested that the usefulness of the test probably lies in an instinctive reaction "based on the prosecutor's sense of fair play" rather than any analytic process. These remarks refer to the useful elasticity of the concept of "the issue", and the facts which relate to it, as interpreted in the courts.[34] Hence in *Nagrecha*[35] it

---

[26] I.e., present as part of the evidence-in-chief.

[27] *Goodright* v. *Hicks* (1801) Bull.NP 296: *Edmondson* v. *Amery, The Times.* 28 Jan. 1911.

[28] For evidence of the good character of the defendant in a criminal case, see Ch. 5.

[29] [1966] 1 QB 309

[30] In *Toohey* [1965] AC 595, none of the Law Lords or counsel involved in the court could recall an instance of evidence of reputation for untruthfulness being adduced.

[31] *Harris* v. *Tippett* (1811) 2 Camp. 637.

[32] *A.-G.* v. *Hitchcock* (1847) 1 Exch. 91.

[33] [1990] 2 All ER 482.

[34] See M. Newark, "Opening Up the Collateral Issue Rule" (1992) 43 *LQR* 166.

[35] 22 Apr. 1997 CA: *Archbold News* 6, 8 July 1997.

was held in the Court of Appeal that the denials by a complainant in an indecent assault case that she had made similar allegations against various men in the past were not final, and the defence should have been allowed to contradict her. Disagreeing with the trial judge, the court regarded the matter as going beyond her credibility. The cross-examination had gone "to the heart of the case, in that it bore on the crucial issue as to whether or not there had been any idecent assault".

In an Australian case, *Piddington* v. *Bennet and Wood*,[36] the plaintiff sought damages from the defendant, alleging that he had been injured by a motor car as a result of the defendant's negligence. One of the plaintiff's witnesses claimed to have seen the accident, and was asked in cross-examination to account for his presence at the scene. He replied that he had gone to the bank to deposit or withdraw money in relation to a certain account. There had in fact been no transactions in respect of that account that day, and the defendant was allowed to call the bank manager to say so, despite the plaintiff's objection. The High Court of Australia was divided on the correctness of the trial judge's decision. The three judges in the majority held that the evidence was wrongly admitted, since the credibility of the witness was only collateral. According to the test in *Hitchcock*, the court was right, as Eggleston explains[37]: "[e]vidence about [the] bank account could not have been relevant in any sense if that particular witness had not given that answer in cross-examination. But the case demonstrates the difficulty of drawing the line." The demarcation in fact is so difficult to identify that it would be wrong to apply the rule uncompromisingly. The law of evidence recognises this and has evolved, as it so often seems forced by its own rigidity to do, a set of exceptions to cover those cases where particular issues of credibility are clearly of central importance. Thus, previous convictions, which may be put to a witness in cross-examination,[38] may be proved if the witness denies having them,[39] even though, as collateral matters, they could not have been led in chief by the cross-examiner. Another exception covers allegations of bias, including having an interest in the case,[40] or having a special relationship with the party for whom the witness is called.[41] A third category is where there is evidence of a mental disability going to reliability,[42] but, curiously, there is no common law authority that a physical disability which could affect reliability is included. This has led the Australian Law Commission to recommend statutory extension of the list.[43]

---

[36] (1940) 63 *CLR* 533.

[37] R. Eggleston, *Evidence Proof and Probability* (Weidenfeld and Nicolson, London, 1983), 76–7.

[38] See Ch. 3; for the defendant's special position in relation to previous convictions, see Ch. 5.

[39] Criminal Procedure Act 1865, s. 6. The method of proof is governed by s. 74 of the Police and Criminal Evidence Act 1984.

[40] *A.-G.* v. *Hitchcock* (1847) 1 Exch. 91.

[41] *Thomas* v. *David* (1836) 7 C & P 350.

[42] *Toohey* [1965] AC 595.

[43] Australian Law Reform Commission, *Evidence* (ALRC Interim Report No 26, Canberra, 1985).

A fourth exception allows a witness to be contradicted if he or she denies ever having made a previous inconsistent statement, but provisions, frequently ignored in practice by advocates, exist to protect a witness from being unfairly suprised by the production of a previous inconsistent statement. First, he or she must be asked whether in the past he or she has made a statement inconsistent with his or her current testimony. Then "the circumstances of the supposed statement, sufficient to designate the particular occasion, must be mentioned to the witness, and he must be asked whether or not he has made such statement".[44] Then the witness may indeed be contradicted if he or she denies making it, but, if the previous statement was made in writing, section 5 of the Criminal Procedure Act 1865[45] applies. If the proof that the statement was made is contained in a document, the witness's "attention must, before such contradictory proof can be given, be called to those parts of the writing which are to be used for the purpose". This means that the cross-examiner must go through various stages if it is intended to discredit a witness by showing that he or she has made contradictory statements in the past.

If, for example, Mrs Smith says she saw a tall man at the scene, and the advocate wishes to make use of an earlier description which she gave which claimed that the man was short, she must first be asked whether she has ever said anything to contradict present testimony. Then she must be asked, if she cannot recall it, whether she remembers giving the description in question. Then, and only if she denies ever describing the man as short, may the cross-examiner resort to proof that she did. If her earlier statement was made orally, then any one who heard her say it may offer evidence of that fact.[46] If her earlier statement was made in writing, at this stage counsel may tell her that the written statement exists, and that it contains a contradictory description. These steps in the process are designed to prevent the witness from being wrong-footed by pieces of paper being waved at him or her which he or she may remember little about, without being given the opportunity to explain the circumstances, or that there is no true contradiction there, if that is the case. It would be quite wrong for the advocate to miss out the early steps set out in section 4 of the 1865 Act, wait for Mrs Smith to describe the man as tall, and then produce an unidentified piece of paper declaring, "Well, I've a piece of paper here which shows you don't know your own mind!", or "That's not what you told the police, is it?". Yet these practices are seen in court every day. In some cases, a witness's previous inconsistent

---

[44] Criminal Procedure Act 1865, s.4. It should be noted that this provision applies to civil as well as criminal proceedings, despite the name of the statute.

[45] This provision applies to civil as well as criminal proceedings.

[46] That would not fall foul of the rule against hearsay as the witness would be testifying only that the she made the statement, that is, that she claimed it was a short man. The new witness would not be in a position to know how tall the suspect was, and is not being asked to tell the court that, only what it was that Mrs Smith said.

statements may appear more reliable than the current testimony, for example, if the passage of time has weakened his or her recall. In civil cases, the earlier statement may be relied on by the court as evidence of the facts stated. This exception to the hearsay rule is contained in the Civil Evidence Act 1995 sections1 and 6. However, in criminal cases, the hearsay rule prevents the earlier statement serving as evidence of the truth of what was said, and the significance of the previous inconsistent statement is therefore solely that here is a witness who has said different things on different occasions and so cannot be regarded as a reliable one.[47]

Zuckerman argues most powerfully that the credibility of witnesses is always relevant to the issue in the proceedings, and therefore the distinction between collateral questions and those going to the issue is unsound. He suggests that for this reason the principle is often ignored. In *Busby*,[48] police officers were cross-examined to the effect that they invented alleged admissions by the defendant and had threatened a potential witness. The Court of Appeal held that it went beyond establishing credibility, and related to an issue, which was whether police officers would go so far to get a conviction. Effectively, here the credibility of a particular witness *was* the issue. The reality is that credibility or, more particularly, specific facts connected with the credibility of a witness may or may not be important, given the other evidence before the court in the light of the arguments relied on. Hence the exceptions relating to particular *kinds* of credibility evidence, which all involve recognition that in some cases the witness's credibility is crucial; but the exceptions are too narrow. Zuckerman's example is of an eyewitness, W, who says that he saw a stabbing from 50 yards and identifies the accused as the attacker. The defence has evidence that W cannot see beyond ten yards. In strict law, it cannot use this evidence if W insists on cross-examination that he can see perfectly well. Yet, argues Zuckerman, the court could not properly convict in such a case.[49] Presumably for this reason, many judges would disregard the restriction and allow the evidence to be called. The view of the Australian Law Reform Commission that the rule on collateral issues is artificial and inflexible and may result in the court being misled has led to the inclusion in the Evidence Act (Australia) 1995 of provisions allowing rebuttal evidence where it shows that the witness is unable to be aware of matters to which his or her evidence relates. Problems of this kind appear to arise because the distinction between evidence which goes to the issue and evidence which goes to credibility does not exist in logic, only in the minds of lawyers. In other contexts we recognise that probative value can vary according to the issues and the other available evidence.

The question remains whether the line is worth drawing at all. Facts do not fall neatly into two categories relating either to issues which are collateral (including credit) or central. Sometimes the matter of the state of an

---

[47] *Golder* [1960] 3 All ER 457.   [48] [1982] Crim. LR 232.   [49] N. 17 above, 95.

identifying witness's eyesight is of crucial importance, and should be investigated with just as much vigour as his criminal record, bias or previous
inconsistent statements.[50] But if we have to conclude from Zuckerman's
argument that the kind of general character evidence such as employment
record, which is commonly put to witnesses on the assumption that any
disagreeable characteristics go to credibility, is central, we are putting the
case too strongly. The apparent inability of judges to protect rape
complainants from cross-examination on previous sexual relationships,
despite statutory reform,[51] indicates the blurred line between questions
going to an issue in the trial and questions going to credit. Zuckerman
should not be taken to propose the gratuitous humiliation of even more of
such witnesses. The point is that previous sexual history is of little evidential
value, as it has no bearing on whether or not the witness would invent a
rape. An untrue explanation of why the witness was allegedly at the scene, as
in *Piddington*, is of a great deal more interest. The problem in that case
resulted entirely from the formal structure of the adversarial trial, with its
rigid division between the case in chief and cross-examination, and its insistence that everything be proved "on the day". In an inquistorial process,
genuinely important collateral issues would be identified and investigated
before the trial by the investigating magistrate. In *Piddington* a pre-trial
inquiry might have elucidated the matter of the bank account; in any event,
it seems unfair to D that what might be an important (or trivial) inconsistency in the witness's story should not be brought out at all, just because he
could not have shown the relevance of the bank account evidence to his case
in chief since its significance depended entirely on the explanation given by
the plaintiff's witness during the trial. Abandoning the inflexible dichotomy
between credit and issue, relying instead on the actual probative value of the
evidence in the case, would be far more helpful. The Law Commission of
New Zealand suggests that flexibility is the solution; it proposes the abolition of the rule on collateral issues, and its replacement with a test of
"substantial helpfulness", which would allow rebuttal evidence in any case
where it would serve a genuinely useful purpose.[52]

Remoteness and Probability

Courts have tried to invent devices to draw a line so that the inquiry does not
become too bogged down with detail and peripheral facts, but not all
solutions appear to be entirely successful. For instance, in *Stephenson*,[53] the
defendant was accused of causing an accident which killed three people and

---

[50] Criminal Procedure Act 1865, ss. 4, 5.
[51] See below Ch. 4.
[52] Law Commission of New Zealand *Evidence Law: Character and Credibility, Preliminary Paper
27* (New Zealand Law Commission, Wellington, 1997).
[53] [1976] VR 376.

injured a fourth in another car. Defence counsel wished to introduce evidence of blood tests for the alcohol level of the three dead. It appeared that at least one of them was not over the legal limit, but there was no evidence as to who was driving. It was held that if all the occupants of that car had been over the limit, then that evidence would have been admissible even without evidence as to who was the driver, since logically the driver must have exceeded the limit. But in this case the evidence was so vague that it was inadmissible on the ground of remoteness. Egglestone[54] criticises this reasoning. If only one of the occupants of the car had been drunk, that would increase the probability of the defendant's claim that the other car was to blame being true, even though the chance of that man being the driver was only one in four. Here the probability was higher than that, and the defendant's chances of conviction were greatly increased by the exclusion of the evidence.

Evidence is relevant if it increases or decreases the probability of the existence of a fact in issue. The maxim *res inter alios acta alteria nocere non debet* (nobody should be harmed by a transaction between strangers) sometimes seems to be used as a test, but is not consistently so treated, and nor should it be. In *Manchester Brewery* v. *Coombs*,[55] the question was whether a brewer had sold bad beer to a publican. The fact that the brewer sold good beer to other publicans was regarded as relevant, since the beer was all from the same brewing. But in *Holcombe* v. *Hewson*,[56] with a similar question, Lord Ellenborough dismissed it as *res inter alios acta*. "We cannot inquire into the quality of different beer sold to different persons. The party might deal well with one and not with others. I cannot admit evidence of this general character and habits as a brewer." Here the beer was from various brewings. So the relevance of evidence depends not on a general principle expressed in a maxim, but on the usefulness in probative terms of the facts in question. The probability of bad beer being supplied in the first case, if the brewing was shown to be good, was only slight. In the second, the possibility of one brewing going badly was sufficient for evidence of the quality of other brewings not to take the court much further. It has been argued that some evidence which appears at first sight as highly probative can be excluded under this maxim. If 95 per cent of all motorists at an intersection cut the corner, that fact must have bearing on whether or not the defendant did. His denial asks us to accept that he is exceptional. Yet such evidence would not be admitted. Judges do not wish to involve themselves in sociological inquiries about the probabilities of human beings behaving in a particular way. In *Metropolitan Asylum District* v. *Hill*,[57] the issue was the effect of a smallpox hospital on the health of the inhabitants of the neighbourhood. A majority of the House of Lords held that evidence of the effect of similar institutions on other localities was inadmissible. There is a general dislike of

---

[54] N. 37 above, 83.   [55] (1900) 82 LT 347.   [56] (1810) 2 Camp. 391.   [57] (1872) 47 LT 29.

the style of argument that A caused (or did not cause) B, therefore wherever A occurs B will (or will not) follow and therefore did so here.[58]

It is far from clear, however, that courts can escape this kind of statistical argument entirely. For example, where fingerprint or DNA evidence is adduced, its reliability is assessed in statistical terms. There are data available on the significance of sexual play by young children with anatomically correct dolls,[59] evidence which is frequently used in child abuse cases. This kind of statistical evidence does not trouble judges, and nor should it, since its probative value is in terms of the reliability of other evidence which is used directly in the case, and thus its impact on the outcome is indirect. Koehler[60] gives the example of evidence of the probability that three out of 20 infants in the same household would die of sudden infant death syndrome over a five-year period; that was relevant to rule out the defence of natural causes. But there would be no case without other evidence to implicate the defendant—the death of a child preceded by two similar deaths, the opportunity to cause those deaths, and so on. Rebuttal of a defence is very different from building a case on probability alone, and the statistics in fact only go to show the genuine probative value of the similar fact evidence of the other children's deaths, and therefore is secondary, as far as the issue at trial is concerned.

"Naked" statistical evidence directly on the issue has been allowed in industrial tribunals on the question of discrimination, for example, where the issue is whether a condition of employment is such that fewer women than men can comply.[61] It is also relatively common in the "mass torts" cases, where a process in which the defendant is engaged is alleged to be responsible for an unusually high incidence of disease or other harm in the locality. For example, it was argued for the plaintiffs in *Reay* v. *British Nuclear Fuels: Hope* v. *Same*[62] that, since the occurrence of childhood leukaemia and non-Hodgkin's lymphoma tended to be higher than the national average within populations close to nuclear re-processing plants, the defendant's activities at the Sellafield plant in West Cumbria must be causally linked to the illnesses and subsequent deaths of their children. French J examined the epidemiological evidence with great care, but found it incon-

---

[58] Judges are right to be cautious. Eggleston could perhaps himself face the objection frequently levelled at statisticians that they assume a continuity of circumstances. In his example from *Stephenson*, if it were the case that one occupant of the car was sober and the rest drunk, that does not necessarily make it 75% probable that the driver was drunk. The people concerned could have agreed that three would drink and the other drive—a common agreement amongst party-goers, and, given that the other three were drunk, highly likely.

[59] D. Glaser and C. Collins, "The Response of Young, Non-sexually Abused Children to Anatomically Correct Dolls" (1989) 30(4) *Jnl. of Child Psychology and Psychiatry* 547.

[60] J.J. Koehler "Probabilities in the Courtroom: An Evaluation of the Objectives and Policies" in D.K. Kagehiro and W.S. Laufer (eds.), *Handbook of Psychology and Law* (New York; Springer-Verlag, 1992).

[61] *Meeks* v. *NUUAW* [1976] IRLR 198.

[62] *The Independent*, 22 Nov. 1993.

clusive. It was also substantially contradicted by other evidence. To establish a causal relationship between an industrial operation and an epidemic or other harm solely on the basis of statistical evidence is not impossible, but it is difficult, although the very notion of cause is a probabilistic one. It is rare to be certain that a causal relationship exists, but evidence from many different angles may build a body of support sufficient to convince most reasonable people that it is more prudent to act as though an association were causal than to assume that it is not. And in many cases, evidence of probability is logically in the same bracket as any other evidence by means of which, given the imperfect information before the court, a verdict is reached on what *did* happen.[63] Rosenberg observes that evidence of probability cannot be excluded, because all evidence is probabilistic.[64] In many contexts, however, the judicial objection is that "[t]rials are said to be conducted to determine what actually happened rather than what the probabilities favour",[65] or in simpler terms, as might express it, "[t]hings either happen or they don't; they don't probably happen".

The issue is essentially a moral one, as Judith Thompson has shown.[66] One of her well-known examples is that of Mrs Smith, whom we know to have been injured by a cab. If more Red Cabs are operated in town than Green Cabs so that the probability that the cab which caused the accident was a Red Cab is 0.6, why should we be reluctant to impose civil liability on Red Cabs on the basis of that evidence alone? Yet we are, and are equally reluctant to convict of a crime in another of her examples. T and S both hate Y and independently but simultaneously shoot all the pellets in their shotguns at him. Only one pellet hits Y and kills him. T had 95 pellets, S only five; if the prosecution can show that T shot 95 pellets out of 100, why has it not proved murder by T beyond reasonable doubt? The objection is that the evidence is not individualised against the defendant in either instance. Thompson, in accepting that weakness, warns against assuming that individualised evidence must therefore be "uniquely highly probabilifying"; categories of "real" evidence such as eye-witness identification or confessions have alarming shortcomings of their own,[67] so the explanation cannot be that direct or individualised evidence is more probative than statistical probabilities. She argues that the answer is that it is unjust to act on a probability to someone's disadvantage. To find against a defendant and therefore impose liabilities upon him, to cause him loss, one must feel (rightly or wrongly)

---

[63] B. Robertson and G. Vignaux, "Probability: The Logic of the Law" [1993] Oxford Journal of Legal Studies 457.

[64] D. Rosenberg "The Causal Connection in Mass Exposure Cases: A 'Public Law' Vision of the Tort System" (1984) 97 *Harvard LR* 849.

[65] C. Nesson, "The Evidence or the Event? On Judicial Proof and the Acceptability of Verdicts" (1985) 98 *Harvard LR* 1387.

[66] J.J. Thompson, "Probabilities as Relevant Facts" in J.J. Thompson (ed.), *Rights, Restitution and Risk* (Harvard University Press, Cambridge, Mass. 1986).

[67] See Ch. 3.

that one knows the truth. Knowing that there is a 95 per cent probability of the defendant's guilt is not the same as feeling 95 per centsure that the defendant is guilty.

On similar lines, Nesson argues that it is illegitimate to convict a prisoner of murder of a guard in the prison yard, where it is known that 24 out of 25 prisoners participated in the killing. If the defendant were selected from that group of 25 on a random basis, there is a 96 per cent probability of his being guilty. However, Nesson observes, he is not uniquely identified as a participant and the verdict depends on factors outside his control. His stance is attacked by Koehler, who replies that the reliability of an eyewitness's account can itself be expressed as a probability, and also depends on factors such as the quality of his eyesight or the physical conditions under which the murder was observed, all being matters outside the defendant's control. But the key issue here is not control, but the lack of "individualised evidence". Our preference for individualised evidence is not because it is more cogent or reliable, but because it is perceived to be unjust to act on a probability to someone's disadvantage. Returning to Koehler's example of the unreliability of eyewitnesses, it is quite legitimate for a conscientious juror, having been told that eyewitnesses are (say) 60 per cent likely to be mistaken, to conclude that nevertheless he believes that *this* eyewitness is reliable, and that therefore he is sure beyond reasonable doubt that the defendant is guilty. That situation is morally acceptable; convicting solely on the basis of a probability is clearly not. Following Koehler's argument, it would be logical to convict in individual trials every one out of the 25 prisoners in the group on the basis of probability alone, although, *ex hypothesi*, one of them is most certainly not guilty. Awareness of this problem may account for what Thompson describes as our intuitive judgement that to assess liability by probability alone is wrong. Yet, as will be seen below, in the American case, *Shonubi*[68] the defendant's uniqueness was virtually ignored, so that he was punished on the basis of the frequency of events with which he had no connection.

Whether juries would over-estimate the reliability of statistical evidence, given its apparent precision "in marked contrast to the uncertainties of other testimony",[69] is not clear. Some research suggests that juries dislike evidence of probability and give it insufficient weight.[70] This may be because the evidence is too abstract to have impact[71] or because of lack of perceived causal

---

[68] *US* v. *Shonubi* (1993) F Supp. 460 (sentence reversed on appeal); resentenced 1995 in the US Dist. Ct. (EDNY, unrep.)

[69] L. Tribe, "Trial by Mathematics" (1971) 84 *Harvard LR* 1329.

[70] M.J. Saks and R.F. Kidd, "Human Information Processing and Adjudication: Trial by Heuristics" (1980) I5 Law and Society Review 123.

[71] R.E. Nisbett and E. Borgida *et al.* "Popular Induction: Information is not Necessarily Informative" in J.J. Carroll and J.W. Payne (eds.), Cognition and Social Behavior (Erlbaum, Hillsdale NJ, 1976).

relevance.[72] The Court of Appeal made it clear in *Adams*[73] that criminal courts are not the place to indulge in abstruse and confusing mathematical theorising. In this case, the defendant's DNA profile matched that of semen left by a rapist. He lived in the area where the offence had been committed, but had an alibi, and, according to the victim, looked unlike her attacker. The defence expert witness, with the approval of counsel for the prosecution and the trial judge, embarked on an explanation of how Bayes' Theorem might assist the jury to link together and assign relative weight to these various items of evidence. Not only did the Count of Appeal consider that the court was as a consequence plunged into inappropriately complex realms of theory, but also that Bayes' Theorem was of its nature an inappropriate mechanism for jury trials.[74] It trespasses on an area peculiarly and exclusively within the province of the jury, namely, the way in which they evaluate the relationship between one piece of evidence and another. Certainly, it appears that the Theorem is not only difficult to understand,[75] but even more difficult to apply without controversy in relation to specific items of concrete evidence. Juries, however guided, are hardly in a position to cope with complex evidence of a mathematical nature. Even experts are alarmingly disposed to misunderstand it. Prosecutors and judges may be forgiven for making some obvious and well-known errors about probabilities, but it appears that they can also be committed by expert witnesses. The most well-documented error is The Prosecutor's Fallacy, or "transposing the conditional". The fallacy is to assume that the answer to the question, "What was the probability that an individual would match the DNA profile from the sample if he were innocent?" is the same as the answer to the question, "What was the probability that an individual was innocent given that he matched the DNA profile from the crime sample?[76]

The court must decide the second question. The expert should give evidence on the first. The answer to the second question depends on many factors, which may include the characteristics of the defendant himself. Robertson and Vignaux give the example[77] of a DNA test based on a sample taken from a crime scene in London, where the band pattern is one shared by only one in 100,000 of the relevant population. This evidence makes it 100,000 times more likely that the samples are from the same source than it would appear without the DNA evidence, and therefore amplifies other evidence against the defendant, such as an eyewitness identification. The

---

[72] A. Tversky and D. Kahnman, "Availability: A Heuristic for Judging Frequency and Probability" (1973) 5 *Cognitive Psychology* 207.

[73] *The Times*, 9 May 1996.

[74] For an explanation of Bayes' Theorem see J. McEwan, "Hypothetical or Actual Fact? Common Sense and Probability as Evidence in *U.S.* v. *Shonubi*" (1996) 4 *Expert Evidence* 150.

[75] Robertson and Vigneaux, n. 63 above.

[76] D.J. Baldwin and P. Donnelly, "The Prosecutor's Fallacy and DNA Evidence" [1984] *Crim. LR* 211.

[77] B. Robertson and G.A. Vignaux, "Expert Evidence: Law, Practice and Probability'" [1992] *Oxford Journal Legal Studies* 392.

Prosecutor's Fallacy is to assume that the match means that the odds are 100,00 to one that the accused is guilty. In fact, if there are 10 million people in London, 100 people would match the sample. If there is no other evidence against any particular person, the odds are 99:1 *against* any of them, including the accused, being guilty, since the culprit could be any one of those 100. The answer to the second question above therefore depends on the nature of the case as a whole. In *Deen*,[78] the expert witness himself made the error, agreeing that "the likelihood of [the source] being any other man but Andrew Deen is one in three million". The tendency of scientific experts to commit errors in terms of probability theory, together with the level of disagreement amongst specialists in the field on how probabilities should be computed in any given case, gives rise to concern about the ability of courts to assess the value of statistical evidence and, when it is correct, to apply what they have been told.

The misuse of statistics may also be seen in the famous American case of *People* v. *Collins*.[79] Witnesses to a robbery said that the culprits were a couple, a male negro with a beard and moustache, and a caucasian woman with her blonde hair in a ponytail. They escaped in a yellow car. Collins, his wife and their car answered this description, and the prosecution called a mathematician to give evidence that there was only a one in 12 million chance that "a couple" would possess all these features. They were convicted, but the Supreme Court of California set aside the verdict on appeal. The rival mathematical arguments offered by the Court have themselves been challenged[80]; in fact, the extent of disagreement among specialists, coupled with the impenetrability of the debate for lay persons,[81] suggests that judges have been well advised not to be drawn into the field of probability. But it is obvious to anyone that the evidence in *Collins* suffered from the number of imponderables in the "population of interest",[82] that is, whether the search for the couple was random over the whole country, and if not, how was it limited? Also, the idea that people occupy an item known as a "couple" on a permanent basis is unconvincing. Certainly, Collins and his wife are a couple for some purposes, but there is no particular reason to assume that the robbers were a couple in any context apart from committing a robbery, and none whatever to conclude that they were married to each other!

The case of *Shonubi*[83] might be thought to involve similar difficulties, but there the defendant was unable to resist. The issue, which was relevant to

---

[78] *The Times,* 10 Jan. 1994.

[79] (1968) 438 P. 2d. 33.

[80] M.D. Finkelstein and N.B. Fairley, "A Bayesian Approach to Identification Evidence' (1970) 83 *Harv. LR* 489; A. Kreith, "Mathematics, Social Decisions and the Law" (1976) 7(3) *International Journal of Mathematical Education in Science and Technology* 315.

[81] Eggleston, n. 37 above, 159.

[82] *Ibid.*

[83] *US* v. *Shonubi* (1993) 895 F Supp. 460 (sentence reversed on appeal); resentenced; (1995 US Dist Ct.) (EDNY, unrep.).

sentence, was how much heroin had been smuggled into the United States by the defendant on the seven trips from Nigeria he was believed to have taken prior to the one during which he was apprehended.[84] On the eighth trip he had been found to have swallowed a large amount of heroin contained in balloons. There was no direct evidence of his having smuggled heroin on the earlier occasions, but if he had, the quantity involved would affect his sentence in relation to the offence of which he was actually convicted. The original sentencing court estimated the total weight smuggled over the eight incidents by multiplying by eight the quantity seized on the last trip. On appeal the decision was referred back, and the sentencing judge instructed to rely on specific evidence and testimony, but without explanation of what this specific evidence might be. Judge Weinstein decided that it would be instructive to take the John F. Kennedy Airport customs figures which showed the quantities of heroin smuggled in from Nigeria by other persons, using similar means, during the period between Shonubi's first and final trip. Averaging out these amounts would suggest a weight which Shonubi himself might have swallowed on each of the previous occasions. Elaborate statistical arguments ensued, for example as to whether Nigerian couriers, known as "mules", typically became increasingly proficient through practice at swallowing large quantities, so that these would become greater over time. This led to the judge allowing for a slight learning curve; the estimate for the first trip was based on the assumption that Shonubi carried 225–450 grammes. This was multiplied by a 65 per cent probability that the trip took place at all, and that it was a smuggling trip. This resulted in a figure of 146 grammes for the first trip. Subsequent journeys were dealt with in a similar way, the probabilities and weights increasing each time.

Thus generalisations were made from the behaviour of others to draw inferences about Shonubi's. But it is only acceptable from a statistician's point of view to draw such comparisons if the specific case can reasonably be considered to be a random sample from the relevant general population.[85] It appears to have been assumed that the defendant was a typical member of an identifiable group, namely, Nigerians who swallow balloons containing heroin, and then smuggle it into New York. There was no evidence that this was so, although Judge Weinstein made the comment: "[t]he government. . . assumed that Mr Shonubi was a typical heroin swallower . . . This was a conservative assumption; Shonubi appears to have been a more-effective-than-typical swallower". The only "individualised" evidence against the defendant, as far as the seven earlier incidents are concerned, was his current demeanour (aggressive and confident), his lies on being arrested and the inferences it was thought reasonable to draw from this behaviour.

---

[84] Under Federal Sentencing Guidelines 1994, a sentencing court may take uncharged conduct proved only to the civil standard into account on the issue of the seriousness of the defendant's criminal conduct.

[85] Koehler, Kagehiro and Laufer (eds.), n. 60 above.

The reasoning in *Shonubi*, being based upon judgments of the frequency of activities of persons unconnected with the case, appears to be the same as that which would convict 25 prisoners where 24 out of 25 murder the prison guard. It is the same as the argument that if 98 out of 100 drivers who take a particular road exceed the speed limit, then it may be concluded that the defendant drove at excessive speed, without need for eye-witness evidence, because he did take that road. We may as well assume that because 97 out of 100 rapists carry weapons, then so did the defendant, given that he committed rape. "Naked" statistical evidence like this is most certainly not acceptable in criminal cases, either to establish guilt or to establish seriousness for sentencing purposes. Thompson has shown that using such reasoning to the detriment of another is morally unsound. Yet probabilistic reasoning effectively caused Shonubi to be sentenced to more than 12 years' imprisonment.

Relevance, Policy and Subjectivism: The Similar Facts Rule

Similar Facts Rule: Area of Operation

Concepts of relevance or probative value are highly subjective, as may be seen in the "similar facts" cases. They represent the area of law which prohibits, in general, evidence of the bad character of the defendant (whether in a criminal or civil case). The view of the common law is that any negative characteristics which the defendant may possess, although relevant, are not admissible merely to show that he or she is the kind of person capable of the act alleged. If a house has been burgled and it is necessary to show that D is the culprit, how probative is it that he has a criminal record which includes burglary? Clearly, someone with a history of burgling houses may be more likely to have burgled a particular house than someone who has never done such a thing. But the history shows no more than that he has no moral inhibition about burglary, so that the likelihood of his guilt is slightly increased. The law, therefore, is inclined to ban evidence which shows that the defendant has the disposition or propensity to behave in a particular way. A phrase commonly used to express the principle is that "a defendant must be tried for what he did, not who he is". However, the mere fact that prosecution evidence in a criminal case tends to show the commission of other crimes does not render it inadmissible, if it is relevant to an issue before the jury. Evidence which indicates that a defendant is guilty is admissible. If it puts him or her in a bad light at the same time, that it is simply an unfortunate and unavoidable consequence of admitting valuable, but incidentally damning, evidence of guilt. The two situations have therefore to be distinguished; is the disputed evidence sufficiently indicative of guilt to justify disregard of the inevitable prejudice which it will inspire in the finder of fact, or is it merely an appeal to the tribunal to conclude that the defendant is the kind of person to commit the act alleged?

The facts of the most famous of the similar facts cases, *Makin v. A-G for New South Wales*,[86]show how the principle works. The defendants were a married couple, in whose yard was discovered buried the body of a dead baby. Its mother had given the couple money to take it off her hands. There was no evidence of how the baby came to die, whether by accident or of natural causes, and thus nothing to indicate that the Makins murdered the baby, except that there were three other dead babies found buried at the same place. At their previous home, the bodies of seven babies were discovered. At their home before that, two dead babies were found buried. There was evidence that they had taken money from a number of mothers in return for keeping their babies. This evidence went far beyond simply suggesting to the court that the Makins were an unsavoury pair. It indicated a systematic practice of taking money from mothers and then killing their babies. This evidence was highly probative on the issue of the death of the baby with whose murder they were charged. The nature of this reasoning process is best explained in the famous passage from Lord Hershell's judgment:

> "It is undoubtedly not competent for the prosecution to adduce evidence tending to show that the accused has been guilty of criminal acts other than those covered by the indictment, for the purpose of leading to the conclusion that the accused is a person likely from his criminal conduct or character to have committed the offence for which he is being tried. On the other hand, the mere fact that the evidence tends to show the commission of other crimes does not render it inadmissible if it bears upon the issue whether the acts alleged to constitute the crime are designed or accidental, or to rebut a defence which would otherwise be open to the accused".[87]

Thus evidence which "would only show the prisoner to be a bad man" should be distinguished from evidence which would be "direct evidence of the fact in issue"—here, whether the Makins had deliberately killed the baby.

The judicial discretion to balance probative force against prejudicial effect operates in the same way in civil cases, although possibly less strictly, given the lower standard of proof and the lesser jeopardy for defendants. In *Mood Music v. De Wolfe*[88] the defendants admitted publishing a melody bearing a marked resemblance to a song already published by the plaintiffs, but argued that the similarity was coincidental and not intentional. The fact that they had twice in the past published songs virtually the same as those published by another was held to be admissible to show that they had deliberately copied the plaintiff's song. The Court of Appeal explained that the civil court will admit similar fact evidence if it is logically probative, provided that it is not oppressive or unfair to the other side, and that the other side has had fair notice of it. Although civil courts will admit, where it is probative, similar

[86] [1894] AC 57.   [87] *Ibid.*, at 65   [88] [1976] 1 All ER 463.

fact evidence in copyright, forgery and breach of fiduciary duty cases, it is difficult to persuade them to do so in cases where it is alleged that the defendant has been negligent. The argument that evidence of negligence in the past indicates negligence on this occasion is rarely successful. However, in *Hales* v. *Kerr*,[89] the plaintiff was allowed to adduce evidence that a barber had failed to sterilise shaving equipment twice in earlier incidents, in order to show that he had done on the occasion which allegedly caused him to suffer a skin rash.

It is frequently not obvious that a case involves the similar facts principle, where the "character" evidence complained of does not consist of misconduct. Yet the judgment is the same—is the evidence genuinely probative or does it create an indefensible level of prejudice? The earlier actions may not in fact be either immoral or illegal, and therefore may not comprise misconduct in any sense. In *Butler*[90] the evidence in dispute involved previous acts of oral sex with willing partners, but in circumstances sufficiently unusual to cast grave doubts on the defendant's claim that he had been identified as a rapist in error. If the earlier behaviour is utterly innocuous and could create no risk of prejudice whatever, then the test for admissibility is simply one of relevance. If some risk of prejudice is created, then the test is whether the risk is counteracted by its probative value.[91]

Another source of potential confusion is that evidence indicative of previous misconduct by a defendant, may or may not necessarily consist of previous convictions. In *Smith*,[92] the defendant was being tried for the murder of a woman with whom he had gone through a form of marriage, and who shortly afterwards was found dead in her bath, apparently drowned. Smith admitted that he had been present in the building at the time of her death, and, that, discovering her underwater, he had made no effort to pull her from the water before calling a doctor. He stood to gain financially from her death. The prosecution sought to adduce evidence that Smith had previously committed two murders with which he had never been charged. It had been discovered that two of his former "wives" had died in their baths in similar circumstances, and that he had derived financial benefit from those deaths as well. Evidence of the two earlier deaths was admitted in the case against Smith, the implication being that he had a "system" of marriage and murder, and so the third victim had been murdered by Smith as he had murdered the first two. The logic would be the same even if Smith had been tried for, and acquitted of, either or both of the first two murders. The

---

[89] [1908] 2 KB 601.

[90] (1986) 84 Cr. App. R 12.

[91] Some defence advocates appear to think that any evidence which suggests that their client is guilty of the offence charged is prejudicial. In fact it is the opposite—it is probative. It may, of course, offend some other exclusionary rule. Prejudicial evidence is that which appears to suggest to the court that because the defendant is of such bad character, he or she is perfectly capable of committing the offence charged.

[92] (1915) 11 Cr. App. R 229.

probative value of the evidence of those deaths would have been just as great. If he had been acquitted, there would have been no element of double jeopardy in using the evidence again, since Smith would not have been at risk, at the trial for murder of wife number three, of conviction for the earlier murders.[93] If there is evidence which suggests that the defendant is guilty of the current offence, the outcome in any previous case based on that evidence is immaterial.

The similar fact principle may affect issues of admissibility in a civil or criminal trial, but in criminal cases it also may have a bearing on the issue whether a number of charges against the same defendant should be "joined", or heard together by the same jury at the same trial. An alternative would be "severance", which means that separate trials are held with different juries hearing isolated charges against the same defendant. Under the Indictment Rules 1971, Rule 9, charges for any offences may be joined in the same indictment if those charges are founded on the same facts, or form or are part of a series of offences of the same or a similar character. In *Kray and others*,[94] it was held that a number of offences could constitute a series if there was a sufficient nexus between them, so that the evidence of one offence would be admissible to prove the commission of the other. But a judge will exercise his discretion to direct that the counts be severed, so ordering separate trials, if joinder would be unduly prejudicial to the defendant.[95] Some of the most well-known of similar facts cases concern joinder, the defence argument on appeal being that the jury will have been prejudiced by having heard several allegations against the defendant at once.[96]

We have seen that not all similar fact evidence in criminal cases consists of criminal misconduct. Where it does consist of misconduct, it would not necessarily have resulted in a conviction, and might even have led to acquittal. Where it did in fact lead to a criminal conviction, the prosecution cannot simply present evidence that the accused was convicted of a particular offence. Section 73 of the Police and Criminal Evidence Act 1984 provides that a conviction may be proved by way of certificate of conviction alone. Such proof means that "he shall be taken to have committed that offence unless the contrary is proved".[97] This provision, however, applies to evidence relevant to any matter in issue in the proceedings for a reason other than a tendency to show in the accused a disposition to commit the kind of offence with which he is charged.[98] Where a prosecutor relies on evidence of an earlier transaction claiming that it is probative against the defendant on the current charge, then the logic of that argument demands that the similar fact evidence be included in the prosecutor's case in chief. Since it is the

---

[93] *Caeres Moreira* [1995] Crim. LR 489; *Ollis* [1990] 2 QB 758.
[94] (1969) 53 Cr. App. R 569.
[95] *Ludlow* v. *Metropolitan Police Commissioner* [1971] AC 29.
[96] *DPP* v. *Boardman* [1975] AC 421; *DPP* v. *P* [1991] 3 All ER 337; *R.* v. *H* [1995] 2 All ER 865.
[97] S.74(2).   [98] S.74(3).

nature of the previous incident that, it is claimed, proves the defendant's guilt on this occasion, all relevant details of the earlier conduct must be proved within that case in chief. Therefore the bare facts on a certificate of conviction are insufficient for the purpose, and constitute only hearsay evidence that the defendant committed the actions concerned. The facts must come from someone with direct knowledge of what was done, and this may mean that there is no alternative to calling the victim to give evidence a second time. In *Jones* v. *DPP*,[99] the defendant was accused of the rape and murder of a Girl Guide. He had a previous conviction for the rape of a Girl Guide. He had, in the earlier case, at first given a false alibi to the police during their inquiry, and then, when it collapsed, gave a new alibi and provided an explanation for the lie. His second version of events was identical to the alibi he offered at the murder trial years later. It emerged, however, that during the murder inquiry he had provided a false alibi identical to that employed during the earlier rape investigation, and an explanation for the lie, when it was discovered, identical to the one he had offered at the rape trial. Despite excellent prospects for convincing the judge that all this evidence was relevant to the question of whether Jones' current alibi could be believed, the prosecution did not attempt to introduce evidence of the rape at the murder trial. The rape victim would have had to describe her ordeal all over again.[100]

The rule against evidence of bad character holds that courts will not allow prejudicial evidence to be heard if its probative value is slight. As we shall see below, that involves judges in a balancing exercise, seeking to measure the amount of prejudice caused against the probative force of the evidence. The cases which require this feat of the judiciary are criticised on many grounds, but here Zuckerman's is the most forceful; he has shown[101] that it is entirely inappropriate to compare relevance or probative force (which are matters relating to the proof of fact) with prejudice, which is not solely concerned with the discovery of the truth, or the avoidance of mistakes by the jury, but includes matters of policy and moral choice:

> "Similar fact evidence threatens two central principles of our criminal justice. The first is that in any criminal trial the accused stands to be tried, acquitted or convicted, only in respect of the offence with which he is charged. The second is that convictions must take place only if the jury are persuaded of the accused's guilt beyond all reasonable doubt."[102]

---

[99] [1962] AC 635.

[100] The House of Lords in this case made it quite clear that the statutory provision allowing cross-examination on previous convictions which fulfil the similar fact requirement of relevance to guilt (s.1(f)(i) of the Criminal Evidence Act 1898) may be used only where the prosecution has laid a proper foundation for it by adducing the similar facts evidence during its case in chief. See Ch. 5.

[101] Zuckerman, n. 12 above.

[102] *Ibid.*, at 195.

There is a risk that the jury's moral reaction to the accused's proclivity would affect their judgement, and that knowledge of his criminal past would reduce the standard of proof.[103] This argument derives some support from the comparatively complacent attitude of the civil courts as far as the risk of prejudice is concerned.[104] In civil cases the test for admissibility is more straightforward, and the judge's task can be described as an attempt precisely to measure the probative force of the similar facts without becoming embroiled in issues of policy.

Probative Value v. Prejudicial Effect

The rule that evidence must be more probative than it is prejudicial is not difficult to grasp, but is notoriously difficult to apply. This is partly because individuals have different perspectives on what is and what is not probative. The other main reason for the problem is that the test is not amenable to classifications and categorisation. What is probative in any given case depends upon several variables. The first is the nature of the rest of the evidence available to the prosecution. The second is the issue in the case. The third can be, but is not always, the nature of the defence, which may dictate the issue in the trial. Lawyers seem to panic at the notion that a subject cannot be divided up into several convenient headings, under which they can itemise a set of rules and exceptions. The tendency is either to impose headings anyway, in defiance of all the judicial statements directing them to the individual nature of the case before them, or avoid these problems altogether by refusing to acknowledge that this area of law exists.[105] Many textbooks provide instances of the first approach, dividing the cases on similar facts into "proof of intention" or "rebutting the defence of innocent association". Such headings are instances of probative value, but no list can be exhaustive. The statement of the principle in *Makin* was never intended to restrict courts to specific kinds of evidence, nor to force prosecutors to specify a particular defence (express or implied) that it is intended to rebut. In *DPP* v. *Boardman*,[106] Lord Hailsham LC made it clear that it is wrong to draw up closed lists of specific defences which must be raised before similar fact evidence may be admitted. Admissibility depends on the relevance of the evidence in the specific instance, given the nature of the rest of the prosecu-

---

[103] *Ibid.*

[104] E.g., *Mood Music* v. *De Wolfe* [1976] 1 All ER 463.

[105] Judges and magistrates have been accused of excluding probative evidence because of uncertainty about the operation of the similar facts principle—"if in doubt, keep it out". For instance, in a case the author came across, a motorist was found in possession of drugs concealed in a void between the inner and outer wall of his car. He denied all knowledge. The magistrates' clerk excluded a previous conviction for possession of drugs, although they were also concealed in a cavity in his car wall, and it was the same car! Prosecutors frequently complain of the uphill struggle they face in reassuring courts that admitting similar fact evidence is not an extraordinary or reckless thing to do.

[106] [1975] AC 421.

tion case, the similar fact evidence itself, and, on occasion, the explanation given by the defendant. Yet, despairing courts have from time to time attempted to resurrect "categories", for instance in *Wright*.[107]. Mustill LJ gave examples, in the case of allegations of indecent assault on children, of the kinds of issues which could arise and how this would affect the admissibility of various categories of similar fact evidence. His approach was approved in *Burrage*,[108] but constituted a departure from the greater flexibility of *Boardman* and *DPP* v. *P*.[109]

Boardman v. *DPP* concerned a headmaster who was accused of acts of gross indecency by two male students. Each alleged that the defendant had come to their dormitory in the night, taken them back to his study, and asked them to take the active role as his sexual partner. He flatly denied these allegations. Given that they knew him, and that it was unlikely that they could mistakenly form the view that these things had occurred, the plea of not guilty amounted to an implication that they were lying. The level of resemblance between their stories was regarded as significant. It would be surprising, assuming the absence of collusion, if two individuals could independently invent such similar accounts. Accordingly, the defence was refused separate trials, and appealed to the House of Lords on the ground that the convictions were unsafe as the jury would have been prejudiced by hearing the two allegations together. The House regarded the case as border-line, but thought there was probative value in the similarity between the two accounts. Lord Hailsham's colourful illustration of the process of measuring prejudice against probative value is helpful and accurate:

> "Whilst it would certainly not be enough to identify the culprit in a series of burglaries that he climbed in through a ground floor window, the fact that he left the same humorous limerick on the walls of the sitting room, or an esoteric symbol written in lipstick on the mirror, might well be enough. In a sex case . . . whilst a repeated homosexual act by itself might be quite insufficient to admit the evidence as confirmatory of identity or design, the fact that it was alleged to have been performed wearing the ceremonial head-dress of a Red Indian chief or other eccentric garb might well in appropriate circumstances suffice".[110]

Unfortunately, it seems to have been almost too memorable, in that many lawyers, including appeal court judges have got sufficiently carried away to require in every case such exotic circumstances and "striking similarity"

---

[107] (1990) 90 Cr. App. R 325.   [108] [1997] Crim. LR 440.

[109] (1990) 90 Cr. App. R 325: See also the Law Commission's proposed "structured discretion", designed to make the courts consistent in their application of the principle: Law Commission, *Evidence in Criminal Proceedings: Previous Misconduct of a Defendant*, Consultation Paper No 141 (HMSO, London, 1996). See P. Roberts, "All the Usual Suspects: A Critical Appraisal of Law Commission Consultation Paper No 141". [1997] *Crim. LR.* 75; J. McEwan, "Law Commission Dodges the Nettles in Consultation Paper No 141" [1997] *Crim. LR* 93.

[110] [1975] AC 421 at 454.

between the incidents. But *Boardman* itself is a case devoid of Gothic images or extraordinary headgear. Such extremes were unnecessary, as a careful reading of the passage quoted shows. The issue in *Boardman* was not identification. There was no question but that two students accused their headmaster of homosexual offences against them. Since he denied this, the implication of the not guilty plea was that they were lying. The "similar fact" issue is merely the likelihood of two young men independently constructing the same lie. The similarity between their accounts was hardly striking, but the fact that both alleged that Boardman wished to take the passive role was arresting enough to suggest that the resemblances between the incidents went beyond coincidence:

> "If collaboration is out of the way it remains possible that the charge made by the complainant is false and that it is simply a coincidence that others should be making or should have made independently allegations of a similar character against the accused. The likelihood of such a coincidence obviously becomes less and less the more people there are who make the similar allegations and the more striking are the similarities in the various stories. In the end . . . it is a question of degree".[111]

In contrast, even striking similarities may not justify the admission of previous offences in some cases, as when the defence alleges that the police fabricated or planted evidence for the prosecution.[112] "The question must always be whether the similar fact evidence taken together with the other evidence would do no more than raise or strengthen a suspicion that the accused committed the offence with which he is charged or would point so strongly to his guilt that only an ultra-cautious jury would acquit in the face of it."[113]

The difference, as far as identification cases are concerned, is clearly seen in Lord Hailsham's example. If the only evidence the prosecution has is that a house was broken into, and that Blakeney has a history of committing burglary, then the evidence against him is both weak and prejudicial. A "hallmark", or "signature", would be required, so that it can be said "[t]his is clearly the work of Blakeney, who always draws a pimpernel on the mirror". More prosaically, in *Mullen*,[114] the defendant was one of only 23 burglars in England known to employ the method of cracking glass by means of a blow torch to gain entry to premises. Police statistics were admitted in evidence at the defendant's trial for burglary to show that, given the shortage of burglars of that kind and that the defendant lived in the locality, it was likely that Mullen had committed the burglary under consideration (although the danger remains that there are burglars who use this method who are

---

[111] *Ibid.*, at 457.
[112] See *Wells (Jeffrey)* [1989] Crim. LR 67, and Birch's note, attached to the report
[113] [1975] AC 421 at 457.   [114] [1992] Crim. LR 735.

unknown to the police). Where there is evidence apart from the similar fact evidence to identify the defendant, the need for a signature diminishes. If an eye-witness identifies the defendant, and the not guilty plea implies that that witness is mistaken or dishonest, then the similar fact evidence has less to do. Instead of linking the crime with the defendant purely through the unusual nature of the *modus operandi*, it is directed to the simpler question—how likely is it that this witness is wrong? In *Thompson*,[115] for example, it was not disputed that sexual offences had been committed on some boys by a man who arranged to meet them later, at a particular time and place. Thompson arrived at that time and place, and gave the boys money. They said he was the man in question. On him at the time of arrest were some powder puffs, and later, in his room, indecent photographs were found. It was argued that, given his sexual preferences, the chance that the boys had seized upon the wrong man by mistake was fairly remote. Of course, it was possible that the defendant had been wrongly identified; but the evidence was undoubtedly material to the issue of identity, given the other evidence in the case.

Unfortunately the legal instinct to attach labels and reduce everything to rules has led the courts in the past to insist on "striking similarity" irrespective of the issue and the nature of the rest of the evidence. In *Mustafa*,[116] Scarman LJ said that there must be a striking similarity between the incidents, but in *Mansfield*,[117] Lawton LJ urged lawyers not to attach too much importance to phrases such as "uniquely and strikingly similar" in House of Lords judgments. The test is whether the evidence can be explained away as coincidence. Unfortunately the principle is not susceptible to simplification, and the cases are impossible to categorise, which is why in *Boardman* the House of Lords gave up the struggle to do so. Lord Hailsham gives specific examples of the nature of evidence required in particular circumstances, and it is entirely wrong to generalise from his remarks to every kind of case. Any disputed item of similar fact or disposition evidence must be examined in the light of the issue to be decided and the other evidence available to the court. Zuckerman has attempted to show the importance of the context (the case as a whole) in which the evidence is to be used; it is in fact central to the *Boardman* decision, but many lawyers seem nevertheless unaware of the importance of this.

> "It is . . . very important that due regard should be paid to the other evidence adduced or about to be adduced by the prosecution, for . . . evidence which incidentally shows bad disposition must be substantially relevant for some other purpose, and the degree of relevancy of such other evidence may be greatly affected by the other evidence."[118]

---

[115] [1918] AC 221.   [116] (1976) 65 Cr. App. R 26.   [117] [1978] 1 All ER 134.

[118] R. Cross, *Evidence*, (then 3rd. edn. Butterworths, London, 1967) 303–4 approved by O'Connor J in *Horwood* [1970] 1 QB 133, 139.

All labels, therefore, are potentially misleading. Even the genus "identification cases" is too widely drawn for any conclusion that striking similarity is necessary there. It is not necessary in a case like *Thompson*; what is striking there is the unlikelihood of two boys picking out by mistake a man who is in the right place at the right time for their rendezvous, and who has a sexual preference for young boys. Uncertainty as to whether or not striking similarity is required in identification cases has led to inconsistency of approach where the defendant is charged with several joined offences, and identification is an issue in each one. There appear to be two divergent judicial approaches to these cases,[119] the "cumulative",[120] and the "sequential", taken in *Black*.[121] There it was said that the jury must be sure on the basis of evidence other than the similar fact evidence that the defendant committed the first offence in the series, before using the similar fact evidence to identify him on the second. The sequential approach appears to demand striking similarities between the cases.[122] In *Brown*,[123] the cumulative approach was preferred. Although in relation to each offence in the series the identification evidence was weak, the jury were directed that, if they were satisfied that the two robberies were committed by the same gang, then the identification evidence on each robbery could be used to support the evidence on the other. Thus two weak identifications could enhance each other, and there was no need for striking similarities as long as there was a nexus between the offences.[124]

In *DPP* v. *P*,[125] the House of Lords again stressed that the overriding issue is probative value in context, so that judges must be flexible enough to decide upon the admissibility of similar fact evidence in the absence of guidelines, labels and demands for striking similarity. A father had been convicted on charges of rape and incest against two daughters. There was evidence that his incestuous conduct covered a long period of time, that he had used force, threatened the girls into silence, and that he had paid for abortions for both of them. The Court of Appeal reluctantly concluded that the nature of these allegations was not unusual in incest cases, and so decided that the evidence of one daughter should not have been admitted as evidence of offences committed against the other. The House of Lords, possibly influenced by its Scottish membership into taking the more relaxed approach being adopted in Scottish courts to cases of this kind,[126] declared that where identity is not

---

[119] See R. Pattenden, "Similar Fact Evidence and Proof of Identity" (1996) 112 *LQR* 446.
[120] *Downey* [1995] 1 Cr. App. R 547; *Barnes* [1995] 2 Cr. App. R 491.
[121] [1995] Crim. LR 640.   [122] Pattenden n. 119 above, 448; criticism, 463–9.
[123] [1997] Crim. LR 502.
[124] C.f. *Downey* [1995] Cr. App. R. 547. One of the dangers with this approach is that it makes the assumption that membership of the gang is consistent from one robbery to another. See Ormerod's Note at [1997] *Crim. LR* 504.
[125] [1991] 3 All ER 337.
[126] See JR Spencer and R Flin, *The Evidence of Children: The Law and the Psychology* (Blackstone, London, 1993), 224–5.

an issue, and the question is whether the witness is telling the truth, general similarity is sufficient. In this case, concerning allegations of sexual abuse made against a father, evidence that he similarly abused other young children was admissible (in the absence of collusion) even in the absence of any other "striking similarities". The House of Lords explained the reasoning process to follow: is the similarity sufficiently strong or is there other sufficient relationship between the events described and the evidence of other young children of the family and the abuse charged, so that the evidence, if accepted, would so strongly support the truth of that charge that it is fair to admit it notwithstanding its prejudicial effect?

Some judges may have been rather too eager to find significance in evidence of conduct or misconduct on other occasions. In *Mustafa*,[127] a man bought some meat from a supermarket using a stolen Barclaycard and a forged signature. On arrest for this offence, the defendant was found to have in his possession a stolen Access card. Also, he was identified as the man who purchased meat on the same day from another shop using a forged Barclaycard signature. The forgeries were all of poor quality, and when the police found him he was trying to copy the signature on the Access card. All this evidence was admitted at the trial, as was the evidence of a store detective who testified that on a previous occasion the defendant had been seen placing the same amount of meat in a trolley at the same store, but left it there when he apparently became aware that he was being watched.[128] The admission of all these incidents into evidence at the trial was upheld by the Court of Appeal, even though it might be thought that the first, putting meat into a trolley at a supermarket, was absolutely commonplace and irrelevant. Similarly in *Seaman*,[129] the defendant brought a bag of empty beer bottles into a supermarket, which he exchanged at the wine counter for new ones. He also pocketed some bacon and did not pay for it. He said he forgot. The prosecution sought to admit evidence of two previous occasions where he had taken bacon, first putting it into a wire basket, as here. On the first, the bacon disappeared, and the store was unsure where it went. On the second, he saw that he was being watched[130] and put the bacon back on the counter. The Court of Appeal held that the evidence was rightly admitted at trial, although his behaviour was consistent with that of perfectly ordinary and honest shoppers who pick up supermarket items but put them back again. These two cases are at the weak end of the similar facts spectrum of probative value; they are far removed from others where the Court of Appeal has demanded striking similarity. Problems of inconsistency appear to be inevitable. "Common sense" is a very personal commodity, the content of which is heavily influenced by individual experiences. Sometimes experience

---

127 (1976) 65 Cr. App. R 26.
128 This apparently inadmissible opinion evidence was not commented on in the Court of Appeal.
129 (1978) 67 Cr. App. R 234.
130 See n. 128 above.

is shared, and there is general agreement about what the common sense view actually is. Sometimes the experiences are shared only by a narrow band of people. In *Wells (Jeffrey)*,[131] the issue was whether the items found in the defendant's home on two separate raids were unusual enough to be mututally admissible, or were the commonplace paraphernalia of drug-dealers. They included paper folds with felt-tip pen markings, scales and the cutting agent, Mannitol. The defendant had been found in possession of similar items in the past. Experienced criminal lawyers and police officers would be better placed to answer that question than most, and here the court's view was that the items were commonplace.

It is curious to find, after observing the intellectual agonies suffered by judges who must decide whether to exercise their discretion in favour of admitting similar fact evidence, that in cases where it is a co-defendant who seeks to adduce it, matters are relatively straightforward. The familiar dread of causing undue prejudice to the defendant is nowhere to be seen. It was held in *Miller*[132] that a co-defendant can use similar fact evidence if it is relevant, confined to the purpose of the case and communicated in advance to counsel for the defendant. Relevance could include propensity evidence, including previous convictions. The disposition of the other defendant is more likely to be relevant in a case of "cut-throat" defences, where each of two co-defendants accuses the other of being the sole perpetrator,[133] than in a straightforward joint enterprise, as in *Neale*.[134] The court considered in this case that it did not follow from the existence of a propensity in one defendant to commit arson that his co-defendant was not a participant in a further act of arson, and therefore it was irrelevant to the defence. In the Privy Council case, *R. v. Lowery*,[135] all the defendants were charged with the apparently motiveless killing of a teenager. At the trial, one of them, King, was allowed to present expert evidence as to the personalities of the others, to show that they were more likely to kill than he.[136] The Supreme Court of Victoria held that although in a particular case it might be unjust to allow the Crown to lead disposition evidence, it is another to restrict a co-defendant from running his chosen defence if evidence of another defendant's propensity could rebut the prosecution evidence in his own case. "The considerations applicable when such evidence is sought to be led by the Crown against an accused person are by no means the same as when it is led by an accused person to support his defence, notwithstanding that it may have a prejudicial effect on the co-accused."[137] In *Lobban v. The Queen*[138] the

---

[131] [1989] Crim. LR 67.   [132] [1952] 2 All ER 667.

[133] *Douglass* (1989) 89 Cr. App. R 264; the judge had been correct in a case of causing death by dangerous driving to allow the co-defendant to present evidence of the defendant's previous convictions for driving offences.

[134] (1977) 65 Cr. App. R 304.   [135] [1972] VR 939.   [136] See Ch. 4.

[137] Sup. Ct. of Victoria, [1972] VR 939, 947.

[138] [1995] 2 All ER 602.

Privy Council held that the trial judge has no discretion to refuse evidence which may be more prejudicial than probative where it is led by a co-defendant to support his defence.

The kind of evidence adduced on behalf of the co-defendant in *Lowery*[139]appears to amount to nothing more than evidence of the dispositions of the various co-defendants. The probative value of personality is a matter of great contention. *Burrage*[140] concerned eight counts of indecent assault against the defendant's grandsons. It was held on appeal that the judge had been wrong to allow the prosecution to include his possession of homosexual pornographic material as part of the evidence against him. Since he completely denied anything improper ever taking place, the evidence served only to indicate a propensity. Homosexuality is not in itself sufficiently unusual to entitle a prosecutor to include evidence of the defendant's homosexual preferences in a case involving offences of a homosexual nature. It had been necessary for the House of Lords to make this absolutely clear in *Boardman* because of the entrenched view that the courts regarded homosexuality as a significant fact. This arose out of a particular interpretation of Lord Sumner's remarks in *Thompson*:

> "Persons . . . who commit the offences now under consideration seek the habitual gratification of a particular perverted lust, which not only takes them out of the class of ordinary men gone wrong, but stamps them with the hall-mark of a specialized and extraordinary class as much as if they carried on their bodies some physical peculiarity".[141]

An alternative interpretation would be that by "particular perverted lust", Lord Sumner did not mean homosexuality in general, to which he took the old-fashioned view that it was the propensity of "ordinary men gone wrong", but Thompson's own particular proclivity, which was pædophilia. The misleading version of *Thompson* comes in fact from the judgment of Lord Goddard CJ in *Sims*[142] and is repeated in *DPP v. Kilbourne*,[143] where it was disapproved on that point. In *Boardman*, Lord Cross said that in any event, in a climate where "the attitude of the ordinary man towards homosexuality has changed very much" Lord Sumner "sounds nowadays like a voice from another world".[144] But more particular homosexual proclivities can be relevant. For instance, in *Twomey*,[145] in which previous offences of homosexual acts accompanied by violence were held to have been rightly admitted where a murder victim had been subjected to a violent homosexual attack and where there was evidence that the defendant had been in the vicinity at the time. In *Sims* itself, the question was whether the four accusers were concocting the allegations of homosexual acts by Sims, which, if there

---

[139] [1972] VR 939.   [140] [1997] Crim. LR 440.   [141] [1918] AC 221, 235.
[142] [1946] KB 531, 540.   [143] [1973] AC 729.   [144] [1975] AC 421 at 458.
[145] [1971] Crim. LR 277.

were no evidence of conspiracy between them, seemed unlikely given the similarity of the accounts. In *Boardman*, Lord Cross stresses the importance of context, contrasting cases such as *Sims* and the instant case, where the issue was effectively the veracity of the complainants, from *Smith*[146] and *Straffen*,[147] where the victim was dead and therefore the issue was whether the defendant' was responsible for that death.

The Probative Value of Disposition

Although judges have from time to time spoken disparagingly of "disposition" evidence,[148] there can be no doubt that, on occasion, propensity or disposition is probative, with or without striking similarities. For instance, there was no striking similarity between the incidents which occupied the High Court of Australia in *Pfennig* v. *The Queen*.[149] The defendant admitted speaking to a boy at a place at which he later appeared to have drowned. Another boy testified to the fact that Pfennig had abducted and raped him. The similarities were slight; for instance, the same van was involved both times. But it was held enough to establish a propensity, criminality and a *modus operandi*. *Ball*[150] and *Straffen*[151] have often been cited as cases where the similar fact evidence was relevant *because* of the accused's disposition. In *Ball*, the previous sexual relationship of a brother and sister was admitted against them on charges of incest; it was highly probative given the circumstances in which they were now cohabiting. In *Straffen*, a case similar to *Pfennig* in that the accused's personality was significant in combination with the opportunity he had to commit the offence, Slade J argued that an abnormal propensity was itself a means of identification in the case. There was no direct evidence that Straffen had murdered a little girl, Linda Bowyer, although he admitted meeting her. The child had been manually strangled, but not sexually assaulted. Straffen had escaped from Broadmoor at the time, having been sent there after being found unfit to plead to charges of murdering two other little girls, both found strangled in similar circumstances, which included the absence of sexual assault and any attempt to conceal the body. The unlikelihood of another man with Straffen's propensities being in the same place at the time meant that the jury should hear of the earlier offences. The same probably would apply even if the circumstances had been less similar, because the personality involved was so unusual.

The post-*Boardman* cases require us to apply a coincidence test. Disputed evidence must be considered in its context, and this opens the way for unusual propensities and/or evidence which is not, *prima facie*, strikingly similar. There is, therefore, a sliding scale indicating the level of similarity necessary. In cases such as *Makin* and *Smith*, the similar fact or disposition

---

[146] (1915) 11 Cr.App.R 229. [147] [1952] 2 QB 911. See n. 151 below.
[148] See *Seaman* (1978) 67 Cr.App.R 234. [149] (1995) 182 CLR 461.
[150] [1911] AC 47. [151] [1952] 2 QB 911.

evidence is required to fulfil a large part of the prosecution's task; without it, there was little to suggest that the defendants were responsible for the deaths of their victims.[152] In cases of this nature, a high degree of similarity between the incidents is required in order to establish a sufficient link. In *Boardman*, there was other evidence to perform that function, requiring correspondingly less of the similar fact evidence. The same was true in *Thompson*, where there were witnesses who could identify the accused and describe his actions. A "hallmark" personality would not be required, but it must be sufficiently unusual to give credence to the boys' allegations. Lord Sumner described the difference between an ordinary criminal propensity and one which is sufficiently abnormal to identify an offender where necessary:

> "The evidence tends to attach to the accused a peculiarity which, though not purely physical . . . may be recognized as properly bearing that name. Experience tends to show that these offences against nature connote an inversion of normal characteristics which, while demanding punishment as offending against social morality, also partake of the nature of an abnormal physical propensity. A thief, a cheat, a coiner, or housebreaker is only a particular specimen of the genus rogue, and, though no doubt each tends to keep to his own line of business, they all alike possess the by no means extraordinary characteristic that they propose somehow to get their living dishonestly. So common a characteristic is not a recognizable mark of the individual."[153]

Thompson's pædophilia was significant because his story was that it was sheer coincidence that he approached the boys at the rendezvous, and that they identified him by mistake. The violent abnormal proclivities of Straffen and Pfennig, in conjunction with their presence at the scene of the crime, were regarded as sufficiently unusual to fill a bigger gap in the evidence than occurred in *Thompson*. It indicated that the accused had attacked and murdered a child, whose body, in the case of Pfennig, had not even been discovered.

In some cases, however, courts have disregarded the probative significance of abnormal personality, and demanded striking similarity as well. In *R. v. Beggs*,[154] the defendant was accused of having murdered O, a practising homosexual whom he had met in a club. Beggs claimed that he put up O for the night and awoke to find him indecently assaulting him, so he lashed out with a razor blade in self-defence. O died mainly from throat wounds. The police carried out extensive inquiries which resulted in Beggs being charged with five counts of unlawful wounding. All the incidents took place before the

---

[152] The dead baby found at the Makins' house could not be shown to have been murdered by them but for the numerous corpses of other dead babies found at three houses in which they had lived. Similarly in *Smith*, the death of his "wife" in the bath appeared innocent even though Smith stood to gain financially, until compared with the deaths of his other brides in similar circumstances soon after their weddings.

[153] [1918] AC 221 at 235.   [154] [1989] Crim. LR 898.

alleged murder, and were rather unusual. Beggs was a student, who lived in the same house as S, a fellow student. S had gone to bed and awoke to find Beggs attending to a wound on his (S's) leg. Beggs told him that he had heard him call out in his sleep and had gone to assist. Under the bed was S's penknife. S noticed a protruding bedspring, and told his doctor he had been injured by it. A few weeks later, while S and Beggs were sharing a bed-sit, S awoke to find superficial lacerations on his leg and a razor blade lying on the sheet of his bed. (In evidence, the defendant said he might have cut S's leg when, as a joke, he decided in the night to shave his friend's legs and his own.) A further count concerned R, another occupier of the same students' house, who awoke to find a four-inch laceration in his calf, about five months afterwards. R told his doctor it might have been a bedspring. Three months later, L, another student living in the house, went to bed after drinking with the defendant and awoke with a large gash in his leg. The Court of Appeal held that the judge was wrong to refuse an application to sever the indictment so that the murder could be heard separately, and consequently quashed Begg's conviction for murder. The striking aspect of this case, it was said, was not so much the similarities between the woundings and the fatal incident, but the differences. O was not a student, he did not live in the house, his wound was to the neck rather than the leg, and the death was caused by a razor, of which there was no sign in relation to the woundings.

Reasoning from *Boardman*, how likely is the story put forward by Beggs to be true, given (if the prosecution evidence is believed) a propensity to gore the legs of young men who are asleep, whatever the implement used? It is certainly a remarkable coincidence that someone with such a habit, and who brings home a practising homosexual whom he meets at a club, should be forced to defend himself with a razor, with fatal effect, from an indecent overture during the night. There is an inference of emotional instability from the earlier incidents which diminish the credibility of the self-defence story. As Lord Sumner, albeit in highly coloured language less appropriate these days, appreciated, sexual offenders are different from "career" or "professional" criminals. Their history frequently shows a progression from less serious to downright dangerous behaviour, as one might expect from the mentally or emotionally sick. The reasoning appropriate to cases of burglary or shoplifting will not fit crimes which demonstrate a disturbed personality which the jury ought to know about. The decision in *Beggs* is a denial of the common sense and application of experience which is thought to characterise the similar fact cases. Why insist upon similarities of an entirely superficial nature, such as D attacking the same part of the body, or using the same kind of implement, when the point is that here is someone who appears to enjoy causing injury to men who are asleep? Treating sexual offences in the same way as other crimes belies their peculiar nature, as Lord Sumner attempted to point out.[155]

---

[155] See L. Hanson, "Sexual Assault and the Similar Facts Rule" (1993) 27 *UBC L Rev.* 51.

Suppose a woman alleges rape and the defendant pleads consent; there follows a credibility battle which she is likely to lose, given the standard of proof in criminal cases. How would the jury react if they were told that the same man has been accused of rape before? Even if he had been acquitted in the earlier cases, constantly running the defence of consent on those occasions might alter their perception dramatically. For a man to fall out with more than one former lover to such an extent that they falsely accuse him of rape would seem very bad luck. Michael Maloney[156] was accused by five separate women of rape. Each said that he met them socially, and offered to drive them home. He in fact drove them to remote locations where he was alleged to have raped them. Despite the fact that the defence was consent on each charge, Bathurst-Norman J refused a prosecution application that they should all be heard by the same jury. Fear of causing prejudice meant that the charges were severed, and there had to be five rape trials, with each jury being unaware of the other four allegations. Each prosecution therefore required the complainant to convince the jury to convict on her word alone that she did not consent. Only one of the five persuaded the jury beyond all doubt of her lack of consent, and Maloney was acquitted of four of the rapes. It is highly unlikely that this would have been the outcome if all had been tried together; and it seems a similar fact case *par excellence* fit for joinder. Surely it stretches coincidence too far entirely to suggest that all five of these women willingly had sex with Maloney on a short acquaintance and then immediately took it into their heads to make a bogus allegation of rape to the police?[157] Similar arguments apply in stranger rape cases where the defendant claims to have been wrongly identified. Some courts appear more willing to admit the evidence in these cases than in consent defence cases.[158]

In contrast to the caution demonstrated in *Beggs* and *Maloney*, the Court of Appeal seemed undisturbed by the inclusion of much less convincing evidence when it heard the appeal of Rosemary West, wife of the notorious serial murderer, Frederick West, who killed himself before his trial. Accused of complicity in her husband's abduction, torture, rape and murder of young women, including his own daughter, Rosemary West was faced with wide-ranging prosecution evidence, which placed her entire personality under scrutiny. It included details of a lesbian relationship, Mrs West's own activities as a prostitute, and of her forcing one of her teenage daughters also into prostitution. Although the justification for admitting this evidence appears to be that it showed that she was such a perverted personality as to be

---

[156] *Dispatches*, "Getting Away with Rape", Channel 4, 16 Feb. 1994: S. Lees, *Carnal Knowledge: Getting Away with Rape* (Hamish Hamilton, London, 1996).

[157] See Lees, n. 156 above.

[158] D.P. Bryden and R.C. Park, "Other Crimes Evidence in Sex Offence Cases" (1994) 78 Minn. LR 529.

capable of anything,[159] the judgment on appeal virtually dismissed any risk of prejudice, concentrating instead on the possible impact of press reporting of the murders.[160] A more restrictive approach was taken at some widely reported trials recently. In September 1996, Dennis Chambers was acquitted of causing grievous bodily harm to Margaret Bent through "stalking". The jury was not informed of his previous convictions for offences committed against her, even though his record suggested serial obsessive behaviour as far as she was concerned. On 24 September 1996, Clarence Morris was convicted of stalking Perry Southall for eight months. His 45 previous convictions for theft, burglary and sexual offences, including the rape of a girl of 15, were not disclosed to the jury, nor was the fact that he was a paranoid schizophrenic. Although his history reflects the classic picture of the profile of a rapist,[161] the jury were presented with a misleadingly bland impression of the defendant, while Ms Southall was castigated in cross-examination for taking trouble with her appearance.

The assumption behind such cases appears to be that where the disposition evidence was not highly probative, the jury would attach excessive weight to it and therefore the defendant would not get a fair trial. The Criminal Law Revision Committee[162] pointed out that such fears do not exist in France where the defendant's criminal record is read out at the beginning of the trial. The Committee also suspects that the system in England, where the record is frequently suppressed until, for instance, the accused loses his shield,[163] maximises the damage done, since the jury is suddenly alerted to the existence of a "past" in dramatic circumstances, fairly late in the day. The Committee rightly doubted whether English jurors were congenitally less able than French to take a balanced view of such information about the accused. And the fact that he can "lose his shield" through the nature of his defence discloses considerable inconsistency in our approach. Spencer and Flin point out[164] that in Continental systems such as the Danish, which is closer to the English accusatorial model and uses a jury in serious cases, there is no rule excluding a defendant's criminal record. This means that their juries are not misled as was the English jury in the trial of Colin James Evans. Despite a long history of offences against children, Evans was able to present himself at his trial as an altruistic individual who had carried out voluntary work with problem families, only to be framed for

---

[159] The probative value depended also on the fact that, although all West's activities, including burying the bodies, were carried out in a small house shared by the couple, Mrs West claimed not to have known of them.

[160] *West, The Times*, 3 Apr. 1996.

[161] See J. McEwan, "Similar Fact Evidence and Psychology: Personality and Guilt" (1994) 3 *Expert Evidence* 113.

[162] *Evidence (General)*, Eleventh Report (1972), Cmnd. 4991.

[163] See below, Ch. 5.

[164] J.R. Spencer and R. Flin, *The Evidence of Children: The Law and the Psychology* (Blackstone, London, 1993), 227.

indecent assault. After his acquittal on those charges, he murdered four-year-old Marie Payne. In his house at that time were photographs of him indecently assaulting the children who had accused him at the earlier trial.[165]

Despite the alarm generated by such cases, the Law Commission[166] does not concede that some propensities can be more probative than others.[167] The United States Federal Rules of Evidence, as amended in 1994, allow in sexual cases evidence of the defendant's commission of other offences of sexual assault or child molestation. Thus the general rule of exclusion is retained, while what is regarded as a particularly probative disposition is routinely admitted.[168] The exclusionary rules peculiarly characterise the Anglo-American method of trial, which suggests that there is a relationship between the adversarial system and the desire to exclude the defendant's previous criminality. Why this should be is not self-evident. There is an obvious link between such a desire and the presumption of innocence—but other countries operate the same presumption without following a similar practice. The distinction may be influenced by the extra significance of the trial itself in adversarial structures; the evidence must be marshalled on the day by the party seeking judgment, and the constraints of the time available limit the party to evidence directly related to the issue he has raised. As we saw earlier in this chapter, courts are not prepared to deviate from the most direct of routes towards resolution of this issue. The (slight) materiality of the accused's record to the prosecution's case does not warrant its introduction into evidence unless they can show that of its nature it directly implicates the accused in the offence. Again, the adversarial trial is forced into its demarcation between evidence which goes to credibility and evidence which goes to guilt. The impossibility of drawing a clear line between the two ensures that the cases on similar facts will never be coherent, despite the best efforts of the judiciary. And a further problem arises from the adversarial structure; since the relevance of the disposition evidence may be established only after the nature of the defence is known, the prosecutor has to hope that it will become clear before he closes his case. If not, he will have to ask the judge if he can re-open it, and become involved in a procedural argument that has no bearing on guilt. This problem could be averted either by allowing for more disclosure by the defence or by admitting evidence of the accused's disposition as a matter of course.[169]

---

[165] *Ibid.*, 227–8.

[166] Consultation Paper No 141, *Evidence in Criminal Proceedings: Previous Misconduct of a Defendant* (HMSO, London, 1996).

[167] Although they note that abnormal personality can be a better predictor of behaviour than situational factors R.A. Prentky and R.A. Knight, "Identifying Critical Dimensions in Discriminating Amongst Rapists", (1991) 5 *Journal of Consulting and Clinical Psychology* 595.

[168] Although there are doubts whether the various states will follow suit.

[169] See Ch. 5.

The Danger of Collusion

In *R. v. H*,[170] the defendant was charged with sexual offences against his adopted daughter and his step-daughter. The matter had been discussed between the two girls and with their mother. The trial judge warned the jury that the girls might have put their heads together and concocted a false story. Counsel for the defence argued that the high risk of collusion nullified the probative value of any similarities between the allegations. Room for this argument was in fact created by the remarks in *DPP v. P*[171] to the effect that in cases where allegations of sexual abuse are made against a father, evidence that he similarly abused other young children in the family was admissible *in the absence of collusion* despite a lack of other "striking similarities". The implication appeared to be that the coincidence between accounts would be unremarkable, and therefore lacking in probative value, if complainants had collaborated over their allegations. The argument that collusion explains what otherwise would be a similarity going beyond coincidence, and therefore destroys its significance, is a logical one. However, the defence conclusion that this evidence was in consequence inadmissible presented the House of Lords in *R. v. H* with the prospect of trial judges becoming involved in debates on the nature and extent of any collaboration. Ultimately, they would have to make crucial adjudications of fact in similar fact cases where collusion was alleged. Lord Griffiths declared that the decision in *DPP v. P* recognised the fact that the sophisticated jury of today does not need rigid rules to ensure that a defendant is not convicted on the basis of prejudice. Matters of witness credibility are for the jury to decide. They must determine what inferences they should draw from the facts as they find them. If the judge were to take over this function, it would have to be by way of *voir dire*. The judge would have to decide in advance of the verdict upon the merits of virtually the whole of the prosecution case. The complications which would flow from such a procedure would mean that cases of child abuse within families would never be brought to trial.

Lord Mustill accepted that the logic of the similar facts rule would appear to favour the defence argument, in that it demands that the similarities between the alleged victims' versions should be of a nature which renders coincidence improbable. But to accept that would mean that proof of absence of collusion is a condition precedent to admission of any similar fact evidence. The trial judge would have to decide as a preliminary matter whether two witnesses were lying, and therefore, effectively, whether the defendant was guilty or innocent. This is the province of the jury. A further point was that there is no existing definition of collusion. It could mean a "wicked conspiracy to tell lies about the defendant", but more common would be innocent discussion among siblings, which would inevitably lead to the transfer of recollection between them. It would be impossible for

---

[170] [1995] 2 All ER 865.   [171] [1991] 3 All ER 337.

prosecutors to prove beyond reasonable doubt that "innocent infection" had not occurred. If, in a particular case, the probability was that collusion of the worst kind had been taking place, in Lord Mustill's view, the case would not come to court. Otherwise, it is sufficient that trial judges draw the attention of juries to any risk of collusion. Lord Mustill's view is broadly accepted by the Law Commission, but doubts whether judicial warning constitute sufficient protection for defendants lead it to propose that a trial judge should be entitled to stop the case if it appears that the risk of collusion is such that the issue should be withdrawn from the jury.[172] The principle that judges should be able to withdraw issues from the jury where a conviction would appear unsafe is perhaps one which should be followed in criminal cases in general.[173]

Anticipating the Nature of the Case

Now that the defence must communicate to the prosecution in advance of the trial the nature of its case,[174] it will be less difficult for the prosecution to assess the relevance of potential similar fact evidence. Although in cases of the *Makin* and *Smith* variety, the probative value of the evidence was so overwhelming that it mattered little what the defence chose to do, or whether it raised any specific defence at all, there are also cases where the defence stance is of key importance. In *Harrison-Owen*,[175] the accused was charged with burglary, having been found in a house at night in possession of keys taken from a car outside. He had a history of burglary, which, *prima facie*, was irrelevant. But he raised a defence of automatism, that he had at the time been unaware of what he was doing, and so the judge put the criminal record into evidence at the trial. The Court of Appeal, however, held that despite the nature of his defence, the defendant's criminal record had insufficient probative value. In *Mortimer*,[176] a different line was taken. A man was accused of the murder of a female cyclist by driving a car at her, and he pleaded that he had no memory of the event. Evidence was admitted of his having driven at three other women cyclists at around the same time. *Mortimer* is the better decision. Harrison-Owen's presence in a private house in possession of someone else's car key gave rise to an obvious inference of deliberateness and dishonesty, all helpful to the prosecution. Since the defence raised the question of automatism, or involuntariness, it was relevant to consider his story in the light of a long record for housebreaking and burglary. How likely was it that, by coincidence, someone with such a history had wandered involuntarily into a private house?

---

[172] Consultation Paper No 141, *Evidence in Criminal Proceedings: Previous Misconduct of a Defendant* (HMSO, London, 1996) para. 10.105.

[173] See discussion of *Galbraith* [1981] 1 WLR 1039 in Ch. 3, text to nn. 25–32 below.

[174] Under the Criminal Procedure and Investigations Act 1996: see Ch. 1.

[175] [1951] 2 All ER 726.   [176] (1936) 25 Cr.App.R 150.

The new obligations on the defence to make disclosure should, in theory, enable prosecutors to make more accurate assessments of the probative value of similar fact evidence, and more able to inform witnesses whether they will be required to give evidence. However, if it is the case, as some critics have argued, that courts will not penalise defence lawyers who fail to make disclosure to the prosecution,[177] the equation remains a difficult one, which may only be solved once the trial has begun. And even in cases where full disclosure has been made, prosecutors remain in the difficulty that they must predict the likely judicial response to their own assessment that the evidence in question is more probative than prejudicial.

Burden of Proof

Despite patriotic declarations to the contrary,[178] it is not only in the Anglo-Saxon system of trial that we find a presumption of innocence in relation to allegations of criminality.[179] But in inquisitorial systems this may be at its most evident during pre-trial procedures, where there is a greater possibility of discontinuance than in the English system. Also, the burden of proof on prosecutors in such systems operates rather differently where the court itself has an obligation to elucidate the truth.[180] Damaska argues that where factual inquiry is mainly judicial business, the parties rarely shoulder their burden of proof alone. The judge's fact-finding duties mean a sharing of the responsibility to produce an answer. In the Anglo-American jurisdiction, where judges should be neutral, the polarisation of the parties makes the burden of proof more significant.[181] Rather than castigate the Continental trial for indifference to the plight of those accused, we might do better to consider the fact that the much-vaunted burden of proof is reversed, that is, imposed upon the defendant, in a considerable number of cases in England; in Poland he never carries a legal burden in any circumstances. So, since the complicated exchange of evidential burdens does not take place in an inquisitorial trial, the defendant's only problem is tactical: "if you do not try to prove your own assertions you will heighten the chances of adopting the opposite one."[182] As we go on to examine the curious ping-pong effect of evidential burdens springing from side to side, and the erosion of the presumption of innocence in criminal trials, the simplicity and naturalness of the Continental trial has some appeal.

[177] See Chs. 1 and 8.

[178] E.g., A.C. Wright, "French Criminal Procedure" (1929) 45 LQR 98.

[179] E.g., Polish Code of Criminal Procedure (1969), Art. 3(2).

[180] S. Waltos, *Code of Criminal Procedure of the Polish People's Republic* (Wydawnictwo Prawnicze, Warsaw, 1979).

[181] M.R. Damaska, *Evidence Law Adrift* (Yale University Press, New Haven, Conn., London, 1997), 82–3.

[182] M. Cieslak, *Polish Criminal Procedure* (Nawkowe, Warsaw, 1973).

Legal Burden

The legal burden of proof of any fact in issue generally lies upon the party who positively asserts that fact, to whose claim or defence proof of that fact in issue is essential.[183] It is not always an easy matter to determine in a given case who that person may be. Courts tend to require proof of the party to whom the least difficulty or embarrassment will be caused by imposition of the burden. Generally, the soundest method of achieving that end is to impose an obligation to prove a positive, rather than to establish a negative.[184] The legal burden is often referred to as the "persuasive burden", the obligation to convince the tribunal, at the end of the case, that the party concerned has proved his or her case to the required standard of proof and is entitled to the remedy sought. Although the question whether the case has been satisfactorily proven arises at the end of the case, and after all the evidence for both sides has been heard, the legal burden has initial impact on trials by dictating in general which party must begin and which side should be the first to call witnesses.[185] If there are several issues in the trial, and both parties find themselves carrying legal burdens on individual points, it may appear to shift from one to the other, but in fact it remains fixed on that particular issue. For instance, in *Medawar* v. *Grand Hotel*,[186] the plaintiff had to show that the defendants' negligence led to the loss of his property, and on that point he had the burden of proof. To escape liability altogether, the defendants needed to show that the loss resulted from the plaintiff's negligence, and on that issue they had the burden of proof.

The closing speech of that renowned criminal advocate, Horace Rumpole, typically emphasises in the most moving and poetical terms that there is a "golden thread which runs through British justice"[187;] that is, that in criminal cases the prosecution bears the ultimate responsibility of proving its case. It is not for the accused to prove his innocence. But how true is this? The principle that the prosecution must prove the case against derives not only from paternalistic concern for the fate of accused persons, but is an application of the basic theory of the trial, that a party who wishes the machinery of the law to assist him should have the obligation of proving his case. The principle that the party seeking judgment bears the legal burden applies to the state itself if it seeks to accuse someone of a crime. In *Woolmington* v. *DPP*[188] the accusation was that the defendant had murdered his wife, while the defendant pleaded a shooting accident. The following passage from the judgment of Viscount Sankey is regarded as a cornerstone of the criminal justice system:

[183] *Joseph Constantine SS* v. *Imperial Smelting* [1942] AC 154.
[184] To show that the defendant was guilty of negligence on a particular occasion is more straighfoward than to show that he was not.
[185] RSC, Ord. 35, r 7.   [186] [1891] 2 QB 11.
[187] E.g., Mortimer, *Rumpole's Last Case* (Penguin, Harmondsworth, 1987).
[188] [1935] AC 402.

"Throughout the web of the English Criminal Law one golden thread is always to be seen, that it is the duty of the prosecution to prove the prisoner's guilt ... If at the end of and on the whole of the case, there is a reasonable doubt, created by the evidence given by either the prosecution or the prisoner, as to whether the prisoner killed the deceased with a malicious intent, the prosecution has not made out the case and the prisoner is entitled to an acquittal. No matter what the charge or where the trial, the principle that the prosecution must prove the guilt of the prisoner is part of the common law of England and no attempt to whittle it down can be entertained."[189]

The ringing clarity of these words is somewhat misleading; the omitted section of the passage refers to exceptions to the principle, and in recent decisions it appears that attempts to whittle it down *are* being entertained. Unfortunately, there is now a tendency, both in the courts and in the legislature, to impose upon defendants in criminal trials legal burdens of proof where evidential ones are all that is necessary.

The *Woolmington* principle that the prosecution bears the burden of proof in respect of all elements of the crime alleged is subject to three exceptions. The first, specifically referred to in the judgment, is that the burden is upon the defendant if he pleads insanity.[190] This exception may have been derived from the common law presumption of sanity[191]; however, the standard of proof required of the defence is only on the balance of probabilities.[192] In any other case where the accused denies *mens rea*, the burden of proof remains with the prosecution, who must show that it was present.[193] The second exception exists in relation to statutes which specifically place the legal burden on the accused.[194] There appears to be an increasing readiness in the legislature to add to the list. The Public Order Act 1986 is a recent example of this tendency.[195] Although the standard of proof is never as great where the legal burden is imposed upon the defendant rather than the prosecution, being proof on the balance of probability,[196] it is not clear why protection of the community cannot be achieved by imposing merely an evidential burden on him. It is interesting to note in this context that section 74 of the Police and Criminal Evidence Act 1984 (PACE) has had unexpected consequences. The problem which Parliament had in mind was that caused

---

[189] At 481.

[190] *Woolmington* [1935] AC 402; *Hill* v. *Baxter* [1958] 1 QB 277.

[191] *Imperial Loan Co.* v. *Stone* [1892] 1 QB 599; *Sutton* v. *Sadler* 3 CB(NS) 87.

[192] *Hill* v. *Baxter* [1958] 1 QB 277: in trials where insanity is the issue, the defendant will be the first to address the court and call witnesses.

[193] Non-insane automatism: *Hill* v. *Baxter* [1958] 1 QB 277; *Moses* v. *Winder* [1981] RTR 37; drunkenness: *Kennedy* v. *HM Advocate,* 1944 SC(J) 171; *Foote* [1964] Crim. LR 405.

[194] E.g., Bills of Exchange Act 1882, s.30(2); Prevention of Corruption Act 1916, s.2; Prevention of Crime Act 1953, s.1; Homicide Act 1957, s.2; Theft Act 1968, s.25; Misuse of Drugs Act 1971, s. 28(2); Criminal Damage Act 1971, s.1.

[195] E.g., s.5(3), s.23(3).

[196] *Sodeman* [1936] 2 All ER 1138; *Carr-Briant* [1943] KB 607.

by the operation of the rule in *Hollington* v. *Hewthorne*[197] in criminal cases, which prevented the court from using a court record of conviction as evidence that an offence had been committed. This meant that, for example in a trial for handling stolen goods, the conviction of the thief was inadmissible, and the prosecution had to start from scratch to show the goods were indeed stolen. Section 73 of the 1984 Act allows evidence of the certificate of conviction to be admitted as evidence of the fact of conviction, and section 74 provides that where the certificate is admitted as evidence of the conviction of a person other than the accused, that person shall be taken to have committed the offence unless the contrary is proved.[198] This provision has caused considerable difficulty in cases where one or more co-defendants pleads guilty, if the prosecution seek to use section 74 to bring in the conviction in the trial of those accused who deny their guilt. The situation is worst in conspiracy cases, since section 75 provides that all the details contained in the relevant count on the indictment should be included. The effect on the jury of hearing that one party to the alleged conspiracy has admitted it could be very damaging as far as the other is concerned.[199] The effect of the provision is to shift the burden of proof in some cases where accomplice convictions are admitted under section 74; the judges have attempted to mitigate its effects by using their discretion under section 78 of PACE, in cases which are discussed in detail in Chapter 5.

The third exception springs from the principle that if facts are peculiarly within the knowledge of the defendant, this imposes a burden of proof on him, since it is easier for him to produce the relevant evidence. In *Turner*[200] there were ten possible justifications in the relevant statute for the defendant's possession of pheasants or hares. Since only Turner could know which, if any, applied to him, he should have the burden of proof despite the prosecution allegation that he lacked the necessary qualification. In *Edwards*,[201] the court went much further, arguing that the common law rule did not relate solely to cases where the defendant has peculiar knowledge; it is a burden which applies generally if an offence carries with it exceptions and provisos. Then the accused must show that he is within one of the excepted categories. This meant that section 81 of the Magistrates' Courts Act 1952 (now section 101 of the Magistrates' Courts Act 1980) merely enacted for summary trials the existing common law on the point. The provision states:

"Where the defendant to an action, information or complaint relies for his defence on any exception, exemption, proviso, excuse or qualification, whether or not it accompanies the description of the offence or matter of complaint in the enactment creating the offence or on which the complaint is founded, the burden

---

[197] [1943] KB 587; see Ch. 5.
[198] Police and Criminal Evidence Act 1984, s.74(2).
[199] *O'Connor* [1987] Crim. LR 260.
[200] (1816) 5 M & S 206.   [201] (1974) 59 Cr.App.R 213.

of proving the exception . . . [etc.]shall be on him; and this notwithstanding that the information or complaint contains an allegation negativing the exception."[202]

Edwards applies the same rule to trials on indictment; this is controversial,[203] particularly as the Court of Appeal rejected the argument that the difficulty presented by such cases would be adequately dealt with by construing the defence burden as an evidential one only. "What rests upon [the defendant] is a legal, or as it is sometimes called, the persuasive burden of proof. It is not the evidential burden."[204] This categorical statement seems unnecessarily harsh to the defence and has provoked a storm of criticism.[205]

Despite the hostility to this approach, which was noted by the Court of Appeal in *Hunt*,[206] that court attempted to extend the *Edwards* principle in an inexcusable fashion. The defendant was charged with unlawful possession of morphine, contrary to section 5(2) of theMisuse of Drugs Act 1971. Regulations issued under the statute provided that section 5 had no effect in relation to preparations containing no more than 0.2 per cent morphine. The defence was that the morphine content of the substance in the possession of the accused was too low to amount to a prohibited drug. The Court of Appeal held that he was attempting to bring himself within an exception created by the regulations and the legal burden therefore rested on him. The court conceded that there was a difference from *Edwards*, in that there the defendant was not in a special position with regard to the regulations, as a pharmacist would have been, for example. In *Edwards*, the accused was a publican, and the question was whether or not he had been granted a justices' licence. Here it could not be said that the regulations in question had created a special category of person who could claim a particular excuse or justification. The Court of Appeal considered it significant that its interpretation of the statute meant that the prosecution need not produce an analyst in every case to show the proportion of morphine present. But to require citizens to prove that substances in their possession are not prohibited drugs, in other words, to create a presumption that they are, is absurd and oppressive. Of course it is for the prosecution to show that the substance in question was the substance prohibited in the statute and defined in the regulations. This was the opinion of the House of Lords,[207] which felt that no excessive burden was placed on the prosecution thereby. The House of Lords confirmed the *Edwards* decision that statutes can by implication cast the legal

---

[202] This s. governs summary trials, which include trials of indictable offences in the magistrates' courts.

[203] See A. Zuckerman, "The Third Exception to the Rule in *Woolmington*" (1976) 92 LQR 402.

[204] (1974) 59 Cr.App.R 213 at 271.

[205] See Tapper and Cross, n. 188 above; G. Williams, *Criminal Law, the General Part* (Stephens, London, 1953), 905; Phipson on *Evidence* (Sweet and Maxwell, London, 1990), 4 18. Cf. the Eleventh Report of the CLRC, n. 162 above, which argued at paras 137–42 that all burdens on the accused should be evidential only.

[206] [1986] 1 All ER 184.   [207] [1987] 1 All ER 1.

burden of proof on the accused. Which statutes do this is a matter of construction in every case. The House conceded that the task of construction is not straightforward. Lord Griffiths suggested that generally the court should consider the seriousness of the offence and the fact that any doubt should be resolved in favour of the accused. Lord Ackner added the practical consequences of placing the burden on the defendant to the list.

Although it was a relief to all that the Court of Appeal's decision was overturned, commentators vary in their reaction to the House of Lords judgment in *Hunt*. Zuckerman argues that it stops the rot which began in *Edwards*[208]; Di Birch has valiantly attempted to extract comprehensible guidelines from it[209]; Mirfield is far more sceptical,[210] and Bennion thinks the courts may disregard the whole thing.[211] Certainly, a cynic might feel that the Court of Appeal decision in *Hunt* was merely a wrong-headed effort to save a conviction despite a serious error by the prosecution, who for some reason had no analytical evidence on the day of the trial. No great advance of principle is necessary in such circumstances, and it may be that *Hunt* will be forgotten in due course.

Evidential Burden

The evidential burden is the obligation to "raise" an issue, or to "pass the judge" by introducing some evidence in support of it. If the judge is not satisfied that an issue has been successfully raised by producing some credible evidence which satisfies the evidential burden, then that issue will not be addressed by the court. In a jury trial, this means that there will be no judicial direction on that issue. The prosecution in a criminal case bears a preliminary evidential burden to show that there is a *prima facie* case against the accused, a "case to answer".[212] This means passing the judge on all the constituent elements of the crime charged. Failure to do so will result in the judge directing an acquittal at "half-time", so that the defence is not required to present its case at all. One of the objects of this procedure in criminal cases is to protect an accused person from a prosecutor who might bring a weak case in the hope that, if he or she gets past "half-time", the deficiency in the evidence can be made good through the effect of cross-examination of the defence witnesses. It is also born to some extent of a fear that a jury might return a perverse verdict, and convict despite a lack of any coherent evidence of guilt. But the same principle applies in civil as well as criminal trials. The reasons for the requirement are that the other side should not be forced to

---

[208] A. Zuckerman, "No Third Exception to the *Woolmington* Rule" (1987) 103 LQR 170.

[209] D. Birch, "Hunting the Snark; The Elusive Statutory Exception" [1988] Crim. LR 221.

[210] P. Mirfield, "The Legacy of Hunt" [1988] Crim. LR 19; D. Birch, "An Ungrateful Reply" [1988] *Crim. LR* 233.

[211] F. Bennion, "Statutory Exceptions: A Third Knot in the Golden Thread" [1988] *Crim. LR* 31.

[212] See below Ch. 3.

the trouble, expense and stress of defending itself against an allegation which there is no evidence whatever to support, and that the tribunal is entitled to know what the range of the inquiry is. It avoids wasting the time of the court; a case with little or nothing to support it will be thrown out at an early stage. In civil cases, this is done largely as a preliminary matter, so that any claim or defence which appears from the paperwork to have no evidential support will not be brought before the court at all.

If the defence in civil or criminal cases wishes the court to consider a particular issue, that issue must similarly be raised by evidence in support of it. The court will not even consider the defence relied on otherwise.[213] Thus an evidential burden may be imposed on a party who does not bear the legal burden in relation to a particular issue. In *Woolmington*, for example, the defence of accident would not have been put to the jury if no evidence had been raised to sustain it; on that issue he bore the evidential burden, although the prosecution retained the legal burden. It would be sufficient for the purpose in a case of this kind if the accused person during his own testimony claimed that the shooting was accidental. Whether the claim were sufficient to raise a reasonable doubt, preventing the prosecution from satisfying its legal burden of proof, would then be for the jury to decide. Thus the prosecution retains the overall legal burden (or "persuasive" burden, the obligation to convince the court) throughout. In *Gill*[214] the plea was duress, although the accused never mentioned the alleged threats to himself and his wife when questioned by police. The trial judge told the jury that they must be satisfied that the defendant had lost all will of his own, bearing in mind that his earlier statements suggested that he acted freely. On appeal it was held that the legal burden remained with the prosecution, although the accused had to raise his defence by sufficient evidence to go to the jury. He had to make duress a "live issue". This could be done through cross-examination of prosecution witnesses, or by evidence called on his behalf, or a combination of the two. Once he had succeeded in doing this, it was then for the Crown to destroy that defence in such a manner as to leave in the jury's minds no reasonable doubt that the accused could not be absolved on the grounds of the alleged compulsion.[215] The Court felt that the direction on the whole made it clear that the prosecution had the burden of proving that the appellant had not acted out of duress, and upheld the conviction.

---

[213] E.g., *Critchley* [1982] Crim. LR 524; where the defendant remembers nothing of the killing, and there is no other evidence to support self-defence, counsel may not suggest the defence in his closing speech, and the the jury cannot be asked to consider the question of self-defence.

[214] [1963] 1 WLR 841.

[215] Edmund Davies J at 846.

Standard of Proof

Civil Cases

Although the standard required is frequently given as "proved on the balance of probabilities", the phrase is slightly misleading insofar as it suggests an even balance or 50/50. This is not the case. "If the evidence is such that the tribunal can say that we think it more probable than not the burden is discharged, but if the evidence is equal it is not."[216] This is a low standard of proof, and yet, according to Eggleston, in a case which could be decided on a likelihood of 51 per cent, a judge who thinks the plaintiff's account more believable than the defendant's will say that he believes the plaintiff.[217] Eggleston suggests that in arithmetical terms the plaintiff is entitled to judgment if his case is proved only to a probability of 0.501—resulting in the defendant losing his case and probably costs where his own case has been proved to a probability of 0.499.[218] But such an outcome is extremely unlikely. Trial judges are aware of the consequences of their own decisions, and inevitably will bear in mind what would be the effect upon the defendant of accepting the plaintiff's version of events where that is barely proven. In fact, there is authority (apart from the dictates of common sense) for the proposition that the greater the impact on the defendant of a decision for the plaintiff, the more evidence the latter will have to find. For example, although if a crime is alleged during civil proceedings the standard of proof remains the civil one, there have been suggestions that the degree of proof required in civil cases may vary according to the seriousness of the allegation.[219]

A civil court, when considering a charge of fraud, will naturally require a higher degree of probability than that which it would require when asking if negligence is established. Likewise a divorce court should require a degree of probability which is proportionate to the subject-matter.[220] Judges hearing cases involving accusations against parents of sexual abuse of their children have operated a varying standard of proof according to the nature of the allegation.[221] There have been criticisms of this approach; Carter argues that shifting standards lead to confusion, and that it is hardly fair to impose a

---

[216] *Miller* v. *Minister of Pensions* [1947] 2 All ER 372, *per* Denning J at 373–4.

[217] R. Eggleston, *Evidence, Proof and Probability* (Weidenfeld and Nicolson, London, 1983), 129.

[218] See reply by L.J. Cohen, *The Probable and the Provable* (OUP, Oxford, 1977), also his debate with Professor Williams: [1979] *Crim. LR* 297, 340; [1980] *Crim. LR* 91,103. This kind of mathematical debate will probably stiffen judicial resolve not to become involved in mathematical arguments—see *People* v. *Collins* (1968) 438 P 2d. 33.

[219] *Hornal* v. *Neuberger Products* [1957] 1 QB 247.

[220] *Bater* v. *Bater* [1906] P 209.

[221] *Re H and Re K* [1989] 2 FLR 313; See C. Yates, "Burden of Proof Past and Future: *Re H and Re K* Revisited" (1989) 2 *JCL* 109.

higher standard on a party merely because he has suffered a grievous wrong.[222]But surely that is the point; the more grievous the wrong, the more the plaintiff is asking the court to demand of the defendant by way of redress. He may lose his job, his home, his company or his family. What judge would go so far on a probability of 0.501?

Criminal Cases

R. v. Winsor[223] settled that criminal cases must be proved beyond a reasonable doubt. Society in the present day is so much stronger than the individual, and is capable of inflicting so much more harm on him than he as a rule can inflict on society, that it can afford to be generous. Other countries also demand a high standard before a finding of guilt, but may express it rather differently. For example, the Polish Criminal Code states that the accused shall not be considered guilty before his guilt has been proven as provided by the Code,[224] and that "[u]nresolvable doubts shall not be resolved to the prejudice of the accused".[225] This last does not mean that all doubts have to be resolved in the accused's favour, but that they shall not be resolved to his detriment–allowing a neutral resolution.[226] The Supreme Court takes the view that the agency conducting the proceedings should try to exhaust every possibility, and only when the remaining doubts prove immune to elucidation should the final decision be made, and that without prejudicing the accused's interests.[227] The reasoning process involved in the Polish proceedings is rather clearer, then, than it is in ours. There is great mystery to the idea of beyond reasonable doubt, both in conceptual terms and in terms of how jurors reach an agreement. There is some suggestion in the case law that judges feel that the best course is to leave the matter as vaguely described as possible. Ultimately a verdict in a criminal case is a reflection of the judgement of the people on the action of this particular defendant, and if that is a moral, rather than a rational, reaction that may not be altogether indefensible.

There have been attempts to define what is meant by reasonable doubt for the benefit of the jury, but these have proved to be at least as confusing as the expression itself. Generally, a definition should be avoided,[228] but if the judge is specifically requested by the jury to explain it, he may be forced to attempt one.

"If the judge feels that any of [the jurors] . . . are in danger of thinking that they are engaged in some task more esoteric than applying to the evidence adduced at the trial the common sense with which they approach matters of importance to

---

[222] P.B. Carter, *Case and Statutes on Evidence* (2nd edn., Sweet & Maxwell, London, 1990), 61.

[223] (1865) 4 F&F 363; confirmed by the House of Lords in *Woolmington* [1935] AC 402.

[224] Art. 3(2).   [225] Art. 3(3).   [226] Prawnicze, n. 181 above.   [227] *Ibid.*

[228] *Walters* v. *The Queen* [1969] 2 AC 26.

them in their ordinary lives, then the use of such analogies as that used by Small J. in the present case, whether in the words in which he expressed it or in those used in any of the cases to which reference has been made, may be helpful."[229]

The approach of Small J was as follows:

"But surely, upon reflection, you remember that in dealing with matters of importance in your own business affairs you do not allow slight, whimsical doubts to deter you from going along; you brush them aside and go ahead. But surely, then comes a time when, in dealing with matters of your own affairs, you stop to think, and by reason of that doubt you decide what to do in your business of importance. Well, this is the quality and kind of doubt of which the law speaks when it speaks of reasonable doubt."

It is no criticism of Small J that there is little enlightenment in the business analogy. That has been employed in other cases.[230] But the attempt to equate commercial decision-making with fact-finding in courts is misconceived for two reasons. In the first place, the factors involved are very different. Business decisions involve an assessment of the degree of commercial risk involved, taking account of the consequences of failure against the potential gain. Jurors trying cases are not themselves at risk, and therefore need take no note of consequences, except insofar as their sympathies have been engaged by the accused or the complainant in the case before them. It is doubtful, too, whether all businessmen employ the same standards in their business affairs[231], and, even if they did, whether the jury would recognise them.

The other, and more profound reason that this is a doomed exercise is that jurors are required to determine the truth, as far as they can from the evidence before them, whereas a businessman's decision-making is rarely an exercise in *adjudication*. It is a conclusion based upon *prediction* (whether as to market forces, labour relations, or other variables). Judith Thompson's example of the lottery illustrates this difference. If A knows that B bought five lottery tickets and that 100 were sold altogether, he is entitled to conclude that there is a .95 probability that B will lose. But he does not *know* that B will lose, and would be wrong to tell B to tear up his tickets. Knowing that there is a high degree of probability is not the same as a belief in a fact beyond reasonable doubt. A businessman might well operate on the basis of the former, but would hardly ever be able to make a decision if he waited until he had achieved the latter.

Is the meaning of "beyond reasonable doubt" obvious to juries, so that elaboration is unnecessary, as indicated by the Privy Council in *Walters*?[232]

---

[229] Lord Diplock, *ibid.*
[230] E.g., *Manning* (1849) 30 CCC Sess. Pap. 654, *per* Pollock CB; *Ching* (1976) 63 Cr. App. R 7.
[231] *Hepworth and Fearnley* [1955] 2 QB 600, *per* Lord Goddard CJ.
[232] [1969] 2 AC 26.

Or is the reality that judges are themselves so unsure of what it means that they are best advised to conceal the fact by avoiding definition? Some points are clear; there cannot be an obligation to prove the case beyond *all* doubt, as that would mean that entirely improbable possibilities, which would exist in every case, would entitle the accused to an acquittal. In *Miller* v. *Minister of Pensions*, Denning J explained that "beyond reasonable doubt" does not mean beyond the shadow of a doubt, since the law would not protect the community if fanciful possibilities could "deflect the course of justice". He concluded that therefore if the evidence against a man is so strong that there is only a remote possibility in his favour, such that a juror could dismiss it as possible but not in the least probable, then the case is proved beyond a reasonable doubt.

Although these remarks may look like a step on the way towards understanding, if a trial judge attempts to define a reasonable doubt for the benefit of the jury, he increases the risk of the conviction being quashed on appeal.[233] Lord Goddard CJ said:

> "Once a judge begins to use the words 'reasonable doubt' and try to explain what is a reasonable doubt and what is not, he is much more likely to confuse the jury than if he tells them in plain language, 'It is the duty of the prosecution to satisfy you of the prisoner's guilt."[234]

However, a direction which does no more than urge the jury to be satisfied of guilt is not sufficient.[235] It should be stressed that the jury should be so satisfied that they feel sure,[236] or the judge should tell them to satisfy themselves beyond all reasonable doubt.[237] In sum, although judges must stress the incidence and standard of proof in criminal cases, they are best leaving the jury to interpret that standard for themselves rather than attempting to define what it is impossible to define.[238] Instead, a more contextual approach is preferred; the judge should give a proper direction when going through the facts, explaining what inferences may be drawn from particular items of evidence. However, it may be that variations in language at this juncture affect the readiness of juries to convict. Mock trials staged for the London Jury Project of the London School of Economics resulted in a significantly lower conviction rate where the jury were told that they "must feel sure and certain on the evidence that the accused is guilty",[239] than where they were told: "You should be sure beyond a reasonable doubt and by a reasonable

---

[233] *Summers* [1952] 1 All ER 1059; *Walters* [1969] 2 AC 26; *Ching* (1976) 63 Cr. App. R 7; *Gray* (1973) 58 Cr. App. R 177.

[234] *Kritz* [1950] 1 KB 82, 90.

[235] *Blackburn* (1955) 39 Cr App R 84n.; *Hepworth and Fearnley* [1955] 2 QB 600.

[236] *Kritz* 6 [1950] 1 K6 82; *Walters* [1969] 2 AC 26.

[237] *Hepworth and Fearnley* [1955] 2 QB 600.

[238] *Ching* (1976) 63 Cr. App. R 7.

[239] Per Lord Goddard CJ in *Kritz* [1950] 1 KB 82.

doubt I mean not a fanciful doubt that anyone might use to avoid an unpleasant decision, but a doubt for which reasons can be given".[24].

There is some evidence that juries adopt a sliding scale according to the seriousness of the offence.[241] Such an approach has some limited judicial approval; apart from the observations in relation to civil cases discussed above, there is authority in an elderly criminal case. Holroyd J in *Sarah Hobson*[242] said: "The greater the crime, the stronger the proof required for the purpose of conviction". The introduction of causing death by dangerous driving offences as an alternative to gross negligence manslaughter was an acknowledgment of jurors' reluctance to convict of the latter more serious offence.[243] Carter, while conceding that the commission of a serious crime is "intrinsically less likely than is the commission of a petty crime", objects to the idea of a varying scale. "The policy of the law is that a man ought not to be convicted of even a minor crime except on proof beyond reasonable doubt." He argues that the gravity of the consequences of the verdict has no rational bearing on a fact-finding process concerned only with probabilities.[244] It is hoped that it has emerged from this chapter that trials are far removed from this description, and are certainly not dedicated first and foremost to discovery of actual facts. There is no real cause for alarm for those who share Carter's views, however, since there is no evidence that judges are suggesting to juries that the more serious the crime, the more they must be sure. But there is nothing to prevent jurors from forming such an opinion independently, and applying their own standards based on their conception of fairness—surely a well-known argument for trial by one's peers.

---

[240] W.R. Cornish and L.S. Sealy, "Juries and the Rule of Evidence" [1973] *Crim. LR* 208.

[241] R.J. Simon and L. Mahan, "Quantifying Burdens of Proof" (1971) 5 *Law and Society Review* 319.

[242] (1823) 1 Lewin 261; cf. *Bater* v. *Bater* [1951] P 35, 36–7: "In criminal cases the charge must be proved beyond reasonable doubt, but where may be degrees of proof within that standard", *per* Lord Denning, quoted with approval by Lord Pearce in *Blyth* v. *Blyth*.[1966] AC 643, 673.

[243] Originally in the Road Traffic Act 1956, s.8.

[244] N. 222 above, 61.

3

Telling the Truth:
Witnesses and the Court

"There's no art
To find the mind's construction in the face"

Shakespeare, *Macbeth*, Act I, Scene 4

The evidence before the court consists of more than sworn testimony. The tribunal of fact may be presented with such "real" evidence as a live dog for inspection on the question of its alleged viciousness,[1] may be expected to travel to view a site[2] or may even be required to scrutinise the very bath in which one of the "Brides in the Bath" was drowned.[3] On some matters, a rebuttable inference may follow from proof of some basic facts, if a legal presumption directs the court towards a conclusion, for example the presumption that someone who, despite due inquiries, has not been heard of for seven years by those who normally would hear of him, is dead.[4] But, generally in cases where facts are in dispute, the court will rely heavily on its assessment of the veracity or reliability of witnesses, particularly in the adversarial trial, where the emphasis is on orality. In the adversarial system, the opportunity to see and hear witnesses being examined is considered essential. Therefore, in addition to considering the content of the witness's evidence, the tribunal will consider the appearance and demeanour of witnesses. It might be relevant that a witness is tall, heavily built or deformed. How wisely these observations are used is discussed below.

Influence of the Judge

The Neutrality of the Umpire

The judicial function in the adversarial trial is, in theory, severely curtailed. In civil cases the role of impartial referee is strictly separated from that of

---

[1] *Line* v. *Taylor* (1862) 3 F&F 731.

[2] *Buckingham* v. *Daily News* [1936] 2 QB 524.

[3] *Smith* (1915) 11 Cr App R 229; the bath had in fact already been purchased with a view to exhibition in the Chamber of Horrors at Mme Tussaud's.

[4] *Chard* v. *Chard* [1956] P 259.

tribunal of fact. In criminal cases the judge is supposed to have no opinion of the facts; the special function of the jury in deciding facts is carefully protected from intrusions, as will appear below with regard to opinion evidence. But, as we saw in Chapter 1, it has been doubted whether the judge in modern criminal trials in this country bears much resemblance to the passive referee of the adversarial model. He or she is in any event expected to adjudicate on issues of law such as the admissibility of evidence, and also on facts which affect admissibility; this must be done in the absence of the jury in a trial within a trial, or *voir dire.* The judge's decision therefore may deprive the jury of the opportunity of hearing certain items of evidence or may have the effect of altogether preventing a particular witness from giving evidence if the entire contents of his or her testimony are found to be inadmissible.

Although the subject of admissibility appears to be closely bounded by exclusionary rules, it can be argued that a considerable amount of personal discretion is involved. This factor is most apparent when judges rule on the relevance of particular evidence, but may also underlie the application of exceptions to particular exclusionary rules. An obvious example is the operation of the doctrine of *res gestae*[5]; the concept affords a convenient cloak for discretion and frequently provides a useful escape route from the rigours of exclusionary rules such as the hearsay rule. Many of the rules themselves, such as the old common law rule requiring a corroboration warning, for instance where an accomplice incriminates his co-accused, appear to have developed from the "good common sense of trial judges" over the years.[6] The corroboration rules have now been abolished, partly because of practical difficulties and partly because perceptions of credibility have changed.[7] Delisle argues that rules which evolved gradually from the operation of judicial discretion ossified into utter rigidity; "the so-called exclusionary rules are not meant to be mechanically applied like some calculus, but rather need to be used with discretion".[8] The disappearance of strict rules requiring judges to give warnings about the danger of fabrication from certain categories of witness has left them with more scope to determine for themselves which witnesses should be treated with caution and alert the jury accordingly.[9] This reform could be seen as a return to the flexibility described by Delisle. He has made a strong case for the expansion of judicial discretion at the expense of a code of exclusionary rules; to attempt to exclude it altogether is, in all probability, a hopeless exercise.

In some contexts the existence of discretion in relation to admissibility is

---

[5] See Ch. 7.

[6] R. Delisle, "Judicial Discretion and the Law of Evidence", paper presented at Conference on Reform of the Criminal Law (London, July 1987).

[7] See text to nn. 178–181 below.

[8] N. 6 above.

[9] See text to nn. 182–189 below.

acknowledged; for example, if questions about the accused's previous misconduct are *prima facie* permissible under section 1(f)(ii) of the Criminal Evidence Act 1898, the trial judge may nevertheless refuse to allow them if he considers that justice requires that they should not be put. The balancing of probative value against prejudicial effect required of trial judges by the similar facts rule is another area where discretion is inevitably involved. However, in *Viola*,[10] Lord Lane CJ held that it was wrong to speak of discretion in the context of section 2 of the Sexual Offences Act 1976, which directs trial judges to exclude certain evidence or questions unless it would be unfair to the defendant to do so. The sole question here is relevance, and Lord Lane CJ thought that if a matter is relevant the judge has no discretion to exclude. This opinion ignores the considerable degree of flexibility involved in decisions about relevance. In identifying the borderline between those facts which are too remote from the issue and those which are not, the judge is inevitably involved in evaluation of evidence and therefore is close to trespassing into the jury's territory in the criminal case.

As far as the running of the trial is concerned, it is not entirely true to say that judges do not descend into "the dust of the arena" In civil cases witnesses can be called only with the consent of one of the parties,[11] but in criminal cases the judge may call and cross-examine witnesses himself in the interests of justice, and particularly if the jury request it.[12] In *Edwards*[13] it was said that the power to call witnesses should be exercised sparingly and with great care. Despite this Jackson and Doran found that in the Northern Irish courts they observed, judges quite often at the *voir dire* stage suggested that a particular witness be called.[14] The Crown Court Study[15] carried out on behalf of the Royal Commission[16] found that in 19 per cent of contested cases, judges considered that a material witness had not been called. The Report consequently recommended that the power be used more often.[17] Cross argues that together with the power to recall witnesses, it "serves as a reminder that the English judge is more than an umpire in the strict sense of the word",[18] quoting Denning LJ:

"In the system of trial we have evolved in this country, the judge sits to hear and determine the issues raised by the parties, not to conduct an investigation or

[10] [1982] 3 All ER 73; and see Ch. 4.
[11] *Re Enoch and Zanetsky, Boch and Co.'s Arbitration* [1910] 1 KB 327.
[12] *Chapman* (1838) 8 C&P 558; *Holden* (1838) 8 C&P 606.
[13] (1948) 3 Cox CC 82.
[14] J Jackson and S Doran, *Judge Without Jury: Diplock Trials and the Adversary System* (Clarendon, Oxford, 1995).
[15] M. Zander and P. Henderson, *Crown Court Study*, Royal Commission on Criminal Justice Research Study 19 (HMSO, London, 1993).
[16] *Report of the Royal Commission on Criminal Justice* (chairman Viscount Runciman) (HMSO, London, 1993)Cm 2263.
[17] *Ibid.*, 123.
[18] C. Tapper, *Cross and Tapper on Evidence* (8th edn., Butterwoths, London, 1995) 281.

examination on behalf of society at large, as happens, we believe, in some foreign countries. Even in England, however, a judge is not a mere umpire to answer the question "How's that?" His object, above all, is to find out the truth and to do justice according to law."[19]

Quite how judges are expected to achieve this aim from their lofty and disinterested perch is not clear; certainly, their position is an uneasy one in its ambiguous stance somewhere between detachment and involvement.

Withdrawing an Issue from Consideration

A judge may withdraw an issue from the jury altogether. Generally if the defendant does not raise a particular defence, the trial judge should put it to the jury only when there is evidence from which they could reasonably infer that the defendant acted in a way which provided a defence at law. There is no duty to leave to the jury defences which are fanciful or speculative.[20] So the trial judge must decide whether as a matter of law any evidence has been raised which, if believed, would establish the facts in issue. His duty to assist the defendant in a criminal trial in this way departs from the normal adversarial principle that it is for the parties to select the issues to be tried. Thus although the jury are the tribunal of fact and decide which evidence is to be believed, their ability to do this is circumscribed by the judge's power (and duty) to withdraw an issue from them altogether. Here the judge is deciding whether or not the defence has discharged its evidential burden of proof. In *Metropolitan Railway* v. *Jackson*,[21] P sued the defendant company for negligence, alleging that his thumb had been trapped in a slamming door because the carriage of a train operated by the defendant was overcrowded. He had evidence to show the overcrowding arose from the defendant's negligence, but none to show that his thumb had been in the path of the door because of the overcrowding. The House of Lords therefore held that the judge should have withdrawn the case from the jury. A single judge hearing a negligence case nowadays in the County or High Court would, in theory, go through two stages of reasoning. First, he or she should consider whether there is a case made which demands subsequent adjudication on the facts by him or herself as tribunal of fact. How is the initial decision to be made? In *Ryder* v. *Wombwell*[22] Willes J observed that whereas previously judges would leave an issue to the jury if there was only the slightest evidence to support it, "it is now settled that the question for the judge is . . . not whether there is literally no evidence, but whether there is none that ought reasonably to satisfy the jury that the fact sought to be proved is established".[23] This can be a difficult question, for instance, with circumstantial evidence. A judge will similarly

---

[19] *Jones* v. *National Coal Board* [1957] 2 QB 55, 63.
[20] *Critchley* [1982] Crim. LR 524.   [21] (1877) 3 App. Cas. 193.
[22] (1868) LR 4 Exch. 32.   [23] *Ibid.*, at 39.

withdraw an issue from consideration if a witness asserting the contrary was not challenged on it by way of cross-examination. This is because of the emphasis English courts place on the value of cross-examination as a way to the truth.

In criminal cases, the defence may submit, at the close of the presentation of the evidence for the prosecution, that there is no case to answer. If it is successful, a verdict of not guilty is returned by the magistrates, or by the jury on direction from the trial judge. In a civil case without a jury, the judge must decline to rule on the submission unless the person making it elects not to call evidence[24] it is thought unreasonable to ask a judge who has to decide on the facts as well as the law to make a decision before the evidence is complete. Before the case of *Galbraith*,[25] there was a school of thought that a trial judge who considered that it would be unsafe or unsatisfactory to convict, should stop a criminal case. But Lord Lane CJ decided that this is so only where the judge concludes that the prosecution evidence, taken at its highest, is such that a jury, properly directed, could not properly convict upon it; only then should he decide, on submission being made by the defence, that there is no case to answer. Where the strength or weakness of the prosecution evidence depends on the view to be taken of a witness's reliability or other matters which are, in Lord Lane's opinion, the province of the jury, and where on one possible view of the facts there is evidence on which a jury could properly convict, then the judge should allow the matter to be tried by the jury. Thus the judge should not make a judgment of how safe a conviction in this case would be. But it may be that a ban on any sort of qualitative judgment by the trial judge is not entirely a good thing. To be sure, Lord Lane does allow a trial judge to reject evidence which is inherently weak or vague or inconsistent with other evidence. Lord Diplock has said in *Haw Tua Tua* v. *Public Prosecutor*[26] that evidence which was "inherently so incredible that no reasonable person could accept it as being true" would not prevent a submission of no case from succeeding. But that is a minimal intervention by the judge. The Court of Appeal in *Galbraith* has reverted to the neutral referee position for trial judges abandoned in the kind of matters discussed above. This approach is inconsistent with *Turnbull*,[27] which requires the judge to withdraw the case from the jury if the quality of identification evidence is poor, as with the "fleeting glimpse" cases.

Pattenden observes[28] that the whole object of the no case procedure is to protect the accused from the risk of a perverse jury verdict or from a prosecutor who cannot establish even a *prima facie* case, but who hopes to make

---

[24] *Alexander* v. *Rayson* [1936] 1 KB 169.

[25] [1981] 2 All ER 1060.

[26] [1981] 3 All ER 14.

[27] [1976] 3 All ER 549; see text to nn. 214–235 below.

[28] R. Pattenden, "The Submission of No Case to Answer: Some Recent Developments" [1982] *Crim. LR* 558.

good his deficiency in his cross-examination of defence witnesses. Both Lord Runciman's Royal Commission and the Law Commission consider that *Galbraith* should be overturned.[29] The increased admissibility of hearsay evidence in criminal trials may bring the judge further into the arena of contested facts than Lord Lane anticipated, for when hearsay evidence is admitted it carries less weight than sworn testimony.[30] Under the Criminal Justice Act 1988 judges are given a discretion to exclude hearsay evidence, taking account of the interests of justice. When it is admitted in proper exercise of that discretion, given the lower probative value of hearsay, judges may be forced to consider the question of how safe a conviction based entirely on such evidence would be. Consider *Hovells*.[31] An elderly lady said that she had been raped, but died before the trial began. There was medical evidence of sexual activity and a police record of her statement describing the attack and the attacker, but the latter only in vague terms. Hovells admitted being at her flat but said that he could not remember anything about it as he had been very drunk. The judge, who had a discretion whether or not to admit the hearsay evidence under the New Zealand legislation[32] allowed it, which is not objectionable. The question remains, however, whether he should have let the case go to the jury on the basis of that evidence; he did so, and they convicted Hovells, whose appeal was subsequently rejected.

Influence on Findings of Fact

It seems somewhat artificial to insist on the one hand that judges vacate the fact-finding arena, scrupulously leaving the jury its task, when in the context of the judicial summing-up on the evidence at the close of the trial considerable scope for influencing the jury remains. Of course, on some occasions judges must make up their own minds on questions of fact; in criminal trials judges may have to decide whether confessions were obtained by unfair means,[33] and that decision will affect what evidence will ultimately be put before the jury. On some issues a judge trying a civil case is entitled to form a view on fact in the absence of evidence. Judges may take judicial notice of matters which are so notorious, or clearly established, or susceptible of demonstration by reference to a readily obtainable and authoritative source, that evidence of their existence is unnecessary.[34] Similarly where facts are within the everyday knowledge of the members of the jury they, like the judge, may take judicial notice of them.[35] A judge may also rely on personal local knowledge within reasonable limits. In *Mullen* v. *Hackney London*

---

[29] *Report of the Royal Commission on Criminal Justice*, para. 4.56: Law Commission, *Evidence in Criminal Proceedings: Hearsay and Related Topics* (Law Com. 245, HMSO, London, 1997), Cm. 3670.

[30] See below, Ch. 7.   [31] [1987] 1 NZLR 610.   [32] See below, Ch. 7.   [33] See Ch. 6.

[34] *Brandao* v. *Barnett* (1846) 12 Ch & F 282; *Taylor* v. *Barclay* (1828) 2 Sim & Sim 213.

[35] *Hoare* v. *Silverlock* (1848) 12 QB 624.

Borough Council,[36] the plaintiff alleged that the defendant was in breach of an undertaking to the court to repair the council house in which she lived. Judge Martin Graham QC observed that this was one of "numerous failures" by the council to take promises made to the court seriously, and, in consequence, he fined it £5,000. There was no evidence before him of other failures to honour undertakings to the court, but the Court of Appeal held that he was entitled to take judicial notice of how the council had conducted itself in regard to undertaking to the court in similar cases of which he was aware through his own "special" (or local) knowledge.

Fear of excessive judicial influence has led many states of the United States to restrict the summing-up to an explanation of the law, leaving the jury to untangle the facts for themselves, but in the United Kingdom the judge sums up on the facts as well as the law. This can be a tricky business in a complicated case, since a misdirection could form the subject-matter of an appeal against conviction. The nature of the law of evidence inevitably leads in some trials to some intricate reasoning which must be explained to the jury.[37] That the defence does not have the last word is regarded as extraordinary in France, but there the judge retires with the jury, so his influence is considerable. The advantage of the British system is that the judge, by reviewing the facts as well as the law, can relate the one to the other in a manner avoiding complicated technical definitions. Although the judge can direct an acquittal, he may not usurp the jury's function by directing a conviction.[38] Yet, it is said that it is impossible for him to deal with doubtful points of fact unless he can state some of the facts confidently to the jury.[39] Although the judge may not usurp the function of the jury,[40] he is entitled to express himself strongly on the facts in a proper case, since he has experience on the bearing of evidence and in dealing with the relevancy of questions of fact, and it is therefore right that the jury should have the assistance of the judge:

> "The judge is more than a mere referee who takes no part in the trial save to intervene when a rule of procedure or evidence is broken. He and the jury try the case together and it is his duty to give them the benefit of his knowledge of the law and to advise them in the light of his experience as to the significance of the evidence."[41]

Judges feel free therefore to tell juries that they may find the witness's account "incredible" or "almost beyond belief", as long as they remind the jury that ultimately it is for them to decide whether or not to believe it. In

[36] [1997] 2 All ER 906.

[37] R. Munday, "Jury Trial Continental Style" (1993) 13 *LS* 204.

[38] *DPP* v. *Stonehouse* [1975] AC 55.

[39] *Cohen* v. *Bateman* (1909) 2 Cr. App. R 197.

[40] *West* (1910) 4 Cr. App. R 179; *Beeby* (1911) 6 Cr App R 138, *Frampton* (1917) 12 Cr. App. R 202.

[41] Lawton LJ in *Mutch* [1973] 1 All ER 178.

Pinfold,[42] May J reminded the jury of the defendant's alibi witness as follows:

"How a witness gives evidence is... one of the most important things for a jury to consider. Do you remember Mr [D]? He was the deaf, elderly man who held his head to one side and who had something wrong with one eye. It is a matter entirely for you, but you should always ask yourselves, when a witness gives evidence, whether anything can be inferred, and properly be inferred, from the demeanour of a witness, in conjunction with what he or she is saying. Did Mr [D] give you the impression that he was seeking to assist the Court as best he could, or do you think that he was, as it were, giving his evidence by rote?"

May J himself was asked to conduct the inquiry into the Guildford Four and Maguire family convictions, producing an exceptionally clear and balanced series of reports.[43] The case of the Birmingham Six was not referred to him. It would have been interesting to know his reaction to the summing up of Bridge J, who had, during the cross-examination earlier in the trial, expressed considerable scepticism in relation to the evidence of one of the the witnesses for the defence. He was the prison doctor, who gave evidence of injuries presented by the defendants. He suggested that they must have been inflicted by the police:

Can you believe one single word of what Dr [H] says? There are inescapably many perjurers who have given evidence. If Dr [H] is one of them, is he not the worst? . . . If this man has come to this court deliberately to give you false evidence, he is certainly not fit to be a member of the honourable profession upon which, by perjuring himself, he has brought terrible shame."[44]

It is widely believed by practitioners that a judge who tries to influence a jury strongly in favour of the prosecution may find that the attempt backfires and that the jury deliberately counter what they perceive as his bias. The jury project at the London School of Economics found that most jurors who thought the judge hostile to the defence acquitted; there was an even higher acquittal rate,[45] though, where the jury thought the judge favoured the defence, apparently being happy to follow his line in this. Where the judge was perceived as impartial, the acquittal rate fell to 50 per cent.[46] Despite the

---

[42] Transcript, trial, Nov. 1980.

[43] Culminating in Sir John May, *Return to an Address of the Honourable the House of Commons Dated 30 June 1994 for a Report of the Inquiry into the Circumstances Surrounding the Convictions arising out of the Bomb Attacks on Guildford and Woolwich in 1974: Final Report* (HMSO, London, 1994).

[44] Quotation from, J. Jackson, "Trial Procedures" in C. Walker and K. Starmer (eds.), *Justice in Error* (Blackstone, London, 1993).

[45] 78% compared with 68%. However, the jurors, all participating in a simulation, did not give the summing-up as a reason for the acquittal.

[46] L.S. Sealy, "An Analysis of Jury Studies" in D.F. Farrington, K. Hawkins and S. Lloyd-Bostock (eds.), *Psychology, Law and Legal Process* (Mamillan, London, 1979).

risk of reaction from the jury, some judges clearly do make their scepticism of the defence case plain, as an eminent judge has conceded:

"Some judges almost tell a jury how they ought to find, and so seem to me to assume a function which is not theirs according to our constitution. I have always striven to avoid this and to leave the question really as well as formally to the jury, taking, however, great care that they should never find a man guilty whom I believed innocent."[47]

So we find the judges given licence to comment strongly on the facts, although in strict adversarial theory the judge should be concerned exclusively with the law. There is another contradiction; there seems to be an increasing tendency in the appellate courts to argue that the trial judge's direction on the law should leave the jury with considerable scope to define elements of the crime charged for themselves.[48] This avoids having to find definitions for difficult and sometimes metaphysical concepts, but may lead to different verdicts in similar cases, should different juries disagree on the meaning of intention[49] or dishonesty.[50] The reply that such concepts require no explanation to men and women of good sense is not entirely convincing, and another view might be that the jury is entitled to help in these matters; jurors may have oppressive responsibilities in serious cases, and questions of fact are difficult enough. There seems no reason to encumber them with the task of defining the offence as well. Genuine anxiety may be seen in the reaction of the jury in *Moloney*,[51] but the fact that the jury was troubled by the definition of intention they were given in that case was seen by the House of Lords as an argument for giving them virtually no definition at all.

According to Jackson and Doran, it is entirely consistent with inquisitorial theory to rely on an active investigator, with the parties making their contributions principally during the pre-trial stages of the process. In contrast, judicial intervention during the course of a trial defeats adversarial objectives; it thwarts the parties' purpose by disrupting the way they want to present their case, and disturbs the impact of the testimony of particular witnesses.[52] Yet, contrary to adversarial theory, trial judges in criminal cases have considerable influence on the way in which evidence is presented. They may question any witness at any stage,[53] although not in a way indicating the

---

[47] Fry LJ, quoted in A. Fry, *Memoirs of Sir Edward Fry* (OUP, London, 1921).

[48] The leading case is *Brutus* v. *Cozens* [1972] 2 All ER 1297 where the House of Lords held that the meaning of "insulting behaviour" in the Public Order Act 1936 could safely be left to the jury.

[49] *Hancock and Shankland* [1986] 1 All ER 641.

[50] *Feely* [1973] 1 All ER 341.

[51] [1985] 1 All ER 1025.

[52] J. Jackson and S. Doran, *Judge Without Jury: Diplock Trials and the Adversary System* (Clarendon, Oxford, 1995).

[53] *Hopper* [1915] 2 KB 43; *Cain* (1936) 25 Cr. App. R 204, per Du Parq J at 205 "a judge may put such questions as the interests of justice require".

belief that the accused is guilty.[54] They may cross-examine the accused if he or she gives evidence, but not in a manner suggesting that they wish to help the prosecution rather than the defence.[55] If a judge's intervention indicates that he or she thinks that the witness is not to be believed, the judge must remind the jury that the question of credibility is for them.[56] But if the judge goes so far as to invite the jury to disbelieve the defence evidence, the conviction must be quashed.[57]

The judge's interruptions must not prevent counsel from presenting his case. In *Perks*,[58] the defendant was giving his evidence in chief. Out of a total of 700 questions put to him, 147 were asked by the judge, who also interrupted defence counsel's final address. The Court of Appeal held that the point was not the number of interruptions so much as their hostile nature, which hindered the development of the defendant's evidence in chief.[59] Such interventions should be kept to a minimum. However, discourtesy to counsel as such is not a sufficient reason to overturn a conviction[60]; there must be positive interference with counsel in pursuit of his or her task.[61] Even a Lord Chief Justice has been known to cause concern on this ground; Lord Hewart CJ was criticised more than once in the Court of Appeal for failing to keep an open mind[62]; more recently, the Court of Appeal expressed disapproval of a judge who during the defence address to the jury made gestures of impatience, sighed and several times "observed in a loud voice 'Oh God' and then laid his head across his arms and made groaning noises". Despite this behaviour, the Court did not feel it necessary to quash the conviction.[63]

In *Sharp*,[64] however, the conviction was quashed on appeal. Not only did the tenor of the judge's frequent interruptions of defence cross-examination of key prosecution witnesses seriously hamper the defence advocate and deflect him from his path, but also clearly conveyed to the jury the judge's opinion of the merits of the defence case. Stuart-Smith LJ advised judges as follows: "[i]n general, where a cross-examination is being conducted by competent counsel a judge should not intervene, save to clarify matters he does not understand, or thinks the jury may not understand. If he wishes to ask questions about matters that have not been touched upon, it is generally better to wait until the end of the examination or cross-examination." He explained that one of the objections to interventions from the judge in an adversarial trial by jury is that

---

54 *Rabitt* (1931) 23 Cr. App. R 112.
55 *Cairn* (1936) 25 Cr. App. R 204.
56 *Gibson and Cohen* (1944) 29 Cr. App. R 174.
57 *Ibid.*
58 [1973] Crim. LR 388.
59 See also *Matthews* (1984) 78 Cr. App. R 23.
60 *Photophopoulos* [1968] Crim. LR 52.
61 *Leggett* [1970] 1 QB 67; *Wilson* [1979] RTR 57; *Sharp* [1993] 3 All ER 225.
62 See C.P. Harvey, *The Advocate's Devil* (Stevens, London, 1958); *Hobbs* v. *Tinling* [1929] 2 KB 1.
63 *Hircock and others* [1970] 1 QB 67; see also *Sharp* [1993] 3 All ER 225.
64 *Sharp* [1993] 3 All ER 225.

the judge may appear to be partial to one side or the other. However, Jackson and Doran could see no connection between the tendency to interrupt a witness's evidence in chief and the presence or absence of a jury in the courts of Northern Ireland.[65] There were a great many interruptions in both kinds of courts, and these were observed quite frequently to impede the flow of a line of questions in cross-examination, particularly where the judge insisted on an explanation of its relevance just as counsel embarked on it. In the Diplock Courts, some judges, because there they were the sole arbiters of fact, effectively took over the task of cross-examination from counsel. Yet the adversarial tradition held; judges did not take the opportunity presented by the lack of a jury to launch into inquisitorial-style questioning to elicit new information. But the chief determinant of whether or not a particular judge will interrupt an advocate appears to have nothing to do with whether or not there is a jury, but the personality of the individual judge, and also the judicial response to the personality of counsel.[66]

Witnesses

The Witnesses Who May be Called

There are few restrictions on the parties in civil cases as to whom they may call to give evidence on their behalf. The position of child witnesses is complex and is discussed below in Chapter 4. Persons of defective intellect may not give evidence if incapable of understanding the nature of the oath, a decision for the judge.[67] If the judge allows such testimony to be introduced, it is for the tribunal of fact to adjudge how much credit to give it. Non-compellable witnesses include the Sovereign and foreign sovereigns and ambassadors.[68] In criminal cases, there are restrictions on the competence and compellability of accused persons,[69] and in the past there were complicated rules governing the competence and compellability of their spouses. These elaborate prescriptions were a source of inspiration to the writers of detective stories; the simplification of the position under the Police and Criminal Evidence Act 1984 has therefore cost us a fascinating oddity, but even so, is to be welcomed as a step towards some coherence. Some of the traditional explanations for the limited availability of spouse witnesses were brushed aside by the Criminal Law Revision Committee: "Objections . . .

---

[65] Jackson and Doran, n. 52 above. The Diplock Courts were set up in 1973; they deal with serious crimes that may have terrorist connections. There is no jury.

[66] *Ibid.*, 120–6.

[67] *Hill* (1851) 2 Den. 254.

[68] M.N. Howard, P. Crane and D.A. Hochberg (eds.), see *Phipson on Evidence*, (14th edn., Sweet and Maxwell, London, 1990), 9.14.

[69] See below, Ch. 4.

based on the theoretical unity of the spouses or on the interests of the accused's wife in the outcome of the proceedings,[70] and in particular on the likelihood that his wife will be biased in favour of the accused, can have no place in the decisions as to the extent of competence and compellability nowadays".[71] However, the Committee did give serious consideration to issues such as the "objection on social grounds to disturbing marital harmony more than is absolutely necessary", and "what many regard as the harshness of compelling a spouse to give evidence against her husband".[72] But the interests of marital harmony were not thought to demand restrictions on the *competence* of spouses as prosecution witnesses. For if a wife chooses to give evidence against her husband, it seems excessively paternalistic to prevent her from doing so on the grounds that the state is anxious to preserve goodwill in her marriage even if she no longer cares. Some lawyers have warned against the vindictive spouse who seizes the opportunity provided by the witness box to settle old grudges, but the fact remains that there may be other prosecution witnesses who are similarly motivated, and it is up to the defence to bring this out in cross-examination and to emphasise the point to the jury.

Reformers seem to make heavy weather of the question whether spouses should be compellable for the prosecution. Section 80 of the 1984 Act rightly assumes that the spouse is potentially as damaging to the defence case if she gives evidence on behalf of the co-accused, whose interests may directly conflict with her husband's, as if she acts as a prosecution witness. Whether this justifies dealing with both situations in the same way is more doubtful; Zuckerman argues that if the co-defendant requires the spouse to show his innocence, he is entitled to her testimony, whatever the effect on their marriage might be.[73] Be that as it may, the Police and Criminal Evidence Act provides in section 80(3):

> "In any proceedings the wife or husband of the accused shall . . . be compellable to give evidence for the prosecution or on behalf of any person jointly charged with the accused if and only if—
>
> (a) the offence charged involves an assault on, or injury or a threat of injury to, the wife or husband of the accused or a person who was at the material time under the age of sixteen; or
>
> (b) the offence charged is a sexual offence alleged to have been committed in respect of a person who was at the material time under that age; or
>
> (c) the offence charged consists of attempting or conspiring to commit, or of aiding, abetting, counselling, procuring or inciting the commission of, an offence . . . [in (a) or (b) above]."

---

[70] A reference to the old common law rule that persons with an interest in the trial were inherently unreliable and should not give evidence.

[71] *Evidence (General)* (Eleventh Report of the Criminal Law Revision Committee (HMSO, London, 1972), Cmnd. 4991, para. 147.

[72] *Ibid.*

[73] A. Zuckerman, *The Principles of Criminal Evidence* (OUP, Clarendon, 1989), 295.

Before this, spouses were effectively not compellable for the prosecution except, arguably, for the common law exceptions of high treason and forcible marriage.[74] The new exception relating to offences against children is justified in the Eleventh Report in relation to the seriousness of "some of these cases",[75] and because of the difficulty of proof where the victim is a young child. The lack of alternative evidence is a pragmatic argument which is not altogether convincing. Difficulty in securing a conviction is held to justify abandoning our erstwhile concern for the stability of the defendant's marriage; this difficulty will not exist in every case where a child has been injured, but may exist in some cases of injury to a 17-year-old—and there the spouse is not compellable. A further argument is put forward by the Committee: "[s]he may have been a party to the violence or at least acquiesced in it, although it may not be possible to prosecute her. For similar reasons we think that the wife should be compellable on a charge of a sexual offence against a child under sixteen *belonging to the accused's household*".[76] It is alarming to find changes in the law being advocated on the strength of what appears to be a wild and unsupported generalisation. If the wife's compellability is to serve as some sort of punishment, then there ought to be a better case against her than that.

There have been suggestions in the past that to call a reluctant spouse-witness would be counterproductive, in that her distress or refusal to co-operate on the day might alienate the jury from the prosecutor or bring the trial to a complete standstill. The emotional conflict suffered by the spouse, who may face imprisonment for contempt of court if she refuses to testify, with the alternative of incriminating her husband or perjuring herself, is not unique, however. There may be others who feel equally anguished on the accused's behalf, and there is no legal bolthole for them. The possibility of an alternative approach which takes account of the emotional involvement of the accused's family never seems to have been addressed in this country. In the French *Code du Procédure Pénale* the father, mother or other ascendant of the accused, his children, siblings, relatives by marriage to the same degree or wife should not take the oath.[77] In our system there is no halfway house, but if in any case it appears to a prosecution that the spouse-witness is unlikely to further its cause, the witness will not be called.

Why, if spouses were to become compellable only in exceptional circumstances, introduce as an exception cases where they have suffered violence to themselves? For they are unlikely to place another person at risk if they refuse to give evidence voluntarily in cases of domestic violence. The Criminal Law Revision Committee said, "On the whole we think that the public interest in the punishment of violence requires that compellability

---

[74] *Phipson on Evidence* (13th edn., 1982), 31.24.
[75] N. 71 above, para. 60.
[76] *Ibid.*, para. 150. The qualification, italicised for convenience, does not appear in s. 80(3)(b).
[77] Art. 335.

should remain".[78] They added that the fact that the wife therefore would have no choice whether to give evidence or not "should make it easier to counter the effect of possible intimidation by her husband and to persuade her to give evidence". The suggestion that a violent husband will participate in a rational debate upon contempt of court and accept that his wife's participation in the trial is not a betrayal is astonishing. The Committee goes on blithely to conclude, "[a]t any rate, there does not seem to us to be any evidence that the present rule of compellability[79] does any harm so it seems safest to preserve it".[80]

The Report of the New South Wales Task Force on Domestic Violence[81] says that to place a choice in the hands of a woman who suffers from domestic violence is "almost an act of legal cruelty". A contrary view is that forcing her to give evidence when she is afraid or does not wish to destroy her marriage is just as cruel. And it appears to be the case that in jurisdictions where victims of domestic violence can be compelled to give evidence, they are rarely forced to do so, probably for pragmatic reasons.[82] Policies of this kind reduce the cogency, if any, of arguments that women are helped by having no choice, since the ability to choose seems to survive a change in the law. On the other hand it is difficult to imagine circumstances where the prosecutor would benefit by invoking the power to compel, although it may be that more women give evidence voluntarily precisely because the power exists. In 1987 Scotland Yard announced a new approach with an increased willingness to use compulsion in domestic violence cases.[83] Even so, in 1989 Edwards writes: "In the United Kingdom compellability has not been enforced"[84]; it is impossible to tell whether the publicity on the subject made it unnecessary in that women became more co-operative, but this seems doubtful. A reluctant witness may prefer a short sentence of imprisonment for contempt of court to the consequences which may flow from testifying. Another option is simply to tell lies in the witness box. Prosecutors can do little about witnesses who change their stories except to treat them as hostile, a procedure from which they frequently find there is little to gain.[85] The most useful and humane way of dealing with the problem of the intimidated witness is probably to rely on his or her written statement, if the court will allow it, under the common law and statutory exceptions to the hearsay rule.[86]

---

[78] This view, that wives were compellable at common law in domestic violence cases, was subsequently rejected by the House of Lords in *Hoskyn* v. *MPC* [1979] AC 474.

[79] See the pre-*Hoskin* view.   [80] *Eleventh Report.*, above, para. 149   [81] 1981:55.

[82] Evidence to New South Wales Report on Domestic Violence (1985:31); Evidence to Law Reform Committee of Australia (1986: Report No. 30 *Domestic Violence*); see S. Edwards, "Compelling a Reluctant Spouse" [1989] *NLJ* 691.

[83] The *Independent*, 24 June 1987.   [84] Edwards, n. 82 above.

[85] See the text to nn. 132–134 below.

[86] Some statements by victims of domestic violence could be part of the *res gestae*: see Ch. 7.

Whatever the force of the arguments for and against the compelling of spouse victims, the fact remains that the position of cohabitees who suffer domestic violence has always been that they enjoy no special protection from the general obligation to give evidence. Despite this, furore followed the decision of Judge Pickles to sentence to seven days' imprisonment for contempt an unmarried girl who declared herself too frightened to give evidence against her boyfriend.[87] This seems to demonstrate considerable public sympathy with the dilemma of battered women who seem to seek the protection of the law without being willing to participate to the extent required by the trial process, a dilemma which our system of criminal justice has not seriously addressed. It is widely believed that battered women are prone to making complaints, perhaps summoning the police in an emergency, but withdrawing them later and refusing to take any further part in the investigation or prosecution process. The evidence for this is anecdotal,[88] but nevertheless convincing, being supported by many experienced practitioners. As a result, it is said, the police are slow to intervene in "domestics", because they believe that the woman will change her mind and so their time would be wasted. The police may be being maligned unfairly; there is research suggesting that there is in fact a high response rate.[89] If the allegations are true, it may be that police lack of interest stems from too narrow a view at all levels of the force as to the proper role of the police. It is wrong to assume that the police function is entirely bound up in arrest, prosecution, trial and conviction. Much may be achieved in protecting society without the consummation of a guilty verdict.[90]

The Eleventh Report pays surprisingly little attention to the issue of whether spouse compellability should be limited at all. In view of the comparative weakness of the arguments adduced in favour of the excepted cases, it might have been instructive to include a discussion of whether it would be best to make spouses compellable in all cases, given the recommendation that they should be generally competent. Instead, there is only the following, baffling, passage:

> "We do not think that the wife should be compellable for the prosecution in the case of offences other than those mentioned above . . . It might be argued that the wife should be compellable in very serious cases such as murder and spying or perhaps in all serious cases of violence; but the law has never, except perhaps in treason, made the seriousness of an offence by itself a ground for compellability, and we do not favour doing so now."[91]

[87] *Williams*, Leeds Crown Court, Dec. 1989.

[88] See Edwards, n. 82 above.

[89] See E.S. Buzawa, "Explaining Variations in Police Responses to Domestic Violence: A Case Study in Detroit and New England", in E.T. Hotaling, D. Finkelhov and E. Kirkpatrick (eds.), *Coping with Family Violence* (Sage, Newbury Park, 1988).

[90] P. Smith, "Victims Who Know their Assailants" in *ibid.*

[91] N. 71 above, para. 152.

There is no apology for the earlier passage emphasising the seriousness of violent crimes against children. Perhaps the explanation for the apparent refusal to explain precisely what, then, *is* the ground for compellability is a natural caution from a Committee which did not wish its proposals to appear so radical that they would not be implemented, which would be ironic in the light of what happened to the Eleventh Report because of the recommendations on the accused's right to silence.[92]

Questions of competence and compellability are of particular significance in an adversarial procedure which relies heavily on sworn oral testimony, preferring it to depositions and other kinds of hearsay evidence. Time and again we hear appeal court judges emphasise that those who saw the witnesses give their evidence are far better able to form a view of the facts than anyone subsequently reading transcripts.[93] The insistence on the importance of the opportunity to watch the witness at first hand has coloured the debate on videotaped depositions[94] and is the reason behind decisions such as *Dunne*[95]; in this case, the trial judge questioned a 7 year-old girl in the absence of the jury to see whether she understood the nature of the oath. She was subsequently sworn and gave vital evidence for the prosecution. The Court of Appeal quashed the conviction. Lord Hewart CJ appreciated the kindly motives of the trial judge but held that witnesses should not be assessed in this way, without the jury or the defendant being present. In *Reynolds*[96] Lord Goddard CJ observed that although the decision whether the child should be sworn is for the trial judge, the jury should see her demeanour and manner of answering questions, even at that preliminary stage, in order to assess the credibility of her testimony, should she be allowed to give it.[97] Although child witnesses no longer take the oath, question-and-answer sessions with the judge to determine competence still occur in some cases.[98]

Believing Witnesses: Testimony

Evidence in Chief

All witnesses give their testimony as evidence in chief. This means that they are initially questioned by the advocate calling them. Once they have identified themselves, or dealt with other matters which are not disputed, no leading questions may be asked.[99] The requirement is for spontaneity; witnesses should be able to describe without prompting the events of which they claim to have knowledge. This notion has dogged the debate

---

[92] See below, Ch. 5.   [93] *Yuill* v. *Yuill* [1945] P 15.   [94] See Ch. 4.
[95] (1929) 21 Cr. App. R 176.   [96] [1950] 1 KB 606.
[97] But now see *Hampshire* [1995] 2 All ER 1015; see Ch. 4.
[98] See Ch. 4.
[99] *Robinson* (1867) 61 JP 520. A leading question is one that suggests the answer to the witness, or assumes the existence of facts in issue or not proven.

surrounding child witnesses. The analogy drawn between conventional evidence in chief and videotaped interviews has caused major problems for those striving under the new provisions to produce evidence which a court can use.[100] But the claim that a witness's evidence in chief is entirely spontaneous and is therefore reliable is unconvincing.

Witnesses may re-read statements or notes made reasonably close in time to the events in question in order to refresh their memories before they go into court.[101] Most witness statements fall into this category, since absolute contemporaneity is not required. Further, in *Da Silva*,[102] it was held that if a witness has not so refreshed his or her memory, the document may be consulted if necessary and, if the judge gives leave, once the testimony has begun. In *R. v. South Ribble Magistrates' Court, ex p. Cochrane*,[103] the Divisional Court envisaged the extension of this principle, at the discretion of the court, to a witness who did consult his or her statement before coming into the witness-box, but failed to take in what he or she was reading. It even suggested that witnesses who faced particular difficulties of recall, for instance the elderly, or witnesses in complex serious fraud cases, might take non-contemporaneous documents with them into the witness-box as *aides-mémoires*. Thus witness are generally primed with the information they are to impart, having mulled over their statements "in the corridor". There may have been considerable contribution from others to the contents of those statements. A witness statement in itself gives no clue to the number or nature of the questions that were asked to assist in its production. It has been observed that with the best will in the world, a statement compiled at the behest of a police officer inevitably will reflect the officer's subjective assessment of the facts, particularly if the witness was suffering from stress or tiredness at the time it was made. "Often a statement owes as much to the officer's controlling hand as to the witness's actual memory."[104]

The legitimacy of a witness, during evidence-in-chief, using a contemporaneous note to refresh the memory is well established in common law and recognised in statute. Traditionally, such a note must have been made or verified by the witness personally, and, if made after the event, while it is still fresh in his or her mind.[105] If the contents of the original contemporaneous

---

[100] See Ch. 4.

[101] *Richardson* (1971) 55 Cr. App. R 244. If the witness is for the prosecution, the defence must be informed: *Westwell* (1976) 62 Cr. App. R 251. The opposing party is entitled to see the memory-refreshing document: *Owen* v. *Edwards* (1983) 77 Cr. App. R 191.

[102] [1990] 1 WLR 31.

[103] *The Times*, 24 June 1996.

[104] D. Wolchover and A. Heaton-Armstrong, "Tape Recording Witness Statements" [1997] *NLJ* 855, 856.

[105] There is considerable latitude here; contemporaneity is a "matter of fact and degree": *Simmonds* [1969] 1 QB 685. Periods of a fortnight and 22 days have been held to be not too long: *Langton* (1877) 2 QBD 296; *Fotheringham* (1975) 119 SJ 613. In *Woodcock* [1963] Crim LR 273, three months was held to be too long.

note become transferred to another document, that document may be used to refresh the witness's memory, even if made a long time after the original note, as long as the new document was personally verified.[106] The document itself is not evidence in the case, as the contents are incorporated into the witness's oral testimony. However, the opposing side is entitled to inspect it, as are the finders of fact. It was said in *Senat* v. *Senat*[107] by Sir Jocelyn Simon:

> "The mere inspection of a document does not render it evidence which counsel inspecting it is bound to put in . . Where a document is used to refresh a witness's memory, cross-examining counsel may inspect that document in order to check it without making it evidence. Moreover he may cross-examine upon it without making it evidence provided that his cross-examination does not go further than the parts which are used for refreshing the memory of the witness: . . . But if a party calls for and inspects a document held by the other party, he is bound to put it in evidence if he is required to do so."

Cross-examination upon parts of the document not used to refresh the witness's memory makes the document evidence in the case. In criminal cases the statements in it go only to the witness's credibility, and are not evidence of the facts stated.[108]

Apart from the accused, a special case, no party can *lead* the credibility of its own witnesses, as it is assumed.[109] A witness may appear more credible if he or she has held to the same story consistently over a period of time. But in general, a witness cannot be asked in chief whether he or she has formerly made a statement consistent with his or her evidence on another occasion, nor can other witnesses be called to prove that this is the case.[110] It is thought that any witness could easily give an inflated impression of his or her credibility by repeating a false story on many occasions. There are exceptions to the rule.[111] The reasoning behind them varies. For example, defendants in criminal cases are entitled to lead evidence that an explanation when first accused of an offence is identical to their present testimony in court. Juries may take account of such consistency in assessing defendants' credibility.[112] The rationale appears to be that it is significant that someone who provided a particular account on the spot has not changed it since. Juries otherwise might suppose that the defendant has had a long time to come up with an explanation. Other exceptions seem to be based merely on necessity. Complaints in sexual cases, or "recent complaint", may be proved to support

---

[106] *Chisnell* [1992] Crim LR 507; *Cheng* (1976) 63 Cr. App. R 20.

[107] [1965] P 172.

[108] *Virgo* (1978) 67 Cr App R 523; for civil cases, see Civil Evidence Act 1995, discussed at Ch. 7.

[109] *Attorney-General* v. *Bowman* (1791) 2 Bos. & P 522 (n).

[110] *Roberts* [1942] 1 All E R 187.

[111] E.g., rebutting allegations of recent fabrication: *Oyesiku* (1971) 56 Cr. App. R 240; prior identification: *Christie* [1914] AC 545.

[112] *Storey* (1968) 52 Cr. App. R 334; *Pearce* (1979) 69 Cr. App. R 365; see Ch. 7.

the testimony of male or female complainants[113]: the justification for it appears to be simply that these are cases where the credibility of the complainant is of crucial importance. And, in an effort to reduce the risk of manufacture, the Court of Appeal has said that the complaint must not be a response to suggestive, intimidating or leading questions. However, it does not have to be made immediately after the event, if it was made at the first opportunity which reasonably presented itself.[114] In civil cases, the previous consistent statement of a witness maybe admitted as evidence of the fact stated, but only where adduced to rebut allegations of fabrication.[115]

Cross-examination

Cross-examination by the opposing side follows the witness's evidence in chief. Sometimes the questioning is lengthy and detailed because the opponent proposes to contradict all the statements of fact in the testimony given in chief. Any fact alleged by a witness during the evidence in chief is conceded by the other side unless it is put to him or her during cross-examination that he or she is wrong.[116] Cross-examination should follow on from the facts and arguments which form the party's case; therefore "fishing" will not be allowed. Counsel should not in cross-examination cast aspersions upon the witness or upon other witnesses, if there is no sufficient basis for it in the information in his or her possession.[117] However, questions of considerable nicety may arise as to what constitutes sufficient foundation or relevance to justify a particular aspersion.[118] Questions should be as to fact and not invite the witness to explain the evidence of others, or to enter into an argument with counsel. The testimony of other witnesses should not be quoted.[119] A cross-examiner may use leading questions. He or she may attack the credibility of the witness, unless the questions are vexatious or irrelevant,[120] for instance, if they concern events remote in time and character, or if there is a lack of proportion between the evidence of misdeeds in the past and the importance of the witness's evidence to the case in hand. The cross-examiner may remind the witness of his previous convictions, although there may not be an unfettered right to do this,[121] and, generally, "spent" convictions under the Rehabilitation of Offenders Act 1974 would not be put

---

[113] *Osborne* [1905] 1 KB 551.

[114] *Ibid.*

[115] Civil Evidence Act 1995, s. 6(2).

[116] *R. v.Wood Green Crown Court, ex p Taylor* [1995] Crim. LR 879. The rule does not, strictly speaking, apply to magistrates' courts, but represents good practice there: *O'Connell* v. *Adams* [1973] Crim. LR 113.

[117] *Rondel* v. *Worsley* [1969] 1 AC 191, *per* Lord Reid at 227.

[118] *Saif Ali* v. *Sydney Mitchell & Co. (a Firm)* [1980] AC 198, 220, *per* Lord Diplock.

[119] *Baldwin* (1925) 18 Cr App R 175; unfortunately, many advocates appear to ignore these principles, and some instead seem to rely heavily on tactics of that kind.

[120] *Hobbs* v. *Tinling* [1929] 2 KB 1.

[121] *Sweet-Escott* (1971) 55 Cr. App. R 316.

without the leave of the judge.[122] Coss-examining prosecution witnesses on their bad character could cost defendants with criminal records their "shield",[123] so that the previous convictions could be revealed to the jury. This may inhibit the way the defence is conducted.[124] As we saw in Chapter 2, however, courts in adversarial proceedings are forced to curtail the ambit of cross-examinations, in order to save themselves from becoming bogged down in endless peripheral details. These may be relevant, but if they are of only collateral importance as far as the main issue is concerned, there are limits to the amount of time the court is prepared to spend pursuing them. There can be no doubt that in some cases the arbitrary effect of the rules which deal with collateral questions deprives the court of relevant information.[125] The emphasis on the trial itself as opposed to any pre-trial inquiry means that issues such as the character of witnesses have to be dealt with in an abrupt fashion in order to cut down the time devoted to what are necessarily classified as collateral issues.

The case of *Edwards*[126] is authority that a police officer may be cross-examined as to credit in respect of a previous trial at which he or she gave evidence for the prosecution and where an acquittal resulted, if on that occasion it was alleged that the officer had fabricated an admission, and the acquittal correspondingly demonstrated the jury's disbelief in the officer's evidence. By the same token, police officers may be asked questions in cross-examination about any relevant criminal offences or disciplinary charges found proved against them. Unproven charges or complaints may not be the subject-matter of a cross-examination. Nor may cases where the officer previously has testified in a case resulting in acquittal, if the verdict did not of itself necessarily indicate that the officer was not believed.[127] But it is not clear to what extent other prosecution witnesses may be cross-examined about earlier trials in which acquittals were returned in the face of their evidence. In *Thorne*,[128] a "supergrass" witness[129] had given evidence in earlier cases, at some of which acquittals were returned. This was held to be irrelevant; there was no consistent pattern to suggest disbelief, and in any event acquittals in themselves did not necessarily indicate that the witness was disbelieved. The reasoning adopted in these cases involves judges in a

---

[122] Ss. 4(1), 7(3); *Practice Note* [1975] 2 All ER 1073. In a civil case, of course, a judge deciding to exclude the convictions would know about them anyway.

[123] Under Criminal Evidence Act 1898, s.1(f) (ii); see below, Ch. 5.

[124] See Ch. 5.

[125] See Ch. 2.

[126] [1991] 2 All ER 266.

[127] Making this distinction involves consideration of all the evidence heard at the previous trial, and of what alternative considerations might lie behind the jury verdict. See e.g. *Lucas* [1993] Crim. LR 599.

[128] (1977) 66 Cr. App. R 6.

[129] Not a police officer, as stated in *Edwards*. See D. Wolchover and A. Heaton-Armstrong, "Cross-examining the Police on their Past" [1991] *NLJ* 1182.

time-consuming diversion from the matter immediately in hand. It forces them to re-open a previous criminal case, and to analyse the verdict in the light of the prosecution evidence presented at the time, solely in order to determine what questions may in the present case legitimately be put to a witness for the prosecution. Thus a criminal court becomes bogged down in issues which are not of even collateral relevance. Scrutiny of transcripts of earlier trials or hearings is hardly an appropriate procedure for the middle of a criminal trial, and pressure of time might easily cause the later court to misunderstand the issues before the first. Pre-trial review is the only sensible way of dealing with it. Even then the process appears to be a departure from the adversarial principle that matters of credit are only of collateral relevance. It seems that it is not only common sense that would suggest otherwise. In the case of certain officers of the constabulary, so does experience.

It is easier to point out the inconsistency or unreliability of the opponent's witness than to indicate the consistency or reliability of one's own witness, which is assumed until disproved by the opponent. Witnesses are clearly identified as being on one side or the other, which means, in effect, that parties are taken to guarantee the credibility of their own witnesses.[130] If a witness makes a statement which appears to support the case for one side, but then during the course of testimony on that party's behalf departs substantially from it, the caller may apply to the court to deem that witness "hostile". But for this to succeed, the witness should have done more than merely to disappoint the caller by failing to come up to proof. There must be evidence of a clear determination not to tell the truth. The court can test this by looking at previous statements, but for a witness to be regarded as hostile, more than contradictory remarks are needed. The contradiction must be on a scale which shows that disregard for the truth, as opposed to forgetfulness, is the only explanation for the discrepancy.[131]

The Criminal Procedure Act 1865, section 3, provides that a party producing a witness shall not be allowed to impeach his credit by general evidence of bad character. The effect is that, although turning a witness hostile entitles the caller to cross-examine the witness, this is only to the extent that the earlier statement can be put to him or her as a previous inconsistent statement. The effect of this may be sufficiently devastating to persuade the witness to admit that the earlier statement is the true one, thus adopting it into evidence-in-chief. Bringing the witness "back on board" in this way is the best that can be hoped for by the caller, although the evidence he or she wanted is now being offered by a witness who is manifestly unreliable. But many hostile witnesses will stick to their new story, and in criminal trials this deprives the advocate of the testimony they were called to provide. Their previous statements, put to them in cross-examination, are relevant

---

[130] M. Newark, "The Hostile Witness and the Adversary System" [1986] *Crim. LR* 441.
[131] *Price* v. *Manning* (1889) 42 Ch.D 372.

only to the issue of credibility[132]; the most that can be achieved is to discredit the current, unhelpful, testimony. To be able to counter the effect of the witness's evidence at trial may be of little comfort to an advocate who has effectively lost a key witness. Few advocates would choose to venture into a court knowing that the witness will turn. Newark has argued[133] that the hostile witness procedure is unsatisfactory and confusing because of the adversarial character of the proceedings. The rigid, two-sided structure of the trial means that the only way to attack the credibility of your own witness is to treat him as "gone over" to the other side. The hostile witness's relationship with the other side is not clearly defined, however. It is not settled whether he or she is now its witness (which may or may not suit it) and therefore whether it can launch a cross-examination as well.[134] The absence of a pre-trial inquiry exacerbates the risk of collapse in the prosecution case because the betrayal of the hostile witness could be a complete surprise. And when it comes, the dominance of the hearsay rule and the principle of orality ensure that previous statements, which may well be true, are almost completely useless.

Believing Witnesses: Credibility

How is judgment made about the veracity of witnesses? Jury studies are unanimous in showing that evidence has a far greater effect on the verdict of the jury than the individual character of jurors,[135] but there is a general tendency for people to over-estimate their capacity to identify persons who are telling the truth.[136] This may be because they have indeed managed to identify obvious lies they are told, but have not known when they have been successfully deceived. It may be, however, that they were relying on misleading indicators; there is a tendency to believe witnesses who have a great deal of confidence.[137] Lawyers have recently been accused of applying inappropriate criteria to witnesses, and therefore of drawing the wrong conclusions,[138] in an experiment where various subjects were shown videotaped interviews with children purporting to describe sexual abuse. Lawyers were seen to stress irrelevant criteria such as spontaneity and confidence, placing little value on non-verbal

---

[132] *Golder* [1960] 3 All ER 457; and the previous statements must be put in accordance with the terms of Criminal Procedure Act 1865 ss. 4, 5. They may be taken as evidence of the facts stated in civil trials, as long as the procedure in the 1865 Act is followed.

[133] N. 130 above.

[134] Newark, n. 130 above.

[135] M.J. Saks and R. Hastie, *Social Psychology in Court* (Van Nostrand Reinhold, New York, 1978).

[136] G. Köhnken, "The Evaluation of Statement Credibility: Social Judgment and Expert Diagnostic Approaches", in J.R. Spencer, R. Nicholson, R. Flin and R. Bull (eds.), *Children's Evidence in Legal Proceedings* (Faculty of Law, University of Cambridge, Cambridge, 1990).

[137] K.A. Daffenbacher and E. Loftus, "Do Jurors Share a Common Understanding Concerning Eyewitness Behaviour?" (1982) 6 *Law and Human Behaviour* 184.

[138] E. Vizard, M. Wiseman, A. Bentovim and J. Leventhal; "Child Sexual Abuse Videos—is Seeing Believing?", Paper given to the British Paediatric Association, 11–14 Apr. 1989.

behaviour and child play. They were accused of becoming irritated by hesitant or ambiguous accounts. Police officers and social workers had more success at identifying genuine cases. But Richard White, a participant in the study and a leading family lawyer, objected to the tiny scale of the research, which used only four lawyer-subjects, and argued that the lawyers' more cautious approach was connected to the anticipated use of the interviews as evidence in the trial. His defence of the lawyers involves a circular argument, however. Judicial assumptions about witness reliability are behind the difficulties of admissibility which they were trying to predict.

Are there indicators of truthfulness? It seems that confidence and fluency are misleading, and are easily copied by a clever liar.[139] Most people look for the wrong clues; "the eyes are very efficient instruments of deception[140] According to Köhnken, lying behaviour is not similar from person to person, and may even vary in the same person. Rather than being fidgety and tense, habitual liars are still and calm. Non-psychologists assume that the best way to expose them is to show suspicion and ask them tough questions. This does not work; a skilful liar will notice this and adjust his behaviour to conform to an honest stereotype. On the other hand, an honest witness may become nervous if subjected to a grilling and appear less convincing. The only genuine characteristics of truthful stories pertain to their contents, and include such factors as internal consistency and accordance with other known facts. Truthful people are more likely than liars to make spontaneous corrections or to admit that they have forgotten something—but an intelligent liar knows this and imitates it.[141] Some years ago naïve faith in technological development encouraged flirtations with truth drugs and lie detector machines, but experience has since proved these guides to truthfulness to be unreliable. Courts have tended to dismiss evidence so obtained on technical grounds, as inadmissible previous consistent or hearsay statements. Lie detector or polygraph machines are not allowed in courts.[142] They are in fact simple devices which measure the level of moisture on the palms of the hands, and so may indicate nervousness, but nothing more.[143] Truth drugs such as sodium pentathol, which releases inhibitions, have been shown not to prevent people fabricating or concealing matters of which they speak.[144]

Eggleston's observations on the propensity of witnesses to lie is an example of the tendency, possibly a chronic one amidst lawyers, to assume that falsehoods can be recognised. He suggests that witnesses are more likely to lie to protect their good name or that of friends or relations where the matter does not seem to them to have any bearing on the case[145]; the old adage *falsus in*

---

[139] Köhnken, n. 136 above.   [140] *Ibid.*   [141] *Ibid.*

[142] *Phipson on Evidence*, n. 68 above, 32.10.

[143] L. Saxe, P. Dougherty and M. Cross, "Validity of Polygraph Testimony" in L.S. Wrightsman, C.E. Willis and S.M. Kassim (eds.), *On the Witness Stand* (Sage, Newbury Park, 1987).

[144] Saks and Hastie, n. 135 above.

[145] R. Eggleston, *Evidence, Proof and Probability* (Weidenfeld and Nicolson, London, 1983), 195.

uno, falsus in omnibus[146] is, therefore, quite wrong. But, traditionally, "witnesses were regarded categorically as being either truthful persons or not".[147] According to Wigmore, the maxim was no more than a working rule, but he supported it, arguing that a man who would lie about a collateral matter is perhaps more likely to be a determined liar than one who would lie on oath about a material fact.[148] However, Wigmore was against the principle hardening into a rule of law, and today it does not appear in the evidence textbooks at all. Egglestone thinks that in fact people will lie more readily where they regard the suppression of the truth as more important than the issue in the case, or if they think that the question is irrelevant to the facts in issue. Withholding the truth may be seen by some as less reprehensible than actually telling lies. If Egglestone is right, the basic assumptions behind many cross-examinations as to credit are misconceived and are being allowed to mislead the court. Revealing previous convictions, shady business practice or proven lying in the past is not a reliable indicator of dishonesty in the present. Yet much may be made of these. The wide-ranging nature of cross-examination on credibility is redolent of the belief that he who has lied about anything will have lied in everything.

Believing Witnesses: Corroboration

Although, in Scotland, there is a corroboration requirement in the sense that the evidence of more than one witness is not full proof of a civil[149] or a criminal case, it is facts, not witnesses, which must be corroborated.[150] The rule is born of scepticism of witnesses and facts in general, and does not represent an opinion on particular kinds of evidence or witness. Thus even the confession of the defendant should be supported by evidence from another source. Circumstantial evidence appears to be sufficient for the purpose, however, and a previous identification by the same witness can support an identification in court.[151] In England, there are statutory provisions said to require corroboration for particular cases, but these can vary in their effects. There have been statutes, such as the Sexual Offences Act 1956, which insisted on corroboration in terms.[152] Others require the evidence of more than one sworn witness to sustain a conviction.[153] The Road Traffic

[146] A witness had to be treated as telling nothing but the truth, or as having lied throughout.

[147] M. Stone, *Proof of Fact in Criminal Trials* (W. Green and Sons, Edinburgh, 1984), 100.

[148] Wigmore, *Evidence* (3rd edn., Little, Brown & Co., Boston, Mass., 1940), 676.

[149] With the exception, under Law Reform (Miscellaneous Provisions) (Scotland) Act 1960, s.9, regarding personal injury suits.

[150] A.B. Wilkinson, *The Scottish Law of Evidence* (Butterworths, Law Society of Scotland, London, Edinburgh, 1986); the rule does not demand corroboration in the English sense, as long as one source of evidence is supported by other evidence which tends to confirm it.

[151] D. McBarnett, *Conviction* (Macmillan, London, 1983).

[152] S. 2–4, 22, 23 (corroboration requirement abolished, Criminal Justice and Public Order Act 1994); Affiliation Proceedings Act 1957, s.4 (abolished, Family Law Reform Act 1987)).

[153] Such as the Treason Act 1795, s.1; Perjury Act 1911, s.13.

Regulation Act 1984, section 89(2), lays down that in relation to an offence of driving a motor vehicle at a speed greater than the maximum allowed, an accused shall not be liable to be convicted solely on the evidence of one witness to the effect that in the opinion of that witness the vehicle was being driven at a greater speed. That wording permits convictions where there is only evidence which would not be regarded as corroboration in the strict sense; an example is where a police officer's opinion of excessive speed is supported from his reading of the speedometer on his car.[154] There is no need for independence, as is required for corroboration proper—the weakness of the evidence in a speeding case derives not from doubts as to the veracity of the witness, but doubts as to the reliability of a subjective judgement of the speed of a car.

In other instances, a "corroboration warning" had to be given by judges in relation to witnesses presumed by the law to be likely to be untruthful; mothers who claim that a certain man is the father of their child,[155] those who allege that they were victims of a sexual offence, and accomplices of the accused. Other witness used to be singled out by the common law for especial distrust. These were all children[156]; complainants in sexual cases[157]; and former accomplices of the defendant.[158] In the case of especially young children, courts were expected to become particularly suspicious. The Children and Young Persons Act 1933[159] provided that no defendant in a criminal case should be convicted solely on the testimony of an unsworn child.[160] For slightly older children, who did take the oath, judges had to give the jury a corroboration warning. As in the cases of accomplice evidence and that of a complainant in a sexual case, jurors had to be told of the need for caution before relying on this witness's evidence; it had to be explained (giving the reason) that it was regarded as dangerous to convict on it unless there was corroborative evidence. The judge had then to identify for the jury's benefit any items of evidence which could, if accepted by them, serve as corroboration, or, if there was nothing which could be regarded as potentially corroborative from a legal point of view, explain that this was the case. A full corroboration warning was therefore a different matter from a simple reminder, without more, of the possible weaknesses or underlying motives of a particular witness. Also, the definition of corroboration was so narrow that in many cases, without an eye-witness, there was no corroborative evidence available. From *Baskerville*,[161] corroboration meant evidence which was

---

[154] *Nicholas* v. *Penny* [1950] 2 All ER 89.
[155] The affiliation proceedings set up under the Affiliation Proceedings Act 1957 have been replaced, under the Family Law Reform Act 1987.
[156] See Ch. 4.
[157] *Midwinter* (1971) 55 Cr. App. R 523; *Marks* [1963] Crim. LR 370; *Trigg* [1963] 1 WLR 305.
[158] *Davies* v. *DPP* [1954] AC 378.
[159] S.38(1).
[160] These tended to be aged between 8 and 10. See Ch. 4.
[161] [1916] 2 KB 658.

independent of that evidence which required corroboration. It must also implicate the accused in a material particular.

The corroboration rule has been said to have developed at a time when jurors often were uneducated and illiterate, and when the penal laws were of such harsh severity that "men could be hanged for stealing a shilling, and could not be heard in their own defence".[162] The common law rules evolved out of fear of bias, but in the case of complainants of sexual offences became offensive and, as the Law Commission observed, patronising.[163] Yet the assumption that alleged victims of sexual offences are more likely to be untruthful (knowingly or otherwise) than the alleged victims of other kinds of crime has been made by many eminent lawyers. Professor Williams wrote in 1963 that there was a sound reason for the requirement of a corroboration warning.[164] This view is not exclusive to men. The Heilbron Report is the work of a woman judge and is a great deal more recent: "We are not unaware of the fact that from time to time women do make false charges from a variety of motives".[165] But few could put the common law anxiety more colourfully than Lord Hailsham:

> "The evidence of Lady Wishfort complaining of rape may be dangerous because she may be indulging in undiluted sexual fantasy. A Mrs Frail making the same allegation may need corroboration because of the danger that she does not wish to admit the consensual intercourse of which she is ashamed."[166]

Not until 1988 did the Court of Appeal finally recognise that even where that was the case, it does not explain the common law's insistence on corroboration in the strict sense in cases where the fact of rape is actually conceded by the defence, so that the sole issue in the trial is the identity of the culprit.[167] A remaining mystery is why the sexual offences warning had to be given where the complainant was male.[168] Were men thought falsely to cry rape as frequently as women?

There seems to be no clear evidence to support either contention.[169] Although many judges in their warnings to juries stressed how easy it is to

---

[162] *R. v. H*, [1995] 2 All ER 865, *per* Lord Griffiths at 879. Defendants were unable to give evidence at their own criminal trials until 1898: Criminal Evidence Act 1898 s.1. See Ch. 5.

[163] Law Commission, *Corroboration of Evidence in Criminal Trials*. (Law Com. No 202, (HMSO, London, 1991),Cm 1620, at 2.19.

[164] G. Williams, *The Proof of Guilt* (Stevens, London, 1968).

[165] *Report of the Advisory Group on the Law of Rape* (HMSO, London, 1976) Cmnd. 6352.

[166] *DPP v. Kilbourne* [1973] AC 729 at 748.

[167] *Chance* [1988] 3 All ER 225; the correct direction in such cases is an identification evidence warning in accordance with *Turnbull* [1976] 3 All ER 549, discussed in the text to nn. 214–235 below. This is still the case.

[168] *Gammon* (1959) 43 Cr. App. R 155.

[169] J. Temkin, *Rape and the Legal Process* (Sweet & Maxwell, London, 1987); cf. Law Commission Working Paper 115 (HMSO, London, 1990), 4.31.

invent an allegation of rape,[170] the experience awaiting complainants in court[171] gives rise to doubt about the correctness of that assertion.[172] It is also difficult to understand why it is frequently said that the charge is a difficult one to refute; it might be thought that, on the contrary, the burden and standard of proof on the prosecution demand an extraordinarily convincing complainant if there is to be a conviction, since there is often no other evidence. The Home Office view is that it is difficult to know to what extent, if any, false charges are made[173]; a police surgeon who acted for the RUC claimed that of the rape allegations investigated by him 16 out of 18 were inventions.[174] A case study regarded by the Home Office as "more careful"[175] found 29 per cent claims were definitely false, and a further 18 per cent probably were so.[176] The debate tends to provoke strong reactions, but is clouded by the failure to clarify one basic point. Is the argument that women (and men?) in general commonly invent sexual attacks, or is it that women who suffer from mental or emotional illness are particularly prone to do so—in other words, that such fabrications are a symptom of disorder? The latter contention is much easier to believe, and might even be susceptible to verification. As it was, the legal position was absurd, as Cross, using the example of a summary trial involving a sexual assault showed:

"Is it not somewhat odd to require a magistrate to reason as follows on a charge of indecent assault brought by a respectable middle-aged female: 'I believe her evidence, but I must think twice before acting on it because sex is a mysterious thing'; whereas, on a charge of assault brought by a man with numerous convictions for violence, the magistrate can simply say to himself, 'I believe his evidence and I need not think twice before acting on it because there is no danger that charges of violence will be made on account of neurosis, jealousy, fantasy or spite'?"[177]

The Royal Commission[178] agreed with the Law Commission that this rule should be abolished, as should the rule requiring a warning when a prosecu-

---

[170] A contention which can be traced back as far as 1680: "It must be remembered that [the] accusation [is] easily to be made and hard to be proved, and harder to be defended by the party accused, tho never so innocent": E. Hale, *Pleas of the Crown* (ed. E. Sollom, Nott & Gosling, London, 1680), vol. 1, c.58, 635.

[171] See below, Ch. 4.

[172] M. Smith and W. Young, *Rape Study—A Discussion of Law and Practice* (Department of Justice and Institute of Psychology, Wellington, New Zealand, 1983).

[173] Home Office, *Sexual Offences, Consent and Sentencing* (HORS No 54)(HMSO, London, 1979).

[174] L.M. Stewart, "A Retrospective Survey of Alleged Sexual Assault Cases" (1981) 17 *Police Surgeon* 28.

[175] N. 173 above.

[176] N.M. MacLean, "Rape and False Accusations of Rape" (1979) 15 *The Police Surgeon* 56.

[177] Tapper and Cross *Evidence* (6th edn., Butterworths, London, 1985) 237; quoted in Law Commission, *Corroboration in Criminal Trials*. Working Paper 115 (HMSO, London, 1990) 4.22.

[178] *Report of the Royal Commission on Criminal Justice* (chairman Viscount Runciman) (HMSO, London, 1993), Cm 2263, 127–8.

tion witness amounted to an "accomplice", as defined in *Davies* v. *DPP*.[179] In some cases, persons with particular reasons to incriminate the defendant fell outside this definition, and in others very credible witnesses who fell within it were damaged by the mandatory warning in the eyes of the jury. The Law Commission argued that it was inappropriate to give the accomplice warning in some cases, for with a particular witness it might be "obvious that he has no ill-feeling towards the accused and that he is repentant and anxious to tell the truth".[180] There was no requirement to give a corroboration warning where a co-defendant incriminated a defendant, because the *Davies* rule applied only to prosecution, not defence, witnesses. The Law Commission regarded these restrictions on trial judges as obstacles to the performance of their obligation to use their experience to guide juries through the evidence that they have heard. Proper exercise of this function, which must take account of the testimony actually heard in the context of the whole of the case, is not assisted by demanding the recital of rigid catechisms without regard to the particular circumstances.[181] The corroboration rules for sexual complainants and accomplices were abolished by section 32(1) of the Criminal Justice and Public Order Act 1994.

Will the abolition of the common law corroboration rules with no replacement, leaving the judge with unfettered discretion to warn only in respect of witnesses or evidence where he or she perceives a need for caution, give rise to confusion and to endless appeals? Even before abolition, there were decisions stipulating where judges merely alert juries to possible weaknesses or hidden motives in a witness. There they have been allowed to express themselves in the most appropriate way. Such cases include the evidence of psychiatric patients[182]; evidence from persons who are not accomplices in the technical sense but have purposes of their own to serve[183]; and evidence of identification.[184] In *Spencer*,[185] allegations of violence by members of staff were made by patients at Rampton Hospital. Not only were these patients mentally ill, but they had been committed to the hospital by way of sentence for various criminal offences. The House of Lords held that the complainants did not occupy any category of witness then requiring the full common law corroboration warning. Judges ought to point out the need for caution in such cases, but not according to any formula. In relation to children's evidence, Parliament abolished the rules and left the courts to their own devices, without, apparently, generating extensive mystification. But the problems which could arise from an unfettered judicial discretion, once the old corroboration rules disappeared, were noted by the Law Commission:

> "In the absence of legislative rules defendants would have greater scope to argue that the judge had failed to give adequate warning to the jury about suspect

---

[179] [1954] AC 378.   [180] Law Commission, n. 177 above, 4.12.   [181] *Ibid.*, at 2.7.
[182] *Spencer* [1987] AC 128.   [183] *Beck* [1982] 1 All ER 807.
[184] See text to nn. 201–213 below.   [185] [1987] AC 128.

testimony ... appellate courts would then have the burden of deciding whether to formulate new rules in place of the old. ..."[186]

Although after abolition some commentators argued that judges could give a full *Baskerville*—style warning if they chose to, and others insisted that they should,[187] the courts have given effect to the intentions of the Law Commission and, presumably, Parliament by allowing judges to make their own assessments of the needs of individual cases. The Court of Appeal laid down guidance for judges who must direct the jury on the credibility of witnesses. In *Makanjuola and Easton*,[188] two defendants separately convicted of indecent assault appealed against conviction on the basis that the trial judges, albeit in their discretion, should have warned the juries that it is dangerous to convict on the uncorroborated evidence of a complainant in a sexual case. They argued that the rationale of the common law approach could not have disappeared overnight. Rejecting this view, the Court of Appeal favoured as much flexibility as possible: "[w]here a warning is required, it will be for the judge to decide the strength and terms of the warning. It does not have to be invested with the whole florid regime of the old corroboration rules." Rarely would the Court interfere with the trial judge's exercise of his or her discretion:

"In some cases it may be appropriate for the judge to warn the jury to exercise caution before acting on the unsupported evidence of a witness. This will not be so simply because the witness is a complainant of a sexual offence nor will it necessarily be so because the witness is alleged to be an accomplice. There will need to be an evidential basis for suggesting that the evidence of a witness may be unreliable. An evidential basis does not include mere suggestions by cross-examining counsel."[189]

In the two cases being considered by the court, no evidential basis had been laid to suggest that the two complainants should be particularly distrusted; the fact that each made an allegation of a sexual nature did not oblige the judge to deliver a warning to the jury.

Believing Witnesses: Reliability

The Home Office at one stage took seriously the idea of obtaining evidence under hypnosis, but more recently issued a circular to all police forces instructing them to discontinue the practice.[190] This would be disappointing, if it were the case that hypnotism is an aid to memory.[191] It could

---

[186] Law Commission, n. 177 above, 5.7.

[187] For a review of the arguments, see D. Birch, "Corroboration: Goodbye to All That?" [1995] *Crim. LR* 524.

[188] [1995] 3 All ER 730.   [189] *Per* Lord Taylor CJ at 733.   [190] [1988] *NLJ* 528.

[191] M. Reiser "Hypnosis as an Aid in a Homicide Investigation" in L.S. Wrightsman, C.E. Willis and S.M. Kassim (eds.), *On the Witness Stand*, (Sage, Newbury Park, 1987).

be helpful to the police in investigation, even though evidence so obtained would be likely to be inadmissible at trial. However, there is no apparent consensus whether hypnotism does facilitate recall. Wagstall suggests that the effect is not greater than that arising from any other relaxation techniques,[192] and there is research which indicates that people in a hypnotic trance are more than usually vulnerable to suggestion.[193] The courts have so far resolutely refused to address an apparent inconsistency in their treatment of suggestion. For example, cross-examination makes extensive use of the leading question and is regarded as an admirable forensic skill. But the courts refuse to accept evidence in chief so obtained,[194] and there has been considerable discussion of the issue with regard to disclosure interviews with children, designed to elicit an allegation of sexual abuse.[195] The courts take the view that it is one thing to attempt to discredit a witness's evidence by leading him to contradict himself (even if in fact this is not as significant as lawyers think) since the effect of that is to cancel out his testimony. It is altogether different to obtain the allegation on which the court is expected to decide, and possibly take coercive action, by means of suggestion.

There is no doubt that all potential witnesses are highly suggestible. Elizabeth Loftus has led the work in this area, and shown that not only do descriptions of events and participants alter on an alarming scale to reflect facts "planted" by the questioner, but the questioning process can have a permanent effect on memory.[196] The style of questioning used by police officers is highly suggestive, and not without good reason. It is extremely difficult to obtain spontaneous descriptions without leading questions.[197] Memory appears to be divided into available and accessible information; a witness can provide available information without prompting, but to go further will need cues.[198] So suggestive or leading questioning reduces the number of omissions, but increases the overall number of errors.[199] To make

---

[192] G.F. Wagstall, "Hypnotism and the Law: A Critical Review of Some Recent Proposals" [1983] *Crim. LR* 152.

[193] W.H. Putnam, "Hypnosis and Distortion in Eyewitness Memory" in Wrightsman, Willis and Kassim (eds.), n. 191 above.

[194] Although there may have been considerable influence through suggestion at the time the original witness statement was put together: see the text to nn. 103–104 above.

[195] See Ch. 4.

[196] E.F. Loftus, "Reconstruction of Automobile Destruction: An Example of the Interaction between Language and Memory" (1974) 13 *Journal of Verbal Learning and Verbal Behaviour* 585; E.F. Loftus and J.C. Palmer "The Malleability of Eyewitness Accounts" in S. Lloyd-Bostock and B.R. Clifford (eds.), *Evaluating Witness Evidence* (Wiley, Chichester, 1983).

[197] R. Bryden, *Identification Proceedings under Scottish Criminal Law* (HMSO, Edinburgh, 1978), Cmnd. 7096 1.03.

[198] G. Davies "Research on Children's Testimony: Implications for Interviewing Practice" in C. Hollins and K. Howells (eds.), *Clinical Approaches to Sex Offenders and their Victims* (Wiley, Chichester, 1991).

[199] K.H. Marquis and S. Oskamp, "Testimony Validity as a Function of Question Form, Atmosphere and Item Difficulty" (1972) 2 *Journal of Applied Social Psychology* 167.

matters worse, it appears that the more knowledgeable the interrogator appears to be about the matter in hand, the more likely is the witness to adopt any suggestion in the question asked.[200] Thus the capacity of the police, whether inadvertent or not, to influence the testimony given may depend on whether at the time of the interview they seemed to know a great deal about the offence—which may depend on the stage the investigation has reached. It cannot be long before judges will be faced with this issue; it has already been discussed to some extent in Family Division cases which involve disclosure interviews with children. It is a growing concern in relation to confessions obtained from the accused by the police. Once advocates become aware of the effect of suggestion, they may attempt to introduce the issue into trials, with a view to discrediting evidence so obtained. If they do, all the aforementioned anxieties about extrapolating from the experimental to the real situation will surface with a vengeance.

Believing Witnesses: Reliability of Identification

Warning the Jury

The inaccuracy of eyewitness memory became known to most trial lawyers through the influence of the Devlin Report[201] and its effect on appellate decisions.[202] Long before publication of the report there was an increasing body of knowledge obtained by psychologists which substantially undermined faith in identification evidence. It seems that people remember action details better than descriptive details.[203] Even so, they tend to give fragmented and limited accounts of events that they have witnessed. They are also prone to making errors in identifying the actors at subsequent line-ups.[204] It has been found that an error-free report is the exception, rather than the rule, that the more full of detail it is the more errors there will be, that time lapse increases unreliability[205] and that cross-racial identification is even more unreliable than identification within the same racial group.[206]

---

[200] V.L. Smith and P.C. Ellsworth, "The Social Psychology of Eyewitness Evidence Accuracy: Misleading Questions and Communicator Expertise" (1987) 72 *Journal of Applied Psychology* 294.

[201] *Report of the Departmental Committee on Evidence of Identification* (HMSO, London, 1976), Cmnd. 338.

[202] See *Turnbull* [1976] 3 All ER 549.

[203] J. Lipton, "On the Psychology of Eyewitness Testimony" (1977) 2 *Journal of Applied Psychology* 90.

[204] B.R. Clifford and R. Bull, *Psychology of Person Identification* (Routledge and Kegan Paul, London, 1988); J. Shepherd, J. Ellis and G. Davies, *Identification Evidence: A Psychological Evaluation* (Aberdeen University Press, Aberdeen, 1982).

[205] B.R. Clifford, "Eyewitness Testimony; The Bridging of a Credibility Gap" in D.P. Farrington, K. Hawkins and S. Lloyd-Bostock (eds.) *Psychology, Law and Legal Processes* (Macmillan, London, 1979).

[206] J.W. Shepherd, J.B. Deregoswski and H.D. Ellis "A Cross-cultural Study of Recognition Memory for Faces" (1974) 9 *International Journal of Psychology* 205.

Some psychologists have found that even a good view of a person for several minutes does not guarantee the accuracy of identification on a later occasion.[207] Confidence is no indicator of accuracy.[208]

Some of these findings are not unchallenged,[209] but even so, the implications are alarming, for example, the finding that accuracy of description ranges from only 25 per cent to 35 per cent,[210] accuracy of recognition between 40 per cent and 65 per cent, but with variations according to the conditions in which the observation was made.[211] At identification parades at which the real actor is not present, there is a one-third likelihood of a volunteer being selected. Gardner found that estimates of height varied from four feet to six feet six, with 50 per cent of subjects over-estimating height by eight inches.[212] Devlin concluded that although powers of recognition are better than those of description, juries should be warned that it is not safe to convict upon eyewitness evidence unless the circumstances of the identification are exceptional or the eyewitness evidence is supported by substantial evidence of another sort.[213]

The Court of Appeal did not go so far; the guidelines in *Turnbull*[214] apply to cases which depend wholly or substantially on the correctness of one or more identifications of the accused which the defence alleges are mistaken. The judge should withdraw the case from the jury if the prosecution consists of nothing more than poor quality identification evidence, such as a "fleeting glimpse", unless there is evidence which goes to support the correctness of the identification, insofar as it reassures the jury that there has been no mistake. This other evidence may consist of another disputed identification; the two identifications may support each other, but only if they are of sufficient quality that a jury may be safely left to assess them.[215] A confession, the defendant's lies,[216] or forensic evidence, might also support a poor quality identification. It seems that some "fleeting glimpses" may amount to higher quality identification evidence, according to the identity of the witness. The Court of Appeal has taken the view that the police are better at identifying and recognising individuals than members of the public. In *Ramsden*,[217] a police officer

---

[207] Shepherd, Ellis and Davies, n. 204 above.

[208] G.L. Wells and J. Murray "Eyewitness Confidence" in G. Wells and E. Loftus (eds.) *Eyewitness Testimony: Psychological Perspectives* (Cambridge University Press, Cambridge, 1984); Daffenbacher and Loftus, n. 137 above.

[209] E.g., R.C.L. Lindsay and G.L. Wells, "What Do We Really Know about Cross-race Identification Evidence?" S. Lloyd-Bostock and B.R. Clifford (eds.), in *Evaluating Witness Evidence* (Wiley, Chichester, 1983).

[210] B.R. Clifford, "Police as Eyewitnesses", (1972) 22 *New Society* 176.

[211] Shepherd, Ellis and Davies, n. 204 above.

[212] G.D. Gardner, "The Perception and Memory of Witnesses" (1933) 18 *Cornell LQR* 391.

[213] *Report on Evidence of Identification*, n. 201 above, para. 8.4.

[214] [1976] 3 All ER 549.

[215] *Weeder* [1980] CLR 645; two independent witnesses identified D. The judge must warn the jury that even a number of honest witnesses may be mistaken.

[216] *Goodway* [1993] 4 All ER 89.   [217] [1991] Crim. LR 295.

saw the suspect for about three seconds over a distance of about ten yards, but the trial judge suggested that a police officer's identifying evidence might be more impressive than an ordinary witness's. The Court of Appeal agreed, and even went so far as to approve a passage in *Archbold* which argued that anyone who has been involved in the criminal justice system, whether police officer, advocate or judge, is likely to have a greater appreciation of the importance of identification and, accordingly, to look for some particular identifying feature. The police, in particular, may be regarded as reliable because they are trained on the importance of these matters and are less likely to be misled by the excitement of the situation. In *Williams (John)*,[218] a police constable saw two men walking to a car. He saw them from a moving vehicle for a couple of seconds. The recorder, at Williams' trial for burglary, refused to stop the case although there was no other evidential support for the identification of the defendant. The Court of Appeal agreed with him that this police witness could be regarded as more reliable than an ordinary member of the public, given that his suspicions had been aroused, and that he made a particular effort to memorise the suspect's appearance. The empirical evidence, however, is against the judicial opinion. It appears that a police officer's powers of recognition are no greater than average.[219]

In cases where the identification evidence is more solid, the judge should nevertheless warn the jury of the need for caution and explain the reasons for it. The judge must warn the jury of the particular dangers attached to the evidence by drawing their attention to two things which they are unlikely to know; first, that in a number of cases over the years erroneous identifications by apparently honest witnesses have led to wrong convictions. Secondly, the substantial degree of risk that honest witnesses may be wrong in their evidence of identification .[220] No particular form of words is needed, but the "full force of the *Turnbull* direction" must not be blunted.[221] The direction should be given even where the witness knows the suspect; there is a tendency in witnesses to assume recognition where the offender resembles someone they know. In *Beckford*[222] a warning was necessary even though the witness knew the defendants and the main issue was his veracity rather than his accuracy. To avoid a successful submission of no case, the prosecution must lead evidence of the circumstances of the identification to show that it is not of poor quality.[223]

The *Turnbull* direction, in no particular form of words, asks the jury to consider carefully the circumstances in which the witness saw the offender, and reminds them that even a confident witness can be mistaken. This is seen by some as a half-hearted acknowledgement of the weaknesses of identification evidence, for researchers have found that even when warned of

---

[218] *The Times*, 7 Oct. 1994.   [219] Clifford, n. 210 above.
[220] *Reid* v. *R.* (1990) 90 Cr. App. R 121.   [221] *Pattinson and Exley* [1996] 1 Cr. App. R 51.
[222] [1993] *Crim. LR* 944.   [223] *Daley* v. *R.* [1993] 4 All ER 86.

adverse conditions, mock jurors do not make sufficient adjustment.[224] Loftus found that they were more impressed by eyewitness testimony than by any other forensic evidence.[225] But criminal courts are hardly in a position to dispense with it altogether:

> "There is a tension in the law in relation to identification evidence. It is universally recognised that mistaken identifications have in the past led to wrongful convictions. But any law that said no person could be convicted on visual identification evidence alone would lead to what the full court in the case of *Turnbull* referred to as 'affronts to justice', and to serious consequences to law and order."[226]

Defendants have themselves been known to offer identification evidence to establish an alibi.

The Devlin Committee were criticised for rejecting procedural change to reflect psychological findings,[227] but there are, and should be, doubts about the extent to which the results of simulations for experimental purposes can be applied to concrete situations involving real crimes. Yuille and Cutshall[228] interviewed 13 eye-witnesses to a real-life shooting, and found a very high level of accuracy which did not diminish over time and was not affected by the nature of the questioning or by the amount of stress affecting the individual witness. Those who reported having nightmares were the most accurate. Wells argues[229] that the police, unlike psychologists using human guinea pigs, rely solely on those witnesses who claim that they can make an identification. The subjects who take part in experiments (often students) are selected before the event rather than after it and are not especially likely to express great confidence. Even if they did, they would do so in very different circumstances in which nothing hangs on any error they might make. A major contributor to the apparent *impasse* between lawyers and those psychologists who feel that the courts could take more account of current knowledge of the reliability of evidence is the conflict between the two systems of reasoning which trials attempt to utilise jointly in uneasy harness. From an empirical point of view identification evidence is extremely suspect. But deductive logic would suggest that the testimony of a witness to a crime has very high probative value—if it is not mistaken, there is none better.

---

[224] R.C.L. Lindsay, G.L. Wells and C.M. Rumpel, "Can People Detect Eyewitness and Identification Accuracy Within and Across Situations?" (1981) 66 *Journal of Applied Psychology* 78.

[225] "Reconstructive Memory. The Incredible Eyewitness" (1974) 8 *Psychology Today* 116.

[226] *Pattinson and Exley* [1996] 1 Cr. App. R 51, 53, *per* Henry J.

[227] R. Bull and B.R. Clifford, "Identification Evidence: The Devlin Report" (1976) 70 *New Scientist* 307.

[228] J.C. Yuille and J.L. Cutshall, "A Case Study of Eyewitness Memory of a Crime" (1986) 71 *Journal of Applied Psychology* 291.

[229] "Applied Eyewitness Testimony Research" in Wrightsman, Willis and Kassim (eds.), n. 191 above.

A further problem which is not faced by psychologists, who stage their own experiments in the best way to achieve scientifically acceptable results, is that trials involve more than one issue. *Turnbull* is an attempt by the judges to devise guidelines which bring scientific knowledge to bear on proceedings; but the note of caution to be introduced relates to identification evidence, and it is not always obvious whether a case is an identification case or not. If the judge gets it wrong, and fails to warn the jury of the dangers when the case does involve primarily identification evidence, then the conviction is likely to be quashed on appeal. It has been said that *Turnbull* does not apply to cases where the defendant admits presence at the scene, but denies participation in the offence, despite having been selected by the eye-witness from a group of people as being the culprit.[230] This statement, however, has proved a misleading over-simplification. Clearly, even in cases where presence is conceded, an identification may have crucial importance. In *Thornton*,[231] the host of a wedding reception was punched and kicked by several persons he did not see. D agreed that he had been a guest, but denied taking part in the attack. He was identified as a participant by the next-door neighbour, and by the victim's 12-year-old son. It was held in the Court of Appeal that there should have been a *Turnbull* direction, because a disputed identification did arise. The Court agreed with Birch's view[232] that persons who admit their presence at a scene should not be in a worse position in evidential terms than someone who claims not to have been there at all. Yet, in *Slater*,[233] it was held that there is no need for a *Turnbull* direction if the defendant admits his presence on the scene, where the issue at trial is what he was doing. The facts do not appear to be materially different from those in *Thornton*. A fight broke out in a club at which the defendant admitted being present. He denied being involved in the incident, but was identified by several witnesses. The Court of Appeal did not regard the case as one of disputed identification; it concerned disputed conduct. Rose LJ explained:

> "For example, such a direction would not, in our view, generally be necessary if the defendant admitted he was the only person present when the complainant received his injuries, or if a black man and a white man were present and the complainant said the white man caused the injuries, or if four men were present, three dressed in black and one in white, and the complainant said the man in white caused his injuries."[234]

Slater was said to fall within this category, apparently because the defendant was of unusual size—"six feet tall and very broad". The witnesses had all described the attacker as very large. In cases such as this, the court concluded, warning should be given to the jury of any problems adversely

---

[230] *Bowden* [1993] Crim LR 379.   [231] [1995] 1 Cr. App. R 578.
[232] Note to *Hope et al.* [1994] *Crim. LR* 118.
[233] [1995] 1 Cr. App. R 584.   [234] At 590, *per* Rose LJ.

affecting the opportunity of a witness to observe, but such cases did not demand the rigour of the full-scale *Turnbull* warning. It might be thought that the fact that Slater was large enough to meet the description of the attacker was simply a matter for the jury to consider in relation to the accuracy of the identification, rather than one which changed the case from an identification case into a disputed conduct case.

Opinions tend to be divided about *Hewett* [235]; the defendant was charged with driving with blood-alcohol concentration above the prescribed limit. He had been drinking with Mrs G and had got into a BMW with her. Police officers, following in their van, said the car did a violent U-turn. They followed the car until it halted (at a spot in Chelsea, dimly lit) and asked for a sample of breath from Hewett who was sitting in the driver's seat, but insisted that he had not been driving. Mrs G said that she had been the driver and asked to be breathalysed. The two police officers had been sitting in the front of their van; both gave evidence that a man and a woman were in the car, and that the man was driving. They described the driver as having a leather jacket and a beard, and the woman, alleged to have been sitting in the passenger seat, as having long fair hair. Mrs G maintained that a scarf hid her hair, and that she got out of the passenger seat because she had left her shoes that side, and needed to put them on. She claimed that Hewett swapped seats with her in order to help her find her shoes, and that was why he got out of the driver's side when the car stopped. The defence appealed against his conviction on the ground that the jury should have had a *Turnbull* warning. The argument was dismissed by the Court of Appeal on the ground that this was not an identification case, even though the dispute concerned the identity of the driver of the car. The police had been observing the BMW in the dark and through two sets of glass. Although the restricted visibility of the circumstances has overtones of the *Turnbull* paradigm, which prompted the defence to argue that *Hewitt* was an identification case, the Court of Appeal was right. For the police and the court were entitled to infer that the man who was found in the driving seat immediately after being ordered to stop was responsible for the vehicle; the only reason to doubt that he was the driver came from the defence evidence; the prosecution evidence did not turn on eyewitness identification of Hewett. The police officers' descriptions were relevant only because the defence tried to rebut the common sense inference by arguing that Mrs G had been driving all the time.

Identification Parades

The law further acknowledges the difficulty of identification by holding that, in general, in-court identifications are not a substitute for identification parades. They are not generally allowed if the witness has not previously identified the defendant at a parade or in other controlled

---

[235] [1978] RTR 174.

circumstances.[236] The expression "dock identification" usually describes a situation where there has been no such prior identification. There is little probative value in a witness pointing to the person in the dock and claiming that he or she is sure that this was the culprit; the defendant's very presence there is suggestive of guilt.[237] Nevertheless, a dock identification is not actually inadmissible, but is likely to be excluded by the court in its discretion to reject evidence more prejudicial than probative.[238] Breach of Code D issued under the Police and Criminal Evidence Act 1984 may lead to exclusion of the identification evidence.[239] It has been held that a parade is unnecessary where the witness already knows the defendant.[240] However, a redrafted Code stipulates that a parade must be held "whenever a suspect disputes an identification".[241] A literal reading of this provision in a recognition case would produce absurd results. It cannot be the case that the police are required to hold a parade so that an eyewitness, who named his own grandmother as the perpetrator of an offence, can select her from the line-up if she denies that it was she he saw.

Nor is necessary to hold a parade in the event of a street identification which is regarded as legitimate. In *Oscar*,[242] it was held that a person identified near the scene was not yet a suspect and therefore Code D did not apply. The latest version of the Code specifically provides that where the identity of a suspect is not known, a police officer may take a witness to a particular neighbourhood or place to see whether he or she can identify the person allegedly seen on the relevant occasion. Before doing so, where practical, a record shall be made of any description given by the witness of the suspect.[243] In *Hickin*,[244] about seven West Yorkshire men stamped on and kicked two men in Blackpool. Two bystanders offered to assist, and the police took them round in a car to look at a large group of men which had been detained, to see if they could identify the attackers. Some of the men fitted general descriptions of the attackers, but these were vague. The defence objected to the identifications, arguing that, since at the time the appellants were under arrest, they were therefore suspects "known to the police", and so a parade should have been held. In the Court of Appeal it was held that cases such as *Oscar* showed that Code D was not to be interpreted to require the police to act in such a way as to affront common sense. On the defence

---

[236] Police and Criminal Evidence Act 1984, Codes of Practice, Code D2.3–2.6, provides for the case where it was not possible to hold an identification parade (impractical to hold one, D would not co-operate, or impossible to find others who resemble D). In such cases, the witness should have the opportunity to see the defendant in a group identification, or there should be a video identification, or a confrontation if practical.

[237] *Hunter* [1969] Crim. LR 262.   [238] *Fergus* (1993) 98 Cr. App. R 313.

[239] *Gaynor* [1988] CLR 242.

[240] *Reid* [1994] Crim. LR 442. A dock identification, admitted by the judge because the case involved recognition, was upheld in the Court of Appeal, but a *Turnbull* warning is still required.

[241] Code D2.3.   [242] [1991] Crim. LR 778.   [243] D2.17.

[244] [1996] Crim. LR 584. See also *Macmath* [1997] Crim. LR 586; *Malashev* [1997] Crim. LR 586.

argument, there would have had to be 14 parades that night, which was highly impractical. And even if the Code had been breached, the identifications would not automatically be excluded. Apart from possible breaches of the Code, the test was that of fairness under section 78 of the Police and Criminal Evidence Act 1984.[245] The trial judge had given that issue insufficient consideration. The witnesses had travelled together; no detailed descriptions had been taken until they has seen the group of suspects,[246] and no detailed record was kept of what the witnesses had said when viewing the group of men. Convictions affected by those police failures were quashed.

Identifications are undermined by previous exposure to photographs of the defendant from police books of photographs of known offenders. There is a danger that the witness, when selecting the defendant at an identification parade, and, subsequently, in court, in fact is recalling that photographic image rather than the person who committed the offence. In *Wainwright*,[247] it was held that such an identification had little probative value, and ran the danger of informing jury of the defendant's criminal record. In *Haslam*,[248] three witnesses were shown photographs of the defendant after his arrest and before a parade, conduct described as "indefensible" on appeal. The Code,[249] providing more recent guidance on the matter, clearly states that witnesses must not be shown photographs or other images of the suspect if he is known to the police and available to stand on an identification parade.

Although in theory it is a witness's in-court sworn testimony which is crucial, the reality in identification cases is that the earlier out-of-court identification has far more probative value. Technically, the prior identification is admitted as an exception to the prohibition on previous consistent statements, and so in theory should go only to the *consistency* of the witness in identifying the defendant in court. But, in making a selection from a parade, a witness has to choose from a number of superficially similar-looking individuals. This makes the exercise reasonably scientific, providing substantial support to the sworn testimony That it is the earlier identification, out of court, which is the crucial one, is borne out by a Court of Appeal decision relating to those witnesses who by time of trial are unable to remember who it was they identified at the parade. Such a witness may nevertheless prove to be of value. The prosecutor may call the police officer who observed the identification at the parade being made to describe the event, and name the person indicated. The witness should, however, be able to say in court words to the effect "I did select someone at the parade but cannot remember who it was".[250] This is a significant departure from the orality principle, creating in effect a new exception to the rule against

---

[245] See Ch. 6.

[246] Making it unsatisfactory even to let them describe the men to the court if the identification evidence were excluded.

[247] (1927) 27 CAR 52.   [248] (1925) 19 CAR 59.   [249] D 2.18.

[250] *McCay* [1990] 1 WLR 645.

hearsay. As with all exceptions to the hearsay rule, it is an acknowledgement that in some instances the sworn oral testimony of a witness is far less reliable than what he or she has said on other occasions.

4

Witnesses With A Legitimate Grievance; Victims Of The Adversarial Trial

> "I was terrified up there. My legs were quaking."
> D. McBarnett, *Conviction*, 90

Giving evidence in English courts is a largely unrewarding task. Expert witnesses are paid for their services, but for others, time at work is lost and expenses are meagre.[1] Most courts do not have separate car parking space for witnesses[2]. Although it is generally accepted that giving evidence is an intimidating experience, there is little done to reassure the witnesses, who may find that there is no microphone to amplify their answers, in which case they are obliged to project their evidence, no matter how sensitive, into a court-room which may be large and crowded. These problems are worst in criminal cases tried by jury, but lawyers report severe attacks of "stage-fright" in witnesses of all kinds, even those asked to give evidence in civil cases in which they have no direct interest. Involvement in criminal trials, however, is much more traumatic. If the witness is afraid of retaliation, the criminal justice system is able to provide little in the way of reassurance, such dramatic measures as a change of identity and/or police protection being reserved for major matters such as the "Supergrass" informer cases in Northern Ireland. In Denmark, witnesses are allowed to give evidence anonymously if it appears that they will be otherwise exposed to danger, but this operates to the disadvantage of the defence.[3] In many cases where genuine fears exist, such as domestic violence, anonymity could not be achieved. Meanwhile,

> "[i]nvolvement in the operation of the criminal justice system often presents witnesses with so many major inconveniences and problems such as wasted time

[1] D. McBarnett, *Conviction* (Macmillan, London, 1983).
[2] N.A. McKittrick, "Witnesses: The Most Precious Resource" (1987) 51 *Journal of Criminal Law* 192.
[3] J.P. Anderson, "The Anonymity of Witnesses: A Danish Development" [1985] *Crim. LR* 363.

caused by trial delays, loss of income and inappropriate physical accommodation at court that, all too frequently, even civic minded, initially co-operative witnesses wish they had never stepped forward and vow never to do so again."[4]

Witnesses of all kinds should be treated better than they are at present, but this would involve the administrators of justice in some forethought and expense. This chapter looks at those witnesses who are particularly ill-served by our adversarial system of trial.

Rape Complainants

". . . Once a woman sets in train a complaint that she has been raped, she has to undergo a prolonged ordeal. In the first place there will be a police interrogation, one of the purposes of which is to ensure, as far as possible, that she is not making a false charge . . .Next she has to answer further questioning by the police surgeon . . .and to undergo a thorough as well as an intimate and inevitably distasteful gynaecological examination. Furthermore, if her story of the rape is true she will, at this stage, probably be in a state of shock and possibly also have suffered painful injuries; yet she may have to spend many hours at the police station before she is able to return home . . .At the trial, which will take place some considerable time later, she has to relive the whole unpleasant and traumatic experience. In many cases, she will be cross-examined at length. . ."[5]

Some small steps have been taken to reduce the severity of the ordeal for the complainant in a rape case. Some trial judges have permitted the use of a screen in the manner employed in child witness cases, to shield her from the defendant. However, the Court of Appeal expressed reservations about the practice, apparently based on the risk of prejudicing the jury against the defendant,[6] and the number of cases where this has occurred is tiny.[7] It is to be hoped that note will be taken of the more robust attitude expressed by the court more recently in *Foster*,[8] in which it was held that the danger of prejudice could be avoided by an explanation to the jury of the potential embarrassment of the complainant because of the nature of the evidence. A combination of common humanity and the fear that a large number of rapes go unreported and therefore unpunished because of the brutal treatment of victims of which the legal system was suspected influenced the Heilbron Committee,[9] whose proposals were the spur to the introduction of the Sexual

---

[4] M.H. Graham, *Witness Intimidation* (Quest Books, Westport, Conn., 1985).

[5] *Report of the Advisory Group on the Law of Rape* (Heilbron Report) (HMSO, London, 1975), Cmnd. 6352.

[6] *Cooper and Schaub* [1994] Crim. LR 531.

[7] Victim Support, *Women, Rape and the Criminal Justice System* (Victim Support, London, 1996), It was denied to Sinitra Vij because she knew the defendant well and so apparently could not be intimidated: *The Times*, 19 Sept. 1997.

[8] [1995] Crim. LR 333.   [9] *Ibid.*

Offences Amendment Act 1976. Unfortunately, section 2, designed to protect complainants from degrading and irrelevant cross-examination, appears to have had astonishingly little effect. Not only is the predicament of these vulnerable witnesses largely an incident of the adversarial nature of the criminal trial, but it appears that evidential reform is ineffectual because related matters such as relevance, particularly the difference between credibility and the issue, are too complicated for many lawyers to understand them—and if the reform is not understood, it does not achieve anything.

In a rape trial, the prosecution must show that intercourse took place, that it took place without the consent of the complainant and that the accused was the person responsible. Unfortunately, in some cases there is no evidence apart from that of the complainant herself.[10] Medical evidence provides support if there was violence of a kind to cause discernible injury, but will only identify the rapist if there is material available which would enable a DNA fingerprint to be taken. Thus it is virtually inevitable that the complainant will give evidence. Her evidence has traditionally been regarded as highly suspect. Glanville Williams has written in support of Wigmore's view that women who make allegations of sexual assault should be subject to scientific evaluation, the results of which would be revealed to the court. Rather than warn the jury of the dangers of uncorroborated evidence, it would be better, thought Wigmore, to employ:

"expert scientific analysis of the particular witness's mentality as the true measure of enlightenment . . .No judge should ever let a sex offence charge go to the jury unless the female complainant's social history and mental make-up have been examined and testified to by a qualified physician."[11]

Such statements suggest that these gentlemen regard a complaint by a woman that she has been raped as an inconvenient and unseemly slur, and that she must anticipate a cautious and sceptical reaction from the criminal justice system before it assists her. Although the requirement for a corroboration warning in sexual cases has been abolished,[12] prosecutors may nevertheless feel that a case which depends entirely on the complainant's word is not a realistic prospect for a conviction.

The nature of cross-examination of rape complainants is known to be a major source of distress. It appears to be thought legitimate to quiz them upon the way they care for their children, what underwear they were wearing at the time of the alleged rape, whether they use make-up and take trouble with their hair, and upon the details of their menstrual cycles, for no

[10] Although a man may be a victim of rape, following the amendment of the Sexual Offences Act 1956, s.1, by s.142 of the Criminal Justice and Public Order Act 1994, most reported rapes are of women.

[11] J.H. Wigmore, *Evidence* (3rd edn., Little, Brown & Co., Boston, Mass., 1978), 924.

[12] See Ch. 3.

apparent reason other than to humiliate and embarrass them.[13] In addition, there have been notable examples of cross-examination by the defendant in person being used to enable him to play power games with the complainant in the courtroom itself. In particular, in 1996, Ralston Edwards cross-examined Julia Mason for six days, and was at the time wearing the clothes he wore at the time of the rape. In 1997, Floyd Bailey made his victim describe his genitals in graphic detail. The right of defendants in rape cases to cross-examine in person may soon be abolished in the way it has been for defendants in child abuse cases.[14]

One of the most vexed questions in this context still is the extent to which a rape complainant may be questioned on previous sexual relationships. In a case where the issue is consent, this might be done simply to discredit the complainant, on the footing that because of her sexual habits she is not a person to be believed when she claims that she did not consent. On the other hand, the object may be to show that, given the circumstances, there was in fact consent on this occasion. The logic of a cross-examination on sexual history designed to discredit the prosecutrix is not obvious; the most extensive promiscuity does not suggest that a woman is not honest. Some lawyers argue that such reasoning has not been employed for many years, and that anyone who attempted to use it would only alienate the jury from his client's cause. Unfortunately, this view appears to be over-optimistic. The Heilbron Committee found that such cross-examinations were established practice, despite being degrading and irrelevant. In Scotland the same was more recently found to be the case, prior to the introduction of the Law Reform (Miscellaneous Provisions) (Scotland) Act 1985.[15] Most of the women interviewed by Chambers and Millar[16] found the experience of testifying confirmed their worst fears. It is not clear whether advocates employing such tactics genuinely thought that these questions were relevant to the woman's credibility; the suspicion remains that some of the motive was to cause as much distress as possible, thereby undermining her performance in the witness-box.

The solution arrived at in the Heilbron Report was to introduce a general prohibition with an inclusionary discretion. The result was section 2 of the Sexual Offences (Amendment) Act 1976:

"(1) If at any trial any person is charged with a rape offence to which he pleads not guilty, then, except with the leave of the judge, no evidence and no question in

---

[13] S. Lees, *Carnal Knowledge: Rape on Trial* (Hamish Hamilton, London, 1996), 146; Cf. Newby's research in Western Australia, identifying tactics designed to demoralise rather than clarify: "Rape Victims in Court: The Western Australian Example" in J.A. Scutt (ed.), *Rape Law Reform* (Australian Institute of Criminology, Canberra, 1980).

[14] *The Times*, 17 Jan. 1998.

[15] S.36 introduced a general prohibition on questions about sexual behaviour, including evidence of prostitution, but there is an inclusionary discretion where to deny the defence would be "contrary to the interests of justice".

cross-examination shall be adduced or asked at the trial, by or on behalf of any defendant at the trial, about any sexual experience of a complainant with a person other than that defendant.

(2) The judge shall not give leave in pursuance of the preceding subsection for any evidence or question except on an application made to him in the absence of the jury by or on behalf of a defendant; and on such an application the judge shall give leave if and only if he is satisfied that it would be unfair to that defendant to refuse to allow the evidence to be adduced or the question to be asked . . . ."

The offences to which the section applies include attempted rape and being an accessory to it, but not indecent assault.[17]

The Court of Appeal has said that leave should be refused if the object of the cross-examination is merely to say to the jury "that's the kind of girl she is",[18] but has not ruled out all questioning which goes to credibility, although it is not at all clear when questions going simply to credit are permissible.

> "If the proposed questions merely seek to establish that the complainant has had sexual intercourse with other men to whom she was not married, so as to suggest that for that reason she ought not to be believed on oath, the judge will exclude the evidence . . . In other words, questions of this sort going simply to credit will seldom be allowed . . . On the other hand, if the questions are relevant to an issue in the trial in the light of the way the trial is being run, for instance relevant to the issue of consent, they are likely to be admitted, because to exclude a relevant question on an issue in the trial as the trial is being run will usually mean that the jury are being prevented from hearing something which, if they did hear it, might cause them to change their minds about the evidence being given by the complainant."[19]

The impossibility of establishing a clear dividing line between matters of credit and the issue in the trial was recognized by the Court of Appeal and is manifest in this passage. The concluding words appear to bring the whole argument full circle by referring again to what the jury might think of the complainant herself, rather than the fact of consent.

An example of how utterly confused a court can get over the distinction between credibility and the issue in the case is the recent case of *Funderburk*.[20] The charge was of unlawful sexual intercourse with a girl under the age of consent.[21] The defendant alleged that the 13-year-old complainant's allegations that he engaged in a number of acts of unlawful sexual intercourse with her were false. She described the alleged offences in detail, including a graphic account of how she lost her virginity on the first

---

[16] G. Chambers and A. Millar, "Proving Sexual Assault: Prosecuting the Offender and Persecuting the Victim", in P. Carlen and A. Worrall (eds.), *Gender, Crime and Justice* (Open University Press, Milton Keynes, Philadelphia, 1987).

[17] S. 7(2).   [18] *Viola* [1982] 3 All ER 73.   [19] *Ibid.*, 77.   [20] [1990] 2 All ER 482.

[21] Since the offence here was not a rape offence, the complainant did not have such protection as is afforded by s.2; the court seemed to think that nevertheless the spirit of the section should apply.

occasion. The defendant wished to testify to conversations with himself and with others in which, he said, she had claimed to be sexually experienced, so that she could not have been a virgin as described. Whether such further evidence could be adduced depended on whether the matter of her virginity was relevant solely to her credibility as a witness or whether it was relevant to the issue. The Court of Appeal quoted with approval the description on the former kind of evidence by Lawton LJ in *Sweet-Escott*[22]: "[s]ince the purpose of cross-examination as to credit is to show that the witness ought not to be believed on oath, the matters about which he is questioned must be related to his likely standing after the cross-examination". Applying this test, there was no doubt that the opinion of the jury of her credibility might have altered if they had heard that she had spoken of experiences which, if true, would mean that she could not have been a virgin at the material time. Her standing as a witness would have been much reduced,[23] but the court failed to recognise that this was because her alleged remarks amounted to previous inconsistent statements which happened, in this case, to concern previous sexual relationships. The defence questions, therefore, would not have been designed to suggest that a girl with such a past ought not to be believed, but would have been directed to her consistency as a witness—a different kind of credibility issue. The Court of Appeal's confusion on this point led Henry J to conclude that the conversations in fact went to the issue in the case, and that therefore if she had denied making the statement, she could have been contradicted by other evidence. Being previous inconsistent statements, such contradictory evidence indeed could have been adduced, but not because her status as a virgin was an issue in the trial; it is not an element of the offence with which Funderburke was charged. Henry J stressed the degree of emotion shown by the complainant during her description, and seemed to think that this made whether or not she lost her virginity at that time an issue in the case:

> "This particular detailed account of that first incident would be the most vivid picture which the jury took back with them into their retiring room. Even disregarding the tears and the pathos it was an account of something which only happens once in a lifetime . . . If a detail of such significance is successfully challenged it can destroy both the account and the credit of the witness who gave it. Therefore . . . this is not a challenge which goes merely to credit but . . . to the issue."[24]

The passage demonstrates the impossibility of establishing a clear dividing line between matters of credit and the issue in the trial. Henry J here acknowledges by implication that in some trials the credibility of the witness *is* the issue.

---

[22] (1971) 55 Cr. App. R 316, 320.   [23] [1990] 2 All ER 482, 488, *per* Henry J.   [24] At 491.

From the *Viola* judgment it appears that there are circumstances in which questions going to credit may properly be put.[25] The Court of Appeal does not trouble us with examples of these in that decision, but *Funderburke* may be an example. Nevertheless, there appears to be an alarming void confronting the courts which have to identify appropriate cases. Adler's research at the Old Bailey in fact found judges permitting questions solidly in the There you are, members of the jury; that is the sort of girl she is category.[26] But, in addition, a more sophisticated manipulation of the statute was observed. There the justification for the questions is said to be the need to establish that the woman has no aversion to intercourse, or to intercourse with an older man (such as the defendant) or to intercourse with black men (such as the defendant). It is difficult to believe that such an argument is seriously entertained, but if it is, of course, counsel could even argue that such questions go beyond the matter of credit to the issue of consent itself.

A further problem arises in relation to cross-examination which seeks to establish that the complainant is a prostitute. Given the authority of *Krausz*,[27] a case decided before the 1976 Act, it is not clear whether such questions are still permissible.[28] If the assumption is that such questions go to credit, it is not at all clear why this should be. Is it to be supposed that it is known that prostitutes are more prone to telling lies than most people? Or is it that prostitutes are particularly prone to making up allegations of rape? It is difficult to see why an admitted prostitute should deny consent after the event—presumably not being as subject to sexual fantasy as Lady Wishfort, nor as prone to embarrassment as Mrs Frail.[29] It might equally be supposed that a prostitute would be reluctant to make an accusation of this sort in public, since it could be damaging from a professional point of view. However, in *Bashir*[30] it was held that the matter was relevant to the issue, rather than to credibility, and so not only are the questions permissible, but the complainant's denials can be contradicted by other evidence. This kind of reasoning has so little merit that it looks positively antediluvian. However since section 2 does not expressly forbid it, cross-examination of this kind is allowed as a matter of course. Adler has found that some defence lawyers put it to the complainant that she is a prostitute, knowing that they will be answered (honestly) "No".[31] The motive is to raise a doubt in the jurors' minds.

[25] The words "will seldom be allowed" in the passage from the *Viola* judgment quoted above leaves an unquantifiable loophole.

[26] Adler, "Rape: The Intention of Parliament and the Practice of the Courts" (1982) 45 *MLR* 664; cf., for Scotland, B. Brown, M. Burman and L. Jamieson, *Sexual History and Sexual Character in Scottish Sexual Offence Trials* Scottish Office, Central Research Unit Papers, (Edinburgh, 1992).

[27] (1973) 57 Cr. App. R 466.

[28] The editors of *Archbold*, while suggesting that the law may be unchanged, argue that "the attitude which it exemplifies is exactly the attitude which the 1976 Act sought to outlaw": *Archbold on Criminal Pleading, Evidence and Practice* (Sweet and Maxwell, London, 1997), 20–48.

[29] See above, n. 166.   [30] [1969] 1 WLR 1303.

[31] Z. Adler, "The Relevance of Sexual History Evidence in Rape: Problems of Subjective Interpretation" [1985] *Crim. LR* 769.

The Heilbron Report made it an overriding principle that "in general, the previous sexual history of the complainant with other men . . .ought not to be introduced".[32] Despite this and the introduction of section 2, Adler reports that questions on the subject are allowed in a great many cases. In 40 per cent of the cases she observed[33] the defence made applications for leave, and 75 per cent of the applications were wholly or partly successful. Most of the applications submitted that the previous sexual relationships were relevant to an issue in the trial; in 80 per cent of these cases that was said to be consent. It must be the case that if the questions *are* relevant to an issue, to disallow them would inevitably be unfair to the accused, and therefore the judge ought to permit them, under the terms of section 2(2). What neither Parliament nor the Court of Appeal appears to have noticed is that it is significantly within the control of the defence what the issues in the trial actually are. In an adversarial trial, the parties decide which battlefield they wish to fight in.

The leading case of *Viola*[34] attempts to provide guidance to judges dealing with applications under section 2, but raises as many questions as it answers. In that case, there were three alleged incidents on which the defence wished to cross-examine the complainant, and the trial judge refused to give leave in relation to all of them. The accused claimed that he happened to call at her flat and she made advances to him which led to consensual intercourse. His counsel wished to question her about an alleged visit by two other men who claimed that she made advances to them when they chanced to visit her flat earlier that day. The Court of Appeal held that the incident (which appears to suffice as "sexual experience" within the language of section 2[35]) was sufficiently similar to the circumstances of the alleged rape to merit inclusion. The reasoning there presumably was that if she made overtures to these visitors, she must have made them to Viola as well (resembling the "not averse to sexual intercourse" argument). The other incident, also held by the court to have been relevant to the issue of consent and which therefore should have been allowed, was that a naked man was seen in the complainant's flat about nine hours after the alleged rape. The court considered that the fact that intercourse with her own boyfriend took place a day after the alleged rape was not relevant. It appears, then, that incidents of a sexual nature in the life of the complainant might be relevant to the issue on the "similar facts" principle, that, if they are close in nature to the circumstances of the alleged rape, this suggests that there is such a pattern in her sexuality as to suggest that she consented on this occasion also. "Evidence of sexual promiscuity may be so strong or so closely contemporaneous in time to the event in issue as to come near to, or indeed reach the border between mere credit and an issue in the case."[36]

---

[32] Heilbron Report, n. 5 above, para 134.
[33] Adler, n. 26 above.   [34] [1982] 3 All ER 73.
[35] In *Hinds and Butler* [1979] Crim. LR, evidence of conversations about previous sexual relationships were treated as falling within the terms of s. 2.
[36] [1982] 3 All ER 73, 77, *per* Lord Lane CJ.

Also, incidents may be of more direct significance, as in the *Viola* case, where it was presumed that victims of rape do not generally choose to indulge in consensual intercourse soon after the event. Other examples of direct relevance include cases where the defence seeks to explain medical evidence of the presence of semen in the complainant at the material time by citing other acts of intercourse. In *Fenlon* [37] the trial judge was held to have been right to allow questions only insofar as they concerned the complainant's last act of sex before the alleged rape, which the Court of Appeal thought allowed D to develop his point without causing undue distress. Courts have allowed leave in cases where young girls have been found not to be virgins, which, in conjunction with their allegations against their fathers or stepfathers, is extremely prejudicial unless the defence is allowed to show that in fact relationships outside the home could explain this. It might be thought that if the defendant should deny *mens rea*, his knowledge of the complainant's habits would become relevant if he claimed that as a result he thought she consented or, at least, was not reckless. For the defence can control how the trial is run, and in *Viola* the Court of Appeal stressed that issues become relevant in the light of how the trial is being run. It also held that the judge has no discretion to exclude under section 2—he must use his judgment on whether to disallow the questioning would be unfair to the defendant. [38]

These principles seem irreconcilable with the case of *Barton.* [39] The defendant claimed that his belief that the complainant consented was reasonable, although it was admitted that he broke down the door of her hostel bedroom, and that she screamed and kicked. He said that she had always behaved like this during acts of group sex at which he was present. The trial judge refused to allow questions on these lines, and was upheld on appeal. Whether or not a belief is reasonable is a jury issue to be decided on the basis of the evidence put before them, but to allow questions of this kind would be to deprive complainants of the protection that section 2 was designed to give them. Although the Court of Appeal proved commendably sympathetic to the predicament of rape victims in this case, its solution does not seem to be justifiable, given the relentless logic of the adversarial trial. Although Barton's story was ludicrous, he *had* made recklessness, and therefore the reasonableness of his belief, an issue in the case. The degree to which the defence can control which issues should figure in the trial and therefore ensure exposing the alleged victim to a humiliating ordeal is one of the least appealing features of the adversarial proceeding, and the court seems to have been forced by the manifest unfairness of Barton's tactics to disregard it. It also places the judge in a difficult position; he is required to adjudge whether the proposed cross-examination of the prosecution witness is relevant to the

[37] (1980) 71 Cr. App. R 307.
[38] Since there is no discretion involved, his decision can be overturned on appeal.
[39] (1987) 85 Cr. App. R 5.

issue before he has heard the defence evidence. The Court of Appeal acknowledged the problem in *Viola*: "at this stage it may not be easy for the judge to reach a conclusion", but Lord Lane CJ consoled himself with the thought that the trial structure frequently requires a judge to make decisions in the absence of the appropriate information, for example, on the issue of separation of trials: "[h]e has to reach the best conclusion that he can".[40]

The "similar facts" account of sexuality evinces fascinating insight into individual preconceptions; for example, Professor Elliott[41] says that any rule which could produce the result in *O'Sullivan*[42] must be a bad rule. In that case, a chapter of Hell's Angels were alleged to have raped the wife of a rival gang leader. They were refused leave to ask whether she had not voluntarily indulged in intercourse with numbers of motor cycle gang members in the past. The incidents were held not to have been sufficiently similar. But Elliott's argument appears to suggest that if the woman consented with one gang of motor cyclists, she is likely to consent to any. Temkin asks[43] whether incidents would be sufficiently similar if both involved the woman wearing a miniskirt. The absurdity of this kind of argument is confirmed by the fact that if the previous history is genuinely relevant to the issue, then the witness's denials of the allegations are not final and can be rebutted by evidence. Thus the court could actually be faced with evidence of what she was wearing on the previous occasion, or whether she really has a proclivity for sex in a Morris Minor as opposed to a Rolls-Royce. It may be that the similar facts argument is behind the assumption that evidence that the complainant is a prostitute is always admissible. The Heilbron Committee seemed to think so,[44] and concluded that to disallow questions on the subject as in *Krausz*, [45] *Clay*[46] (where the acts of prostitution were about 20 years before the alleged rape) and *Bashir*[47] must be unfair to the accused.

Adler's research shows that not only are judges consciously giving leave for cross-examination under section 2, but questions are frequently asked without application having been made and without objection from either prosecuting counsel or the judge. The apparent indifference of the prose-cutor is odd, given that it seems that juries are more reluctant to convict those accused of rape when they have heard of the complainant's sexual history.[48] It is far from clear that some of the lawyers involved in sexual cases are aware of the precise nature of the issues; woolly logic is bad enough in itself, but catastrophic in cases where prosecution witnesses pay the price for it. Another problem is that although complainants come into court as

---

[40] [1982] 3 All ER 73, 77, *per* Lord Lane CJ.

[41] Elliott "Rape Complainants' Sexual Experience with Third Parties" [1984] *Crim. LR* 4.

[42] (1981) CA, ref. 3292/BZ/80.

[43] J. Temkin, "Evidence in Sexual Assault Cases: The Scottish Proposals and Alternatives" (1987) 47 *MLR* 625.

[44] Heilbron Report, n. 5 above, para. 135.

[45] [1969] 1 WLR 1303.   [46] (1851) 5 Cox CC 146.   [47] [1969] 1 WLR 1303.

[48] H. Kalven and H. Zeisel, *The American Jury* (Little, Brown & Co, Boston, Mass., 1966), 249.

witnesses for the prosecution, they do not enjoy a lawyer–client relationship with counsel. There is a potential for conflict of interests; counsel for the prosecution may consider that tears strengthen the witness's credibility, and consequently might sit back and let the defence do its worst. It is inconsistent with adversarial theory to allow legal representation for prosecution witnesses, but that is not an insuperable obstacle; we have seen that there are many aspects of the criminal trial which are not strictly adversarial. In non-adversarial jurisdictions such as Germany, all victims are entitled to representation; in France, they can put in a claim for nominal damages, making themselves *parties civiles,* or co-plaintiffs, with the same effect. It is not established, however, that this makes much difference in practice; Pizzi's observation of the treatment of rape complainants in German courts shows a very similar experience to that undergone in the Anglo-American jurisdictions.[49]

The Law Commission of New Zealand attributes many of the wrongs suffered by complainants in rape trials to the "rape myths" which have coloured the way rape is handled in courts, possibly within inquisitorial as well as adversarial traditions. These it lists as follows;

- women are prone to fabricate complaints of sexual assault;
- promiscuous women or female sex workers deliberately provoke sexual assault ("they ask for it") and are therefore less deserving of protection;
- women are prone to fantasise about rape to the extent of actually desiring it.[50]

These myths are not the product of the adversarial trial, but it is clear that the adversarial trial is the worst kind of forum in which to encounter them. It has been argued that legal representation[51] would alleviate the position of all victims who give evidence for the prosecution; if it were combined with a non-adversarial structure, so that the issues in the case were not dictated by the defence, their protection would be considerably improved. The law of evidence could itself be reformed to widen the scope of and put some real teeth into section 2; questions designed to do no more than suggest that the complainant is not a respectable member of society should be disallowed.[52]

---

[49] W.T. Pizzi,"The American Adversary System" [1997] *NLJ* 986.

[50] New Zealand Law Commission, *Evidence Law: Character and Credibility* (New Zealand Law Commission, Wellington 1997).

[51] As urged by J. Temkin, *Rape and the Legal Process* (Sweet & Maxwell, London, 1987), 178.

[52] Such reform would be unnecessary, in the view of Sir Frederick Lawton, if judges took control of cases and confined cross-examination to matters of genuine relevance as they used to in the days when he himself practised at the bar. Cross-examination as to consent lasted "minutes, not hours". (Letter to *The Times*) 11Mar. 1998.

Children

Vulnerability

There can be no doubt that children are particularly vulnerable witnesses. Cases which involve suspected abuse of children may involve them in a potentially harrowing investigative process. The Cleveland Report[53] observed that repeated interviewing of suspected child victims could amount to abuse in itself. For example, in *Re E*[54] a child, Z, was questioned by parents, a social worker, and then seven times by a child protection officer of the NSPCC, four of which interviews were videotaped.[55] Inter-agency co-operation has since been introduced to unite police and social services in Child Protection Units which consist of specialists in child abuse.[56] Joint investigation should reduce the number of interviews child victims have to give in those cases where both criminal and civil proceedings are likely. It also provides the means to control the way these children are dealt with. However, the outcome of the investigation may be proceedings which cause the child to be removed from home, which can feel like punishment for another's wrong.

Once in court, few children are likely to comprehend the exact nature and purpose of the proceedings; some children think they are there to prove their own innocence.[57] The ordeal of child witnesses involves such potentially distressing features as facing the accused; the imposing atmosphere of a crowded court; the fact that in a jury trial they must speak loud enough to be heard over some distance[58]; relating intimate and embarrassing details, if the case involves sexual abuse; in some cases, a genuine fear of the accused if there have been threats in the past; there may be a moral and emotional dilemma if the consequences of denouncing a loved relative are understood.[59] Where child victims of sexual abuse have given evidence in court, they have been found to be suffering greater psychological damage than victims who have not.[60] On the other hand, the Thompson

[53] *Report of the Inquiry into Child Abuse in Cleveland 1987* (HMSO, London, 1988), Cm 412.

[54] *The Times*, 2 Apr. 1990.

[55] This despite the recommendation in the Cleveland Report that there should be no more than two interviews, and these should not be too long: n. 53 above, para. 12.34.

[56] *"Working Together"* (HMSO, London, 1988:1991).

[57] J. Cashmore and K. Bussey, "Children's Conceptions of the Witness Role" in J.R. Spencer, G. Nicholson, R. Flin and R. Bull (eds.), *Children's Evidence in Legal Proceedings* (Faculty of Law, University of Cambridge, Cambridge, 1990).

[58] This problem is best overcome by the clip-on lapel microphone, still not universally available in all courtrooms.

[59] D. Libai "The Protection of the Child Victim of a Sexual Offence in the Criminal Justice System", (1969) 15 *Wayne LR* 977, 984.

[60] T.C. Gibbens and J. Prince, *Child Victims of Sex Offences* (Institute for the Study and Treatment of Delinquency, London, 1963); Cf. Dr Jane Wynne, "The Court Appearance is Child Abuse Itself", Address to the British Paediatric Association, *The Times*, 17 Apr. 1986; M. Avery, "The Child Victim: Potential for Secondary Victimization" (1983) 7 *Criminal Justice Journal* 1.

Committee[61] reported that a majority of psychiatrists and social workers who made representations to them thought that children should continue to participate in the trial, and that they were not so seriously affected by giving evidence as was generally supposed.

The criminal trial presents a more daunting prospect to the child witness than the civil, partly because of its public nature and physically grand scale, since courtrooms have to be large enough to accommodate the jury, but also because of its more adversarial character. In an entirely adversarial trial, the child witness must be cross-examined by the opposing side on every fact which it proposes to deny. This not only frequently prolongs the child's ordeal but forces the defence into a hostile posture which might in fact be counter-productive from its point of view. Some judges, alive to this difficulty, indicate to opposing counsel a willingness not to insist on full cross-examination. The child is unlikely to have met the advocates in advance. 16 per cent of child witnesses in a Home Office Study met prosecuting counsel prior to trial, and only 2 per cent met defence counsel.[62] The Children Act 1989 gave jurisdiction for civil cases concerning child abuse to the new-style care proceedings set up under that Act. These are regarded as not strictly adversarial, since the participants are not necessarily those with something to deny.[63] Allegations of child abuse may be made in other varieties of civil proceeding, however, most commonly during divorce and matrimonial cases. But children rarely have to attend; the hearsay rule is effectively abolished in regard to child-centred hearings[64] and, indeed, for civil proceedings generally.[65]

Reducing Stress: Screens and Live Link

Increasing public concern that the processes faced by child witnesses in criminal cases in the first place lacked compassion, and in the second probably led to abusers escaping retribution, led to dramatic changes in law and practice. The use of screens to shield the child from the defendant in criminal cases was pioneered by Judge Pigot QC in 1987. There have been

[61] Scottish Home and Health Department, *Report on Criminal Procedure in Scotland*, (HMSO, Edinburgh, 1975).

[62] G. Davies C. Wilson, L. Mitchell and J. Milsom, *Videotaping Children's Evidence: An Evaluation* (Home Office, London, 1995), 25.

[63] *Humberside* v. *R.* [1977] 3 All ER 964; although "essentially non-adversary" (*per* Lord Widgery CJ) in nature the hearsay rule applied. In *Re L* (*A Minor*) (*Police Investigation: Privilege*) [1996] 2 All ER 78, the House of Lords agreed that care proceedings are non-adversarial, but nonetheless stressed the importance of legal professional privilege. See Ch. 1.

[64] Children (Admissibility of Hearsay Evidence) Order 1993: "[i]n civil proceedings before the High Court or a county court; and (b) civil proceedings under the Child Support Act 1991 in a magistrates' court, evidence given in connection with the upbringing, maintenance or welfare of a child shall be admissible notwithstanding any rule of law relating to hearsay".

[65] Civil Evidence Act 1995 (see Ch. 7).

numerous practical problems affecting the provision of screens.[66] Legislative intervention so far has been untidily piecemeal, a product of hasty reaction to difficulties as they have emerged over the last few years. The messy scissors-and-paste technique employed in the relevant statutory amendments has prevented until very recently a remotely coherent approach to the problem of child witnesses.

Parliament has acted to reduce the stress suffered by child witnesses in a variety of ways. A child witness may not be cross-examined by the accused in person.[67] Where once the defence was able to cross-examine child witnesses at the committal stage in a magistrates' court, in order to test whether there was a case to answer which should be heard in the Crown Court, it is now able to make challenges only to a case presented on paper.[68] Unfortunately, this reform has failed to secure the expected expedition of child abuse trials.[69] Technology has inspired more sophisticated methods to assist child witnesses. They may now give evidence through a live television link on a trial on indictment[70] if under the age of 14 and the offence is one of violence, or 17 in a sex case.[71] The procedure requires the leave of the trial judge, who need not give reasons for refusal.[72] In *Guy*,[73] Judge Herrod ruled that a judge should not grant permission for the live link automatically, but should balance the risk of harm to the child against the risk of creating prejudice against the defendant by allowing it to be used. In principle, if the prosecution request use of the live link, it should produce some evidence that it is likely to be harmful to this particular child to give evidence in the traditional way. In the case of a very young child, however, "there must come a time when the very fact of the child's age is almost sufficient in itself to show that

---

[66] J. Morgan and J. Plotnikoff, "Children as Victims of Crime: Procedure at Court" in Spencer, Nicholson, Flin and Bull (eds,) n. 57 above; J. Spencer and R. Flin, *The Evidence of Children: the Law and the Psychology* (2nd edn., Blackstone, London, 1993), 101.

[67] If the witness is the person against whom the alleged offence was committed or was a witness to it and is a child or is to be cross-examined following the admission under s. 32A of the Criminal Justice Act (CJA) 1988 as amended of a video recording of testimony from him. (New s.34A of the 1988 CJA as amended by the 1991 Act, s.55.) This provision effectively forces the accused to have legal representation, but in *Mills* [1997] Crim. LR 604, the accused sacked counsel during the trial. Since Mills could not cross-examine the 12-year-old alleged victim of offences including rape, abduction and wounding with intent, the trial judge carried out the cross-examination himself. The Court of Appeal appeared to approve, although made the point that this was not a course of action which should lightly be undertaken.

[68] For child abuse proceedings, see ss. 53, 55 of the CJA 1991. Committal proceedings in general are now to be done entirely on paper: s.46 of and Sch ed. 1 to the Criminal Procedure and Investigations Act 1996.

[69] J. Plotnikoff and R. Woolfson, *Prosecuting Child Abuse* (Blackstone, London, 1995).

[70] Or an appeal to the criminal division of the Court of Appeal or the hearing of a reference under s. 17 of the Criminal Appeal Act 1968.

[71] S.32A of the CJA 1988 as amended by s.54 of the CJA 1991 and s.62 of the Criminal Procedure and Investigations Act 1996.

[72] CJA 1988, s.32(2); Crown Court Rules 1982, rr.23A, 23B.

[73] 21 Dec. 1989, Leeds Crown Court. See Spencer and Flin, n. 66 above, 105.

it would be detrimental for the child to have to give evidence in open court and to be cross-examined in the usual way". The decision will normally be made at a plea and directions hearing before the trial. Once made, it is binding on any subsequent judge, and irrespective of any change of advocate,[74] unless it appears to be contrary to the interests of justice to do so, given that a material change of circumstances has been shown to have occurred.

The judges who hear these cases are specialists and receive specific training. They assert that they never refuse a request,[75] but Plotnikoff and Woolfson found that the live link was used in only 16 out of 41 cases in which the facility was available.[76] The explanation for the low take-up rate appears to lie in the reluctance of some prosecutors to apply for the live link.[77] A number of practising lawyers appear to believe that a screen image of the child lacks the power of his or her actual presence,[78] the accused being seen as more real as a person to the jury through constant presence in the court itself. Crown Prosecution Service lawyers and prosecution advocates have reported a fear that the impact of the evidence would be lost on live link. Some Scottish prosecutors admitted that in their view a frightened child made a more effective witness.[79] The loss of rapport and eye contact, frequently presented as an objection to the live link by prosecution lawyers, is hardly a serious disadvantage in those cases where otherwise the child could not proceed at all. Some judges have consequently become relatively interventionist, and suggest at the plea and directions stage that an application would be appropriate. It appears that the child is rarely consulted on the issue,[80] and that applications are only half as likely to be made in cases of stranger assaults because of the lack of involvement of the Child Protection Unit.[81]

Whether the removal of the child from the immediate scrutiny of the jury makes it harder to obtain a conviction is not known. Certainly, the conviction rate is low, standing at 16 per cent against a national average of 50 per cent. One victim support officer blamed the live link for this—"[y]ou don't get the emotion".[82] Yet jurors in Australia did not feel disadvantaged by the

---

[74] Criminal Investigations and Procedure Act 1996, s.62(2), inserting new subs. (6)–(10), s.32A of the CJA 1988. The same applies to a decision on the use of a videotaped interview in lieu of evidence-in-chief or part of it (see text to nn. 92–105 below).

[75] Judicial Training Seminar, Judicial Studies Board, 18 Dec. 1997.

[76] J. Plotnikoff and R. Woolfson, *Prosecuting Child Abuse* (Blackstone, London, 1995).

[77] *Ibid.*

[78] S. B. Smith, "The Child Witness" in *Representing Children: Current Issues in Law, Medicine and Mental Health,* (National Association of Councils for Children, London, 1987), 13.

[79] K. Murray, *Live Television Link: an Evaluation of its use by Child Witnesses in Scottish Criminal Trials* (Scottish Office Central Research Unit, HMSO, Edinburgh, 1995).

[80] Plotnikoff and Woolfson, n. 76 above.

[81] *Ibid.*

[82] Social Services Inspectorate, *The Child, the Court and the Video* (Department of Health, London, 1994).

fact that a child witness was visible only on a screen.[83] In New Zealand, professionals were positive about the live link.[84] The attitude of legal practitioners in the United Kingdom seems rather more conservative. Murray reported considerable resistance to the live link in Scotland,[85] where the videotaped interview has still not been introduced: "[w]ithout exception, the lawyers who were interviewed believed that the use of a live television link offends against the general principle that the accused person is entitled to be faced directly by his accuser".[86] Both prosecution and defence lawyers, while recognising that children benefited from the live link, considered that it made them more likely to lie.[87]

The live link has reduced the levels of stress suffered by many child witnesses, who consequently have been more forthcoming in their evidence,[88] although it is most successful in this respect where the child actually expresses a preference for giving evidence that way.[89] Murray has described how some defence advocates in Scottish cases, being deprived of the unnerving effect their client's gaze might have upon the young witness, compensate by announcing at commencement of cross-examination that the defendant is present—"[y]ou realise he is here with me, watching this?". This tactic, although apparently accepted by the Scottish courts observed, is unlikely to be countenanced in England.[90] On the whole, children seem not to have found the live link intimidating.[91] The concern to avoid "coaching" of children has resulted in courts tending to use a neutral, the court usher, to sit with the child in the transmitting room, but most of these officers ensure that they have met the child beforehand.

Reducing Stress: Videotaped Interview

More innovative yet is the new exception to the rule against hearsay introduced in 1991, inserting new section 32A into the Criminal Justice Act 1988. [92] The intention behind the reform was to provide the court with the

---

[83] *Jurors' Responses to Children's Evidence Given by Closed-Circuit Television or with the Aid of Removable Screens* (Ministry of Justice, Strategic and Specialist Services Division, Perth, Western Australia, 1995).

[84] Law Commission of New Zealand, *The Evidence of Children and Other Vulnerable Witnesses: a Discussion Paper*, Law Commission of New Zealand, Preliminary Paper 26.

[85] Ss.56–60 Law Reform (Miscellaneous Provisions)(Scotland) Act 1990.

[86] Murray, n. 79 above, para. 8.8. See text to nn. 149–151 below.

[87] *Ibid.*, 8.6.

[88] G. Davies and E. Noon, *An Evaluation of the Live Link for Child Witnesses* (Home Office, London, 1991), 133.

[89] Plotnikoff and Woolfson, n. 76 above 96-7: some children are actually anxious to face the defendant.

[90] Judicial Training Seminar, 18 Dec. 1997.

[91] Davies and Noon, n. 88 above.

[92] S.54 of the CJA 1991.

most reliable evidence available,[93] bringing to justice those who commit offences against very young children and reducing the stress suffered by children who give evidence in the present conditions. It was hoped that it would lead to more pleas of guilty, making the ordeal in court unnecessary for all concerned,[94] although the American evidence cited in support of this expectation was admitted to be ambiguous.[95] There is no evidence to date that it is having this effect[96]. The Pigot Report accepted that a contemporaneous account is frequently more accurate and detailed than one given much later in court, particularly in the case of child witnesses Accordingly, section 32 provides for the admission into evidence of a video recording of an interview conducted between an adult and a child[97] who is not the accused or one of the accused and which relates to any matter in issue in the proceedings. The leave of the court is required and should generally be given, unless the court is of the opinion, having regard to all the circumstances of the case, that in the interests of justice the recording ought not to be admitted.[98] Where the video is used, the witness shall not be examined in chief on any matter which, in the opinion of the court, has been adequately dealt with in his recorded testimony. The scheme envisaged in the Pigot Report would have required cross-examination of the child to be carried out in chambers and recorded on a second tape which the jury would watch after the first video. This scheme was recommended also for Scotland[99] and New Zealand.[100] Since the Government decided not to implement this aspect of the proposals, child witnesses have to attend court in order to be cross-examined,[101] albeit, in some cases, by way of live link.

The defence is equally entitled to produce a video, but also should comply with guidelines on the manner of questioning and the technical standard of the recording. These are contained in the Memorandum of Good Practice,[102]

---

[93] *Report of the Advisory Group on Video Evidence* (Pigot Report) (Home Office, London, 1989), para. 2.10.

[94] *Ibid.*, para. 2.11.

[95] Pigot Report, n. 93 above, para. 2.11: cf. K. Murray, *Evidence from Children; Alternatives to In-Court Testimony in Criminal Proceedings in the United States of America,* SLC Research Paper (Apr. 1988). Those few recorded changes of plea where defendants had seen videotaped interviews might have been forthcoming anyway. Also, the particular procedure may include videotaped cross-examination in advance of trial, so that a defendant considering his plea is precisely aware of the child's performance in cross-examination—not usually the case when entering a plea.

[96] G. Davies, C. Wilson, L. Mitchell and J. Milsom: *Videotaping Children's Evidence: an Evaluation* (Home Office, London, 1995).

[97] S.32A(7).   [98] S.32A(3).

[99] Scottish Law Commission, *Report on the Evidence of Children and Other Vulnerable Witnesses* (Scot Law Com. No 125, HMSO, Edinburgh, 1989); provisions to effect the recommendation were included in the Prisoners and Criminal Proceedings (Scotland) Act 1993, which has not in that regard been implemented.

[100] Law Commission of New Zealand, n. 8 above.

[101] CJA 1988, s.32A(3).

[102] *Memorandum of Good Practice on Videorecorded Interviews with Child Witnesses for Criminal Proceedings* (Home Office, Department of Health, London, 1992).

issued jointly by the Home Office and the Department of Health, in fact to assist the interviewers from Child Protection Units who will normally produce these videotaped interviews.[103] The aim is to produce a videotape which will be acceptable to both the criminal and the family courts. Although designed for non-lawyers, and not to operate as a rigid Code, the Memorandum tends to be complex and legalistic. There is a brief summary of the exclusionary rules of evidence[104]; a six-page chart of offences; and an explanation (surely unnecessarily heavy-handed?) that the child may admit an offence, rendering the document to that extent a confession, which should be subject to the Codes of Practice issued under the Police and Criminal Evidence Act 1984.[105] It demands a good clear picture of the head and face, and if possible, the rest of the body, consistent and clear audibility, and sets out a recommended pattern for interviews, which should take no more than an hour. It is not entirely clear that it prohibits the presence of a parent at the interview, although the Cleveland Report considers it undesirable, but family courts have treated the presence, and particularly the participation of, a parent as a serious breach.[106]

These guidelines were developed in the wake of controversy following the disapproval of Family Division judges[107] of some videotaped interviews offered as evidence in care or custody cases, which were based on a style of questioning devised at Great Ormond Street Hospital for use during therapy for children known to have been abused. The objective was to overcome the child's tendency to denial, which might derive from guilt, fear or love, so that counselling could begin.[108] The techniques used, for example, pressure, leading and hypothetical questions, rendered the videotapes inappropriate for evidential purposes. Bearing this in mind, the Pigot Report endorsed Professor Yuille's "step-wise" approach[109] to interviewing such children. This requires the interviewer to proceed from the most general and open aspects of the interview to the more specific. The emphasis is on allowing the child to be spontaneous. Thus the Memorandum requires a four-phase structure. As far as the suspected abuse is concerned, the interviewer should begin with a "free narrative" phase, in which there should be only general, open-ended questions. If it is thought necessary, the questioner may move to more

---

[103] As recommended in Pigot, n. 93 above, para. 4.8; although these are officially joint agency intestigations, in reality it appears that the lead in questioning tends to be taken by the police officer (Social Services Inspectorate, n. 82 above).

[104] Pt. 3.B.   [105] See Ch. 6.

[106] *Re A & B (minors)(investigation of alleged abuse)(no1)* [1995] 3 FCR 389; *Re N (a minor)(sexual abuse: video evidence)* [1996] 4 All ER 225.

[107] *"Tranter Cases"* [1987] 1 FLR 269–310; see also G. Douglas and S. Willmore, "Diagnostic Interviews as Evidence of Child Sexual Abuse" (1987) *Fam. L* 191.

[108] E. Vizard, "Interviewing Young, Sexually Abused Children; Assessment Techniques" [1989] *Fam. L* 28.

[109] J.C. Yuille, R. Hunter, R. Joffe and J. Zaparmink, "Interviewing Children in Child Sexual Abuse Cases" in (eds) G. Goodman and B. Bottoms (eds.), *Child Victims, Child Witnesses*, (Guilford, New York, 1993).

specific questions, but this must be done without pressure. Leading and closed questions[110] should be avoided as much as possible. The child should feel that it is acceptable not to know or not to remember, must not be interrupted and may be assisted with props not including anatomically correct dolls.

These guidelines are designed to reflect judicial concern about the use of suggestion. After all, evidence in chief in court has to be elicited without the use of leading questions. The analogy is a false one, however. Witnesses may in fact refresh their memory from their witness statements before going into court[111] or even interrupt their testimony to look through them if having trouble remembering the facts.[112] These statements, frequently compiled with considerable assistance from police officers, could be, and often are, the compilation of a large number of leading questions—a matter not indicated in the text itself. It is not clear that children are more susceptible to suggestion than adults. Marin thought that they were[113], and Cohen and Harnick[114] found 12-year-olds more suggestible than adults, with 9-year-olds more suggestible still. But more depends upon the strength of the impression created by the event than the child's age[115]; it is much harder to get a child to accept "planted" information where he or she had central, as opposed to peripheral, involvement in it. Davies concludes that the evidence shows that suggestibility in children is more a function of setting and task than state of mind.[116] However, most of the experiments on which that conclusion is based deal with morally neutral matters. More disturbing findings were the result of an experiment[117] in which the questioner deliberately assumed guilt or innocence on the part of the actor. Children of 5 and 6 saw incidents in which a janitor was tidying up toys. In the case of half of them, the janitor became "Chester the Molestor" in that he ceased work to play with the dolls in a suggestive way, adopting malicious and aggressive behaviour towards them. When questioned neutrally afterwards by

---

[110] Requires a yes/no answer or forces a choice between two answers.

[111] *Richardson* (1971) 55 Cr. App. R 244. See Ch. 3.

[112] If they did not in fact read them outside the court: *Da Silva* [1990] 1 WLR 31; and even where the statement has been read previously: see *R. v. South Ribble Stipendiary Magistrate ex p. Cochrane*, *The Times*, 24 June 1996. See Ch. 3.

[113] B. Marin, D. Holmes, M. Guth and P. Kovac, "The Potential of Children as Eyewitnesses" (1979) 3 *Law and Human Behaviour* 295.

[114] R.L. Cohen and M.A. Harnick, "The Susceptibility of Child Witnesses to Suggestion" (1980) 4 *Law and Human Behaviour* 295; Cf. G.S. Goodman and R.S. Reed, "Age Differences in Eyewitness Testimony" (1986) 10 *Law and Human Behaviour* 317.

[115] G.S. Goodman, C. Aman and J. Hirschman, in S.J. Ceci, M.P. Toglia and D.F. Ross (eds.), *Children's Eyewitness Memory*, (Springer-Verlag, New York, 1987).

[116] G. Davies "Research on Children's Testimony: Implications for Interviewing Practice" in C. Hollins and K. Howells (eds.), *Clinical Approaches to Sex Offenders and their Victims* (Wiley, Chichester, 1991).

[117] A. Clarke-Stewart, W. Thompson and S. Lepore, "Manipulating Children's Interpretations Through Interrogation", In Ceci, Toglia and Ross, n. 115 above. See Davies, n. 116 above.

"Chester's boss", the children were generally accurate in describing his behaviour. But in some cases, the questions were designed to incriminate the "cleaning" Chester, or to exculpate the "playing" character. There fewer than half the children stuck to their story, instead adopting the questioner's interpretation or saying that Chester had both cleaned and played. This shows, says Davies, the "devastating effect" on these children of assumptions of guilt or innocence, although the authors could not reproduce the results with older children.[118] Against this is work that shows that even 3-year-old non-abused children will resist suggestion implying impropriety after an intimate medical examination.[119] Although it may be that overall there is not sufficient evidence to justify a conclusion that children are more suggestible than adults, who are extremely suggestible themselves,[120] the difficulty remains that children are peculiarly at risk of suggestion from investigators or from members of their own families.

The Memorandum does not entirely rule out the use of leading questions. It has been customary for many years to allow a little leading of a shy child during conventional evidence-in-chief.

> "Has anyone, in this country or elsewhere, yet found a way of leading a child along without use of these methods? It is how it is done that matters, and then the interpretation to be put on the answers and reactions of a child. The fact is in this case that a good deal of what was elicited from [the child witness] was spontaneous."[121]

In *G v. DPP*,[122] the Court of Appeal explained that not all breaches of the Memorandum should lead to exclusion of the interview. Here the interviewer did not explain that the child could say "I don't know". Some of the questions were leading, some grossly leading, but it was held that the issue is not simply a question of the number and nature of the breaches. There is also a question of the extent to which passages in the evidence affected by the breaches are supported by other passages in respect of which no complaint can be made. It depends also on the other evidence in the case and the extent to which it corroborates the evidence in the video interviews. Once a trial judge is satisfied on these grounds that the evidence should be admitted, the Court of Appeal will rarely interfere. The Court declared that this approach does not condone failure to comply with the Memorandum; it recognised that it is of great importance that the Memorandum is followed.

---

[118] But work with adults suggests that the relationship, particularly the degree of trust, between the subject and the suggester is crucial: G.H. Gudjonsson, "Retracted Confessions: Legal, Psychological and Psychiatric Aspects" (1988) 28 *Med. Sci. Law* 187.

[119] K. Saywitz, G.S. Goodman, E. Nichols and S. Moan, "Children's Memory for a Genital Examination" Paper presented to the Society for Research on Child Development, Kansas City, USA, 1989.

[120] See Ch. 1.

[121] *C v. C* [1988] FCR 458, *per* Latey J.

[122] [1997] 2 All ER 755.

A judge, in considering whether to allow a videotape to replace a child witness's evidence-in-chief, will consider the manner of questioning, the quality of the recording[123] and will, in many cases, have to direct the editing out of inadmissible parts of an otherwise acceptable interview.[124] It may be that the child no longer holds to the allegation made in the video, as in *Parker*.[125] After making accusations during the course of a taped interview, B retracted them and made it clear he did not wish to give evidence. The prosecution proceeded, and obtained the admission of the videotaped interview. On appeal it was held that the interview should have been abandoned, and B called to give evidence through the live link.[126] Some judges watch the video prior to the plea and directions hearing; others have no opportunity to do so until the trial itself. The unfortunate consequence of this is that the child has to wait until the last minute to know whether the video will be used or whether he or she will have to give evidence after all.

The Memorandum suggests that once the interview has been successfully conducted and recorded, an abused child may receive therapy, as long as the Child Protection team has consulted the Crown Prosecution Service. The Service's stated policy is to allow counselling to take place, but there are suggestions that this practice is far from uniform.[127] This is not surprising, since counselling prior to trial could seriously undermine a prosecution. There is no guarantee that a videotaped interview will be used as evidence. If it is rejected, whether by prosecutors or by the trial judge, the child will have to give conventional evidence in chief, albeit perhaps by live link, and will have to be cross-examined in any event. The defence may damage the credibility of the child's evidence by alleging that the counselling received amounted to coaching or, at least, that the offence has been discussed during the therapy sessions.[128] Although open to this kind of attack, the child's evidence is probably admissible,[129] even if it may have been discussed beforehand. The risk is that prosecutions will be abandoned or fail if therapy has taken place, as it is virtually inevitable that counselling would have included discussion of it. It is difficult to see what value it would have if it did not.

---

[123] Any party who applies for leave must provide *inter alia* information of recording times, the location of the interview and a description of the equipment used.

[124] There may be hearsay statements or descriptions of offences against others committed by the defendant falling outside the similar facts principle, for example.

[125] [1996] Crim. LR. 510.

[126] Given the reluctance of the witness to participate in the trial, the case raises interesting issues as to the compellability of children and the consequences of their refusal to give evidence. (See text to nn. 149–152 below).

[127] Plotnikoff and Woolfson, n. 76 above; Social Services Inspectorate, n. 82 above; Davies, Wilson *et al.*, n. 96 above.

[128] The normal prosecution obligations of disclosure to the defence may be subject, as far as the contents of therapy sessions are concerned, to public interest immunity. If the defence demands such information, the trial judge should first consider those contents himself or herself, and order disclosure if they are material to the development of the defence. *Re K(DT)* [1993] Crim. LR. 281.

[129] *Dye and Williamson, The Times*, 19 Dec. 1991; *R v. H* [1991] Crim. LR. 516.

Where a jury requests a second viewing of the video, the trial judge must follow the guidance set out in *Rawlings and Broadbent*.[130] In this case, the Court of Appeal acknowledged that the video may legitimately be regarded as an exhibit, and that the jury is usually allowed to see an exhibit again if available. However, the video also represents testimony, and it was thought potentially unfair to allow the jury to see a particular witness's examination in chief more than once. The normal practice, if a jury wishes to be reminded of the content of a witness's testimony, is for the judge to read it from his or her own notes. The practice of note-taking developed when there was no other record available. Although in this case there was an available and accurate record of the testimony, and of that witness's demeanour, replaying it carried a risk that the jury would place excessive reliance on it. It is for the trial judge to decide, on request from the jury,[131] whether there should be a replay. If tthe jury seek a reminder as to contents, it may be best for the judge to read from his or her note. If their concern is the witness's demeanour, the judge may in his discretion allow this, but the replay should be watched in court with judge, counsel and the defendant present, and the judge should warn the jury not to give the evidence disproportionate weight. Also, to maintain fair balance, the judge should, afterwards, remind the jury from his or her own notes of the terms of the cross-examination, whether the jury ask for it or not.[132] In *Mills*,[133] the jury asked to be shown part of a video again, because the 12-year-old victim of alleged abduction, false imprisonment and rape might have been heard to refer to the defendant by his Christian name, which could be relevant to his defence of consent. This was allowed, and approved on appeal. In *Atkinson*,[134] the jury requested and were granted a reshowing in the jury room. However, here the video had not been given in lieu of evidence in chief; the defence had intended to use it during cross-examination, and, presumably to defuse the effect of this, the prosecution successfully applied to run it during its own case. The Court of Appeal appeared satisfied with the procedure. A jury might, alternatively or in addition, ask to consult the transcript of the videotape. (Trial judges have successfully campaigned for transcripts to be provided,[135] to assist them in their preliminary decisions in relation to admissibility and possible editing.)

---

[130] [1995] 1 All ER 680.

[131] *R. v. M, The Times*, 29 Nov. 1995; retrial ordered because the tape was replayed in the absence of a jury request.

[132] This did not happen in *R. v. B*, [1996] Crim. LR. 499, however, but the jury had a transcript in that case by agreement from both sides. In *Saunders* (unreported, 14 Feb. 1995) also, the judge did not go through the cross-examination and yet the conviction was upheld on appeal because he had already taken the jury through it during "his impeccable summing up".

[133] [1997] Crim. LR. 604.

[134] [1995] CLR 490; this case pre-dates *Rawlings*, which stipulates that reshowing should take place in the courtroom.

[135] The Crown Prosecution Service has taken responsibility for this; tapes are to be transcribed at York, and should be available within a few days of request.

But there may be occasions when access to the transcript could assist the jury, for example where the sound is indistinct.[136] The Court of Appeal made it clear in *Coshall*[137] that the transcript should not be taken into the jury room unless by consent of both sides.

The legal status of a videotaped interview is unclear; as the Court of Appeal observed in *Rawlings*, it in many respects resembles an exhibit, as with items of real evidence, but in others appears to be a kind of witness statement. Adult witnesses may refresh their memories of the contents of their written witness statements before going into the witness-box, but it is unclear how many times a child may re-acquaint himself or herself with the contents of the videotape interview. The Crown Prosecution Service view, based on the analogy, is that the child can see it the day before, if appropriate. Judicial practice, however, seems to vary quite considerably.[138] If a tape should be in fact held to be inadmissible, so that a child must give conventional evidence in chief, it is arguable that the child should be able to use it as a memory-refreshing document according to the principle in *Richardson*.[139] Defence lawyers, in using any inconsistency between an unused video interview and current testimony as the basis of cross-examination, employ an analogy with a written witness statement. Potentially, such an interview may in some cases constitute a previous consistent statement, which might be admissible under the exceptions dealing with recent complaint in rape cases, a previous identification or to rebut accusation of afterthought.[140]

In England and Wales, only just under half of the barristers, and just over half of the judges interviewed in the Home Office study felt that the videotaped interview would serve the interests of justice or the interests of the child; 20 per cent of judges and 50 per cent of barristers thought they would make it harder to detect false allegations.[141] That research[142] could find no evidence to suggest that it increases or, indeed, decreases the prospects of conviction, although it did appear to reduce the levels of stress suffered by children who gave evidence by that means. There is no evidence that it increases the number of guilty pleas. Davies' team found much criticism from the legal profession of the standard of interviewing in many videos. The tapes examined in the study contained a number of frequently-occurring breaches of the Memorandum guidelines, including "inappropriate comfort" or encouragement during the course of the interview with a distressed child. This particular problem highlights the dilemma faced by interviewing teams, some members of which are responsible for the child's welfare and may know a great deal about the child's family background. Yet if the evidence obtained is to be of value to the criminal court, such interjections undermine the child's perceived reliability.

---

[136] *Welstead* [1996] Crim. LR. 48.   [137] *The Times,* 17 Feb. 1995.
[138] Davies, Wilson *et al.*, n. 96 above.   [139] (1971) 55 Cr. App. R 244.   [140] See Ch. 3.
[141] Davies, Wilson *et al.*, n. 96 above.   [142] *Ibid.*

At present, few children are receiving the benefit of videotaping, although many videotape interviews exist.[143] Out of 1,199 trials involving child witnesses between October 1992 and April 1994, there were 470 successful applications to show videos as evidence-in-chief.[144] There is unlikely to be in existence a videotape interview in cases of stranger abuse, since child protection units tend not to handle inquiries in those cases. Even if the videotape interview is available and passes the judge, the child has to undergo cross-examination. Although judges claim[145] that defence lawyers do not harass child witnesses at trial, because it would be counter-productive and alienate the jury, researchers have observed what they perceive to be bullying by counsel.[146] During the long trial of a pædophile ring in Swansea in 1993–4, it appears that Kay J felt powerless to prevent a "barrage of hostile questioning".[147] In any event, it is clear that the linguistic style of defence counsel is significantly less accommodating of the child's than that of prosecution counsel,[148] and the obsession with peripheral detail characteristic of many second-rate cross-examinations pertains in these, as in other, trials.

In a climate of concern to protect children from abuse, the legal provisions for child witnesses in England and Wales appear to many to be unnecessarily technical and legalistic. It is not clear why it is thought appopriate to restrict the new technology to cases involving violence, where the witness is aged under 14, and sexual offences, where the witness is aged under 17. Those lawyers who stress the importance of the defendant's right to confront his or her accuser, might bear in mind that there is no such constitutional right in English law,[149] and that the European Convention on Human Rights merely requires that an accused person must have the opportunity to "examine or have examined" witnesses against him.[150] And, as the New Zealand Court of Appeal observed, "[c]onfrontation in the sense of being in the presence of one's accusers is one thing; but confrontation merely to afford the opportunity to glower at and thereby intimidate the witness is another".[151] Scepticism in the legal profession may explain the difficulty facing those law reform bodies which favour a flexible approach. But, so far, even law reform agencies have declined to consider introduction of an entirely different procedure. Child abuse cases could be primarily inquisitorial, allowing of informal questioning by the judge, who could also examine any available hearsay evidence. Rather than put children through a formal cross-examination, which would prove little in many cases beyond how easy it is to confuse a child, the judge could ask the pertinent questions

---

[143] Between Oct. 1992 and June 1993, 14,912 interviews were taped; only 24 % of those were forwarded to the Crown Prosecution Service: Davies, Wilson *et al.*, n. 96 above, 17.
[144] *Ibid.*, 25.　　　[145] Judicial Training Seminar, 18 Dec. 1997.
[146] Plotnikoff and Woolfson, n. 76 above.　　　[147] *Ibid.*
[148] Davies, Wilson *et al.*, n. 96 above.
[149] *Smellie* (1919) 14 Cr. App. R 128; *X, Y, and Z, The Times*, 31 Nov. 1989.　　　[150] Art. 6 (d).
[151] *R.* v. *Accused* [1989] 1 NZLR 660, *per* McMullin J at 672.

to establish what opportunities for suggestion there might have been, and the accused would be able to raise further points, about which he would request the judge to ask.[152] Utter devotion to the adversarial trial might appear somewhat irrational in ordinary circumstances; to insist on retaining it while going to the lengths comprised in the child witness legislation to escape its traditional features might seem thoroughly eccentric.

Reliability of Child Witnesses

Without the victim's evidence, an offence committed against a child may be difficult to prove. John Spencer[153] argued forcefully that very young children ought to be able to give evidence in some form so that they are protected by the law. Some of the arguments on this issue turn on how much credence it is appropriate to give the evidence of small children; but, additionally, on the risk that the nature of our proceedings, particularly criminal trials, might weigh against introducing small children as witnesses simply on humanitarian grounds. The use of live link and the videotaped interview has transformed the physical conditions under which some, but by no means all, children give evidence in criminal courts; the remaining problems of comprehension and communication obviously depend heavily on the child's age and stage of development.

The assumption that children's evidence is inherently suspect was behind the common law requirement that a warning to the jury of the need for corroboration be given to jurors, and the statutory requirement in relation to unsworn children that no-one should be convicted solely on the strength of what such a child might say.[154] These requirements were abolished in the Criminal Justice Act 1988.[155] In *Pryce*,[156] the Court of Appeal held that, although the language of the provision was unclear, the effect was to place children on the same footing as adults so far as their evidence was concerned, and that there is no specific requirement for a warning. Here the judge had in fact told the jury that they should take into account the fact that the witnesses were children[157]; that was held to be sufficient. The issues in the case were complicated by the prevailing judicial obligation to issue a warning to juries on the subject of corroboration where the crime alleged was sexual in nature. This requirement is now abolished also,[158] and in *Makanjuola and Easton*[159]

---

[152]　See J. McEwan, "Child Evidence: More Proposals for Reform" [1988] *Crim. LR* 813.

[153]　E.g., J. Spencer, "Child Witnesses and Video-technology: Thoughts for the Home Office" (1987) 51 *Journal of Criminal Law* 44 and "Reforming the Competency Requirement" [1988] *NLJ* 147.

[154]　Children and Young Persons Act 1933, s.38(2).

[155]　S.34.

[156]　[1991] Crim. LR 379.

[157]　Aged 6 and 7; the charges were of indecent assault and indecency with a child.

[158]　S.32 of the Criminal Justice and Public Order Act 1994.

[159]　[1995] 3 All ER 730A.

the Court of Appeal rejected the argument that in cases where previously a corroboration warning had to be given, there should be some alternative obligation on trial judges to issue warnings to the jury.[160] Judges might now be found to observe to the jury that the evidence of a child witness may have been influenced by fantasy or suggestion, but the modern summing-up is unlikely to reflect the rigour of the old corroboration warning.

The legislative changes discussed above represent not only increasing concern to protect children from abuse, but an increased faith in the credibility of child witnesses. An influential lobby of opinion argued that children are equally as reliable as adults,[161] but the question of the reliability of the evidence of children is in fact a particularly complicated one. There is no doubt that children can be helpful in identification[162] although stress reduces their performance,[163] making it advisable to screen them from the suspect during any identification parade. But tests have found that an 8-year-old is more likely than an older child to select a face from a series of photographs when that of the real subject is not there.[164] This may be because young children do not understand the object of the exercise and assume it is some sort of test of themselves,[165] increasing the likelihood that they will hazard a guess and select the person most like the subject. In a famous article, Dr Jones describes the case of Susie, aged 3,[166] who was able to pick out a photograph of her attacker from six pictures. Although her ability to describe the events and to remember who was responsible is encouraging, the problem that children may be more likely to pick out the wrong person because the real one is not shown should not be forgotten.

If a child is required to describe an event rather than describe or identify a person, more is required of his or her memory, and he or she is more likely to make errors.[167] A child's capacity to remember events increases with age, apparently in direct relation to his or her understanding of what he or she observes.[168] The research on children's ability to recall and describe events

---

[160] See Ch. 3.

[161] Notably J. Spencer, "Child Witnesses Video Technology and the Law of Evidence" [1987] *Crim. LR* 76.

[162] J.F. Parker, E. Haverfield and S. Baker-Thomas, "Eyewitness Testimony of Children" (1986) 16 *Journal of Applied Psychology*; G. Davies, Y. Stevenson-Robb and R. Flin, "The Reliability of Children's Testimony" (1986) 11, *International Practitioner* 81.

[163] Davies, Stevenson-Robb and Flin, n. 162 above.

[164] J.C. Yuille, J.L. Cutshall and M.A. King, "Age-related Changes in Eyewitness Accounts and Photo-identification" (unpublished; quoted, Hedderman, *Children's Evidence; the Need for Corroboration*, Home Office Research and Planning Unit Paper 41 (Home Office, London, 1987), 13–14.

[165] S. Moston, "The Suggestibility of Children in Interview Studies" (1987) 7 *First Language* 67.

[166] D. Jones, "The Evidence of a Three Year Old Child" [1987] *Crim. LR* 677.

[167] M.A. King and J.C. Yuille, "Suggestibility and the Child Witness" in S. Ceci, M. Toglia and D. Ross (eds.), *Children's Eyewitness Memory* n. 115 above.

[168] G. Davies, "Research on Children's Testimony: Implications for Interviewing Practice" in C. Hollins and K. Howells (eds.), *Clinical Approaches to Sex Offenders and their Victims* (Wiley, Chichester, 1991).

suggests that they are not as good as adults at searching their memories or categorising them to order.[169] Unprompted, children of under 10 recall five or six times less than adults and furnish accounts which are more fragmentary and selective than older children or adults.[170] The explanation for this appears to be that young children are only learning to think conceptually and have only a limited range of concepts.[171] The greatest development here takes place between the ages of 5 and 10.[172] However, if a child possesses a body of knowledge, for instance about cars, which enables him or her to organise information systematically, he or she may well be more accurate describing a car than an adult without such knowledge.[173] More significantly, observation of and ability to recall details depend very much on how important the event was to the child. Being immediately involved in it has a far deeper impression on the memory than when the child is merely a bystander.[174]

Children are quicker to forget than adults, and so the younger they are, the faster the memory fades[175]; this means that the departure from the principle of orality with regard to these young witnesses is entirely appropriate. The court otherwise merely deprives itself of the most accurate account. The risk that a child will forget important details means that it is vital that evidence be obtained shortly after the event; but it may be difficult for the child to describe it unaided. It has been shown that prompting can assist children to search their memories, since the questions asked can themselves organise their thinking. Marin's study[176] found that when structured questioning guided the children's efforts to remember, they were much closer to the adults in performance.[177] However, "structured questioning" is rather easier to achieve when the researcher knows the facts, as Marin's questioners did, and as Dr Jones did, when questioning Susie about what happened.[178] This raises the question of suggestion, particularly as Tschirgi has argued that people testing a hypothesis preferentially search for evidence which will support it.[179] It is extremely difficult to put questions non-suggestively where the inquisitor does not know what, if anything, happened. Dent found that a

---

[169] G. Davies and L. Brown, "Recall and Organization in Five Year Old Children" (1978) 69 *British Journal of Psychology* 343; N. Perry, "Child and Adolescent Development—a Psychological Perspective" in J.E.B. Myers (ed.), *Child Witnesses; Law and Practice* (Wiley, New York, 1987).

[170] Marin, Holmes, Guth and Kovac, n. 113 above. 295.

[171] Davies, Stevenson-Robb and Flin, n. 162 above.

[172] L. Brown, "Learning and Development: The Problem of Compatibility, Access and Induction" (1982) 25 *Human Development*, 89.

[173] *Ibid.*

[174] Goodman, Aman and Hirschman, n. 15 above.

[175] C. Brainerd, J. Kingma and M.J. Howe, "On the Development of Forgetting" (1985) 56 *Child Development* 1103.

[176] Marin, *et al.*, n. 170 above.

[177] Cf. S.J. Ceci, D.F. Ross and M.P. Toglia, "Suggestibility of Children's Memory; Psycho-legal Implications' (1987) 38 *Journal of Experimental Psychology* 116.

[178] Jones, n. 166 above.

[179] J.E. Tschirgi, "Sensible Reasoning: A Hypothesis about Hypotheses" (1980) 51 *Child Development* 1. See Hedderman, n. 164 above.

major problem in his experiment, where the interviewers did not know the facts, was their tendency, whatever their training, to reach a premature conclusion and then attempt to elicit confirmatory information from the young witnesses. In such cases were the least accurate descriptions obtained.[180] Leading questions are, of course, allowed as a last resort but sparingly, in the Memorandum of Good Practice. It may be the anxiety to avoid these that has led, apparently, the majority of interviewers to employ closed, single-response type questions despite Memorandum exhortations to ask open-ended questions.[181]

Whether or not children would invent stories of abuse of their own accord is a vexed question. The law has in the past been influenced by an instinctive feeling that the temptation to lie might be stronger for children than for adults. Professor Williams suggests[182] they might lie for reasons such as gaining attention or because of dislike of a step-parent or new "uncle". Spencer and Flin, arguing that children are unlikely to lie about abuse, suggest that children lie more usually to avoid trouble than to create it.[183] But it should be remembered that children often have different concerns from adults. There is a view that a child may go to extreme lengths to cover up behaviour for which they fear rebuke—for instance playing with children disapproved of by their parents, or accepting sweets from strangers, having been told not to do it—because they are unaware of the triviality of the incident about which they are concerned in comparison with the story they are telling.[184] There are claims that children of particular ages could not invent allegations of sexual abuse because they do not have the essential knowledge,[185] but this is doubted by the Royal College of Physicians.[186] It may be that there is a gap between what adults wish a small child to know and what is in fact gleaned from much older friends.[187] American research suggests that interviewing techniques for children may result in a large number of unfounded allegations, particularly in cases involving warring adults, such as custody or access disputes.[188] The problem with such claims is

---

[180] H.R. Dent, "The Effect of Interviewing Strategies on the Results of Interviews with Child Witnesses" in A. Trankell (ed.). *Restructuring the Past* (Kluwer, Deventer, 1982).

[181] Davies, Wilson *et al.*, n. 96 above.

[182] G. Williams, "Child Witnesses" in P. Smith (ed.), *Essays in Honour of J. C. Smith* (Butterworths, London, 1987).

[183] J. Spencer and R. Flin, "Child Witnesses—Are they Liars?" [1989] *NLJ* 1601.

[184] A. Trankell, "Was Lars Sexually Assaulted? A Study on the Reliability of Witnesses and of Experts" (1961) 56 *Journal of Abnormal Psychology*, 385.

[185] DHSS Paper, *Child Abuse—Working Together* (HMSO, London, 1991): "[a] child's statement that he or she is being abused should be accepted as true until proved otherwise. Children seldom lie about sexual abuse."

[186] Evidence to Butler-Sloss LJ, Cleveland Report, n. 53 above.

[187] E. Smith, "How to Deal with Children's Evidence" in Spencer, Nicholson, Flin and Bull (eds.), n. 57 above.

[188] D.C. Raskin and J.C. Yuille, "Problems in Evaluating Interviews of Children in Sexual Abuse Cases" in Ceci, Toglia and Ross (eds.), n. 167 above.

that it is extremely difficult to prove or disprove a tendency to lie. Yet there are assertions to the opposite effect, for instance, in the work of Jones and McGraw,[189] who estimate that only about 2 per cent of allegations by children of sexual abuse are false. The totality of the findings is inconclusive, to say the least, but there are two legitimate conclusions which may be drawn. The first is that it is no more possible to say that children are as reliable as adults than that they are not. The second is that, although opinions may vary as to whether children would or could spontaneously invent allegations of sexual abuse, there is some cause for concern about their vulnerability to suggestion, particularly where there is an adult with considerable opportunity to influence the child who has a motive for fostering a belief that abuse has occurred.

Identifying the cases where this has happened may be especially difficult, as there is evidence that adults have more trouble differentiating truthful from untruthful children when they are very young.[190] It is suggested[191] that it would be safer to rely on interview evaluation techniques such as Statement Validity Analysis, which test the contents of the child's statement against criteria based on findings that true statements share various characteristics.[192] Such assessment is employed in Canada,[193] the United States and Germany, where there are court psychologists to carry it out. Whether or not this is the way forward for us may be arguable, but judges should approve of the stance that there can be no initial assumptions about the credibility of a child who makes an allegation. One of the tests in Statement Validity Analysis is whether the statement accords with other evidence, including medical. Indeed, in certain civil cases, one problem was that expert conclusions on the matter of abuse were reached without any attempt to check the contents of the child's story against ascertainable facts. In *Re E*[194] there was ample independent evidence that the father worked in London during the week and could not have committed the acts of which he was accused. In *Re H and Re K*[195] the child referred to acts occurring while she and her father were "in their pyjamas" and on "Nona's bed", which could not have been true. In *Re G*[196] a boy's earlier statement was shown by a subsequent questioner to be unreliable by the simple means of asking him when and where the acts took place; his answers were fantastic. Butler-Sloss LJ stresses

[189] D.P. Jones and J.M. McGraw, "Reliable and Fictitious Accounts of Sexual Abuse in Children" (1987) 2 *Journal of Interpersonal Violence* 27.

[190] H. Westcott, G. Davies and B.R. Clifford, "Lying Smiles and Other Stories: Adults' Perceptions of Children's Truthful and Deceptive Statements", Paper presented at the First European Congress of Psychology, Amsterdam; cited by Davies, n. 168 above.

[191] For example by Davies, *ibid.*

[192] C.F. Faller, "Criteria for Judging the Credibility of Children's Statements about their Sexual Abuse", (1988) 67 *Child Welfare* 389.

[193] E.g. J.C. Yuille, "The Systematic Assessment of Children's Testimony" (1988) 29 *Canadian Psychology* 247.

[194] *The Times*, 2 Apr. 1990.   [195] [1989] 2 FLR 313.   [196] [1987] 1 FLR 310.

that adults as well as children must be interviewed to obtain background information,[197] but, although it is clearly vital that no conclusion is drawn before it is known, the Cleveland Report does not make it clear whether it should be known at the time of the interview itself. Specialists differ about the importance of this; the Great Ormond Street approach[198] now is to consult any available information before interviewing, but the NSPCC model[199] recommends interviewers to ignore it, in order to avoid forming preconceptions. Statement Validity Analysis would, *inter alia*, systematically test the contents of the child's statement, once made, against known facts in order to evaluate its reliability.

Competence and Compellability of Child Witnesses

It is now clear that the law sets no minimum age for child witnesses,[200] and that they are presumed to be competent[201] The test to be applied by the trial judge is contained in section 33A of the Criminal Justice Act 1988[202]:

"(1) A child's evidence in criminal proceedings shall be given unsworn.

(2) A deposition of a child's unsworn evidence may be taken for the purposes of criminal proceedings as if that evidence had been given on oath.

(2A) A child's evidence shall be received unless it appears to the court that the child is incapable of giving intelligible testimony.[203]

(3) In this section "child" means a person under fourteen years of age."

Hampshire[204] involved an alleged indecent assault on a girl of 5, S. The Court of Appeal held that the recorder was entitled to regard her as competent. In *DPP* v. *M*[205], it was held that the recorder at that trial should not have excluded the evidence of a child of five solely on the basis of her age without a preliminary investigation of the competency issue.

It is clear from Murray's research in Scotland[206] that individual judges have different expectations of the narrative abilities of children from particular age groups, and therefore it is reasonable to conclude that the court is neither the best assessor of, nor the ideal environment in which to estimate, a child's level of sophistication. Encouragingly, it has been recently established

---

[197] Cleveland Report, n. 53 above, 12.2–9.

[198] E. Vizard, "Interviewing Children Suspected of being Sexually Abused; A Review of Theory and Practice", in Hollins and Howells (eds.),n. 168 above.

[199] A. Bannister and B. Print, *A Model for Assessment of Interviews in Suspected Cases of Child Sexual Abuse*, NSPCC Occasional Paper No 4 (NSPCC, London, 1988).

[200] *Norbury* (1992) 95 Cr. App. R 256.

[201] *R*. v. *D*, [1995] 2 All ER 1019.

[202] Inserted by CJA 1991, s. 52(1).

[203] Amended by Criminal Justice and Public Order Act 1994, Sched. 9, para. 33.

[204] [1995] 2 All ER 1019.   [205] [1997] 2 All ER 749.

[206] K. Murray, *Live Television Link: An Evaluation of its Use by Child Witnesses in Scottish Criminal Trials* (Scottish Office Central Research Unit, HMSO, Edinburgh, 1995).

that in England the traditional preliminary inquiry conducted by the trial judge into the child's understanding, in order to see whether he or she is capable of giving sworn or unsworn evidence, is no longer obligatory in every case. In the leading case of *Hampshire*,[207] S was asked by the police interviewer at the end of the videotaped interview about the differences between telling a lie and telling the truth. The recorder watched the tape before the trial, and decided that it was admissible. At the trial, the tape was played to the court, after which the recorder realised that he had not investigated S's competence himself. So she was recalled, and in the presence of the jury was asked the difference between the truth and lies. The Court of Appeal held that there is no longer a duty on trial judges to conduct an inquiry of this kind into a child's competence, but there is a power to do so if it is considered necessary, for example if the child is very young or has difficulties in expression or understanding. The video alone will normally enable the judge to form a view on this, but if there is remaining doubt, there should be a preliminary investigation into the matter. Here, the recorder was entitled to decide that S was competent from the video alone. Earlier cases had insisted that where the preliminary discussion between the judge and the child is held, it should be conducted in the presence of the jury, but the Court of Appeal in *Hampshire* disagreed. Although it had been said in the past that observation of the discussion with the trial judge enabled the jury to assess how much weight to give the child's evidence, there was in fact ample opportunity to make that judgement when hearing the evidence itself. As with other witnesses, questions of competence can be investigated and ruled upon in the absence of the jury, but it should be in open court with the accused present.

Judges are no longer to required to put the child through a little interview; in the past, it was crucial to discover whether the child understood the difference between truth and lies. The test for competence is now intelligibility rather than an understanding of the importance of telling the truth[208]; judges should approach the matter on the basis laid down in *D*.[209] The test is whether the child is able to understand the questions put to him or her, to communicate and to give a coherent and comprehensible account of the matters in relation to which he or she is giving evidence. If a child, by reason of extreme youth or for any other reason, is unable to distinguish between truth and fiction or between fact and fantasy, then that child will be unable to give a coherent and comprehensible account of the matters in issue. "It is a matter of [the judge's] perception of the child's understanding demonstrated in the course of ordinary discourse."[210] However, a softly worded and spoken

---

[207] [1995] 2 All ER 1019.

[208] As required in the now repealed provisions of the Children and Young Persons Act 1933, s.38(1).

[209] [1995] 2 All ER 1019.

[210] *Hampshire*, [1995] 2 All ER 1019, *per* Auld J at 1026.

reminder to the child, in the presence of the jury, of the importance of telling the truth, may be appropriate.[211] In *DPP* v. *M*,[212] a 12-year-old was accused of indecent assault against a child at the time aged 4, who was aged 5^{1}/2 by time of trial. There were objections from the defence to the admission of the video in evidence, partly because of her age and partly because of the risk of contamination from the various members of the family with whom she discussed events. In the Court of Appeal, Phillips LJ stressed that the new provisions are mandatory.[213] If the assessment of competence could not be made from the videos alone because there was an objection to their admissibility, the recorder should have questioned the child and not simply have excluded the evidence solely on the grounds of the child's age. If a child satisfies the competence test, the judge has no discretion to exclude his or her evidence, and the question whether he or she is telling the truth is a matter for the jury.

Generally, child witnesses are 4 or 5 years old at the youngest, but there have been child witnesses of 3 in cases of "same abuse", where older siblings gave evidence. The difficulties surrounding the treatment of child witnesses who are very young should not, however, distract courts from the fact that the evidence of older children may present pitfalls. In *Sharman*,[214] the defendant was convicted on two counts of indecent assault, two counts of gross indecency with a child, one count of attempted rape and two counts of rape. The evidence in chief of one of the witnesses consisted in part of the contents of a videorecorded interview which took place when she was 13, but she gave additional evidence orally, by live link. She was at no stage sworn, nor did she affirm, although, as it emerged on appeal, she was aged 14 by time of trial. The seriousness of the error prompted the Court of Appeal to quash the conviction and order a retrial.

Although with an adult witness competence normally implies compellability, under pain of imprisonment for contempt of court, the notion clearly sits awkwardly in the case of child witnesses, particularly as the minimum age for conviction of a criminal offence is 10, and some witnesses are younger than that. At the same time, however, judges are reluctant to be thwarted by a child who declines to appear, especially as refusal by a young child is likely to be parent-led. In *R.* v. *Liverpool City Magistrates' Court, ex p. Pollock*,[215] an important witness to alleged domestic violence was aged only 7. The mother refused to let the child attend court. The stipendiary magistrate considered that the court must balance the best interests of justice

---

[211] *Ibid.*; this echoes the provision of the Memorandum which suggests that a child should be made aware, in as sensitive a fashion as possible, of the importance of the truth.

[212] [1997] 2 All ER 749.

[213] Apart from the possible application of the discretion to exclude on the basis of unfairness under s.78 of the Police and Criminal Evidence Act 1984 (see Ch. 6).

[214] *The Times* 18 Dec. 1997.

[215] Unreported, 14 Mar. 1997.

against the best interests of the child, and refused to issue a warrant, but in the Queen's Bench Division Curtis J doubted whether such a discretion existed. Even if it did, since the only effect of a warrant would be to ensure the child's attendance at court, it should be issued. The court then should assess the situation and take steps to mitigate any problems flowing from its decision. In the civil jurisdiction, however, there certainly is a judicial discretion. The court will not order the attendance of a witness where it would be oppressive or contrary to the welfare of the child. Age is a relevant factor here.[216]

Experts in Child Witness Cases

The criminal court does not require expert assistance on the issue of a child's competence. In *G* v. *DPP*,[217] psychiatrists were instructed by either side to test the children before trial by discussing hypothetical cases with them. Phillips LJ described the procedure as a complete waste of money; it might also be thought to be an unnecessary source of extra stress on the child. The question is simply one of intelligibility, and the judge is able to assess that. Although *DPP* v. *A&BC Chewing Gum*[218] might be thought to suggest that child development is an area of special expertise, criminal courts are very wary of expert witnesses advising magistrates and jurors on the credibility of a child witness. In *R.* v. *D*,[219] Swinton-Thomas LJ explained:

"It is fundamental that experts must not usurp the function of the jury in a criminal trial. Save in particular circumstances, it is the function of the jury to make judgments on the questions of reliability and truthfulness. Particular circumstances arise where there are characteristics of a medical nature in the make-up of the witness, such as mental illness, which could not be known to the jury without expert assistance. These circumstances do not arise in the case of ordinary children who are not suffering from any abnormality. It may well be open to parties in a particular case to call general expert evidence in relation to the Cleveland guidelines and, for example, to tell the judge or jury that over interviewing as a matter of generality has been shown to have a much more adverse effect on children than on adults, but the witness cannot express an opinion whether a particular child is a reliable or truthful witness. That is precisely the province of the jury in a criminal case, or the judge when considering the admissibility of evidence . . ."[220]

It is common to find experts assisting the civil courts on the matter of the credibility of child witnesses, however. Previous uncertainty as to how close the expert can come to the ultimate issue has been resolved in *Re M and R*

---

[216] *Re P* [1987] 2 FLR 447.   [217] [1997] 2 All ER 755.
[218] [1968] 1 QB 159. For admissibility of expert evidence, see text to nn. 234–278 below.
[219] *The Times*, 15 Nov. 1995.
[220] Quoted with approval in *G* v. *DPP* [1997] 2 All ER 755, 759.

(minors) (sexual abuse: expert evidence).[221] The Court of Appeal took the point that the 1972 Civil Evidence Act[222] allows expert evidence on any issue. Earlier cases[223] which sought to prevent experts from stating that they believed or disbelieved the child's complaint were dismissed as *per incuriam* because the effect of the Civil Evidence Act had not been argued before the court. A judge is perfectly capable of hearing, and disagreeing with, expert evidence on the ultimate issue.

Other vunerable witnesses

Here the Pigot Report was a grave disappointment, in that without apparent reason it concentrated on the problems of child witnesses in particular, unnecessarily[224] leaving other vulnerable witnesses to one side. The hothouse atmosphere surrounding the issue of child abuse should not blind lawyers to the fact that there are other witnesses who may be at least as vulnerable as children. The predicament of rape complainants, addressed above, would clearly be eased by applying the proposals to them.

> "[They] will do so only where the circumstances clearly require them both in the interests of justice and in the interests of the witnesses themselves. Such caution will, we think, impose its own restrictions, but will do so more flexibly and more appropriately than would be the case if somewhat arbitrary restrictions were to be imposed by statute.[225]"

A neglected group of victim-witnesses easily as vulnerable as children are the mentally handicapped. Vizard has shown that there is a reluctance to accept that symptoms of abuse indicate adult interference, placing the mentally handicapped in a position previously occupied by battered wives and children, who were similarly the subjects of denial by society.[226] The problems of the mentally handicapped in communicating their distress and describing their experiences can be just as acute; if in institutions, it seems that they may be just as vulnerable to physical and sexual abuse as children.[227] There may be communication difficulties more difficult to overcome than is the case with children, particularly as the reaction to abuse

---

[221] [1996] 4 All ER 239.   [222] S.3.

[223] E.g., *Re N (a minor: child abuse: evidence)* [1994] 4 All ER 225.

[224] The Home Secretary's letter of invitation does not so limit the Committee's scope.

[225] Scottish Law Commission, *Report on the Evidence of Children and other Potentially Vulnerable Witnesses* (Scot. Law Com. No 125, HMSO, Edinburgh, 1989), para. 5.19.

[226] E. Vizard, "Child Sexual Abuse and Mental Handicap: A Child Psychiatrist's Perspective", in S.M. Brown and A. Craft (eds.), *Thinking the Unthinkable; Papers on Sexual Abuse and People with Learning Difficulties* (FPA Education Unit, London, 1989).

[227] V. Sinason, "Uncovering and Responding to Sexual Abuse in Psychotherapeutic Settings" in Brown and Craft (eds.), n. 226 above.

may involve withdrawal, creating the impression of a more severe handicap than is in fact the case.[228] The disclosure techniques used with young children—play and the use of anatomical dolls—may be necessary to uncover abuse. The additional problem of competence[229], which could be alleviated, although not solved, by the Pigot proposals, exacerbates the problem of proof, as does the obligation to warn the jury about the reliability of those of defective intellect.[230] Although it was thought that the mentally handicapped were poor at retaining information over time,[231] it subsequently appeared that, as with children, difficulties related to the level of initial understanding of the event itself, rather than to deficiencies in memory capacity.[232] The court would inevitably benefit in these cases from the assistance of an expert in interpreting the witness's behaviour; there is no legal authority against it, as long as the expert does not usurp the function of the court by expressing an opinion on whether or not abuse took place. In New Zealand mentally handicapped complainants in sexual cases may avail themselves of screens, audio links, closed circuit television and videotaped interviews. The Law Commission there has recommended that these facilities be extended where appropriate to other kinds of case to increase the likelihood that that all relevant evidence is available to the court.[233]

Expert witnesses

The admissibility of expert opinion

There can be no doubt that courts could improve their assessment of child and mentally handicapped complainants by allowing experts to explain how their memories work; this is permissible under current case law, but the fact that witnesses are called by the parties, and that therefore the expert has been selected because of the compatibility of his or her views with the arguments to be put forward by that party, undermines the authority with which they speak. Anecdotal tales of American trials being dominated by queues of "hired gun" expert witnesses lined up for either side have led not to judges questioning the wisdom of a trial structure under which there is no other means of hearing expert evidence, but to a reluctance to allow experts to

---

[228] *Ibid.*

[229] M. Gunn, "Sexual Abuse and Adults with Mental Handicap; Can the Law Help?" in Brown and Craft (eds.), n. 226 above.

[230] *Ibid.*

[231] N.R. Ellis, "The Stimulus Trace and Behavioural Inadequacy" in N.R. Ellis (ed.), *Handbook of Mental Deficiency* (McGraw-Hill, New York, 1963).

[232] J.M. Belmont and E.C.Butterfield, "Learning Strategies as Determinants of Memory Deficiencies" (1971) 2 *Cognitive Psychology* 411.

[233] New Zealand Law Commission, *The Evidence of Children and Other Vulnerable Witnesses: A Discussion Paper*, Law Commission of New Zealand, Preliminary Paper 26 (New Zealand Law Commission, Wellington, 1997).

express opinions except within narrowly and obscurely drawn limits. Judicial restrictiveness is particularly noticeable in the cases concerning expert evidence on the credibility of witnesses. This field which, naturally, is the domain of the "trick cyclists"[234] is wide open to the scepticism and disdain of lawyers.

> "The fact that an expert witness has impressive scientific qualifications does not by that fact alone make his opinion on matters of human nature and behaviour within the limits of normality any more helpful than that of the jurors themselves; but there is a danger that they may think that it does . . . Jurors do not need psychiatrists to tell them how ordinary folk who are not suffering from any mental illness are likely to react to the stresses and strains of life."[235]

Thus psychiatrists may not explain what the effect of provocative acts would be on a "normal" person,[236] nor may they give an opinion on whether there was intention behind such a person's act.[237] Where he or she has an expertise outside the experience of the tribunal of fact, as a psychiatrist has with the defences of diminished responsibility[238] or insanity,[239] the expert may express an opinion on the ultimate issue, but only on the presence or absence and nature of the condition in question. In *Toohey* v. *MPC*,[240] medical evidence was held by the House of Lords to be admissible to show that a witness's own hysterical personality was as likely to have caused his hysteria as the defendant's alleged attack, but not whether the witness could be believed on oath or not. On the other hand, if there were a disease present that actually prevented a witness from telling the truth, then the condition should be brought to the notice of the court.[241] The difficulty of drawing the line between evidence of credibility and evidence on the issue at trial may be seen in *Re S and B.*[242] A psychiatric social worker could legitimately describe the witness's illness, which involved a tendency to fantasise, and express the belief that the witness's claim to have been abused as a child herself was true. But, even as an expert witness, she could not go on to say that she believed the witness's evidence in the case, namely an allegation that her brother had

---

[234] Psychiatrists and psychologists are still so regarded in certain quarters of the legal profession: G. Clapham, "Introducing Psychological Evidence in the Courts: Impediments and Opportunities" in S. Lloyd-Bostock (ed.), *Psychology in Legal Contexts* (Macmillan, London, 1981).

[235] Lawton LJ in *Turner* [1975] 1 All ER 70, 74.

[236] *Ibid.*

[237] *Chard* (1971) 56 Cr. App. R 268.

[238] *Matheson* (1958) 42 Cr. App. R 145; an opinion on the ultimate issue is in strict theory inadmissible, but allowed in such cases "time and again without any objection": Lord Parker CJ in *DPP* v. *A and BC Chewing Gum* [1968] 1 QB 159.

[239] *Holmes* [1953] 1 WLR 686.

[240] [1965] AC 595.

[241] Compare *MacKenny* (1981) 72 Cr App R 78; May J refused to allow a psychologist to say that the principal prosecution witness was a psycopath and therefore highly likely to lie.

[242] *The Independent*, 1 June 1990.

abused his children. In general, the credibility of witnesses cannot be supported by "oath-helpers", even if there is a risk that testimony might be disbelieved because of their innate limitations. In *Robinson*,[243] a fifteen year old complainant in a rape case was alleged to have the mental capacity of a seven or eight year old. It was held on appeal that expert evidence to the effect that she was not unusually suggestible could not be led by the prosecution as part of their case in chief in the absence of a defence allegation to the contrary in cross-examination.

An interesting facet of the case law in this area is that an expert may give evidence on personality only if the personality in question is unusual or abnormal. Whether there is a disorder of the nature claimed is for the judge to decide. This means that it is possible for judges to operate a legal definition of mental abnormality which may have little to do with psychiatric assessment. For example, in *Reynolds*,[244] the court rejected expert evidence on a person who allegedly could not separate fantasy from reality. In *Weightman*,[245] the same fate befell expert evidence on the nature of a histrionic personality disorder. Yet in the well-known case of *Lowery*,[246] the Privy Council approved the admission of evidence of the sadistic tendency of one co-defendant and the passive dependent personality of the other, the object of which was to suggest that the first led the other into murder.[247] In *Masih*[248] the Court of Appeal upheld the trial judge's refusal to admit expert evidence on the mental capacity of a man with an IQ of 72 (the boundary between dull-normal and subnormal intelligence) on the issue of his alleged recklessness; if the defendant had had an IQ of 69 or less (mental defective) the evidence might have been admissible. However, in *Silcott and others*[249] Hodgson J acknowledged the arbitrariness of this approach, and it was held that expert evidence was admissible on the issue of the psychological effect of interview conditions on a teenager with a mental age of 7 and an IQ of between 70 and 80.

The Court of Appeal to some extent clarified matters in *Ward*[250]; evidence of a psychologist or psychiatrist is admissible on the issue of the reliability of a confession, if its reliability is alleged to be affected by mental illness or by a personality disorder so severe as to be categorised as a mental disorder. However, whether or not the alleged condition constitutes such a disorder is still a decision for the trial judge; before it can be decided whether the evidence is admissible, the judge may first have to decide upon the nature of an alleged illness. Obscure or recently-identified conditions are less likely

---

[243] [1994] 3 All ER 346.   [244] [1989] Crim. LR 220.   [245] (1990) 92 Cr. App. R 291.
[246] [1974] AC 85.
[247] Decided on its own special facts, according to Lawton LJ in *Turner*; a cynic might regard it as significant that, unusually, deciding that the evidence was admissible enabled the conviction to be upheld.
[248] [1986] Crim. LR 393.   [249] [1987] Crim. LR 765 [1988] Crim. LR 293.
[250] [1993] 2 All ER 537.

than familiar ones to be regarded as genuine fields of expertise. Psychiatrists constantly complain that judges think they know more about psychiatry than they do. The reality appears to be that judges have invented techniques for excluding experts whom they do not trust. There is a select band of expert witnesses including psychiatrists who are known to the judges and are treated with enormous respect. The whole problem is a result of judicial fear of the "hired gun" syndrome, and could be avoided completely by detaching expert witnesses from the interests of the parties to the cause.

The amount of weight attached by courts to expert evidence probably depends on the tribunal and the issue. Courts with no claim to superior expertise are entitled to reject even unanimous expert opinion[251]; jurors may choose to rely on their own view of the defendant's mental state in a diminished responsibility case notwithstanding the view of all the psychiatrists called,[252] depending on their own assessment from his performance in court (even unsworn), the circumstances of the killing and his conduct at the time. This has led to the curious fact that "sympathy" cases such as mercy killing are more likely to result in a diminished responsibility verdict than horrific crimes such as those of Peter Sutcliffe (the Yorkshire Ripper), who was found to be insane by every psychiatrist who saw him. In a study where half the subjects, who all acted as jurors in mock trials, heard psychological evidence on the weakness of identifications and the other half did not, the first half were more reluctant to believe the identification witness. But they were no better at discriminating between accurate and inaccurate testimony.[253] It seems that the expert evidence there was too non-specific; what was needed was more individualised opinion as to who was most likely to be reliable— the very ground into which experts are not allowed to tread.

Appropriateness of Adversarial Process

The most common complaint of experienced forensic scientists and psychiatrists who act as expert witnesses is the way that counsel can use his or her ability to control what they say in court. The witness depends on counsel to ask the right question; this presupposes that counsel has a grasp of the scientific issues involved—increasingly difficult in view of the pace of technological development. The accuracy of the evidence may be undermined if the witness is not allowed to qualify or explain his answer; expert witnesses are frequently cut off precisely because the qualification is unhelpful to counsel's case, and some advocates insist on "Yes" and "No" answers which are entirely misleading in areas of complexity. It has been said that lawyers love to emphasise the witness's expertise in glowing terms, thus making it psychologically

---

[251] *Lanfear* [1968] 1 All ER 683.

[252] *Walton* v. *R* [1978] 1 All ER 542.

[253] G.L. Wells, R.C.L. Lindsay and J. Tousignant, "Effects of Expert Psychological Advice on Testimony" (1980) 4 *Law and Human Behaviour* 275.

difficult for him or her to admit that he or she does not know the answer.[254]
There are other well-known tricks; one is to ask the witness whether he knows
a particular book (usually old and obscure), pour scorn on him if he has not
heard of it, read aloud apparently contradictory passages out of context and
then ask him to explain them. Others include humiliation, even going so far
as demanding to inspect a doctor's extremely grubby handkerchief, bullying,
complaining if the witness cannot be more precise when it would be wrong to
do so, calling an expert who uses entirely inappropriate techniques which
yield no result and suggesting that therefore there is something suspect about
a technique which does, and translating testimony into simpler language
which makes it sound absurd.[255] Although lawyers may reply that expert
witnesses are often well paid for their pains, the hostile reception from lawyers
to their evidence and the resultant publicity has made some experts reluctant
to have anything at all to do with cases such as child abuse.[256]

The expert witness for the defence at the trial of the Maguire Seven had
previously worked at the Royal Armaments Research and Development
Establishment, which employed the prosecution expert witnesses.
Nevertheless, he was subjected to a stinging cross-examination by Sir
Michael Havers QC, which attacked both his professional competence and
his honesty. He was accused of being selective with the facts to prove the
defence case; in fact, it was the prosecution expert witnesses who were doing
that. The witness was severely undermined by this; he became hesitant and
confused. The result was disastrous. Defence lawyers became aware of a vital
piece of scientific evidence which would have sunk the prosecution case
without trace. They felt unable to exploit it to that effect because it would
require their expert witness to go back into the witness box, the scene of his
earlier humiliation. Instead, they struck a deal with the prosecution which
meant that the evidence had little impact on the trial.[257]

A major problem in an adversarial procedure is that since experts are
initially instructed by one side or the other,[258] there is a danger that experts
for each side will form an allegiance with their client and lose detachment,[259] The most notorious example of bias in a civil case is *Vernon* v.
Bosley (No 2),[260] in which mental health professionals were severely criti-

---

[254] G.H. Gudjonsson, "The Psychology of False Confessions" (1989) 57 *Medico-Legal Journal* 93.

[255] See e.g. L.R. Haward, *Forensic Psychology* (Batsford, London, 1981).

[256] Vizard, n. 108 above.

[257] Sir John May, *Return to an Address of the Honourable the House of Commons Dated 30 June 1994 for a Report of the Inquiry into the Circumstances Surrounding the Convictions arising out of the Bomb Attacks on Guildford and Woolwich in 1974: Final Report* (HMSO, London, 1994).

[258] Albeit that they may have to acquire a loftily detached position later on, see text to nn. 269–271 below.

[259] E.g., see Lord Taylor of Gosforth CJ commenting that during his career at the Bar, he frequently encountered experts who would ask at conference, "What do you want me to say?"(The Lund Lecture (1995) 35 *Med Sci Law* 3, 5).

[260] [1997] 1 All ER 614.

cised by the Court of Appeal. The case originally sprang from the tragic deaths of Mr Vernon's two daughters. The defendant, the children's nanny, admitted negligence but disputed the scale of damages sought.[261] The dispute centred on the plaintiff's claim that post-traumatic stress disorder had rendered him incapable not only of working, but of looking after himself. This contention was supported by expert evidence from a clinical psychologist and a consultant psychiatrist. The trial involved a mass of detailed evidence, and so the judge, Sedley J, delayed giving judgment. In the meantime, Mr Vernon, who was engaged in a matrimonial dispute, called the same two expert witnesses to give evidence in the Family Court that he was capable of looking after his children. The medical evidence was that he was unexpectedly much recovered from his severe depression. However, neither Miss Bosley's lawyers nor Sedley J were informed of this, and she was duly ordered to pay damages of £1.3 million. By the time the negligence case came before the Court of Appeal, however, the information had (somewhat mysteriously) come into the hands of Miss Bosley's legal team; at the appeal stage, the experts modified their evidence yet again. The Court of Appeal ruled that expert witnesses have a continuing duty to disclose a change of opinion, even after evidence has been given in court, if it is so fundamental as to alter a material fact on which a client's case is based. The court denounced the excessive loyalty these experts afforded their client. Attention was drawn to:

"The readiness of [the expert witnesses] to do their best to present the plaintiff's condition on different dates in different proceedings in the light that seemed most helpful to the immediate cause, ignoring their equal or greater duty to the court."[262]

Judges have recently taken steps to emphasise the overriding duty of the expert witness, which is to the court,[263] particularly in cases concerning the welfare of children.[264] Here it has been spelled out that not only must entirely honest opinions be presented, but evidence should be properly researched,[265] and, if insufficient data are available to support a conclusion, the witness must say so. Hypothetical opinions must be clearly presented as such. All material must be made available to other expert witnesses in the case.[266]

"For whatever reason, whether consciously or unconsciously, the fact is that expert witnesses instructed on behalf of the parties to litigation often tend to espouse the cause of those instructing them to a greater or lesser extent, on occasion becoming more partisan than the parties."[267]

---

[261] *Vernon v. Bosley (No 1)* [1997] 1 All ER 577.

[262] *Vernon v. Bosley* (No 2) [1997] 1 All ER 614, *per* Thorpe LJ at 647.

[263] *Whitehouse v. Jordan* [1981] 1 WLR 246.

[264] *Re R (a minor) (expert evidence)* [1991] 1 FLR 293.

[265] In other varieties of cases, opponents must rely on cross-examination to discredit expert evidence.

[266] *Re AB (child abuse) (expert witness)* [1995] 1 FLR 181.

[267] *Abbey National Mortgages plc v. Key Surveyors Nationwide Ltd* [1996] EGCS 23.

From the other side, it has been claimed that it is common for solicitors to apply improper pressure on experts.[268]

Lord Woolf in his Report observed that it runs contrary to the principles of proportionality and access to justice to have an expensive support industry consisting of highly-paid expert witnesses.[269] When in 1992, a test case was brought against British Nuclear Fuels to recover damages in respect of the death from leukaemia of a child living near one of their nuclear plants, 50 experts were called as witnesses. The costs are prohibitive for many prospective litigants. Lord Woolf observes: "The purpose of the adversarial system is to achieve just results. All too often it is used by one party or the other to achieve something which is inconsistent with justice by taking advantage of the other side's lack of resources or ignorance of relevant fact or opinions".[270] Although the number of experts required to some extent depends upon the number and complexity of the scientific issues in the case, the Report suggests that in some instances the number could be drastically reduced.

The Woolf Report recognises that when scientific evidence is highly technical, it is far from clear that the just result is achieved by allowing a judge to choose between two conflicting views.[271] Although the recommendation is that the benefits of the adversarial system should be retained, the features which make adversarial trials the inappropriate forum for the presentation and analysis of scientific evidence should be reformed. The Report recommends that judges, taking much greater control than before of civil litigation, should be able to restrict the number of experts called and direct that they meet beforehand to identify and possibly reduce the number of areas of disagreement. The judge should be able to order the parties to supply lists of names of potential expert witnesses for the judge to choose from. The court should be allowed to insist on the selection of only one single expert who could inform the court of all relevant shades of opinion. This would mean that the witness should not feel impelled to adopt the extreme position many experts currently feel forced to adopt, or choose to adopt.

It is curious to note that the Royal Commission on Criminal Justice rejected the suggestion that the court should be able to influence the choice of expert witnesses, a notion that seems to be regarded as acceptable in civil cases. Yet the relevant fields of expertise in civil cases could be far more esoteric. The Commission opted instead for limited case management, recommending pre-trial dialogue between prosecution and defence expert witnesses, who should make a genuine effort to reduce areas of contention.[272] These matters would be discussed with the judge at a prepara-

---

[268] *Access to Justice: final report by Lord Woolf MR, to the Lord Chancellor on the civil justice system in England and Wales* (HMSO, London, 1996) para. 13.25.

[269] *Ibid.*   [270] *Ibid.*, para. 13.7.   [271] *Ibid.*

[272] A potentially alarming situation for their respective lawyers, who may not be able to prevent damaging concessions being made: P. Roberts, *Just Science? A Critical Review of the Royal Commission's Recommendations on Forensic Science and Other Expert Evidence* (University of Nottingham Department of Law, 1994).

tory hearing; agreement could be reached on any further tests which might be needed. The experts might in a position to produce a joint report for the court.[273] Certainly reduction of the impact of the gladiatorial ethic of adversarial procedures upon expert witnesses would be beneficial. It has in the past led experts to identify themselves with the prosecution so that the police were not informed of adverse results—the government research scientists had convinced themselves that these were irrelevant.[274] A more neutral police culture clearly would assist greater scientific objectivity in forensic testing by government scientists during criminal investigations. That would also support the Royal Commission's preferred solution to the acknowledged problems faced by defence lawyers seeking to instruct expert witnesses,[275] namely, to facilitate greater defence access to the central forensic facility—an establishment which is treated with suspicion by some defence lawyers because of its involvement with the notorious miscarriage of justice cases.[276]

Co-operation at present seems to be only an ideal. The Crown Court Study[277] found that defence lawyers frequently failed to comply with the defence duties of disclosure in relation to expert evidence.[278] This study found also, as did the Bristol Study,[279] that defence lawyers and courts were frequently inconvenienced by late or non-disclosure of forensic evidence by prosecutors. Again, attempts to achieve rational decision-making by informed tribunals assisted by transparent procedures appear to be thwarted by circumstances, particularly the inability of the criminal justice system to conform to timetables.

---

[273] *Report of the Royal Commission on Criminal Justice* (chairman Viscount Runciman) (HMSO, London, 1993), Cm 2263, para. 9.63.

[274] Sir John May, *Return to an Address of the Honourable the House of Commons Dated 30 June 1994 for a Report of the Inquiry into the Circumstances Surrounding the Convictions arising out of the Bomb Attacks on Guildford and Woolwich in 1974: Final Report* (HMSO, London, 1994).

[275] P. Roberts and C. Willmore, *The Role of Forensic Science Evidence in Criminal Proceedings*, Royal Commission on Criminal Justice Research Study No 11 (HMSO, London, 1993).

[276] Following these recommendations, the Forensic Science Service became an independent agency, and has to compete for police business. It now treats defence reports as confidential, and in recent years gained 20% of the market for defence work: R. Bramley, "Developments in Forensic Science", Judicial Seminar, Crown Court, Stafford, 1 June 1998.

[277] M. Zander and P. Henderson, *Crown Court Study*, Royal Commission on Criminal Justice Research Study 19 (HMSO, London, 1993).

[278] Crown Court (Advance Notice of Expert Evidence) Rules 1987 (SI 1987 No 716).

[279] Roberts and Willmore, n. 275 above.

5

The Accused In
The Criminal Trial

Not an Ordinary Witness

The principles which normally apply to adversarial trials are modified in the case of someone facing trial for a criminal offence. The accused's position is also to some extent protected by the operation of the presumption of innocence; other qualifications of adversarial theory may flow from recognition that defendants are not voluntary participants in the proceedings, and therefore it would be unfair to treat them as free agents. The defence duty to disclose evidence has been, as we have seen in Chapter 1, considerably increased, but is still less onerous than that of the prosecution. Other limitations upon the duty to disclose depend upon the common law privileges, such as the privilege against self-incrimination, a principle of confidentiality where it is in the public interest, and legal professional privilege.

There can be no doubt that in some cases legally privileged material could be of probative value but is excluded from the trial. Privilege operates only to resist discovery[1] of documents and privileged material. It is admissible if it comes into the hands of the other party by any means; the holder of the privilege can recover his material or restrain its use in breach of confidence at any point during the case.[2] No privilege, however, attaches to information in the hands of a lawyer which is actually held to further some criminal purpose,[3] but if a lawyer hears his client confess to the crime charged, that revelation is entirely confidential.[4] If the client changes his or her story a dozen times, a fact which would be suggestive of unreliability were the court to hear of it, the defence lawyer may not disclose it. On the other hand, there is a principle that legal professional privilege cannot be invoked where to allow it would prejudice the case of an accused person—an indication of the

[1] Being required to hand over documentation prior to trial.
[2] *Nationwide* v. *Goddard* [1986] 3 WLR 734; although the exercise of the court's power to order an injunction may not in fact be automatic: *per* Scott J in *Webster* v. *James Chapman & Co. (a firm) et al* [1989] 3 All ER 939.
[3] Police and Criminal Evidence Act 1984 (PACE), s.10(2).
[4] Counsel should not represent his client on a plea of not guilty in such a case.

imbalance of procedural rights at criminal trials which follows from the presumption of innocence. But the principle was watered down recently by the Court of Appeal in a case where the competing interests were those of two co-defendants. In *Ataou*,[5] H, originally a co-defendant, gave evidence against the defendant on a charge of conspiracy to supply heroin. At first, the alleged conspirators had shared the same solicitor, who still represented Ataou. A member of the firm passed a note to counsel during the trial to the effect that H had told his original solicitor that Ataou was not involved. The trial judge refused counsel leave to cross-examine H on his previous inconsistent statement, since he declined to waive his privilege. The Court of Appeal quashed Ataou's conviction, not because the questions should necessarily have been allowed, but because the judge had failed to recognise that each case requires a balancing of competing public interests; the due and orderly administration of justice against the production of all evidence supporting the defence. The Court of Appeal did take note of the fact that H had already pleaded guilty and therefore was unlikely to be prejudiced by such a breach of confidence. There has been criticism of this case on the ground that it is entirely inappropriate to balance against the risk of convicting the innocent the somewhat nebulous public interest in a general freedom to communicate in confidence with one's lawyers.[6]

The existence of a privilege in relation to lawyer–client communications could be seen as a reinforcement of the adversarial pattern of trial; free from any obligation to disclose what their clients tell them, lawyers can prepare a case for trial with as much of a "surprise" element as they can muster. It is entirely up to the other side to gather its own evidence in support of its case, therefore it cannot expect to rely on its opponents' lawyers to provide it for it. (The usual justification for the privilege, that clients would not be frank with their lawyers without it, is not supported by any known evidence.) However, Continental jurisdictions such as Germany adopt a similar approach in relation to communications between lawyer and client in order to encourage frankness and thereby to enhance the effectiveness of legal advice. Also, the House of Lords has recently affirmed the importance of legal professional privilege even in care proceedings, which are non-adversarial, even, apparently, if the welfare of the child might be threatened by treating admissions as confidential.[7]

The privilege against self-incrimination may have its roots in the right of accused persons to remain silent.[8] It may be the rationale of the rather mysterious terms of section 1(e) of the Criminal Evidence Act 1898:

---

[5] [1988] 2 All ER 321.

[6] M.J. Allen, "Legal Privilege and the Accused: An Unfair Balancing Act'"[1988] *NLJ* 668.

[7] *Re L* [1996] 2 All ER 78; however, "litigation privilege" (attaching to third party reports commissioned by a solicitor on behalf of a client) does not apply in care proceedings.

[8] L.W. Levy, *Origins of the 5th. Amendment* (Oxford University Press, Oxford, New York, 1968); doubted M. MacNair, "The Early Development of the Privilege Against Self-incrimination" (1990) 10 *OJLS* 66.

"A person charged and being a witness . . . may be asked any question in cross-examination notwithstanding that it might tend to criminate him as to the offence charged."

The simplest interpretation of this provision is that once accused persons elect to exercise the right, bestowed by section 1(1), to give evidence in their own defence, they may not pick and choose which questions they will answer solely on the ground that to do so would not serve the interests of their case. The provision may have been thought necessary because otherwise the privilege against self-incrimination might have been invoked (although probably unsuccessfully), or because in Continental trials, which have no general right to silence, a defendant *can* decline to answer any question he chooses. Section 1(e) ensures that, in this respect at least, an accused person in the witness box is in the same position as other witnesses.[9]

The Right to Silence

Silence during investigation

The right to silence during interrogation and the right to choose whether or not to give evidence could be seen as applications of adversarial principles. There can be no duty on adversaries to supply explanations unless they choose to do so. The old common law principle *nemo debet se prodere ipsum*[10] was said in *Sang*[11] to incorporate the right to silence. It involves more than simply the right not to make oral reply. All evidence obtained from the person, including samples of hair, bodily fluids and fingerprints, is included. The Royal Commission on Criminal Justice, despite its concern that abolition or modification of the right to silence could put unfair pressure on suspects to talk in police stations,[12] was nevertheless content with the provision that allows "such inferences as appear proper" to be drawn from an arrested suspect's refusal without good cause to consent to intimate samples being taken from his or her body.[13] In conjunction with the power to take non-intimate samples[14] and fingerprints[15] without the suspect's consent, this erosion of the right to silence demonstrates that it is not regarded as absolute. Derogations from the right have tended to be justified on pragmatic grounds, the foremost of which is that convictions of the

---

[9] See discussion of s.1(e) in the text to nn. 130–131 below.

[10] No one should be forced to condemn himself out of his own mouth.

[11] [1980] AC 402.

[12] *Report of the Royal Commission on Criminal Justice*, (Runciman Report) (HMSO, London, 1993), Cm 2263, 4.

[13] S.62(10) of PACE; according to the Report, the evidence provided by the samples may be as probative of innocence as guilt, or may establish the innocence of others (*ibid.*, 14).

[14] S.62.

[15] S.61 of PACE.

guilty are too difficult to achieve if suspects are entitled not to co-operate with investigations.

Given the utilitarian approach, it is perhaps not surprising that the right to refuse to answer questions was effectively removed in the case of serious and company frauds—cases which may not be the most heinous of crimes, but may be particularly difficult to unravel. The Department of Trade and Industry can demand that persons attend, answer questions, furnish information and produce documents[16]; the sanction is punishment for contempt of court.[17] These powers, however, have recently been held to infringe the right not to be forced to incriminate oneself under the European Convention on Human Rights.[18] The Serious Fraud Office has rather less sweeping powers, but can demand attendance before the Director and a description of the location of documents. Failure to comply is an offence,[19] but the intervention of the European Court of Human Rights is less likely in respect of these provisions since the evidence supplied under these powers normally cannot be used as evidence in criminal proceedings.

In Northern Ireland the right to silence during interrogations and the right of defendants not to give evidence at their trials was dramatically curtailed. This was especially controversial, since it was done by statutory instrument and therefore without full Parliamentary debate.[20] Similar provisions now apply to England and Wales despite furious opposition to the reforms. Much of the debate, however, is curiously overheated; extreme statements which bear little proportion to the issue have been made by both sides. The right to remain silent represents to some a bastion of liberty, so that its removal would "dismantle the venerable fortress built by many generations of British lawyers to protect the innocent".[21] For the other side, spokesmen for the abolitionist school of thought have certainly exaggerated the extent to which the right to silence hampers criminal investigation. Sir Peter Imbert, the former Commissioner for the Metropolitan Police, said that abolition would be the most important single step legislators could take to control and reduce crime.[22] It appears to be virtually impossible to prove the contention, frequently made by police officers, that the right is used exclusively by guilty men and is effective in helping them avoid conviction.[23] In fact, there are grounds for believing that the "right to silence" has been of little practical importance.

---

[16] Companies Act 1985, ss. 431, 432 and 434, as amended by Companies Act 1989, s. 56.

[17] Companies Act 1985, s. 436.

[18] *Saunders* v. *UK*, *The Times* 18 Dec. 1996.

[19] Criminal Justice Act 1987, ss. 2–3.

[20] Criminal Evidence (Northern Ireland) Order 1988.

[21] M. Manfred Simon, letter to *The Times*, 5 Oct. 1972.

[22] *Daily Telegraph*, 16 Sept. 1987.

[23] See the debate on conviction rates of "professional criminals": M. Zander, "Are Too Many Professional Criminals Avoiding Conviction? A Study in Britain's Two Busiest Courts" (1974) 34 *MLR* 26; J.A. Mack, "Full-time Major Criminals and the Courts" (1976) 39 *MLR* 241.

Research shows few suspects availed themselves during questioning of the right to silence, even though the caution reminded them of it. American research suggests that suspects either take no notice of the caution or, hearing it, assume that the police know everything and confess at once.[24] Research carried out for the Policy Studies Institute in the early 1980s found that not one subject remained silent under questioning, and remarked that the caution had so little effect that there was no incentive for the police not to caution.[25] Other studies, carried out on behalf of Lord Phillips' Royal Commission on Criminal Procedure, also prior to PACE, confirmed that rarely did the caution encourage silence. About 12 per cent of those in the study exercised the right to some degree, but only 5 per cent of those aged under 17 did so.[26] Irving comments:

> "To remain silent in a police interview room in the face of determined questioning by an officer with legitimate authority to carry on his activity requires an abnormal exercise of will . . . When it does occur, the observer would be forgiven for making the fallacious assumption that the abnormal behaviour is associated with some significant cause (in this context guilt as opposed to innocence)."[27]

The irony is that it is the psychologically vulnerable suspects, who really ought to remain silent, are the least able to withstand the pressure and therefore most likely to incriminate themselves unwittingly. The psychological pressure was acknowledged in the Phillips Report, which concluded that, rather than remind a suspect of a right which it is almost impossible to exercise, it would be better to have safeguards designed to increase the reliability of what he says.[28] To this end, PACE reinforced the right to legal advice and began the move towards tape-recording of all police station interviews.

There is no empirical evidence for the contention that it is hardened and experienced criminals and terrorists who avail themselves of the right to refuse to answer police questions, nor that the result is that they escape justice.[29] In fact, there is reason to suppose that the "No comment" interview is more often associated with conviction than acquittal.[30] Certainly, there are

---

[24] M. Wald, R. Ayers, D.W. Hess, M. Schantz and C.H. Whitehouse, "Interrogations in New Haven: The Impact of *Miranda*" (1967) 76 *Yale LJ* 76.

[25] D.J. Smith and J. Gray, *Police and People in London*, vol. 4 *The Police in Action* (Policy Studies Institute, London, 1983).

[26] P. Softley, *Police Interrogation: An Observational Study in Four Police Stations*, Royal Commission on Criminal Procedure Research Study No. 4 (HMSO, London, 1980).

[27] B. Irving, *Police Interrogation: A Case Study of Current Practice*, Royal Commission Criminal Procedure Research Study No. 2 (HMSO, London, 1980).

[28] *Report of the Royal Commission on Criminal Procedure* (Phillips Report) (HMSO, London, 1981) Cmnd 8092 para. 4.51.

[29] I. Dennis, "The Criminal Justice and Public Order Act 1994: The Evidence Provisions" [1995] *Crim. LR* 4, 11.

[30] M. Zander and P. Henderson, *Crown Court Study*, Royal Commission on Criminal Justice Research Study 19 (HMSO, London, 1993).

fewer such interviews than might be supposed from police propaganda. Figures from the Metropolitan and West Yorkshire Police[31] show between 12 per cent and 23 per cent respectively of suspects exercising the right to silence to some degree; this figure suggest a slight increase since the Act. Only a small minority of suspects refuse to answer any police questions at all (from 2 per cent to 6 per cent). The take-up rate is greater for those with criminal records, but the difference is slight.[32] In the Crown Court study, 70 per cent of those interviewed did not exercise the right to silence at all; between 20 and 28 per cent exercised it to some extent, of which at least half ultimately pleaded guilty. 26 per cent of suspects were advised by solicitors to say nothing; 23 per cent were advised to be selective with their answers.[33]

Although there has been since 1984 an increase in the number of suspects receiving legal advice in some form—from about 7 per cent to 24 per cent,[34] it has hardly made dramatic impact upon the balance of power in police stations. The research conducted on behalf of the Runciman Commission found that the legal adviser was usually an unqualified legal representative,[35] and that this lack of experience and consequent nervousness on the professional's part was one of the reasons suspects were advised to say nothing. However, the most frequent reason a lawyer would advise silence was insufficiency of information from the police about the nature of the case and the state of the evidence. Police have been accused of being reluctant to reveal the case to the legal adviser, making it impossible to advise.[36] Sometimes lawyers use advising silence as a weapon—a bargaining chip to get the police to explain the position.[37] Even so, 78 per cent of the legal advisers recommended co-operation with the police. The withholding of information by the police amounts to unfair pressure on the suspect according to Zuckerman, who argues that requiring answers from a suspect who does not know the nature of the case being assembled against him or her is tantamount to an ambush.[38] Although, in the absence of a proper explanation by the police of their case, silence is not likely to justify an adverse inference, the

---

[31] Home Office, *Report of the Working Group*, App. C, 60–2.

[32] *Ibid.*

[33] Zander and Henderson, n. 30 above.

[34] D. Brown, *Detention at the Police Station under the Police and Criminal Evidence Act 1984* Home Office Research Study No. 104 (HMSO, London, 1990); similar figures appear in A. Sanders, L. Bridges, A. Mulvaney and G. Crozier, *Advice and Assistance at Police Stations and the 24 Hour Duty Solicitor Scheme* (Lord Chancellor's Department, London, 1989).

[35] M. McConville and J. Hodgson, *The Right to Silence in Police Interrogation: A Study of Some of the Issues Underlying the Debate*, Royal Commission on Criminal Justice Research Study No 10 (HMSO, London, 1995).

[36] J. Mackenzie, "The Great Fiasco" [1994] *NLJ* 1104.

[37] *Ibid.*, 90–5; In *Argent* [1997] Crim LR 347, the Court of Appeal was sympathetic to the information deficit problem even if police have good reasons for non-disclosure at the time. See text to n. 65 below.

[38] A. Zuckerman, "Trial by Unfair Means: The Report of the Working Group on the Right of Silence" [1989] *Crim. LR* 855.

suspect is unlikely to realise that at the time the decision whether to answer or not has to be made.[39] Zuckerman argues that it is unfair to expect suspects to answer if they do not know how their answers might incriminate them; courts should use section 78 of PACE[40] to exclude answers if information is withheld by the police.[41]

To what extent is silence an indicator of guilt? The Runciman Commission accepted that suspects may remain silent during interview out of fear, shock, because the truth is embarrassing or because they belong to an ethnic minority which is deeply suspicious of the police. The suspect may be unclear about the legal definitions of offences, unaware of the definitions of terms such as dishonesty or intention, and hence his or her answers should be treated with extreme caution.[42] The argument that police investigations have been hampered by the regulation of the treatment of suspects under the PACE does not hold water.[43] The separate problem of the ambush defence is more properly dealt with as a pre-trial procedural issue of disclosure, not of demanding answers from those held in intimidating surroundings likely to overwhelm and confuse them.[44] To those who consider that the police are over-reliant on confession evidence, it has been replied that curtailment of the right to silence would cause them to place less emphasis on admissions.[45] This argument is difficult to follow; telling suspects that silence could be used as evidence against them is surely a means of pressurising them into confessing. It must be noted, however, that in Singapore, where few remained silent even before the law was changed to allow adverse inferences to be drawn,[46] the behaviour of suspects appears relatively unchanged since.[47]

It is not clear that suspects who choose to exercise their right to silence under the common law rules necessarily protect their interests. In some circumstances, remaining silent in the face of an accusation is tantamount to an admission of guilt. This is where a person is accused by someone with whom he or she could be said to be psychologically "on even terms", in that the accuser is not in a position to influence any criminal investigation. Then the court or jury is entitled to interpret a failure to respond to the accusation

---

[39] *Ibid.*

[40] P. Mirfield, *Silence, Confessions and Improperly Obtained Evidence* (Clarendon, Oxford, 1997) 244; see Ch. 6.

[41] A. Zuckerman. "The Inevitable Demise of the Right to Silence" [1994] *NLJ* 1104. Under s.78, the trial judge has a discretion to exclude evidence which would adversely affect the fairness of the trial: see Ch. 6.

[42] *Report of the Royal Commission on Criminal Justice*, chaired by Lord Runciman (HMSO, London, 1993), Cm 2263 52.

[43] n. 40 above, 244.

[44] See Chs. 1 and 8.

[45] N. 42 above, para. 4.10.

[46] M.H. Yeo, "Diminishing the Right to Silence: The Singapore Experience" [1983] *Crim. LR* 89.

[47] A.K.J. Tan "Adverse Inferences and the Right to Silence: Re-examining the Singapore Experience" [1997] *Crim. LR* 471.

as acceptance of it, and thus as an admission of guilt.[48] The Eleventh Report of the Criminal Law Revision Committee assumed that silence in the face of an accusation by a police officer could never amount to an acknowledgement of guilt,[49] but in fact the common law showed signs of considerable confusion on the point.[50] In any event, it has always been open to juries to assume the worst from a failure to answer, whatever the guidance from the Bench might be. And in the classic case where a defendant made no comment during interview by the police, a judge could, pre-1994, legitimately comment that it was "unfortunate" that the accused gave no answer.[51] In *Gilbert*,[52] the Court of Appeal confirmed that judges could point out that a particular defence was not put forward until trial, and thus could not be investigated by the police, but insisted that no adverse inferences in terms of guilt or the credibility of the defence should be allowed. This common law position is retained by section 34(5)(b) of the Criminal Justice and Public Order Act 1994 for those cases which fall outside the scope of the new power to draw adverse inferences.

The Phillips Report was against any change in the law unless interrogation procedures were dramatically reformed, so that suspects were given at all stages of the investigation full information on their rights and on the nature of the evidence against them.[53] Inevitably, the Committee concluded, this would involve a move towards an inquisitorial system of trial, for the interrogations would have to be supervised by a judicial official to ensure that the suspect was indeed so informed. The obligation to answer could be justified "only if the critical phase of the investigation, that is the phase at which silence could be used adversely to the accused, was to become more structured and formal than it is now; in effect responsibility for and conduct of this phase of the investigation, close to charge, would have to become a quasi-judicial rather than a police function".[54] The Committee drew a distinction between questioning before arrest, where there should be no obligation to answer, and afterwards, where the suspect would be fully informed as to his position. Although the suggestion envisages a considerable step towards an inquisitorial process, there was support for it.[55]

Despite these arguments, and the opposition of the two government-appointed Royal Commissions, the law was changed in 1994 out of "political expediency prompted by the rhetoric of the law and order lobby".[56] The Criminal Justice and Public Order Act 1994 provides, in section 34:

---

[48] *Hall* v. *R.* [1971] 1 All ER 322.

[49] *Evidence (General)* (Eleventh Report of the Criminal Law Revision Committee, HMSO, London, 1972), Cmnd 4991, 28–30.

[50] See *Chandler* [1976] 3 All ER 105: *Lewis* (1977) 57 Cr. App. R 860; *Gerard* (1948) 32 Cr. App. R 215.

[51] *Davis* (1959) 43 Cr. App. R 215.　　[52] (1977) 66 Cr. App. R 237.

[53] Phillips Report, n. 28 above, para. 4.53.　　[54] Para. 4.52.　　[55] Editorial [1988] *NLJ* 737.

[56] M.J. Allen and S. Cooper, "Howard's Way: a Farewell to Freedom?" (1995) 58 *MLR* 364.

"(1) Where, in any proceedings against a person for an offence, evidence is given that the accused—

(a) at any time before he was charged with the offence, on being questioned under caution by a constable trying to discover whether or by whom the offence had been committed, failed to mention any fact relied on in his defence in those proceedings; or

(b) on being charged with the offence or officially informed that he might be prosecuted for it, failed to mention any such fact,

being a fact which in the circumstances existing at the time the accused could reasonably have been expected to mention when so questioned, charged or informed, as the case may be, subsection (2) below applies."

Subsection (2) allows a court, in considering the issue of guilt or of whether there is a case to answer, to "draw such inferences as appear proper". In *Murray* v. *UK*[57] the European Court of Human Rights held that the drawing of adverse inference from silence is not a breach of the European Convention on Human Rights, although denial of access to legal advice is.

There is no requirement under section 34 that the suspect should have been arrested, and so, theoretically, he has no right to legal advice at the point at which he acquires the obligation to answer.[58] However, the police should not conduct what amounts to an interview outside the police station,[59] so, as Mirfield argues, the man holding the smoking gun should not be asked anything until he gets to the police station.[60] If a police officer should delay arrest improperly, in order to have the advantage of section 34 in the absence of legal advice, then any answers so obtained are likely to be excluded under section 78 PACE. Clearly it is also important that the suspect understands the consequences of failure to answer. The new caution which must be uttered by the police officer is as follows: "[y]ou do not have to say anything, But it may harm your defence if you do not mention when questioned something which you later rely on in court. Anything you do say may be given in evidence." Only one person in eight out of a random sample understood the second section of this caution.[61] Meanwhile, it is the interests of the police to persist with a "No comment" interview where previously they would have given up in defeat; each separate silent reaction to each particular allegation could enhance the prosecution case.

It has been argued that this Act constitutes a "bonanza" for duty solicitors, who now must attend police stations and keep detailed notes.[62] Advice given

---

[57] *The Times,* 19 Feb. 1996.

[58] Under s.58 of PACE suspects arrested and held in custody at a police station have the right to consult a solicitor.

[59] Code C, 11.1(Codes of Practice issued under PACE).

[60] Mirfield, n. 40 above, 264.

[61] E. Shepherd, A. Mortimer, and R. Mobasheri, "The Police Caution: Comprehension and Perceptions in the General Population" (1995) 4(2) 60 *Expert Evidence.*

[62] D. Wolchover and A. Heaton-Armstrong, "Labour's Victory and the Right to Silence" [1997] *NLJ* 1382.

will now have to be very carefully considered; it is not likely to be regarded on its own as sufficient reason for not mentioning facts relevant to the defence. If the advice is thought to have been reasonable, the explanation for it should be given to the court.[63] But if the police have told the solicitor little or nothing, so that the solicitor is not in a position usefully to advise, the court should be informed and adverse inferences will not then be drawn.[64] In *Argent*[65] there was useful guidance from the Court of Appeal; the court should consider the circumstances at the time of the questioning, including the time of day, the defendant's age, experience, mental capacity, state of health, sobriety, tiredness, knowledge, personality and legal advice. References to "the accused" do not mean some hypothetical, reasonable accused of ordinary phlegm and fortitude,[66] but the actual accused with the qualities, apprehensions, knowledge and advice he is shown to have had at the time. In *R. v. N*[67], the Court of Appeal took a common sense view of facts " the accused could reasonably have been expected to mention".[68] The trial judge invited the jury trying an indecent assault case to draw adverse inferences from the defendant's failure, when questioned by the police, to explain the presence of semen on the victim's nightdress. However, the presence of the fluid was not known at the time of the interview, and the defendant had not been asked about it. It was held that no adverse inferences could be drawn from the lack of explanation.

Unlike section 34, sections 36 and 37 do not depend on a defence being raised at trial which has not been mentioned earlier. The obligation to answer (insofar as otherwise "proper" adverse inferences may be drawn) is therefore to that extent an absolute one which arises from circumstances. The police do not have to explain the nature of their case, neither is there a requirement that the suspect should reasonably be expected to know relevant facts; that knowledge is also assumed from the circumstances. Section 36 provides:

"(1) Where—
    (a) a person is arrested by a constable, and there is—
        (i) on his person; or
        (ii) in or on his clothing or footwear; or
        (iii) otherwise in his possession; or
        (iv) in any place in which he is at the time of his arrest,
    any object, substance or mark, or there is any mark on any such object; and

---

[63] *Roble* [1997] Crim. LR 449.   [64] *Ibid.*   [65] [1997] Crim. LR 347.

[66] However, see *Condron and Condron*, [1997] Crim. LR 215 where it availed the defendants nothing that the stated reason that their solicitor advised them to say nothing was that he thought they were unfit by reason of withdrawal from drugs, although the Force Medical Examiner had passed them fit for questioning. The jury convicted them, having been told that it was for them to decide whether or not to draw adverse inferences.

[67] *The Times* 13 Feb. 1998.

[68] S.34(1) of the Criminal Justice and Public Order Act 1994.

(b) that or another constable investigating the case reasonably believes that the presence of the object, substance or mark may be attributable to the participation of the person arrested in the commission of an offence specified by the constable; and

(c) the constable informs the person arrested that he so believes, and requests him to account for the presence of the object, substance or mark; and

(d) the person fails or refuses to do so . . ."

adverse inferences again may be drawn, and taken into account in determination of the issue of guilt or whether there is a case to answer.[69] The accused must be told in ordinary language by the constable when making the request what the effect of this section would be if he failed or refused to comply with the request.[70] The same applies to section 37,[71] where adverse inferences may be used with the same effect.[72] Section 37 is as follows:

"(1) Where—

(a) a person arrested by a constable was found by him at a place at or about the time the offence for which he was arrested is alleged to have been committed; and

(b) that or another constable investigating the offence reasonably believes that the presence of the person at that place and at that time may be attributable to his participation in the commission of the offence; and

(c) the constable informs the person arrested that he so believes, and requests him to account for that presence; and

(d) the person fails or refuses to do so,

then if, in any proceedings against the person or the offence, evidence of those matters is given . . ."

adverse inferences may be drawn as appears proper, but only in relation to the offence for which he was arrested.[73]

No one can be convicted solely on the basis of an adverse inference drawn under any of these sections, or, indeed under section 35 (see the text to notes 130–131 below)[74] but it is difficult to see how the jury could be prevented from doing so in a case where they regarded the silence as significant but rejected the other prosecution evidence.[75] It is not clear either whether a conviction could be sustained on the strength of nothing more than a combination of silences from sections 35, 36, 37 and 34, or whether there should be some non-silence evidence in every case.[76]

---

[69] S.36(2).   [70] S.34(5).   [71] S.37(5).   [72] S.3792).   [73] S.38(2).   [74] S.38(3).
[75] Mirfield, n. 40 above, 269.   [76] *Ibid.*

Silence in Court

When a plaintiff in a civil case shows a *prima facie* case against a defendant who elects not to give evidence, that case is proved on the balance of probabilities.[77] Since 1851,[78] a party to civil litigation has been in a position to insist that the other gives evidence; the extension of this principle to proceedings instituted in consequence of adultery[79] suggests that the availability of relevant evidence was regarded as more important than allowing litigants to decide entirely for themselves how and to what extent they will participate in the trial. Curiously, Anglo-American systems are willing to tolerate less information being available to the criminal court than to the civil—the exact reverse of the Continental approach.[80] In England, the defendant in a criminal trial cannot be compelled to give evidence.[81] In Continental trials, the accused cannot decline to be questioned, but he can decline to answer. If he does elect to explain himself, he does this unsworn. In most systems, the courts may not draw adverse inferences from a refusal to answer all or any of the questions put, but there is considerable psychological pressure to answer because unfavourable common-sense inferences are almost inevitable, given that the refusal always relates to a particular question.[82] The position of Continental defendants may at first sight appear to be similar to that of the Anglo-American, but their decision whether or not to answer is in fact more difficult, since they are questioned before any of the prosecution witnesses. They are to some extent in the dark. To this extent such defendants are in fact being treated as a primary evidentiary source themselves,[83] which many adversarially-trained lawyers would regard as entirely incompatible with the presumption of innocence. But although it is true that at the trial itself the prosecution has no need to show a case to answer, the preparatory stages of Continental proceedings will have established that already, and acquainted the accused with the nature of the case against him or her.

Why should a defendant elect not to give evidence? A poor performance in the witness box should go only to credibility, at the most, not to indicate guilt. There is an obvious risk, however, that once the jury regard the accused as a person not worthy of belief, he or she will be convicted. It is true that prosecution witnesses also have to perform as well as they can, and must satisfy a higher standard of proof before they may be believed. The accused

---

[77] *Francisco* v. *Diedrick, The Times* 3 Apr 1998.

[78] Evidence Act, s. 2.

[79] Evidence Further Amendment Act 1869; *Tilley* v. *Tilley* [1949] P 240.

[80] M.J. Damaska, *Evidence Law Adrift* (Yale University Press, New Haven, Conn., 1997), 116–17.

[81] Criminal Evidence Act 1898, s.1(1). The failure of any person charged with an offence to give evidence shall not be made the subject of any comment by the prosecution (s.1(1)(b)).

[82] M.J. Damaska, "Evidentiary Barriers to Conviction and Two Models of Criminal Procedure: A Comparative Study" (1973) 121 *U of Penn. LR* 506.

[83] *Ibid.*

needs only to raise a doubt. But prosecution witnesses do not run the risk of being convicted. Also, to produce a system designed to force the defendant into the witness-box renews the emphasis on demeanour and presentation, relying more than ever on the limited ability of most of us to tell lies from the truth.[84] The jury may attach too much importance to factors such as fluency and confidence.

The leading case on the judge's summing-up at common law in such cases is *Bathurst*,[85] where it was established that a judge may comment on the accused's failure to give evidence[86] as long as he points out that it is the right of an accused person not to do so. Lord Parker CJ said that the accepted form of comment was:

> "To inform the jury that, of course, he—the defendant—is not bound to give evidence, that he can sit back and see if the prosecution have proved their case, and that while the jury have been deprived of the opportunity of hearing his story tested in cross-examination, the one thing they must not do is to assume that he is guilty because he has not gone into the witness box."[87]

These remarks were observed to have been *obiter* in a later case, *Sparrow*,[88] in which Lawton LJ concluded that the Lord Chief Justice could not have intended the judges to parrot a rigid formula in every case. What is said must depend on the nature of the case before them. In *Sparrow*, a police officer was shot dead by a gun which the defence claimed was not intended to do more than frighten anyone who tried to apprehend the two accused. Sparrow declined to enter the witness box. Lawton LJ said that if the trial judge had not commented on this "in strong terms" he would have been failing in his duty, given that he must not expressly or impliedly suggest that a defence cannot succeed unless the defendant gives evidence. Despite the fact that keeping the accused out of the witness-box runs the risk of alienating the jury, the recommendation in 1973 of the Criminal Law Revision Committee that adverse inferences should be legitimised by reform were received with shock in some quarters. The Committee thought that the case for allowing inferences to be drawn was "even stronger in the case of failure to give evidence" than for failure to respond to police interrogation.[89] The judge should warn the accused about the consequences of his failure to give evidence.[90]

A Home Office Working Group recommended that the prosecution should be able to comment on the defendant's failure to testify in similar terms to the trial judge, while giving the defence the opportunity to explain

---

[84] See Ch. 3.   [85] [1968] 2 QB 99.

[86] The prosecutor may not do so: Criminal Evidence Act 1898, s. 1(b).

[87] [1968] 2 QB 99, 107.   [88] [1973] 1 WLR 488.

[89] Eleventh Report, n. 49 above, para. 110.

[90] Although it would not assist the prosecution in establishing a case to answer.

it.[91] Its Report anticipated difficulty with unrepresented defendants, but disposed of this by requiring that unspecified but "adequate safeguards" be devised. The cure seems rather worse than the disease, particularly since the disease which necessitates such changes is never identified. Neither the Phillips nor the Runciman Royal Commission could see any reason to follow the recommendation of the Eleventh Report of the Criminal Law Revision Committee that pressure should be brought to bear on criminal defendants who declined to give evidence. The 1993 Runciman Report did not even trouble to rehearse arguments: "[g]iven the principle that the burden of proof should rest on the prosecution to prove its case, it must be wrong for defendants who leave the prosecution to prove its case to be exposed to comment by either the prosecution or the judge".[92] Nevertheless, the Criminal Justice and Public Order Act allows for the drawing of such adverse inferences "as appear proper"[93] where the defendant declines to give evidence, if he or she has attained the age of 14 years for an offence, unless either:

"(a) the accused's guilt is not in issue; or
(b) it appears to the court that the physical or mental condition of the accused makes it undesirable for him to give evidence".[94]

Where this applies, the court shall, at the conclusion of the evidence for the prosecution, satisfy itself (in the case of proceedings on indictment, in the presence of the jury) that the accused is aware that the stage has been reached at which evidence can be given for the defence and that he can, if he wishes, give evidence and that, if he chooses not to give evidence, or having been sworn without good cause refuses to answer any question, it will be permissible for the court or jury to draw such inferences as appear proper from his failure to give evidence or his refusal, without good cause, to answer any question.[95]

Under the Criminal Evidence (Northern Ireland) Order 1988,[96] the trial judge is required formally to call upon the accused to give evidence, but the Lord Chief Justice of England successfully campaigned to have a similar provision removed from the 1994 Act.[97] Section 35 differs from the other sections in the Criminal Justice and Public Order Act which deal with the right to silence, in that the adverse inferences it permits cannot be used to establish a case to answer. In terms of logic this is inevitable, since the prosecution must have produced a prima facie case to get past 'half-time', that is, they must show that there is a case to answer before the defence even open

---

[91] *Report of the Working Group on the Right to Silence* (Home Office, London, 1989), 116.
[92] *Report of the Royal Commission on Criminal Justice* (HMSO, London, 1993), 55.
[93] S.37(3).   [94] S.37(1).   [95] S.37(2).   [96] Art. 4(2).
[97] Trial judges should, at the close of the prosecution case, proceed on the lines of *Practice Direction (Crown Court: Evidence: Advice to Defendant), The Times,* 12 Apr. 1995.

their case. In terms of principle, however, it is vital that silence from the defendant is not used to bolster a thin prosecution case, or that fear of adverse inferences being drawn does not force an unconvincing defendant into the witness-box where a disastrous performance in cross-examination masks the intrinsic weakness of the evidence against him.

This concern seems to lie behind the case law on section 35. The courts have explained that the jury must be satisfied that the prosecution has established a case to answer before any adverse inference may be drawn under section 35.[98] At face value, this requirement appears meaningless; by definition there will be a case to answer before the question of evidence from the defence arises. But in *Murray*,[99] the House of Lords elaborated thus: if the prosecutor cannot establish a *prima facie* case there is no case for the accused to answer. Equally, if parts of the prosecution case have so little evidential value that they call for no answer, a failure in the defendant to deal with those specific matters cannot justify an inference of guilt.[100] If, on the other hand, aspects of the evidence taken alone or in combination with other facts clearly call for an explanation which the accused ought to be in a position to give, if an explanation exists, then a failure to give any explanation may as a matter of common sense allow the drawing of an inference that there is no other explanation than that the accused is guilty.[101] Thus evidence that Murray had been in a car linked with a shooting did not call for an answer from him; but evidence that linked him directly with the shooting itself did.

Not only does a "case to answer" requirement in the technical sense appear otiose, but there must be a question as to the appropriateness of asking a jury the question, given that the judge has already adjudicated on the point. *Murray*, a Northern Ireland case, was tried in a "Diplock Court" with no jury, and may operate more easily there or in the magistrates' court. But in fact the phrase appears to be used in this context to mean rather more; that there is a case against the accused which demands an answer. In *Cowan*,[102] the offence charged was unlawful wounding, and related to an incident outside a public house in relation to which two witnesses identified Cowan. He did not give evidence, but two witnesses testified on his behalf to say that someone else had inflicted the wound. The Court of Appeal approved the model direction issued for the benefit of trial judges by the Judicial Studies Board:

"The defendant has given evidence. That is his right. But, as he has been told, the law is that you may draw such inferences as appear proper from his failure to do so. Failure to give evidence on its own cannot prove guilt but depending on the circumstances, you may hold his failure against him when deciding whether he is guilty. [There is evidence before you on the basis of which the defendant's

---

[98] See *Murray* (1993) 97 Cr. App. R 151; *Cowan* [1995] 4 All ER 939.
[99] (1993) 97 Cr. App. R 151.
[100] Lord Slynn at 160.   [101] *Ibid.*   [102] [1995] 4 All ER 939.

advocate invites you not to hold it against the defendant that he has not given evidence before you namely . . . If you think that because of this evidence you should not hold it against the defendant that he has not given evidence, do not do so. But if the evidence he relies on presents no adequate explanation for his absence from the witness box then you may hold his failure to give evidence against him. You do not have to do so.] What proper inferences can you draw from the defendant's decision not to give evidence before you? If you conclude that there is a case for him to answer, you may think that the defendant would have gone into the witness box to give you an explanation for or an answer to the case against him. If the only sensible explanation for his decision not to give evidence is that he has no answer to the case against him, or none that could have stood up to cross-examination, then it would be open to you to hold against him his failure to give evidence. It is for you to decide whether it is fair to do so."

The appeal was upheld on the ground that it was not explained to the jury that adverse inferences may be drawn only when the only sensible explanation for the silence is that the defendant has no answer to the charges. In *Birchall*,[103] this was expressed as a requirement that the prosecution evidence be "sufficiently compelling" to call for an answer from the defendant at the close of the prosecution case.

Although this restrictive attitude towards section 35 is to be welcomed, there is, in some cases, evidence of judicial over-enthusiasm to apply it. In *Friend*,[104] the defendant, who was accused of murder, had the mental age of a 9-year-old child. The judge nevertheless refused to rule under section 35(1), that his condition made it undesirable that he gave evidence, because a 9-year-old child can give evidence. Hence the jury was told that adverse inferences might be drawn from his failure to give evidence. The Court of Appeal agreed, even though this would not have been possible in the case of a witness in fact aged 9, as section 35 applies only to defendants aged over 14. The decision was justified in terms of the reluctance of the Court of Appeal lightly to interfere with the exercise of the trial judge's discretion, given that he has heard the expert evidence and made his own assessment of the case. Support was given to the view expressed in *Cowan* that it is only exceptional cases which fall outside section 35. As for the passage in the Model Direction which deals with defence explanations of the reason for the refusal to testify, it seems that there must be more evidence than speculation or "enigmatic assertions". In *Ricciardi*[105] defence counsel had claimed that there was a good reason, but declined to state it on the ground that it was too sensitive to repeat.

The Court of Appeal has shown itself to be unsympathetic to the essential dilemma facing a defendant with a criminal record.[106] As will be seen below, the accused may be cross-examined on his previous convictions if he attacks

---

[103] *The Times*, 10 Feb. (1998).   [104] [1997] 2 All ER 1011.
[105] [1995] 4 All ER 939.   [106] *Cowan* [1995] 4 All ER 939.

the character of any witness for the prosecution.[107] The abolition of the right of the accused to make an unsworn statement from the dock (on which he could not be cross-examined[108]) leaves any defence counsel faced with a prosecution witness whose bad character he wishes to expose with a tactical problem more appropriate to a game of Risk than a criminal trial. To discredit the prosecution witness will lose the defendant his shield against being cross-examined on his criminal record. Thus counsel must either spare the prosecution witness, and potentially throw the case away, or go ahead and hope the jury will not be excessively influenced by the defendant's previous convictions, or go ahead and keep the defendant out of the witness-box, with the attendant risk of adverse inferences being drawn.

Evidence of the Defendant's Character

"Good Character" Evidence

It has been argued[109] that to allow the accused to adduce evidence of previous good character whether or not relevant to the charge allows the jury to reach a verdict which may reflect little more than their perception of his or her moral standing. There have recently been some notable acquittals which appeared to be based on a moral judgement by the jury on the character or behaviour of the accused or, indeed, his or her accusers, rather than the evidence. It is sometimes said that one of the principal arguments in favour of trial by one's peers is that it makes possible "perverse" verdicts which nevertheless implement the reaction of the community. Hence the jury must know the nature of the individual whose fate they are to determine. However, they may never discover the dark side of a defendant who chooses to keep his or her character out of the debate. This state of affairs is more difficult to defend. In Continental trials the antecedents of the defendant are the first items of information presented; it is thought imperative that the tribunal of fact should know with what sort of person it is dealing.

Strictly, at common law, evidence of good character should consist of testimony from witnesses who can speak to the defendant's reputation within a community with which they are familiar, and not of specific meritorious acts. In *Rowton*,[110] it was held that although a character witness can be cross-examined about particular matters within his knowledge which reflect badly on the accused, he may not, in chief, speak from his own experience or opinion, but should testify to that of the neighbourhood or community in which the accused has a good reputation. Also, the character proved must be

---

107 Criminal Evidence Act 1898, s. 1(f) (ii); see text to nn. 140–191 below.
108 Criminal Justice Act 1982, s. 72.
109 A. Zuckerman, "Similar Facts: The Unobservable Rule" [1987] *LQR* 187.
110 (1865) Le. & Ca .520.

of the specific kind impeached and should relate to a period proximate to the date of the alleged offence. *Phipson*[111] objects that it is impossible for anyone to give evidence of his own reputation, and therefore *Rowton* does not apply to the accused giving evidence himself.[112] The preference for reputation evidence, which by definition relies on hearsay composed of gossip and speculation rather than direct knowledge, is itself baffling. In fact the rule is ignored on a daily basis in every criminal court in the land, where character witnesses may be found attesting to all kinds of impressions and experiences of the defendant. Nevertheless, it was upheld in *Redgrave*,[113] where the defendant was accused of importuning for an immoral purpose in a public convenience. He sought to adduce evidence of heterosexual relationships to rebut the inferences of homosexuality derived from his conduct as observed by the police. It was held that he could not adduce evidence of particular acts to show he was of a heterosexual disposition. He should show that by way of general reputation he was not the kind of young man who would behave in the way charged. The Court of Appeal thought, however, that Redgrave's trial judge "might, as an indulgence," have allowed evidence of marriage or a relationship with one woman.

One problem with this case is that it is nonsense to argue that evidence of heterosexuality, however established, has something to do with credibility on oath. Redgrave was not asking the court to believe what he said in the witness-box because he was really a heterosexual. He was suggesting that his sexual proclivities made it unlikely that he would approach men in a public lavatory. The fact is that "character" evidence is a broad category, at times relating to honesty and at others to very different attributes. A defendant might suggest that he has a gentle disposition incompatible with the violent offences alleged. He might wish to establish lifelong patriotism in order to suggest that he would not betray his country. He might even argue that as a committed homosexual he is an unlikely rapist. None of these arguments has anything to do with credibility as a witness; whether or not he gives evidence has absolutely no effect on its relevance. The proper direction to the jury must therefore depend on the purpose for which the evidence is admitted, rather than some *ex post facto* categorisation by the judge. It would be absurd, as *Phipson* argues, to demand that if the accused gives evidence of these matters he should do so by way of establishing his own reputation, and he should not be dependent on the generosity of judges to get it in. It would be better simply to acknowledge, as Continental courts do, that it is irrational to try a person without knowing what sort person is before the court.

The legal effect of evidence of the defendant's good character has become a

---

[111] *Phipson on Evidence* (14th edn. by M.N. Howard, P. Crane and D.A. Hochberg, Sweet and Maxwell, London,1990), 18.15.

[112] Citing *Samuel* (1956) 40 Cr. App. R 8.

[113] (1981) 74 Cr. App. R 10.

complex issue. It was recognised by Viscount Sankey in *Maxwell* [114] that inevitably it would in some case establish more than credibility, and would be taken to suggest that the accused is a person unlikely to have committed the offence charged. His remarks indicate a realistic acceptance of the likely reaction of jurors to disposition evidence. [115] But the courts have become increasingly persuaded that only out of tolerance do judges allow evidence of good character in the first place to be called and then to go to the issue of guilt [116]; this has led them into disarray. Although there are cases to the effect that it goes only to credibility, [117] the earlier common law was that such evidence went to the issue of guilt, a natural consequence of the fact that before 1898 defendants were not allowed to give evidence and so the issue of their credibility as witnesses did not arise. [118] However, judges began more recently to give directions that good character is relevant to credibility, as in *Mendez*, [119] where the Court of Appeal upheld the practice as correct. The jury should be told that evidence of good character goes to credibility, although if the accused does not give evidence they may then ask themselves whether, in the light of the character evidence, he is the sort of person likely to have committed the offence charged. To enhance the incoherence of this reasoning the court added "[t]hat may also be done when he does give evidence but should be done in cases where he does not give evidence".

It was clearly of vital importance, in the wake of *Mendez*, to clarify the position relating to evidence of good character, particularly whether it goes to the issue of guilt, as propensity evidence, or to the credibility of the defendant. In *Vye, Wise and Stephenson*, [120] the Court of Appeal decided that judges should direct juries that evidence of good character affects credibility where the defendant has either given evidence or made pre-trial exculpatory statements. They should also, in every case, explain the relevance of the good character evidence to the likelihood of the defendant's having committed the offence charged. This should happen irrespective of whether the defendant is charged jointly with a co-defendant who has no good character evidence to offer, and therefore may suffer in comparison with the defendant. The judge must do "what he thinks best" in terms of advising the jury about the position of a co-defendant in such a case. The House of Lords declared recently in *Aziz* [121] that there should always be a direction about the relevance of any good character evidence because "it is of probative significance". [122] However, in *Hickmet*, [123] the Court of Appeal was unimpressed by the

---

[114] [1935] AC 309, 315.

[115] A reasoning process rarely permitted if the disposition evidence is negative in effect.

[116] *Rowton* (1865) Le & Ca 520; *Hunt* v. *Evans* [1917] 1 KB 352; *Miller* [1952] 2 All ER 667; *Redgrave* (1982) 74 Cr. App. R 10.

[117] E.g. *Falconer-Atlee* (1973) 58 Cr. App. R 348.

[118] The change came in s.1 of the Criminal Evidence Act 1898.

[119] [1970] Crim. LR 397; contradicted in *Bryant* [1979] QB 108.

[120] [1993] 3 All ER 241.   [121] [1995] 3 All ER 149.   [122] *Ibid., per* Lord Steyn at 156.

[123] [1996] Crim. LR 588.

defence argument that the defendant's lack of (recent) previous convictions made it less likely that he would commit the act of rape. It seems that the relevance, or probative significance, of the evidence inevitably will be considered by the trial judge in the light of the totality of the case; here the issue was whether or not the complainant had consented to sexual intercourse, and the trial judge was entitled to conclude that the character evidence had no bearing on that.

There have been doubts expressed as to the wisdom of assuming, as some courts have done, that the absence of previous convictions necessarily amounts to evidence of good character.[124] In *Aziz* itself, two co-defendants admitted to acts of dishonesty which had not resulted in criminal convictions. Noting this problem, Lord Steyn stated that a trial judge has a residual discretion to decline to give any character directions in the case of a defendant without previous convictions, if it would seem to be an insult to common sense to do so. However, *prima facie*, a direction is necessary. Where previous convictions should be regarded for most purposes as "spent", within the meaning of the Rehabilitation of Offenders Act 1974, the court should not be misled as to the defendant's character. The defendant therefore cannot necessarily be put forward as a person of good character.[125]

Previous Convictions

The logic of the similar facts principle is that previous misconduct may form part of the prosecution's case if its effect is to supply evidence that the accused is guilty of the offence currently charged[126]; this is irrespective of whether it resulted in a criminal conviction. It has been argued above that the similar fact decisions are inevitably incoherent and inconsistent; this is a result of the fallacious assumption that the amount of probative value can be weighed in an imaginary scale against the amount of prejudicial effect. That exercise is all the more difficult, given that it relies heavily on the imaginary divide between evidence which goes merely to disposition and evidence indicative of guilt. These confusions are apparently given statutory approval in the more well-trodden field of cross-examination of an accused person on his criminal record. This is a less rarefied area than similar facts. It is a matter for the everyday criminal court. It is a creature of statute, the Criminal Evidence Act 1898, and therefore the courts cannot be blamed if the philosophical framework in which it operates is obscure. The legislature have, in fact, added confusion to confusion; not only is the similar fact doctrine

---

[124] R. Munday, "What Constitutes Good Character?' [1997] *Crim. LR* 247.

[125] *O'Shea* [1993] Crim. LR 951.

[126] The previous offences may in some cases not be at all similar and nevertheless provide a link between the accused and the offence for which he is being tried. Yet the courts insist that they eschew reasoning from proof of a generally bad disposition to a conclusion that therefore he must be guilty. See above, Ch. 2.

apparently imported wholesale; in addition, the statute creates categories of case in which the accused can be cross-examined on previous convictions. This resulted in a minefield in which even a former Lord Chief Justice had to declare defeat.[127]

The 1898 Act in question was a landmark which allowed for the first time every accused person to give evidence in his own defence.[128] Previously, it was thought that no man should be placed in a position where he might be tempted to perjure himself in order to escape a human punishment. The Criminal Evidence Act 1898 Section 1 reads as follows:

> "(1) Every person charged with an offence, shall be a competent witness for the defence at every stage of the proceedings, whether the person so charged is charged solely or jointly with any other person provided as follows . . . [*inter alia*]
>
>> (e) A person charged and being a witness . . . may be asked any question in cross-examination notwithstanding that it might tend to criminate him as to the offence charged.
>>
>> (f) A person charged and called as a witness in pursuance of this Act shall not be asked, and if asked shall not be required to answer, any question tending to show that he has committed or been convicted or been charged with any offence other than that wherewith he is charged, or is of bad character unless—
>>
>>> (i) the proof that he has committed or been convicted of such other offence is admissible evidence to show that he is guilty of the offence wherewith he is charged; or
>>>
>>> (ii) he has personally or by his advocate asked questions of the witnesses for the prosecution with a view to establish his own good character, or the nature or conduct of the defence is such as to involve imputations on the character of the prosecutor or the witnesses for the prosecution; or the deceased victim of the alleged crime[129]; or
>>>
>>> (iii) he has given evidence against any other person charged in the same proceedings."

Although the wording of section 1(e) appears sufficiently wide to allow any questions whatsoever, including questions about the defendant's bad character or previous misconduct, the courts have interpreted it narrowly. After all, to do otherwise would deprive 1(f) of any significance. In *Cokar*,[130] the prosecution was not allowed to ask the defendant about his previous acts of trespass, which had led to acquittals. It sought to show that he knew trespass without intention to steal was not a crime, but section 1(e) was held not to justify such prejudicial evidence being adduced. Neither did section

---

[127] *Watts* [1983] 3 All ER 101; *Powell* [1979] 2 All ER 1116.

[128] Other statutes, such as the Metalliferous Minerals Regulation Act 1872 and the Criminal Law Amendment Act 1885, had allowed accused persons in specific kinds of trial to do so. These statutes appeared to permit unfettered cross-examination.

[129] The last category was inserted by s.31 of the Criminal Justice and Public Order Act 1994; see R. Munday, "A Sample of Lawmaking" [1995] *NLJ* 855, 895.

[130] [1960] 2 QB 207.

1(f)(i), which requires evidence to satisfy the similar fact principle that evidence of previous misconduct must go beyond the merely prejudicial in order to be probative of guilt. In *Jones* v. *DPP*,[131] the House of Lords found it difficult to justify the cross-examination of the accused in his trial for murder of a Girl Guide about his previous conviction for the rape of another Girl Guide. He had given a demonstrably false alibi for the murder. When that was exposed, he gave an alibi improbably identical to the one he gave at the rape trial. Lord Denning took the common sense view that the history of Jones and his alibis incriminated him as to the offence charged, and therefore fell within section 1(e). But the majority held to the view that the subsection was confined to questions tending directly towards guilt, not questions about previous misconduct. The prosecution could have adduced the evidence of the earlier rape as similar fact evidence. In fact, it forbore to require the victim to undergo a second ordeal in court.[132] Hence the admissibility of this vital evidence appeared to depend upon whether Jones would throw away his shield under section 1(f)(ii).[133]

Section 1(f)(i) assumes that evidence of the commission of previous offences may be indicative of guilt. Bad character *simpliciter* and charges which did not lead to conviction are not included here. The courts have dealt with this omission somewhat haphazardly,[134] but generally the wording mirrors their conviction that such evidence does not indicate guilt. This effectively limits the operation of section 1(f)(i) to matters of similar fact. The House of Lords in *Jones* held that if the subsection is used to justify questions about similar facts evidence, then the prosecution should have laid a proper foundation in chief by adducing that evidence as part of its case.[135] The reason for this is explained in the judgment of the Court of Criminal Appeal:

> "It might in general be undesirable that such matters should first be addressed in cross-examination; in such a case . . . in which the accused desired to dispute or explain the alleged similarity of circumstances or pattern of the two offences he would thereby be deprived of any opportunity to cross-examine prosecution witnesses and be exposed to the gravely prejudicial effect of suggestive questions to which his negative answers might be of no avail."[136]

---

[131] [1962] AC 635.

[132] See text to n. 135 below.

[133] The House concluded that these problems did not arise since the cross-examination did not "tend to show" the jury about the conviction, Jones having already mentioned that he had been in trouble with the police before in order to explain why he gave a false alibi. See text to nn. 137–138 below.

[134] See C. Tapper, "The Meaning of Section 1(f)(i) of the Criminal Evidence Act 1898" in Tapper (ed.), *Crime, Proof and Punishment: Essays in Memory of Sir Rupert Cross* (Butterworths, London, 1981).

[135] [1962] AC 635, *per* Lord Morris at 685.

[136] [1962] AC 635, 646.

Tapper suggests that questioning might be permitted under the subsection even in the absence of evidence in chief from the prosecution, for example, if the defence is sprung on it at a late stage.[137] However, the argument that the defence is prejudiced if unable to cross-examine on the extent of the alleged similarity is no less persuasive in such a case. It is better to ensure that the prosecution receives prior notice of all special defences. Going further, the Continental practice of acquainting the court with the defendant's history at the outset might be adopted. Then the facts could be established without the artificial division into in-chief and cross-examination which causes so many problems. The decision in *Jones* is a reaction to the problems the distinction causes. The House of Lords decided that Jones' cross-examination fell outside the protection of the preamble in section 1(f), which disallows questions "tending to show" bad character or convictions. Jones had explained that he at first gave a false alibi out of fear, because he had "been in trouble with the police before". It was held that the words "tending to show" mean "make known to the jury". Thus Jones' answers to questions about the earlier rape of a Girl Guide were said to tell the jury nothing they had not already heard from Jones himself. As a result, he had no shield to lose. It might be thought that mentioning having been in trouble with the police before has rather less impact upon a jury than the details of a brutal rape. Also, this decision[138] renders otiose the whole of section 1(f)(i); for if the similar fact evidence has been presented as part of the prosecution case, the jury know about the previous misconduct already, the exclusionary preamble in section 1(f) does not apply and therefore the exception in section 1(f)(i) is unnecessary.[139]

Losing the Shield

Defendants can escape from the terms of section 1(f)(ii) in three ways: they can avoid throwing away their shield by not bringing their character into issue or attacking that of the prosecution witnesses; they can decline to give evidence in their own defence so that they cannot be cross-examined at all; or, if they appear *prima facie* to have brought themselves within the subsection, they can appeal to the discretion of the trial judge,[140] who may decide that justice would be best served by refusing leave to cross-examine on criminal record. The risk attached to the second course of action is that adverse inferences may be drawn from the failure to give evidence.[141] At common law, also, the prosecution has a right to rebut any evidence of good character given on behalf of a defendant who declines to give evidence. This

---

[137] Tapper, n. 134 above.

[138] Cf. *Anderson* [1988] 2 All ER 549.

[139] It might in any case be thought that if similar fact evidence is introduced by the prosecution in its case in chief, then it would be absurd if the prosecution could not follow it up by referring to it when the accused, should he elect to give evidence, is cross-examined.

[140] *Selvey* v. *DPP* [1970] AC 304.

[141] See text to nn. 94–95 above.

must be done, however, by calling rebuttal witnesses who can testify to the defendant's bad reputation; they should not describe specific incidents or individual views.[142] A significant case which appears to be widely overlooked is *Waldman*,[143] which holds that whether or not the defendant gives evidence, a good character witness called by the defence may be cross-examined by the prosecution to show that the defendant has previous convictions.

The theory behind the first limb of section 1(f)(ii) is reasonably clear. The purpose of the questioning is to rebut the favourable impression induced by the defence evidence. However, this rationale appears to apply even if the aspect of character presented for the defence bears no logical relation to the previous convictions produced in rebuttal. At least, so runs the decision in *Winfield*,[144] where Humphreys J announced that "there is no such thing known to our procedure as putting half a prisoner's character in issue and leaving out the other half". The Court of Appeal thus upheld the trial judge in allowing cross-examination on previous offences of dishonesty when the defendant on an indecent assault charge had called a witness to establish his generally proper conduct towards women. Although criticised,[145] the decision was upheld by the House of Lords in *Stirland* v. *DPP*.[146] The rationale of the second limb of the subsection is rather more elusive. The fact that the defence has tried to discredit prosecution witnesses is taken to justify a reciprocal discrediting of the defendant on a "tit for tat"[147] basis; if the defence has asked the court to disbelieve the witness for the prosecution because of his or her bad character or criminal record, the court would be misled when it came to assess the evidence as a whole because of the misleadingly superior moral light in which the accused would otherwise be entitled to appear. Although at first sight it would appear that the subsection restores proper balance, as far as relative credibility is concerned there is a problem, in that the accused is in greater jeopardy from prejudice than are the prosecution witnesses.

Since the courts are adamant that disposition is generally not evidence of guilt, and that criminal record is relevant only to the credibility of the accused as a witness,[148] the cases have come to a logical *impasse*. We have seen that any kind of previous conviction may be brought into the cross-examination under section 1(f)(ii); attempting to impose rationality upon this contradictory state of affairs led the Lord Chief Justice into error in

---

[142] *Rowton* (1865) Le. & Ca. 520; *Butterwasser* [1948] 1 KB 4.

[143] (1934) 24 Cr. App. R 204.

[144] [1939] 4 All ER 164.

[145] E.g. G.D. Nokes "If a man is charged with forgery, cross-examination as to his conviction for cruelty to animals can have no purpose but prejudice": G.D. Nokes, *Introduction to Evidence* (4th edn., Sweet and Maxwell, London, 1967), 140.

[146] [1944] AC 315.

[147] *Selvey* [1970] AC 304; *Powell* [1986] 1 All ER 193.

[148] *Selvey* [1970] AC 304.

Watts.[149] The defendant was being tried for indecent assault. He made imputations on the police evidence which lost him his shield, so the prosecution sought and got leave to cross-examine on his previous convictions, which were for sexual offences against children. Lord Lane CJ conceded that the judge has a discretion once the shield has been lost, and therefore was reluctant to interfere, but could not swallow the notion that these convictions could or would be treated by the jury, even with the most correct of directions from the judge, as evidence going to credibility rather than to the issue. In his opinion, they should, therefore, have been excluded as more prejudicial than probative. However, in the subsequent case of *Powell*,[150] Lord Lane CJ announced that he had been wrong. He had not appreciated the "tit for tat" principle, and therefore that in fact previous convictions should not be analysed for their logical relationship with credibility as such, but admitted whatever their nature. Here the defendant was accused of living off immoral earnings. He claimed ignorance; also that having worked hard to build up his business he had no need of money gained in such a way. In addition, he alleged that police descriptions of his conduct were fabrications. He had previous convictions for allowing his premises to be used for the purpose of prostitution. The trial judge was held to have been right to allow cross-examination on these offences, despite their resemblance to the charge. This case shows the inadequacy of the similar facts principle. It forces courts, which can see that sometimes the record of the accused does have probative value but does not satisfy the requirement of striking similarity, to manipulate the 1898 Act to allow the jury to learn of it. It is absurd to argue that Powell's record had anything to do with his credibility on oath. It was probative, not in itself, but in the light of the defence he ran, which the trial judge said was crucial to his decision to give the prosecution leave under section 1(f)(ii). Relying on the accused to throw his shield away leaves the admissibility of valuable evidence to chance, and also prevents the defence from showing any significant difference between the offence charged and the previous ones—the unfairness indicated by the Court of Criminal Appeal in *Jones* v. *DPP*. Lord Lane CJ was unable to indicate in *Powell* just what the record had to do with his credibility; this is understandable. But it had everything to do with whether he was likely to be guilty—an inference described as "sheer prejudice" in *Watts*.

The same problem arises on a different question in *Duncalf*.[151] The issue was whether the prosecution, cross-examining under section 1(f)(ii), was entitled to go into the details of the offence, or whether it was confined to the mere fact of the conviction. A previous case, *France and France*,[152] had apparently established that it could not ask questions on details.[153] In *Duncalf*, the defendants were charged with conspiracy to steal. They

---

[149] [1983] 3 All ER 101.   [150] [1986] 1 All ER 193.   [151] [1979] 2 All ER 1116.
[152] [1979] Crim. LR 48.
[153] In *Watts* Lord Lane dismissed the case on the ground that the transcript was corrupt.

admitted being at the scene, but denied intent to steal, claiming that they were window-shopping. They lost their shield by attacking the character of police witnesses. The prosecution duly cross-examined them on previous offences of theft in which both were involved, the *modus operandi* being that they waited outside shops until the opportunity arose to run in and snatch goods off the counter. The House of Lords concluded that it was legitimate to introduce details of the *modus operandi*, distinguishing *France and France* on the ground that there the issue was identity, here intention.[154] There can be no doubt that here their Lordships were allowing *quasi*-similar fact evidence in by the back door; it is submitted that section 1(f)(ii) is an inappropriate vehicle for this for the reasons given above. More recently, the Court of Appeal overturned a conviction for affray and assault on a police officer because of the nature of the cross-examination under section 1(f)(ii). The defendant lost his shield by alleging that police witnesses had lied. He was cross-examined on details of his previous convictions for assaulting a police officer. On appeal, it was held that such facts could have no bearing on the issue of his credibility.[155]

A thorough examination of the issue of cross-examination on the facts underlying the conviction took place in *McLeod*.[156]. The defendant pleaded alibi, a defence he had raised before in an earlier case which had led to his conviction for robbery. This fact was averted to in cross-examination on his criminal record[157]; it was also suggested to him that during another robbery for which he had a conviction, he had locked the occupant of a house in a cupboard.[158] The Court of Appeal considered both lines of questioning proper within the scope of section 1(f)(ii), and gave the following guidance. The purpose of cross-examination under the subsection is to show that the defendant is not worthy of belief. The judge must explain this to the jury, and warn them that the previous convictions go to credibility and not propensity. The mere fact that the previous offences are similar in type to the current charge does not make the questions improper.[159] There should not be prolonged or extensive cross-examination in relation to the previous offences, because that would divert the jury from the principal issue, which is guilt of the current offence, not the details of earlier ones. But the similarities between defences raised on previous occasions such as false alibi or allegations of fabrication by the police, are legitimate because they do not go to disposition but to credibility. Underlying facts that show particularly bad

---

[154] But *France* is consistent with *Bradley* [1980] Crim. LR 173, interpreting s. 27(3) of the Theft Act 1968.

[155] *Khan* [1991] Crim. LR 51.

[156] [1994] 3 All ER 254.

[157] McLeod lost his shield by alleging that the police had fabricated evidence including alleged admissions.

[158] The Court of Appeal did not regard this revelation as unnecessarily prejudicial. Violence is a characteristic of the offence of robbery.

[159] *Powell* [1986] 1 All ER 193; *Selvey* [1970] AC 304.

character over and above the bare facts of the case are not necessarily to be excluded, but the judge should be careful to balance the gravity of the attack on the prosecution with the degree of prejudice to the defendant which will result from the disclosure of the facts in question.[160] If the defence object to a particular line of questioning about underlying facts, objection should be taken as soon as it is apparent to defence counsel that it is in danger of going too far. Otherwise it will be very difficult to contend that the judge has wrongly exercised his discretion under section 1(f)(ii).[161]

The courts have encountered a similar problem of interpretation in relation to section 27(3) Theft Act 1968. It reads:

> "Where a person is being proceeded against for handling stolen goods (but not for any offence other than handling stolen goods), then at any stage of the proceedings, if evidence has been given of his having or arranging to have in his possession the goods the subject of the charge, or of his undertaking or assisting in, or arranging to undertake or assist in, their retention, removal, disposal or realisation, the following evidence shall be admissible for the purpose of proving that he knew or believed the goods to be stolen goods:
>   (a) evidence that he has had in his possession, or has undertaken or assisted in the retention, removal, disposal or realisation of stolen goods from any theft taking place not earlier than twelve months before the offence charged; and
>   (b) (provided that seven days' notice in writing has been given to him of the intention to prove the conviction) evidence that he has within the five years preceding the date of the offence charged been convicted of theft or handling stolen goods."

The effect of this provision is to allow the defendant's dishonest past to be used as evidence on the issue of his or her knowledge or belief that the goods were stolen, as long as the prosecution has other evidence to establish the actus reus. In *Bradley*,[162] the Court of Appeal held that the section did not permit the giving in evidence of details of the events during which the accused had come into possession of stolen property in the past. However, since that case was decided, section 73 PACE provided that a previous conviction may be proved by production of the certificate of conviction, and this must give the "substance and effect" of the indictment and of the conviction.[163]. The issue in *Hacker*[164] was whether these innovations had undermined the decision in *Bradley*. The defendant had been charged with handling the bodyshell of a Ford Escort RS Turbo car. He had a previous

---

[160] The Court felt that details of sexual offences against children are especially likely to cause prejudice in the minds of the jury, and that this explained the decision in *Watts*; the court appears to be right; in an Oxford study of mock juries, the effect of disclosure of a previous conviction for indecency with a child was more significant than knowledge of any other kind of criminal record: Law Commission, *Evidence in Criminal Proceedings: Previous Misconduct of a Defendant*, Consultation Paper No 141, Appendix D (HMSO, London, 1996).

[161] *McLeod* [1994] 3 All ER 254, 265.

[162] (1979) 70 Cr. App. R 200.   [163] S.73(2) of PACE.   [164] [1995] 1 All ER 45.

conviction for receiving a stolen Ford Escort RS Turbo; these details were included on the certificate of conviction. The House of Lords agreed that the Recorder had rightly allowed the cross-examination to refer to those, even though the issue in the trial had been whether the car was in fact stolen, rather than Hacker's state of mind.

How the Shield is Lost

We have seen that once an accused brings into evidence any positive aspect of his or her character, any negative traits displayed by criminal behaviour in the past may be brought into cross-examination under section 1(f)(ii), whether or not they appear relevant to the point the defence is making.[165] In *Ellis*,[166] it was held that the issue of good character must be raised through evidence; suggestions of good character in counsel's opening speech do not therefore bring the subsection into operation. In *Samuel*,[167] however, the defendant was charged with larceny and gave evidence that in the past he had returned lost property. This was held to be an attempt to establish his good character, and so the prosecution was allowed to cross-examine him on his previous convictions for theft. On the other hand, if the suggestion of good character is in fact only an ancillary effect of evidence raised primarily for the purpose of developing a defence, the shield is not lost. In *Malindi*,[168] the accused was charged with political conspiracies to commit arson. He claimed that one of the meetings at which he was alleged to have joined a conspiracy was abandoned because he voiced disapproval of violent action. The Privy Council held that he had not given evidence of his own good character.[169]

Considerable cause for concern arises from the manner in which courts have interpreted the words "involve imputations on the character" in section 1(f)(ii). We are told that the accused is entitled to defend himself, which necessarily involves denying the truth of the prosecution case, without losing his shield. Thus, calling a prosecution witness a liar is not an imputation.[170] Yet explaining to the court the reason the witness would want to lie in this context apparently is.[171] We are told that the accused is entitled to describe events in order to develop his defence, even if he emerges creditably from the account, since he is not making his character an issue.[172] The same should apply if a prosecution witness emerges *discreditably* from the account,[173] since the defence is not making his character a separate issue in the trial. From *Rouse*,[174] a defendant ought to be able to contradict a prosecution witness, event to the extent of accusing him or her to be lying. In *Selvey*[175] the House of Lords added that the logic of this included the allegation that

---

[165] *Winfield* [1939] 4 All ER 164; *Stirland* [1944] AC 315.
[166] [1910] 2 KB 246.   [167] (1956) 40 Cr. App. R 8.   [168] [1962] AC 439.
[169] Cf. *Stronach* [1987] Crim. LR 231.   [170] *Rouse* [1904] 1 KB 184.
[171] *Rappolt* (1911) 6 Cr. App. R 156.   [172] *Malindi* v. *R.* [1967] AC 439.
[173] But see discussion of *Selvey* v. *DPP* [1970] AC 304, in the text to n. 181 below.
[174] [1904] 1 KB 184.   [175] [1970] AC 304.

the complainant in a rape case is lying, and in fact did consent to sexual intercourse. Yet a defendant who denies ever making admissions, where he or she is alleged by *police* witnesses to have made them, will lose the shield. Further, even if the defence insists that it has no intention of accusing the police witnesses of dishonesty, the criminal record may become admissible. From *Britzman and Hall*,[176] in such a case the admissibility of the criminal record depends upon the amount of detail in that part of the police account of events which is challenged by the defence. If it is sufficiently long and complicated, then to deny that it took place—without specifically alleging that the police are lying—cannot be by implication a suggestion that they are mistaken. If the logical implication of the challenge is that the police officers are conspiring to fabricate evidence against the defendant, this amounts to an imputation.[177] It also appears to be legitimate for the trial judge to lure the accused into an accusation that the officer is in fact lying, as opposed to being mistaken.[178] In a recent Consultation Paper, the Law Commission seeks to redress the unfairness of this group of cases. The Paper suggests that a defendant who makes an imputation on the character of a prosecution witness should not lose the shield if the imputation relates to the witness's conduct in the incident or investigation which led to the trial.[179] This would also allow the defendant to explain the reason a witness is lying on oath, for example.[180]

Decisions such as *Britzman and Hall* are justified by the Court of Appeal on the ground that they can afford to be strict in the interpretation of section 1(f)(ii), since the trial judge has a discretion to exclude the convictions even after the shield is lost. But the manner in which the discretion was exercised in *Selvey*,[181] the House of Lords case generally cited as authority for this proposition, is not encouraging. The complainant in a buggery case, according to the defendant, told him that he would go to bed with him for a pound, and that he had already gone on the bed for that sum with another man earlier that day. When Selvey refused, he dumped indecent photographs in his room out of pique. The trial judge asked Selvey whether he was asking the jury to disbelieve the witness because he was "that sort of young man". Selvey agreed that he was. The House of Lords upheld the judge in concluding that the shield was lost, and the fact that in his discretion he allowed cross-examination on Selvey's political views, which included approval of illegal activities. Yet it could be argued that no evidence had been

---

[176] [1983] Crim. LR 106.

[177] *Tanner* (1977) 66 Cr. App. R 56; *Britzman and Hall* [1983] Crim. LR 106.

[178] *Tanner* n. 177 above; observers have seen judges deliberately do this—see D. McBarnett, *Conviction* (Macmillan, London, 1983).

[179] Law Commission, *Evidence in Criminal Proceedings: Previous Misconduct of a Defendant*, Consultation Paper No 141 (HMSO, London, 1996), para. 12.71–12.79.

[180] For a critique, see P. Roberts, "All the Usual Suspects: A Critical Appraisal of the Law Commission Consultation Paper No 141" [1997] *Crim. LR* 75, 88–91.

[181] [1970] AC 304.

introduced of the complainant's character extraneous to the events the defendant had to describe in order to present his case (apart from that provoked by the judge). Despite this, Lord Pearce thought the "attack on the chief witness was very thorough and very serious. There was even added to the attack contained in the alleged admissions of the prosecution witness a suggestion that he was inventing the whole charge because the accused would not give him a pound." It is difficult to see how the accused in the absence of legal training could describe the events which gave rise to suspicion without describing the statements made by the complainant.[182] And yet the House of Lords thought the trial judge was right to allow the cross-examination.

The answer to all these difficulties cannot be further to refine the already complicated rules on the defendant's criminal record. The eagerness with which the courts misinterpret them to get the result they want shows that in some cases previous criminality is relevant, though not, strictly, admissible. It would be much simpler and more intellectually honest to place the record before the jury, as Continental courts do. There is clearly a risk that improper inferences will be drawn,[183] but it is difficult to see that the situation would be worse than in cases such as *Powell*, where the jury are presented with evidence of guilt and instructed to apply it to the credibility of the accused. The admissibility of the evidence would not depend on defence tactics, the schooling of defendants not to criticise the police or any other imponderable. And the criminal record would be seen in relation to all the defendant's history, his or her education and employment (if any) and might be more comprehensible as a result. Also, since it would come out in every case, rather than being sprung on the defendant during the course of giving evidence, the defence would be able to dispose of inconsequential information and make any material point about the nature of the criminal record.

The elaborate minuet between prosecution and defence provoked by this legislation, the progeny of the adversarial trial, is indefensible, yet it seems that radical reform is unlikely. The Law Commission's Consultation Paper recognises the illogicality of section 1(f) in a thorough review but proposes only the most modest amendments.[184] This conservativism is surprising in view of the findings of the Paper. It observes that the theory of "indivisibility of character" established in *Winfield*[185] cannot be convincingly defended.[186]

---

[182] Cf. *Bishop* [1974] 2 All ER 1206; accounting for his fingerprints in the room of the prosecution witness, D claimed to have had a homosexual relationship with him. This was held to have been an imputation on his character because, "unless [the Court is] behind the times . . . most men would be anxious to keep from a jury . . . the knowledge that they practised such acts"

[183] M.J. Damaska argues that drawing of inferences contrary to common sense is not likely: "Evidentiary Barriers to Conviction and Two Models of Criminal Procedure: A Comparative Study" (1973) 121 *U Penn. LR* 506, 518.

[184] Law Commission, *Evidence in Criminal Proceedings: Previous Misconduct of a Defendant,* Consultation Paper No 141 (HMSO, London, 1996).

[185] [1939] 4 All ER 164.   [186] *Ibid.*, para. 6.5.

It demonstrates that to look for links between most varieties of criminal record and a tendency to tell lies on oath is a fool's errand.[187] There are suggestions that the traditional dichotomy between credibility and the issue of guilt is unworkable.[188] The difficulty encountered in *Watts*[189] and *Powell*[190] is that if a previous conviction is similar in nature to the offence charged, the jury will be hard put to restrict it to its impact to credibility alone. This problem is exacerbated if aspects of the offences are so alike as to bring them close (albeit not close enough) to "similar facts" relevance.

The Law Commission does not recommend substantial reforms to the rules on admissibility of the defendant's criminal record. However, it does suggest that where the accused raises a particular aspect of good character, previous convictions adduced in rebuttal should be relevant to that. There is no attempt to address the acknowledged illogicality of admitting *all* previous convictions where the shield is lost through an attack on the character of a prosecution witness. Here the provision appears to serve a primarily deterrent function, which is to protect prosecution witnesses from gratuitous slurs from the defence, which will pay for them through loss of the shield—though that will hardly cause sleepless nights to a defendant with no criminal record. This is an ineffective protection for prosecution witnesses against offensive and unnecessary harangues in cross-examination,[191] and affords the crudest means of restoring balance and fairness to the adversarial criminal trial.

Giving Evidence against the Co-Defendant: section 1(f)(iii)

In a leading case in the House of Lords, *Murdoch and Taylor*,[193] section 1(f)(iii)[192] of the Criminal Evidence Act 1898 was interpreted as follows: "I myself would . . . simply say that "evidence against" means evidence which supports the prosecutor's case in a material respect which undermines the defence of the co-accused".[194] In *Crawford*,[195] Lord Bingham CJ thought the simplest way of expressing the principle was to ask, "[d]id the evidence given by the defendant in the witness box, if accepted, damage in a significant way the defence of the co-defendant?". In the earlier case, the defendant Murdoch argued that he had not given "evidence against", since he had no "hostile intent", and had made the damaging remarks during cross-examination rather than during evidence-in-chief. The test laid down in section 1(f)(iii) was satisfied, according to the House of Lords. The House went on to reject the argument that a trial judge should have a discretion whether to allow a co-defendant to cross-examine on previous convictions under the

---

[187] *Ibid.*, para. 6.27.   [188] Paras. 6.74–6.84, 11.10–11.12.
[189] [1983] 3 All ER 101.   [190] [1986] 1 All ER 193.
[191] See J. McEwan, "Law Commission Dodges the Nettles in Consultation Paper No 141" [1997] *Crim. LR* 93, 101–2.
[192] See above, p. 186.   [193] [1965] AC 574.   [194] Lord Donovan. at 592.
[195] *The Times,* 10 June 1977.

subsection.[196] That would involve judges in an invidious choice between two defendants who may have dramatically conflicting interests. Lords Reid and Pearce, however, were less than happy about this even-handed stance. Lord Reid pointed out that if one co-accused with previous convictions has a version of events which materially contradicts that of the other, but that other has no criminal record, he or she will find it very difficult to mount a defence. He could see no answer to the problem, however, whereas Lord Pearce preferred the use of a judicial discretion to ameliorate the harshness of the subsection's effect.

The Convictions of Accomplices: Section 74 of PACE

Prior to the enactment of sections 73 and 74 of PACE, the effect of the rule in *Hollington* v. *Hewthorne*[197] was in criminal cases to prevent a criminal conviction from being regarded as admissible evidence that an offence had been committed. Thus, in a prosecution of D for handling stolen goods, the prosecution had to prove afresh that the goods were stolen, even where the thief had been convicted at an earlier trial. After 1984, the conviction, proved by producing a certificate of conviction,[198] of a person other than the accused may be admitted as evidence that the offence was committed by that person,[199] although the accused may disprove it by adducing evidence of his or her own.[200] These provisions appear at first sight innocuous and sensible, but have had implications not generally anticipated; at their worst they reverse the burden of proof in criminal trials, effectively convicting an accused person by means of evidence adduced and challenged, if at all, at proceedings to which he or she was not a party.

There is a principle that one person's confession is not evidence against another[201]; therefore, if the police statement made by B, D's co-defendant, is read out in the usual way but appears to implicate D, the judge should warn the jury that it is not evidence against D.[202] In practice, prosecutors who wish to rely on B's admissions as far as his own role is concerned, usually omit the passage placing blame on D (otherwise, the nature of the statement may be a ground for separating the trials). The problem caused by section 74 is that if the trials of co-defendants are separated, and one is convicted before the other on a guilty plea or otherwise, it could be argued that the conviction

---

[196] The only exception to this would be in the case where the prosecution seeks leave to cross-examine under s.1(f)(iii). Although this would be a rare case, in the opinion of the House of Lords, it might be appropriate, for instance, if the co-defendants have hatched a plot to run cut-throat defences but leave each other's criminal records out of the trial.

[197] [1943] KB 587.   [198] PACE, s. 73.

[199] *Ibid.*, s.74(1); see *Pigram* [1995] Crim. LR 808.   [200] *Ibid.*, s. 74(2).

[201] An out-of-court statement in which A implicates B would be hearsay if offered as evidence of B's guilt at his trial: see Ch. 7.

[202] *Gunewardene* [1951] 2 KB 600.

of the first to be dealt with is admissible at the trial of the other to show that the offence was committed or that there was a conspiracy. The acts and declarations of a conspirator are admissible against a fellow conspirator to prove the nature and scope of the conspiracy, but there must be independent evidence to implicate the latter in the conspiracy.[203] However, if one conspirator has already pleaded guilty to conspiring with D, evidence of this fact, if admitted under section 74, is very damaging. If such a conviction is admitted, then the burden is on the accused if he wishes to challenge the presumption that the co-defendant is guilty of the offence. The courts have in some cases of this kind felt that the only way to avoid the danger of prejudice is to exclude the evidence concerning the co-defendant altogether under section 78, which deals with evidence that would adversely affect the fairness of the proceedings.[204] Inconsistent use of the discretion has precipitated a haphazard collection of cases.

The traditional view was that a plea of guilty by one co-accused is not in any sense evidence of another's guilt although at the trial of the latter the jury could be told of the other's plea to explain his or her absence from the dock.[205] The courts have been forced to look at the principle again in the light of section 74. In *O'Connor*,[206] the defendant was charged with conspiracy to obtain property by deception. He was alleged to have taken part in a scheme with another man to defraud an insurance company by falsely reporting a vehicle as stolen. He initially admitted the offence but then retracted. The co-defendant pleaded guilty to the offence of conspiracy to defraud before O'Connor's trial, and that conviction was admitted under section 74. The defence argued on appeal that this enabled the prosecution to put before the jury a statement made by one co-accused in the absence of the other, and that the evidential effect of the guilty plea was only that the co-defendant had conspired with the defendant, so that it was not open to the jury to infer that the defendant had conspired with him. The Court of Appeal held that section 74 was clearly designed to deal with the situation where it was necessary as a preliminary matter for it to be proved that a person other than the accused had been convicted of an offence as a condition precedent to the conviction of the accused, for example, proof of theft by another in a trial for handling. Section 75 of PACE provides that where the conviction is admitted in evidence it is admitted with all the detail contained in the relevant count in the indictment. Once that went before the jury in this case, it was not realistic to stress that they would not be entitled therefore to infer that D conspired with the co-defendant. Without deciding the full scope of section 74, it was sufficient for the purposes of the present

---

[203] *R. v. Governor of Pentonville Prison, ex p. Osman* [1989] 3 All ER 701.

[204] For the court's power to exclude evidence which would adversely affect the fairness of the proceedings; see Ch. 6.

[205] *Moore* (1956) 40 Cr. App. R 50.

[206] [1987] Crim. LR 260.

case to say that the evidence should not have been admitted under the discretion given in section 78. (The proviso was applied.)

In *Robertson*,[207] however, section 78 was not invoked. The defendant was charged with conspiracy to burgle. There were convictions of P and L for burglary, allegedly in relation to acts in pursuance of the conspiracy. Their guilt was therefore neutral as far as Robertson was concerned, but there was other evidence implicating him in the agreement, including an eyewitness who saw him with them at about the material time. Taken together, the evidence showed what the object of their joint plan was. The Court of Appeal held that the evidence was rightly admitted, and section 78 was inapplicable. It distinguished *O'Connor*, where the conviction tended to lead the jury to the conclusion that the defendant must have conspired with the other accused. The appeal was dismissed also in *Bennett*[208] where the defendant was jointly charged with theft. The co-accused pleaded guilty, and the resulting conviction was used in evidence against Bennett. The Court of Appeal held that this was acceptable; to omit the guilty plea would "mystify the jury". But since the allegation was that the co-accused, who worked in a supermarket, had passed goods worth £85 to the defendant for a price of £4.99, it caused substantial damage to the defence case. As Birch has noted, juries managed not to be mystified before 1984, when they were told nothing about the fate of the co-accused.[209]

Kempster[210] represents a wish to keep the new law more in line with that of before 1984; there were eight charges, and the Crown led evidence that Kempster had been seen in the company of his co-accused close to the time of the offences. There was also other evidence, none of which was sufficient *per se* to identify any of the offenders. The trial judge admitted the guilty pleas of the co-accused without imposing a limit on the purpose for which the prosecution could use those pleas. This appeal was allowed; the Court of Appeal followed *Moore* [211] in holding that a plea of guilty by a co-defendant is not evidence against the other accused. Section 74 allows the admission of the plea where relevant. Here it was relevant to the issue whether the defendant had taken part in the robberies/burglary to which the co-defendant had pleaded guilty, the offences occurring when the co-defendant was said to have been in the defendant's company. The application of section 78 was an entirely different question. The cases show that whilst evidence which of itself established complicity should be excluded under section 78, evidence which did not of itself have that effect but which was used as a basis for other evidence to that end need not necessarily be excluded. If it is intended to use the plea as evidence against the defendant, the intention must be clear, and may attract section 78. Here it was not clear what use the prosecution wanted to make of it, therefore section 78 was not argued on that point. In the light

---

[207] [1987] 3 All ER 231.   [208] [1988] Crim. LR 686.
[209] [1988] Crim. LR Case commentary 687.   [210] [1989] Crim. LR 747.
[211] [1981] Crim. LR 747.

of less than overwhelming evidence against Kempster, there was a suspicion that the prosecution did intend to use the other's conviction against him, and therefore the conviction was unsafe. Another strong case is *Mattison*, involving a charge against Mattison and one Davis of gross indecency in a public lavatory. Davis pleaded guilty but Mattison pleaded not guilty. His case was that he had been falsely accused by the police who burst into his cubicle, which he had been using for orthodox purposes. He denied any contact with Davis. The trial judge allowed evidence of Davis's guilty plea, and the jury seemed unsure how to deal with it. They returned a note to the judge inquiring whether Mattison had been charged with indecency with anyone other than Davis. Saville J concluded that in such a case the admission of the evidence was inevitably unfair. "If A commits an act of gross indecency with B, it is a strong inference that the converse is also true, in the absence of special circumstances to indicate otherwise."

Why did Parliament place the burden of proving someone else's innocence on the defendant? He was not party to the other's trial and so could not influence the way it was conducted. In *O'Connor* Lord Lane CJ thought that the intention of the legislature had been merely to reverse *Hollington* v. *Hewthorne* to deal with offences such as handling stolen goods or impeding arrest of an offender. But in *Robertson* it was observed that the court was not entitled to ignore the plain meaning of Parliament's words.[212] Although it seems likely that cases such as *Robertson* were unforeseen, the effect is of significance for two reasons. First, it is a further instance of the erosion of the *Woolmington* principle that the defence should not bear the burden of proof.[213] Secondly, judicial reaction to the perceived unfairness of the provision has involved use of section 78 in a way which was entirely unforeseen,[214] with the result that the judge's discretion is becoming more important and more visible in criminal trials. We could see development in the direction that any evidence ultimately will depend for its admissibility on the court's opinion of its probative value against a general principle of fairness. If this were so, Parliament could feel free to introduce more rules which appear to strike at the presumption of innocence, in the knowledge that they would be invoked only in those cases where the judges regard their use as appropriate.

---

[212] See R. Munday, "Proof of Guilt by Association under s. 74 of the Police and Criminal Evidence Act" [1990] *Crim. LR* 236.

[213] [1935] AC 462; see above, Ch. 2.

[214] See Ch. 6.

6

The Prosecutor in the Criminal Trial

A Formidable Opponent

Adversarial theory presupposes two contestants equally matched in a struggle in which the state, which provides them with a forum for contest and a machinery to enforce victory, takes no direct interest. A curious irony is the fact that the proceedings which most closely resemble this model are civil trials, in which the state has no interest unless it is a party; but these are far less committed to the principle of orality than English criminal trials, the closest thing to an adversarial proceeding that exists within any jurisdiction, but in which the state does have a direct interest. The trend in civil cases towards greater pre-trial exchange of information and advance notification to the judge of intended arguments and evidence suggests a move in the direction of the Continental or European Court of Justice mode of trial. Yet, curiously, Continental systems are more content to perceive civil trials as private battles between two parties than criminal proceedings, where the state has an obvious interest.[1] Meanwhile, in England, advocates in criminal trials hang on doggedly to the adversarial tradition, despite increasing pressure to change[2] and a gradual movement away from many of its fundamental features through piecemeal statutory reform.[3] The rules of evidence diminish in importance as the emphasis on orality declines. Yet the parties in a criminal case are not independent, and they do not have equal potency as litigants.

It is certainly possible to devise criminal proceedings which encompass the concepts of equality of risk and independence. Taking a lesson from the Anglo-Saxons, in a case where a suspect is remanded to gaol, the accuser could also be so remanded in order to be fair; if the prosecution fails he could be made to suffer the penalty he sought for the defendant.[4] But

---

[1] M.R. Damaska, *Evidence Law Adrift* (Yale University Press, New Haven, London, 1997).

[2] E.g., Ludovic Kennedy's address to the Conference of the Liberal Democratic Party, 17 Sept. 1990.

[3] E.g. of the hearsay rule, see Ch. 7.

[4] *Lex talionis*; F. Pollock and F.W. Maitland, *History of the English Criminal Law* (Cambridge University Press, Cambridge, 1895).

although equality of risk may appear fairer than a system where the prosecutor hazards nothing, it does little to further the interest of society as a whole in the prevention of crime. The state in this country, however, was slow to take on responsibility for the prosecution of crime. There were private associations for the prosecution of offences until the nineteenth century, although there were efforts to involve representatives of the community such as Justices of the Peace as early as 1349.[5] Public resistance to the introduction of a police force delayed an organised system of prosecution for many years, but once such forces were set up it was obvious that they would make more effective prosecutors than private individuals or associations, and would establish a consistency of approach whereby an offender's prospects of being prosecuted did not depend on the identity of his victim.

It is still assumed, however, that any private citizen is wronged by the commission of crimes, whether or not directly injured by them, and therefore may prosecute in the criminal courts. In complex cases costs are now prohibitive, and even straightforward cases are beyond the means of most people. In 1981 the Phillips Commission noted that the majority of private prosecutions were launched, not by individuals, but by shops which employed their own store detectives or charities such as the RSPCA and the NCPCC.[6] The Commissioners regarded private agencies as inappropriate prosecutors for shoplifting cases, since many offenders are elderly or have medical or personal histories which justify non-prosecution, and recommended that the practice of private prosecution by retailers should cease.[7] Prosecution is regarded as an area where discretion should be exercised in a responsible way, and in which agencies should be accountable.[8] Thus, the citizen who wishes to initiate a private prosecution finds that he or she does not have an entirely free hand. In well over 100 Acts of Parliament the right to prosecute is subject to the consent of a minister, official or a judge.[9] Government agencies may ensure that the case is discontinued, either by the Attorney-General entering a nolle prosequi,[10] or by the Director of Public Prosecutions taking over the prosecution, which he may continue or drop by offering no evidence.[11] Also, if the individual is regarded as a vexatious litigant with a *penchant* for launching unmeritorious criminal proceedings, the Attorney-General may apply to the High Court for an order to prevent him or her from laying an information in future without the leave of the Court.[12]

---

[5] Ordinance of Labourers.

[6] Royal Commission on Criminal Procedure, *The Investigation and Prosecution of Criminal Offences in England and Wales: the Law and Procedure* (Phillips Report, (HMSO, London, 1981) Cmnd 8092, para. 171.

[7] *Ibid.*, para. 7.46.   [8] *Ibid.*, para. 7.3.   [9] *Ibid.*, para. 7.48.

[10] A power not subject to any scrutiny by the courts: *R.* v. *Comptroller of Patents* [1899] 1 QB 909.

[11] Prosecution of Offences Act 1985, s. 6(2).

[12] Supreme Court Act 1981, s. 42, as amended by Prosecution of Offences Act 1985, s. 24; there is a similar power to ban a litigant with a history of vexatious civil proceedings.

There is a recognition, then, that criminal proceedings are not a matter from which the state can stand back with magnificent disinterest. And once the police began to take on the work of prosecution, having the funds and the organisation (although no increased powers) to do it, the question naturally arose whether they had special responsibilities in that regard. The public interest in the bringing of criminal prosecutions was acknowledged by the courts. In *R.* v. *Metropolitan Police Commissioner, ex p. Blackburn (No 1)*,[13] the plaintiff sought judicial review of police prosecution policy. Lord Denning in the Court of Appeal conceded that a chief constable was entitled to make his own decision whether or not to prosecute in a particular case. But his discretion was not absolute. There might be decisions of policy with which a court could interfere, if they amounted to a failure to enforce the law. However, although Lord Denning thought that the writ of *mandamus* provided the individual with the legal equipment with which police prosecution policy could be challenged, the problem of *locus standi*[14] has never been satisfactorily addressed. The police are certainly subject to the law in the way cases are investigated; their powers, which were defined in the main in a series of cases on civil liberties, are now primarily set out in the Police and Criminal Evidence Act 1984 (PACE). This Act was the product of recommendations of the Royal Commission on Criminal Procedure in 1981; the Commission's review of prosecution concluded that the lack of accountability and, in some cases, inefficiency of the then current arrangements demanded the creation of a specialist prosecution service.

The creation of the Crown Prosecution Service in 1985[15] may have succeeded in providing a more professional prosecution system, although there is heated debate on the subject. But the Service is subject to a scrutiny which shows that prosecutors are no longer to any extent regarded as equivalent to private litigants.[16] However, since the police retain the responsibility to investigate offences and gather evidence, they have a substantial influence on the cases which appear in court. The Crown Prosecutor decides whether or not to proceed with cases *as presented to him* by a police officer. The police, then, still act as a filter which may lead to many cases never being produced to the Crown Prosecution Service at all. Prosecution is in fact an enterprise conducted jointly by the police and the Crown Prosecution Service. Since the Service is not involved with a case at the investigation stage unless advice is specifically sought, there is no opportunity to control how the evidence is obtained, although police conduct is subject to the restraints of PACE, the common law and the police disciplinary code. The relative

---

[13] [1868] 2 QB 118.

[14] An interest which the party seeks to defend, and entitles him to seek an administrative remedy.

[15] Prosecution of Offences Act 1985.

[16] The regional structure with local supervisory authorities recommended by the Royal Commission (Phillips Report, n. 6 above, paras. 7.21–37) was not adopted. But the head of the CPS, the DPP, is answerable to Parliament through the Attorney-General.

liberty of the police appears to be inevitable in an adversarial system. Although the Procurator Fiscal in Scotland and the District Attorney in the United States of America are involved at an earlier stage of an inquiry, "in practice the police retain a very large measure of control over the decision to prosecute and, especially where the volume of cases puts pressure on the system . . . the lawyer's decision tends to be little more than an endorsement of that of the police".[17] For the purposes of gathering evidence, police officers might be thought to be in a position of privilege, with powers of search and seizure not possessed by the ordinary citizen. But many police officers complain that the safeguards in the 1984 Act too often tie their hands. A journalist told John Stalker that an investigation by the press was far "deeper and more searching than anything MI5 or Special Branch could undertake . . . 'You have', he said, 'survived the Fleet Street vetting machine'."[18]

In a strictly adversarial system, a decision to prosecute would be based entirely on the merits and potential consequences of an individual case. The reality is that some decisions are to some extent influenced by considerations of the public interest. There were protests that some notorious fraud trials post-1980s were influenced by utilitarian concerns, such as the need to prove to investors that the City of London is not immune from investigation, and that therefore their money is safe. It is alleged that to this end practices which had long been tolerated and were in fact widespread suddenly became the object of attention; individual businessmen, investment consultants and company directors were sacrificed to the greater good of community confidence. Similarly, the 1990 investigation into the dealings of Liverpool councillors has been described as a witch-hunt designed to encourage industrialists to base operations in Liverpool, secure in the knowledge that the widely-rumoured corruption in the area has been stamped out. There is a danger that political expediency may direct prosecution policy, for example, where there has been a vocal campaign in the press about a particular sort of crime, or where for some other reason there is considerable public concern, as with the Zeebrugge ferry disaster of 1987. In that case, the prosecution case for manslaughter against company officials was thrown out by the trial judge,[19] causing observers to wonder why the case against them had been brought in the first place. In the defence of Kevin Taylor and his co-defendants, who included his bank manager and his accountant,[20] it was argued forcefully that the case had been brought to justify the earlier pursuit through disciplinary proceedings of his friend John Stalker, the former Deputy Chief Constable of Greater Manchester.[21] Whether or not the allegations contain any truth, the risk remains that close association between the

---

[17] Phillips Report, n. 6 above, para. 7.11.
[18] J. Stalker, *Stalker* (Penguin, Harmondsworth, 1988), 163.
[19] *P & O (European) Ferries* (1990) 93 Cr App R 72 (Waterhouse J).
[20] *Bowley et al.*, Case No 88.6607, 10 Oct. 1989.
[21] See Stalker, n. 18 above.

government and a highly organised, centralised, prosecution service, could allow influence to be exercised.

There are other bodies which investigate offences and carry out prosecutions, such as the Serious Fraud Office,[22] the Department of Social Security, the Commissioners of Customs and Excise and the Inland Revenue. Some of these agencies have sweeping powers the police would envy, and which add further weight to the argument that the prosecutor in a criminal case has a might on his side which unbalances the criminal trial and demands that strict adversarial theory be modified to protect the accused. The inbalance of power as between the state apparatus and the single suspect has led to significant departures from adversarial principles; the greater duty on the part of the prosecution to disclose evidence has been discussed above in Chapter 1. Also, barristers who are prosecuting should bear in mind the particular jeopardy facing defendants; a prosecutor should not go for a conviction at any cost, but present the case fairly and completely.[23] The most obvious difference, however, is the duty to obtain evidence by legitimate means, although the law on this is unclear from the point of view of both principle and content.

Evidence Obtained by Unlawful Means

The Exclusionary Rule

The fact that prosecutors are now supported by a funded and specialist service with exclusive access to investigative agencies may account for the scrupulousness with which courts examine some of their activities. If a defendant were to obtain valuable evidence by burgling the police station, there is no reason to think that he or she could not use it. In general, relevant evidence is admissible whatever its provenance.[24] If, however, it is so unreliable that it ceases to be relevant then it will be excluded. If the rules of evidence in criminal cases had developed exclusively along those lines. a reasonably coherent system would have emerged. Continental rules did this; oral evidence obtained by oppression is inadmissible,[25] but physical evidence, such as documents unlawfully obtained but reliable in themselves, is not. But the common law and now PACE, together with the cases which interpret it, are less straightforward. Unreliability is not the only factor at work. This state of affairs was conceded by the Criminal Law Revision Committee, which concluded that nevertheless the reliability requirement was the most important influence.[26] Other concerns are not easily identified;

---

[22] Criminal Justice Act 1987, s.1(5).

[23] *R.* v. *Thomas (No 2)* [1974] 1 NZLR 658; *Berger* v. *US* (1935) 295 US 78.

[24] *Lord Ashburton* v. *Pape* [1913] 2 Ch 469; *Nationwide* v. *Goddard* [1986] 3 WLR 734.

[25] Damaska, n. 1 above, 13.

it may be that judges are using the rules of evidence to deter unlawful police practices; it may be that they are mindful of the institutional might of the prosecutor, and wish to even things up; it may be that they would feel themselves or the integrity of the trial contaminated if they admitted evidence discovered by means they regard as repugnant. This is a factor in the extreme position of the American courts: "[o]ut of regard for its own dignity as an agency of justice and custodian of liberty the court should not have a hand in such a 'dirty business' . . . It is morally incongruous for the state to flout constitutional rights and at the same time demand that its citizens observe the law."[27] But once evidence which is itself reliable is excluded for any or all of these reasons, the issue of guilt or innocence has been made a secondary matter in the proceedings: "[w]hat bothers me is that almost never do we have a genuine issue of guilt or innocence today. The system is so changed that what we are doing in the courtroom is trying the conduct of the police and that of the prosecutor all along the line."[28] These remarks of Judge Walter V. Shaefer indicate the anxiety of many American judges during the heyday of the doctrine of the "fruit of the poisoned tree", by which the courts would have nothing to do with any evidence obtained improperly. Even minor breaches which led to the discovery of reliable evidence might fall foul of this doctrine, as in *Orozco* v. *Texas*.[29] Four police officers burst into the defendant's bedroom immediately after a shooting. They regarded him as under arrest, and asked where the gun was. He told them, and they found the murder weapon in his washing machine. Since in the heat of the moment they had not reminded him of his rights to silence and to legal advice, all this evidence was inadmissible. Widespread belief that this approach was leading to undeserved acquittals has led the American courts to adopt unconvincing reasoning to escape the rigours of *Miranda* v. *Arizona*,[30] the decision which demanded elaborate warnings to be given to suspects as soon as there were grounds for suspicion.[31]

The Phillips Report rejected the argument that it was necessary to exclude unlawfully obtained evidence as a sanction against improper police conduct. The intended result would, apparently, be best achieved by

---

[26] *Evidence (General)*, Eleventh Report (1972), Cmnd 4991 para. 56. Mirfield suggests that the more extreme examples of exclusion of perfectly reliable confessions at common law were the result of a preference for generalised principles rather than scrutiny of the facts of each case: P. Mirfield, *Confessions*, (Sweet and Maxwell, London, 1985) 62.

[27] *People* v. *Cahan* (1985) 282 P 2d. 9805, 912, *per* Justice Traynor.

[28] Judge Walter V. Shaefer, quoted in McDonald, *The Center Magazine*, Nov. 1968 at 76.

[29] (1968) 394 US 324.

[30] (1966) 384 US 436.

[31] *Harris* v. *New York* (1971) 401 US 222; it was held that although a confession was inadmissible as evidence of the facts stated, the accused could be cross-examined on it. Further dilution of the spirit of *Miranda* is found in the Omnibus Crime Control and Safe Streets Act 1968, amending United States Code (Title 18, Ch. 350 1(a)). For analysis of the retreat of the Supreme Court from *Miranda,*. see P Mirfield, *Silence, Confessions and Improperly Obtained Evidence* (Clarendon, Oxford, 1997), 327–36.

"contemporaneous controls and good supervision",[32] and "effective arrangement for the investigation of complaints against the police" plus the usual civil remedy.[33] The complaints procedure has (fairly or unfairly) had a poor press, and therefore victims of police malpractice may be unenthusiastic about participating in it, especially as they gain nothing more than vindication and revenge even if the complaint is upheld. To bring civil proceedings for trespass would require extraordinary determination, given the effort and expense likely to be involved. Litigation, therefore, tends to be reserved for the most extreme cases. On the other hand, the Report rightly anticipated that the system established by PACE would provide better controls over what happens to suspects in the police station. The increasing use of tape-recording is designed to reduce the number of allegations that oppression was used to extract a confession; this works to the benefit of suspect and interrogator.[34] But it is more difficult to control what happens outside the police station.

Lord Phillips' Royal Commission decided against a general discretion to exclude improperly obtained evidence, chiefly because it would be exercised in very few cases: only a minority of those stopped and searched are arrested: a sizeable minority of those whose premises are searched are never charged: most defendants plead guilty: and of the rest, who deny guilt, only a small proportion challenge the legality of the manner in which the investigation was conducted. This argument is startling; first, it ignores the fact that, since at the time of the Commission's inquiry such evidence was admissible, this would have encouraged guilty pleas and discouraged any challenge to admissibility. Also, the fact that so few of those searched were subsequently charged or prosecuted is more alarming than reassuring. And to allow the police to make use of evidence obtained where there were no grounds for the search is to encourage "fishing" expeditions, and to maintain a high number of fruitless searches. Lord Hailsham, having stated that one ground for objecting to a discretion to exclude would be prolonged and expensive *voirs dires*, added that the penalty for police misconduct would be levied on the public rather than the police if it led to the acquittal of guilty men.[35] The subsequent Royal Commission chaired by Lord Runciman simply declared satisfaction with present arrangements.[36] It is understandable that some are persuaded by the argument that the rules of evidence should not be used as a means to discipline the police force, since the purpose of the trial is to establish guilt or innocence, but it would be a great deal stronger if the relationship between

---

[32] *Phillips Report*, n. 6 above, 4.118.

[33] At 4.119.

[34] Increased police enthusiasm for tape-recording was noted in J. Baldwin, "Police Interviews on Tape" [1990] *NLJ* 662.

[35] 1983–4 HL Deb. 26 July col. 668 430.

[36] *Report of the Royal Commission on Criminal Justice* (chairman Viscount Runciman) (HMSO, London, 1993), Cm 2263, 58.

the rules of evidence and the truth were more clearly established than it seems to be in the adversarial trial.

Reliability of Evidence or Fairness?

The lack of a consistent approach to the admissibility of evidence unlawfully obtained by the prosecution predates PACE and has to some extent been embodied in its provisions on confession evidence. Section 76 provides:

> "(1) In any proceedings a confession made by an accused person may be given in evidence against him so far as it is relevant to any matter in issue in the proceedings and is not excluded by the court in pursuance of this section.
>
> (2) If, in any proceedings where the prosecution proposes to give in evidence a confession made by an accused person, it is represented to the court that the confession was or may have been obtained—
>
> (a) by oppression of the person who made it; or
>
> (b) in consequence of anything said or done which was likely to render unreliable any confession which might be made by him in consequence thereof,
>
> the court shall not allow the confession to be given in evidence against him except in so far as the prosecution proves to the court beyond reasonable doubt that the confession (notwithstanding that it may be true) was not obtained as aforesaid.
>
> (3) In any proceedings where the prosecution proposes to give in evidence a confession made by an accused person, the court may of its own motion require the prosecution, as a condition of allowing it to do so, to prove that the confession was not obtained as mentioned in subsection (2) above.
>
> (4) The fact that a confession is wholly or partly excluded in pursuance of this section shall not affect the admissibility in evidence—
>
> (a) of any facts discovered as a result of the confession; or
>
> (b) where the confession is relevant as showing that the accused speaks, writes or expresses himself in a particular way, of so much of the confession as is necessary to show that he does so.
>
> (5) Evidence that a fact to which this subsection applies was discovered as a result of a statement made by an accused person shall not be admissible unless evidence of how it was discovered is given by him or on his behalf.
>
> (6) Subsection (5) above applies—
>
> (a) to any fact discovered as a result of a confession which is wholly excluded in pursuance of this section; and
>
> (b) to any fact discovered as a result of a confession which is partly so excluded, if the fact is discovered as a result of the excluded part of the confession.
>
> (7) Nothing in Part VII of this Act shall prejudice the admissibility of a confession made by an accused person.
>
> (8) In this section 'oppression' includes torture, inhuman or degrading treatment, and the use or threat of violence (whether or not amounting to torture)."

The Criminal Law Revision Committee argued that reliability was the dominant common law principle; this explained why evidence discovered as a result of a confession obtained by threats or promises was admissible even though the confession itself was not. That position was restated in section 76(4); it echoes the decision in *Warwickshall*,[37] where the defendant made an inadmissible confession, which indicated that the stolen goods were to be found in her bed. They were indeed found there, and the evidence that they had been was held to be admissible. Their location was incriminating in itself. The confession, however, remained inadmissible notwithstanding that the facts appeared to confirm it as accurate. Similarly, the court could not be told even in gerneral terms that the defendant had indicated where the incriminating articles might be found.[38] This rule is a serious disadvantage to prosecutors; if incriminating items are found in "neutral" circumstances, there is no ostensible link with the defendant. Yet parts, at least, of the inadmissible confession appear to be true; to exclude them from evidence suggests that the reliability principle is not the only one at work here.

Clearly, reliability is not the only concern of section 76. Subsection (2) contains similar contradictions, in that an improperly obtained confession is inadmissible "notwithstanding that it may be true". This proviso appears to espouse a disciplinary rather than a reliability principle. It might be thought that judges are hardly in a position to know whether the confession was true or not, particularly at the *voir dire* stage at which they have to adjudicate on admissibility; but in that case, the proviso is unnecessary. Also, there have been cases where the accused has admitted at the *voir dire* that his confession, despite the claims of police misconduct, was true.[39] A *voir dire* must be held where an issue as to the admissibility of a confession arises. The question of admssibility must be decided by the trial judge[40] or magistrates.[41] An accused person who is unsuccessful in the challenge at the *voir dire* stage may reprise the challenge for the benefit of the jury, in order to suggest that it is unreliable.[42] Where the defendant has admitted guilt at the *voir dire*, but nevertheless succeeded in securing its exclusion, a prosecutor might seek to have the more recent admission admitted in evidence or, at least, to use it to cross-examine on inconsistency. In *Brophy*,[43] the House of Lords argued that to allow the admission to be given in evidence at the substantive trial would curtail the freedom an accused person ought to enjoy to give evidence at the *voir dire* of any improper means used by the police during questioning.[44] The same principle was applied to the issue of cross-

---

[37] (1783) 1 Leach 263.　　[38] Now in s.76(5).

[39] *Wong Kam-Ming* [1980] AC 247; *Brophy* [1981] 3 WLR 103.

[40] *Sat-Bhambra* (1989) 86 Cr. App. R 55.

[41] *R. v. Liverpool JJ, ex p. R* [1987] 2 All ER 66; obviously magistrates, as arbiters of fact and law, must dismiss from their minds, when considering their verdicts at the conclusion of the case, any confession of which they became aware at the *voir dire* but which they decided was inadmissible.

[42] *Chan Wei-Keung v. R.* [1967] 2 AC 160.

[43] [1981] 2 All ER 705.

[44] Although this argument was held not to apply if the admissions made at the *voir dire* are entirely gratuitous, as where they are made out of bravado.

examining the accused on discrepancies between what was said at the *voir dire* and testimony during the substantive trial in *Wong Kam-Ming* v. *R.*[45]

The theoretical position is further confused by the enactment of section 78 of PACE, inserted into the Bill at a late stage by an unwilling government which appeared to think that it had nothing to do with disciplining the police.[46] The section reads:

> "(1) In any proceedings the court may refuse to allow evidence on which the prosecution proposes to rely to be given if it appears to the court that, having regard to all the circumstances, including the circumstances in which the evidence was obtained, the admission of the evidence would have such an adverse effect on the fairness of the proceedings that the court ought not to admit it."

Although in debate on the Bill the Home Secretary emphasised that section 78 was not addressed to the history or origin of evidence, but was concerned only with the fairness of the trial itself, it is not clear whether the courts have taken the same view. It is arguable that not to look at the manner in which the evidence was obtained would render the provision meaningless. After all, an accused person has an absolute right to a fair trial; that is not a matter of judicial discretion.[47] Section 82(3) of PACE adds a further complication in theory, by providing for the retention of any common law discretion to exclude, but in practice judges have used section 78 to give themselves such a wide discretion that section 82(3) is rarely mentioned.

A flexible discretion of this kind seems ideal to protect rights which, Ashworth argues, exist independently of either reliability or disciplinary concerns.[48] For it is one thing to argue that to devise exclusionary rules of evidence is not an appropriate means of disciplining the police—there are other ways of doing this—but another to identify an alternative method of protecting and enforcing the right of the private citizen to be fairly treated by law enforcement officers. Evidence which is obtained by unlawful procedures, he argues, places the suspect at a disadvantage which can only effectively be mitigated by disallowing its use in court. The "protective principle", unlike the disciplinary one, does not depend on whether or not the misconduct was deliberate; the relevant factors are matters such as the seriousness of the breach and its consequences for the accused. However, to allow such a judgment to dictate whether evidence is admitted or excluded introduces into a trial concerns other than the reliability of evidence and the pursuit of the truth. The protective principle is not therefore an application of adversarial reasoning. History confirms the view that it is not trial structure that

---

[45] [1979] 1 All ER 939.

[46] St J. Robilliard and .J McEwan, *Police Powers and the Individual* (Blackwell, Oxford, 1986), 224–6.

[47] *Ibid.*

[48] A.J. Ashworth, "Excluding Evidence as Protecting Rights" [1977] *Crim. LR* 723.

determines whether or not individuals are protected from excesses by the state, nor even whether the reliability or the disciplinary principle predominates. On the Continent, the inquisitorial method replaced adversarial trial by ordeal, which came to be perceived as unreliable. Ironically, the new emphasis on "hard evidence" merely encouraged the use of torture to extract confessions. Defendants found themselves even worse off than before.[49] Subsequently, Continental systems were the first to take exception to evidence obtained in this fashion, even during the "inquisitorial process of the *ancien régime*".[50]

The Reliability Principle at Work

There are two aspects of unreliability. A confession may be given which is not true; this is the concern of section 76(2). But before the universal introduction of the tape-recording of interviews, many court cases involved protracted disputes about whether a confession was made at all. The number of these investigations into alleged "verballing" by police has been dramatically reduced by the insistence in the Codes of Practice that all interviews should be carried out at the police station,[51] and tape-recorded.[52] There are still some interviews taking place outside the police station, however, the most common explanation given by police officers for this being that the suspect insisted on making oral admissions immediately on arrest. In such a case, a contemporaneous note should be made and shown to the suspect as soon as possible.[53] Tape-recorded interviews are admissible at trial.[54] If the video-recording of interviews with suspects became common, presumably these also would be admissible in evidence. It is thought by many commentators that they could be extremely damaging to the defence. A suspect seen throughout the interview uneasily shifting about in his or her chair and staring at the floor is unlikely to be regarded as convincing.[55] McConville argues that to allow the court to watch the whole of a "No comment" interview could be gravely prejudicial.[56] Now that adverse inferences may legitimately be drawn from silence, the effect could be catastrophic. There is also a risk of reinforcing the popular notion that veracity can be measured from the manner in which oral responses are delivered.[57]

The research commissioned by the Phillips Royal Commission clearly

---

[49] D.N. Robinson, *Wild Beasts and Idle Humours: The Insanity Defense from Antiquity to the Present* Harvard University Press, (Cambridge, Mass., London, England, 1996).

[50] Damaska, n. 1 above 13.

[51] PACE Codes of Practice, Code C. 11.1.

[52] PACE Codes of Practice, Code E (not required for minor offences triable only summarily, but compulsory for all other offences).

[53] Code C.11.5, 11.10.

[54] *Maqsud Ali* [1966] 1 QB 688.

[55] M.S. Barnes, "One Experience of Videorecorded Interviews" [1993] *Crim. LR* 444.

[56] M. McConville, "Videotaping Police Interrogation" [1992] *NLJ* 960.

[57] *Ibid.*

established that being held under arrest at a police station is intimidating, to an extent where many suspects would rather confess and end the uncertainty than suffer prolonged questioning.[58] However, the definition of oppression in section 76(8) requires deliberate impropriety of quite an extreme kind. In *Fulling*,[59] the defendant claimed that she confessed because the police had given her distressing news, involving her partner and the woman who was being held in the cell next to her own. It was held in the Court of Appeal that informing her of the affair and of the woman's proximity did not amount to oppression. The word should be construed in the light of section 76(8). Whilst it almost inevitably involves some impropriety on the part of the inter-rogators, not all impropriety would amount to oppression. The language in *Fulling* seemed to require extreme, violent or cruel behaviour from the police. More recently, the test for oppression, has been expressed far less dramatically. In *Miller, Paris and Abdullahi*,[60] Miller had been interviewed over days in a hectoring manner (without objection from his legal representative) which ignored his denials and seemed designed to bully admissions out of him rather than ascertain his version of the facts. The Court of Appeal held that this was oppression; the atmosphere was intimidating, his answers disre-garded. In terms of the legal structure for questioning set up under PACE and the Codes of Practice, there was no identifiable unlawful behaviour; the unlawfulness of this kind of oppression is established by the Court of Appeal decision itself. In *Glaves*,[61] a 16-year-old suspect was told at one point that he should answer. His denials were ignored at least nine times. The solicitor's representative was silent throughout these interviews. It was held that not only should these interviews be excluded, but so should further interviews conducted a few days later, which were tainted by the same oppression.[62]

Cases in which the courts have been rigorous in excluding evidence obtained in breach of the Codes are varied, but breaches which appear to be taken especially seriously are failure to allow access to legal advice (whether the police have failed to remind the suspect of the right to consult a lawyer or whether they have actually denied access to a solicitor) and failure to show the suspect a contemporaneous record of the interview.[63] Wrongful denial of legal advice would lead to the exclusion of a confession under either section 78 or, if the prosecution fails to show the absence of oppression, section 76(2)(a).[64] In *Mason*,[65] police officers falsely told the defendant while he was being questioned that his fingerprints had been found on a piece of glass

---

[58] E.g., B. Irving and L. Hilgendorf, *Police Interrogation: The Psychological Approach: Police Interrogation: A Case Study of Current Practice,* Royal Commission on Criminal Procedure Research Study Nos 1 and 2 (HMSO, London, 1980).

[59] [1987] 2 All ER 65.

[60] (1993) 97 Cr. App. R 99; these defendants became popularly known as "the Cardiff Three".

[61] [1993] Crim. LR 685.

[62] Although it might have been different had he received legal advice in the interim.

[63] Although see Mirfield, n. 31 above, 162–5.

[64] *Samuel* [1988] 2 All ER 135.   [65] [1987] 3 All ER 481.

from the bottle used to start the fire under investigation. They told his solicitor the same lie. Mason's confession was held by the Court of Appeal to be inadmissible under section 78, partly because as a result of the deception his solicitor advised Mason to explain himself to the police, and therefore his right to silence was undermined. The trial judge was held to have paid insufficient attention to the deception of the solicitor, and thus omitted from consideration a vital factor affecting the fairness of the trial. If he had considered it, Lord Lane CJ had "not the slightest doubt", the confession would have been excluded. Since there was no other prosecution evidence, this would have inevitably resulted in an acquittal. The function of the solicitor in the police station is ultimately to remind the suspect of his rights. The curtailment of the right to silence means that it is important that the suspect understands what the consequences of failing to answer questions would be. It can be argued that the importance of legal advice is now greater than ever, and that the practice of sending unqualified staff to police stations must cease.[66]

Despite clear statements in *Mason* that the Court of Appeal rejects the use of the rules of evidence as a means of disciplining and directing the police, the case law in this area sets out some very positive guidelines as to what are and what are not legitimate police tactics in interviews. The deception of the solicitor was taken particularly seriously because of its effect on the quality of his legal advice, but it was also made clear in *Mason* that misleading a suspect into thinking that the police have more evidence against him or her than they in fact have will lead to exclusion of any confession. It might be thought that such a confession would not be unreliable; that an innocent suspect would not fall into a trap of this kind, because he or she would know that the police could not possibly have the evidence they claimed to have. However, there are considerable risks of false confessions being made by persons who either temporarily or permanently become persuaded of their own guilt or, who react to the deception with a gloomy conviction that they will not be believed, and admit everything to avoid further interrogation. Irving and McKenzie[67] report an increased tendency since the 1984 Act for police interrogators to use tactics they describe as "witness manipulation"—convincing the suspect that his case is a foregone conclusion so that he has no option but to confess. But "lying was always seen by expert interviewers as a crude tactic, which, if discovered, handed the advantage immediately to the interviewee. In outlawing it in *Mason* the judiciary happened to be following good police practice."[68] Police misrepresentation of facts is thus described as a problem only where less skilled interrogators have been at work; but unfortunately, exaggeration

---

[66] See Ch. 5.

[67] B. Irving and I.K. McKenzie, *Police Interrogation: The Effects of the Police and Criminal Evidence Act 1984* (Police Foundation, London, 1989), 175.

[68] *Ibid.*, 177.

of the impact of evidence and its damning quality is equally capable of inducing a false confession.[69]

Before the universal tape-recording of police station interviews, it could be argued that the presence of a legal advisor also ensured or increased reliability in terms of the accuracy of the record. Yet in *Alladyce*,[70] wrongful denial of access to a solicitor's advice was not regarded as sufficient reason to exclude the confession, because the defendant said he already knew what his rights were, and so only wanted a solicitor present in order to see "fair play" at the interview. This approach was carried to its logical conclusion in *Dunford*,[71] where it was held that a defendant's criminal record is admissible in the *voir dire* on the issue whether the defendant is sufficiently familiar with the criminal process not to need the advice of a solicitor. This means that in a summary trial magistrates might become familiar with the defendant's criminal record simply because it was led at the *voir dire* to demonstrate that advice was not needed. In *Dunn*,[72] the defendant denied the offence throughout the interview, but police witnesses claimed that he admitted it while checking through the record afterwards, and while his legal adviser, who denied hearing this, was present. It was held that the evidence was admissible, although there was no contemporaneous note of the admission. Apparently, the absence of the note in this case did not handicap the defence (although in most it would) since the lawyer could give evidence that she was there. Here the issue should be tested in the normal way, by introducing evidence and cross-examining witnesses. It was not considered necessary to exclude the evidence altogether. In other words, the requirement for contemporaneous note-taking was seen to be only one way of guarding against the manufacture of admissions by the police; here the presence of the legal advisor filled the gap, although she could not confirm that any admission had been made! But the approach taken here does not depend at all upon the witness's status as *legal advisor*, for any disinterested third party present could in theory have testified to whether or not the accused made the alleged admissions.

The Disciplinary Principle

The case of *Kuruma* v. *R.*[73] is generally taken as authority for the common law position, prior to the 1984 Act, that if evidence is relevant and reliable, it matters not how the prosecution came by it. But even that decision accepted that there are varieties of conduct so unacceptable that the prosecution can never profit from them.[74] The conviction that the court has more to do than merely to ensure that evidence is relevant has influenced the Court of Appeal in its interpretation of section 78 of PACE. For example, in *Quinn*, Lord Lane CJ said:

---

[69] See text to n. 84 below.   [70] [1987] Crim. LR 608.   [71] (1990) 91 Cr. App. R 150.
[72] [1990] Crim. LR 572.   [73] [1955] AC 197.
[74] Cf. *Callis* v. *Gunn* [1964] 1 QB 494; *King* v. *R.* [1964] AC 304.

"The function of the judge is . . . to protect the fairness of the proceedings, and normally proceedings are fair if a jury hears all relevant evidence which either side wishes to place before it, but proceedings may become unfair if, for example, one side is allowed to adduce relevant evidence which, for one reason or another, the other side cannot properly meet, or where there has been an abuse of process, for example where evidence has been obtained in deliberate breach of procedures laid down in an official code of procedure."[75]

In *Matto* v. *Wolverhampton Crown Court*,[76] real evidence contained in a sample of breath, which appeared perfectly reliable, was excluded because the defendant was unlawfully breathalysed on private property. The Divisional Court distinguished *Fox* v. *Chief Constable of Gwent*[77] where the House of Lords held that an unlawful arrest was not a ground to exclude evidence obtained from a breath test subsequently administered. And in *Fennelly*[78] an arrest was unlawful because the suspect was not told the reason for it. The consequence was the exclusion of evidence that, when he was subsequently searched at the police station, heroin was found in his underpants. No other breach of the 1984 Act or Codes had occurred, but the Court of Appeal held that the illegality arising from the unlawfulness of the arrest ran through everything that followed. When Kevin Taylor, the businessman whose relationship with John Stalker led to the police inquiry into the conduct of the Deputy Chief Constable,[79] was tried with others over a loan he negotiated with his bank,[80] the trial collapsed when His Honour Judge Sachs excluded bank documents under section 78. The reason for this was that the court which ordered disclosure of the bank accounts had been deliberately misled by the police. The refusal of the courts in these cases to countenance use of contaminated although reliable evidence suggests an attempt to force prosecutors and their agents to adopt a higher standard of behaviour than any other party going before a court.

Recently, however, the Court of Appeal has stressed that only where the case falls within the *Sang* discretion may the Court reject evidence which is in itself perfectly reliable. In *DPP* v. *Sang*,[81] the House of Lords preferred the reliability principle to any notion of deterring police misconduct; Lord Diplock said that to allow a discretion to exclude the evidence of an *agent provocateur* would be absurd, since the mere fact that the witness is alleged to have provoked the crime indicates that a crime was indeed committed. The common law discretion to exclude relates only to evidence obtained directly from the accused, in the form either of oral admissions or of physical evidence taken from his or her person. It is a manifestation of the principle

---

[75] [1990] Crim LR 581, 583; cf Lord Griffiths in *Lam Chi-Ming* v. *R.* [1991] 3 All ER 171, 179.
[76] [1987] RTR 337.   [77] [1985] 3 All ER 392.   [78] [1989] Crim. LR 142.
[79] N. 18 above.
[80] *Bowley* n. 20 above; the trial ended on 18 Jan. 1990.
[81] [1980] AC 402.

nemo debet se prodere ipsum.[82] Nevertheless, it is possible that in an extreme case the court might use section 78 to exclude evidence by an *agent provocateur* who went too far. In a case which predates the *Sang* decision, *Ameer and Lucas*,[83] a police informer approached the defendant and asked him to sell him some cocaine. The defendant refused, but the informer, who on his own admission used "every trick in the book" to persuade him, eventually got him to agree to supply him with cannabis for a fictitious client who was described as extremely keen. The trial judge excluded the evidence of the *agent provocateur*, although on one view he obtained evidence outside the *nemo debet* principle in that he observed the defendant committing the offence.

Even in *Kuruma*, which also predates *Sang*, Goddard LJ said that evidence obtained by a trick might be excluded, whether it be an admission or any other kind of evidence. In *Mason*[84] the Court denied that it was disciplining the police, arguing that the decision merely ensured fairness in the proceedings:

> "It is obvious from the undisputed evidence that the police practised a deceit not only on the appellant, which is bad enough, but also on the solicitor, whose duty it was to advise him. In effect they hoodwinked both solicitor and client. That was a most reprehensible thing to do. It is not however because we regard as misbehaviour of a serious kind conduct of that nature that we have come to the decision [to quash the conviction] . . . A trial judge has a discretion to be exercised, of course on right principles, to reject admissible evidence in the interests of a defendant having a fair trial."[85]

The language employed by the Lord Chief Justice, however, is in sufficiently strong terms to suggest the objective of deterrence:

> "Despite what I have said about the role of the court in relation to disciplining the police, we think we ought to say that we hope never again to hear of a deceit such as this being practised on an accused person, and more particularly possibly on a solicitor."[86]

Following *Sang*,[87] except for admissions and other evidence obtained from the accused after the commission of the offence, there is no discretion to exclude evidence unless its quality was or could have been affected by the way it was obtained. In *Chalkely*,[88] Auld LJ explained that PACE has not affected the common law position; to exclude evidence as a mark of disapproval of the way it was obtained was not and is not the law. The decision in

---

[82] See Ch. 5. More recent cases, decided in the light of PACE, followed the same line: e.g. *Harwood* [1989] Crim. LR 285; *DPP* v. *Marshall* [1988] Crim. LR 750.
[83] [1977] Crim. LR 104.   [84] [1987] 3 All ER 481.   [85] Lord Lane CJ, at484
[86] *Ibid.*, 485.   [87] [1979] 2 All ER 1222.   [88] [1998] 2 All ER 155.

Matto is an instance of the *nemo debet* principle. In *Khan*,[89] the same test was applied by the House of Lords. Whether or not the evidence was obtained in breach of Article 8 of the European Convention on Human Rights is not the crucial question. The issue is whether any breach affected the fairness of the proceedings.

Unfortunately, even cases falling squarely into the category of *nemo debet*, in that evidence has been obtained from the person of the suspect, are not easy to reconcile. The fairness of the trial was not apparently at risk in *Cooke*.[90] The defendant gave a sample of hair voluntarily, being assured that it would be used solely for the purpose of a particular rape inquiry. However, a match was found in relation to another offence, and the police, being unsure about the admissibility of the sample in relation to that, asked the defendant for another sample of hair. He refused, and was informed that it could be taken by force (several officers wore riot gear to emphasise the point). Cooke duly consented. It was held on appeal that the second sample was properly admitted in evidence. The trial judge had said that he considered that the police were entitled to use force[91] to obtain the second sample, but would not have excluded it even if they were not.[92] The Court of Appeal agreed; such a breach would not have cast doubt on the accuracy or strength of the evidence. The court was more hostile to the admission of apparently reliable evidence in *Nathaniel*[93]; the defendant provided a sample of blood to police investigating the rapes of two Danish women. He was promised that it would be destroyed if he were acquitted, which he was. In fact the DNA analysis from the sample was later adduced in evidence at his trial for a different rape. The Court of Appeal overturned his conviction.

A disciplinary principle could only work if the system is clear about what constitutes proper police practice. Generally, there is now wide awareness of the standards of conduct demanded by the 1984 Act and the Codes.[94] But where police activities fall outside the 1984 framework, court guidance can only develop piecemeal. In recent years, a number of cases have featured police use of undercover officers, surveillance devices and other surreptitious methods of gathering evidence. Increased sophistication amongst the criminal fraternity is said to demand the use of clandestine operations.[95] The idea that individuals might incriminate themselves whilst unaware that they were being observed by police officers to some represents an invasion of civil liberties. In *Christou*,[96] undercover police officers set up what appeared to be

[89] [1996] 3 All ER 289; see n. 116 below.   [90] [1995] Crim. LR 497.

[91] S. 63 of PACE as amended by s. 56 of the Criminal Justice and Public Order Act 1994.

[92] He would, however, have refused to admit the first DNA sample.

[93] [1995] 2 Cr. App. R 565.

[94] Although areas of uncertainty are highlighted in D. Brown, "PACE Ten Years On: A Review of the Research", Home Office, Research Study No 155, (Home Office, London, 1997).

[95] G. Robertson, "Entrapment Evidence: Manna from Heaven or the Fruit of the Poisoned Tree?" [1994] *Crim. LR* 805.

[96] [1992] Crim. LR 729.

an everyday jewellery shop in North London. They let it be known that they would be willing to buy stolen jewellery. Various individuals brought in goods which they admitted to be stolen. These conversations were recorded on videotape and were adduced in evidence against them. In contrast, in *Bryce*,[97] oral admissions made to an undercover police officer were excluded because the officer approached the suspect, pretending to be interested in buying a car. The element of voluntariness was therefore absent, and the conversations amounted to an interview which should be conducted at the police station with the protection of the Codes of Practice. The suspect had not been shown a record of the conversation, bringing authenticity into doubt.

In many common law jurisdictions, entrapment evidence, where the police apparently lure a suspect into committing a crime, has become a major ethical isssue.[98] In the United States, "virtue-testing" (presenting people with a "honey-trap" opportunity to commit crime) has led the Supreme Court to demand in each case evidence that the defendant had a predisposition to commit the criminal act.[99] That approach is reminiscent of the problem in *Ameer and Lucas*,[100] in that the accused had appeared genuinely reluctant to commit the offence. The Canadian Supreme Court prefers an objective approach which concentrates on the behaviour of the alleged *agent provocateur*.[101] The courts in England have so far developed only rough and ready principles in this area. In *Williams v. DPP*,[102] plain clothes officers left an insecure and unattended van in a busy street. It contained dummy cigarette cartons. The defendants were seen lingering near to the van, and eventually they removed the cigarette cartons.[103] The magistrates at first instance found that the police plan had not been directed at the defendants in particular, and that they approached the van voluntarily. On appeal to the Divisional Court, Wright J held that the police had not been acting as *agents provocateurs*; they had done nothing to force, persuade, encourage or coerce the defendants to do what they did, and so the situation was similar to that in *Christou*, or the case of a "heroic WPC" who might act as bait to a known sex attacker, by waiting in an area in which he is thought to strike. The analogy is far from being exact; in a case like *Williams*, the enticement may tempt someone who otherwise would not be involved in crime, to commit one. Nevertheless, such practices were approved in *Dawes v. DPP*,[104] where the bait was a powerful car which in fact was a "rat-trap", which locks in anyone who gets into it hoping to drive off in it. The Divisional Court thought there was nothing objectionable about this kind of lure, as long as the suspect, who is effectively under arrest once the doors

---

[97] [1992] Crim.LR 728. [98] Robertson, n. 95 above.
[99] *Jacobson* v. *US* (1992) 503 US 540. [100] [1977] Crim. LR 104.
[101] Robertson n. 95 above. [102] [1993] 3 All ER 365.
[103] But only after the police had chased away two 8-year-olds who could not resist the temptation!
[104] [1994] Crim. LR 604.

lock, is informed of the fact within a reasonable time. There are cases, however, where the predisposition may be more safely assumed. Shopkeepers are from time to time caught selling illegally fireworks, alcohol, cigarettes and lottery tickets by the simple device of sending in a child volunteer to buy the illicit article. Again, the evidence so obtained is admissible.[105]

In *Smurthwaite and Gill*,[106] two separate appeals involved spouses who had sought a contract killer. Smurthwaite had wanted to dispose of his wife; Mrs Gill to have her husband murdered. In each case, an undercover police officer posed as a contract killer, and tape-recorded the conversations in which the defendants incited murder. The Court of Appeal set out the kinds of factors which might define the *agent provocateur*, such as whether the offence was likely to be committed without police intervention; whether the undercover officer incited its commission; whether the evidence produced consists of admissions[107] or the commission of the offence itself; and whether there is any tangible record of the admissions. But even if a police officer has effectively acted as an *agent provocateur*, that is only a factor favouring exclusion. The evidence may yet be admissible, depending on all the circumstances. In 1994, Keith Hall was acquitted after the trial judge refused to admit into evidence a tape-recording in which he admitted killing his wife and burning her body in an incinerator. The recording had been made by the woman he was seeing regularly and whom he had met at a lonely hearts' club. In fact she was a police officer. Not only was she effectively interviewing Hall outside the terms of the Codes, so that he had not been cautioned, offered legal advice or even informed of the significance of these statements, but she manipulated him emotionally by pretending to be anxious in case his wife returned to him.[108]

The use of covert surveillance gives rise to other issues, particularly the question of a right to privacy. In *Bailey*[109] two suspects were placed together in a police station cell in which listening equipment had been installed. To allay suspicion, the investigating officers pretended that they had not wanted Bailey and his fellow suspect to be kept together, and that the custody officer had insisted. Their subsequent conversations incriminated them as to a number of robberies. The Court of Appeal saw no reason to decry the police conduct in this case, although, intriguingly, announced that it was "manifestly a strategy to be used in grave cases". Here there was nothing to suggest either oppression or something said or done which was likely to

---

[105] *London Borough of Ealing* v. *Woolworths plc* [1995] Crim. LR 58. Cf *Marshall and Downes* [1998] 3 All ER 683, under-age agents were asked to buy alcohol in order to obtain evidence against shop-keepers suspected of breaching the regulations on sale of alcohol.

[106] [1994] 1 All ER 898.

[107] Raising the spectre of an interview being conducted under cover in order to avoid the Codes of Practice.

[108] Leeds Crown Court, transcript no T931483; S. Sharpe, "Covert Police Operations and the Ddiscretionary Exclusion of Evidence" [1994] *Crim. LR* 793.

[109] [1993] Crim. LR 681.

render the confession unreliable. The conversations did not amount to an interview in breach of the Codes; the defendants had simply been given the opportunity to speak to each other. Given this reasoning, it might be thought that, were the police to use a civilian agent to trap the suspect into making admissions by conducting what amounts to an interview outside the terms of the Codes, any such evidence should be excluded.[110] Yet in *Jelen and Katz*[111] the Court of Appeal emphasised the fact that the suspect had not been arrested, so the conversations with the agent fell outside the Codes of Practice. Although there was an element of entrapment, the court considered that the trial judge had been entitled to conclude that the admission of the tape-recorded conversations was not unfair. *Stephen Roberts*[112] did involve breaches of the Codes of Practice, in that conversations between one C and a police officer had not been recorded. It was decided that this was unimportant since the admissions in question were made by the defendant, and not by C, so that C did not need the protection of the Code. After these conversations had taken place, C was placed in a cell with Roberts, and pleaded with him to admit his involvement in an armed robbery. The admissions were recorded, and were held to be admissible. Similarly, in a case of illegal telephone-tapping, what mattered to the Court of Appeal was "the nature and quality of the recordings", not any unlawfulness in the police action.[113]

All these cases, involving oral admissions, fall within the *Sang* discretion. The courts nevertheless emphasised reliability rather than unfairness, although it might be thought that the admissions in *Stephen Roberts* lacked reliability also. When the taperecorded admissions emanate from a private home, the issue of fairness might be superceded by questions about privacy. In *Chalkley*[114] there was no illegality. In order to procure a tape-recording of the two defendants discussing their plan to commit a robbery, the police obtained permission from the chief constable to place a listening device in Chalkley's house.[115] There was nothing illegal about this, but it was decided to suggest to other police officers that they arrest Chalkley and his girlfriend (on reasonable grounds) for credit card fraud. This would get them out of the house so that the officers investigating the robbery could get in and install the microphone unobserved. It was held in the Court of Appeal that, given that the arrests were lawful, the evidence obtained from the tape-recording in relation to the robbery was admissible. There was nothing unfair about this; it was relevant and highly probative evidence, about which there was no dispute as to its authenticity, content or effect.

Khan[116] again involved a private house, although not the defendant's. He was suspected of involvement in importation of prohibited drugs. A listening device was installed outside the house of someone Khan visited. It was capable of transmitting conversations taking place inside the house. There

---

[110] Cf. Keith Hall's trial at n. 108 above.   [111] (1990) 90 Cr. App. R 456.
[112] [1997] Crim. LR 222.   [113] *Effik* [1994] 3 All ER 458.   [114] [1998] 2 All ER 155.
[115] See Police Act 1997, s. 93(4).   [116] [1996] 2 All ER 289.

was technical trespass to the owner's property and possibly very minor damage to the outside brickwork, but the police had complied with the current guidelines on listening devices. The defence argued illegality, and, particularly in the House of Lords appeal, breach of the European Convention on Human Rights.[117] The House of Lords reasserted the proposition that section 78 of PACE did not operate to exclude evidence every time it was obtained unlawfully. The question of fairness is separate. "It would be a strange reflection of our law if a man who has admitted his participation in the illegal importation of a large quantity of heroin should have his conviction set aside on the grounds that his privacy has been invaded."[118]

False Confessions

The Codes of Practice which accompany PACE require that the mentally disordered or mentally handicapped should not be interviewed in the absence of an appropriate adult. Such vulnerable suspects should be questioned with special care.[119] It is clear that persons of below average intelligence have difficulty in understanding the words of the caution and frequently construe it as an injunction to speak,[120] but it appears that detained persons of even average intelligence are likely to find it difficult to grasp the nature of their rights when held on arrest. Gudjonsson[121] applied the Flesch Statistical Formula to analyse the reading ease of the "Notice to Detained Persons" issued by the Metropolitan Police, which was read out to suspects and then handed to them. The notice contained the caution, the right to have someone informed, the right to legal advice, mention of the Codes of Practice and the right to a copy of the custody record. Although understanding of these matters would increase the probable reliability of statements made in detention, only a minority of suspects are likely to fathom them. Gudjonnson found that the Notice required an IQ of at least 111 to understand it—and that would cover only about 24 per cent of the population.[122] The position with the Codes of Practice is even worse. Code C, which directly deals with the detention, treatment and questioning of detained persons and which demands that detained persons and members of the public should be able to consult it, is unlikely to be understood without an IQ of 126; so fewer than 5 per cent of the general population would be able to follow it. To make the Codes more comprehensible, shorter and less involved sentences would be needed.[123]

---

[117] Art. 8: right to privacy.

[118] [1996] 2 All ER 289, *per* Lord Nolan at 302.   [119] Code C.11.14.

[120] G.H. Gudjonnson, "The Notice to Detained Persons, PACE Codes and Reading Ease" (1991) 58 *Journal of Applied Cognitive Psychology* 88; M. Beaumont, "Confessions, Cautions and Experts after *R* v. *Silcott and Others*" [1987] *NLJ* 807.

[121] Gudjonsson, n. 120 above.

[122] This was confirmed by an exploratory study.   [123] *Ibid.*

Work on false confessions is inevitably hampered by the difficulty of knowing whether a confession which is subsequently withdrawn, and which may or may not be excluded by the judge, is genuine or not. Under section 76 of PACE, as we have seen, impropriety by the police would require the exclusion of even genuine confessions. But there are grounds for concern in relation to confessions which were admitted, no impropriety having taken place. Work done on confessions which were the basis of convictions subsequently quashed or set aside with a pardon shows that the confessions tend to fall into three main groups[124]:

(a) Voluntary confessions, offered to the police by someone not under investigation, and usually to publicized crimes. The reason for this may be a desire for notoriety, or to relieve a general feeling of guilt, or an inability to distinguish fact and fantasy;

(b) Coerced-compliant confessions, which account for most false confessions. The best explanation is the desire to escape from a highly stressful situation. The immediate gain, which may include the need to establish some short-term certainty of future events[125] becomes a more powerful influence on the subject's behaviour than the uncertain long-term effects of the confession, even when the alleged offence is serious;

(c) Coerced-internalised confessions; the person is temporarily persuaded that he might have committed or did commit the crime because he does not trust his own memory and begins to accept the suggestions of the police. Such a confession is more likely to be elicited by gentle rather than aggressive interviewing. It may be retracted later on, although the subject is more likely to stick to it than is the coerced-compliant, but even if it is withdrawn later the subject's memory may be permanently distorted.

Gudjonsson and MacKeith argue that interrogative suggestibility and compliance are enduring psychological characteristics relevant to erroneous testimony. The effect of such a trait during police questioning may be to elicit a false admission which could form the basis of a conviction. Gudjonsson's study of 100 cases of people who retracted their confessions and were referred to him suffers from the risk of selection of particularly vulnerable subjects by the solicitors who sought psychological testing. But he compared these defendants with another 100 cases referred to him, and involving persons referred in relation to similar offences. The group which had retracted its confessions had a lower mean IQ, and far higher levels of

---

[124] G.H. Gudjonsson and J. MacKeith, "Retracted Confessions: Legal, Psychological and Psychiatric Aspects" (1988) 28 *Med. Sci. Law* 187; G.H. Gudjonsson, *The Psychology of Interrogations, Confessions, and Testimony* (Wiley, Chichester, 1992).

[125] G.H. Gudjonsson, "The Psychology of False Confessions" (1989) 57 *Medico-Legal Journal* 93.

suggestibility and compliance. These characteristics are to some extent inherent in the personality and can be measured by a reliable test,[126] but they can be aggravated by conditions. Gudjonsson defines the dangerous characteristics as follows: acquiescence, which is the tendency of the person to answer questions affirmatively irrespective of content. This characteristic is most common with people of low intelligence.[127] Suggestibility is a tendency to accept uncritically information communicated during questions.[128] It is greatest in people of low intelligence. Compliance is a tendency to go along with requests of the person perceived to be in authority, even though the subject does not necessarily agree with them.[129] However, analysis of an individual's general personality does not give the whole picture: "[p]eople are generally not passive recipients of suggestive influences from others— they are constantly in a *dynamic* relationship with their social and physical environments".[130] Suggestibility is increased in certain situations. The stressfulness of the police interrogation at the police station may increase it, depending on the coping strategy of the detainee. He or she may become resistant, but if not, then many other factors apart from a generally suggestible personality may operate. The effect of a leading question depends on whether the subject is uncertain what the true answer is. Suspicion of the interviewer makes the subject less suggestible, and so does anger. But if the interviewer is trusted, suggestibility increases.[131] Where there is a high level of suggestibility, even questions requiring only a Yes/No answer are dangerous since, when in doubt, some people have a tendency to give affirmative answers.[132]

To some extent the police use fear as an interrogation device, although Irving and McKenzie found since the 1984 Act a reduced tendency to display authority and use the custodial conditions themselves as a means to intimidate.[133] But CID officers privately admitted using fear as a tactic, and experienced officers "are well aware of the power of suggestion".[134] In 1979 Irving reported that about 12 per cent of detained suspects showed visible symptoms of fear such as trembling, sweating, hyperventilation or incoherence. In 1986 the number had increased to about 22 per cent; but this proportion dropped in the 1987 study to 10 per cent.[135] The authors explain

[126] G.H. Gudjonsson, "A New Scale of Interrogative Suggestibility" (1984) 15 *Personality and Individual Differences* 303.

[127] C.K. Sigelman, J.L. Budd, C.J. Spanhel and C.J. Schoenrock, "When in Doubt say Yes: Acquiescence in Interviews with Mentally Retarded Persons" (1981) 19 *Mental Retardation* 53; G.H. Gudjonsson, "The Relationship Between Interrogative Suggestibility and Acquiescence: Empirical Findings and Theoretical Implication" (1986) 7 *Personality and Individual Differences* 195.

[128] Gudjonsson, n. 127 above.

[129] G.H. Gudjonsson, "Compliance in an Interrogative Situation: A New Scale" (1989) 10 *Personality and Individual Differences* 535.

[130] G.H. Gudjonsson and N. Clark, "Suggestibility in Police Interrogation: A Social Psychological Model" (1986) 1 *Social Behaviour* 83, 86.

[131] *Ibid.*   [132] Gudjonsson, n. 126 above.   [133] Irving and McKenzie, n. 67 above.

[134] *Ibid.*, 169.   [135] *Ibid.*, 167.

this by suggesting that the safeguards under the 1984 Act were becoming better understood and that therefore suspects were more confident that they would not be abused after arrest. There is, however, no suggestion that the police observed by Irving and McKenzie were deliberately generating tension, and some degree of apprehension is inevitable in someone placed under arrest and held, powerless to alter his or her situation, at the police station. The symptoms of fear described indicate only the extreme cases where physical manifestations of near-panic were shown. The most frequently occurring false confessions are the coerced-compliant, where the admission is known to be untrue by the person making it, but he makes it for his own neo-pragmatic reasons. Without being made aware of the research in this area, courts are unlikely to be persuaded that a confession not induced by threats or promises, but uttered during the course of a properly-conducted interview, is not true.

The work of Gudjonsson and other psychologists shows that the most innocuous interrogation techniques could adversely affect the reliability of admissions so obtained. Yet it is conceded that the police must be able to utilise at least some pressure:

> "I think it is important to realise that unless there is some kind of perceived pressure or that people believe that the police have something on them in the majority of cases people would not confess; but clearly the greater the pressure that you place people under the greater the risk that some people falsely confess, particularly if you are dealing with vulnerable individuals. Some people cope very badly with pressure, so that if you put them under even more pressure they may agree with anything that you say. Other people you can place under a great deal of pressure and they would not confess to anything . . . I do believe that a certain amount of pressure is essential in police work."[136]

The judiciary has recently acknowledged that suspects may be vulnerable despite not falling neatly within some clear-cut definition of abnormality. In *Masih*,[137] an IQ of 72 was treated as "normal" by the Court of Appeal; however, in *Silcott, Braithwaite and Rahip*[138] more flexibility was shown in relation to a confession from someone with a borderline IQ. There expert evidence was admissible on the subject of the reliability of his confession.

In *Goldenberg*,[139] a heroin addict alleged that his confession was made because he was suffering withdrawal symptoms. The Court of Appeal held that section 76(2)(b) requires the unreliability to be a result of something *said or done*, and by someone other than the suspect. Thus the confession cannot be excluded under section 76, even if the suspect has inadvertently hurt himself at the police station, or if he is feeling ill, or has an embarrassing digestive problem. If such a confession is to be excluded, that must be done

---

[136] Gudjonsson, n. 125 above.   [137] [1986] Crim. LR 395.
[138] *The Times*, 9 Dec. 1992.   [139] [1989] Crim. LR 678.

under section 78, which was not referred to in this case, and which has two disadvantages for the defence. First, it loses the advantage of the burden of proof being placed on the prosecution, as in section 76. Secondly, the matter turns on the exercise of discretion by a particular trial judge. The individual judge has to be convinced in each case that stress combined with a compliant or suggestible personality could result in a confession so unreliable that fairness demands it be not admitted.

There is little guidance on how the courts will exercise their discretion in cases of self-induced unreliability. In the common law cases before 1984 courts have considered the question of the accused's own mental state. In *Isequilla*[140] the Court of Appeal held that although the accused at the time he made admissions was so hysterical that he was frothing at the mouth, there was no reason to exclude them. The court went on to say, however, that there could be cases where the accused's mental state at the time he confessed was such that the confession should be excluded, but described them as "extreme", for instance, "where the man is a mental defective". In *DPP* v. *Ping Lin*[141] the Privy Council commented on the decision in *Isequilla* in these terms:

> "A confession which is simply blurted out by a criminal caught *in flagrante delicto* is not the sort of thing to which [the exclusionary principle at common law] applies; if it were, anyone caught red-handed who admits 'it's a fair cop' could probably plead self-induced fear and have his remark excluded."[142]

In *Fulling*,[143] the defendant's distress was only in part self-induced, since the police told her of her lover's infidelity. It did not appear to constitute reason to doubt the reliability of her confession. There are, however, cases where unreliable confessions have been excluded, despite *Isequilla*, such as *Davis*,[144] where expert evidence at the *voir dire* suggested that Davis at the time of his questioning was still under the influence of the drug Pethidin. In *Kilner*,[145] the defendant had a low IQ, epilepsy, and became hysterical when he found himself in difficulties. Although there had been no misconduct by the police, the confession was not admitted at trial. There may be instances of similarly unreliable confessions being excluded expressly on the grounds that to admit them would render the trial unfair under section 78 of the 1984 Act. However the language in *Isequilla* and the willingness of the Court of Appeal to uphold the convictions in *Fulling* and *Goldenberg* suggest that the judicial perception of unreliability is a very limited one. Only about 15 per cent *voir dire* submissions that a confession should be excluded are successful.[146]

---

[140] [1975] 1 WLR 716.   [141] [1976] AC 574, *per* Lord Hailsham.
[142] [1976] AC 574, *per* Lord Hailsham at 602.   [143] [1987] 2 All ER 65.
[144] [1979] Crim. LR 167   [145] [1976] Crim. LR 740.   [145] [1976] Crim. LR 740.
[146] J. Vennard, "Disputes Within Trials over the Admissibility and Accuracy of Incriminating Statements: Some Research Evidence" [1984] *Crim. LR* 15.

Using section 78 rather than section 76 leaves everything to the inevitably uncertain exercise of judicial discretion, which would be satisfactory if all judges gave the available scientific research the respect it deserves.

The result of all this uncertainty was a conviction, in the case of *McKenzie*,[147] which affronted common sense, let alone expert medical opinion. The accused had been arrested on suspicion of arson, which he duly admitted in interview. He went on to confess to 12 murders, ten of which the police did not believe he had committed. However, they suspected that the remaining two murders might have been committed by McKenzie, and eventually he was put on trial for them despite the lack of any other evidence to implicate him. Psychological tests showed that the defendant, who was 38 years old, had an IQ of between 73 and 76. He was described by Dr Gudjonsson, as expert witness, as having a guilt obsession due to being sexually abused as a child and as having a suggestible and compliant personality. The Court of Appeal quashed the murder convictions, and held that where the prosecution case depends wholly upon a confession made by a defendant who suffers from a significant degree of mental handicap and the confessions are unconvincing to the point where a jury, properly directed, could not properly convict upon it, then the judge should withdraw the case from the jury.

A more robust safeguard would be to introduce a requirement that confession evidence on its own may not provide sufficient evidence for a conviction, so that further evidence indicating guilt would be needed. For PACE is simply not designed to deal with the problem of self-induced unreliability. In Scotland there is a general requirement for evidence in support in criminal cases. In all but a few United States jurisdictions, an extra-judicial confession by the defendant without corroboration is not considered sufficient to sustain a conviction. It is submitted that the doubtful reliability of all confession evidence demands a requirement of evidence in support, or a mandatory warning at least. The Royal Commission on Criminal Justice observed that the common law tradition that individuals will not make false statements against themselves can no longer be sustained, and that confessions have taken too central a role in police investigations.[148] The Commission nevertheless rejected the suggestion that confessions should never form the sole basis of a conviction; such a change in the law would lead to some genuinely guilty people going free. An even more baffling argument employed by the Commission is that if there were a general requirement that there should be evidence in support, weak confessions backed by unsatisfactory evidence in support would form the basis of prosecutions which currently, in the absence of such a requirement, would probably be

---

[147] (1992) 96 Cr. App. R 98.
[148] Royal Commission on Criminal Justice (chairman Viscount Runciman), *Report* (HMSO, London, 1993) Cm 2263, 64.

dropped.[149] The preferred solution is a reversal of Galbraith,[150] so that if a judge were unhappy about the reliability of any confession, he or she could direct an acquittal.

This seems a feeble response to a major problem. Gudjonsson's review of a number of instances of miscarriage of justice clearly demonstrates how reliance on confession evidence can lead to error. First, it is apparent that confessions are relatively easy to obtain from persons being questioned in situations of stress. Secondly, experience shows that once a confession has been obtained the police may attach too much weight to it, having persuaded themselves that the suspect is guilty. The temptation, then, is to dispense with other lines of inquiry which are more demanding of effort, which might have suggested that the confession is not to be trusted.

---

[149] *Ibid.*, 66   [150] [1981] 2 All ER 1060; see Ch. 3.

7

Hearsay

There is no advocate who has not experienced countless cases where a story that seemed consistent and watertight down on paper was destroyed by a proper and skilful cross-examination. Trials conducted on paper, on the whole, represent second-rate justice.[1]

Hearsay and the Adversarial Trial

Judicial loyalty to the principle of orality has undermined successive legislative attempts to extend the range and application of exceptions to the hearsay rule. This rule effectively requires witnesses to attend a trial to give live, sworn, oral evidence. Out-of-court statements, whether reported to the court by someone who heard them being made or in written form, are likely to fall foul of the rule against hearsay. Statutes which were intended to facilitate the reception of hearsay in civil cases for many years failed to have the desired effect. It has been observed that the liberalising aim of the Evidence Act 1938 was frustrated by restrictive interpretation and led to dissatisfaction, eventually culminating in the passage of the 1968 Civil Evidence Act. First instance judges seemed to take a narrow approach to that statute as well, however.[2] The main fault may have lain elsewhere; although it was commonly supposed that the Civil Evidence Act 1968 fundamentally changed the admissibility of hearsay evidence in civil cases, in fact an opportunity was missed. The statutory framework was over-complicated and over-restrictive. More recently, the legislature has responded to the impasse by effectively abolishing the hearsay rule for civil proceedings.[3] In the House of Lords debates on the Criminal Justice Bill, the then government found that Opposition lawyers would not easily countenance major departures[4] from traditional grounds for exclusion:

---

[1] Lord Irvine of Lairg, *Hansard*, HL Deb., vol. 489, col. 77, 20 Oct. 1987.

[2] C. Tapper, *Cross and Tapper on Evidence* (8th edn., Butterworths, London, 1995), 617.

[3] Civil Evidence Act 1995; see text to nn. 194–200 below.

[4] Although there was less exception taken to the provisions concerning business documents than to those regarding first-hand hearsay documents.

"To mitigate the rule against hearsay and permit documentary hearsay is sensible. To destroy the rule altogether is to damage irretrievably the fairness of the criminal trial."[5]

The Law Reform Advisory Committee for Northern Ireland, on the other hand, considered all possible improvements to the present unsatisfactory legislation governing the admissibility of hearsay evidence in civil trials in the province, and provisionally concluded that the most sensible course would be to abandon the rule except for the safeguard that hearsay evidence should not normally be admissible in civil proceedings where it is reasonable and practical for the maker of the relevant statement to be called as a witness.[6] The qualification was thought necessary to reflect the right of a party to insist on the production of the best reasonably available evidence against him.

At first sight, it seems curious that lawyers are so much more ready to dispense with orality requirements in civil than in criminal trials. The issues are not inevitably so very different from those dealt with in criminal cases. However, we have already seen throughout this book that, although criminal trials venture some way from adversarial theory in the matters of independence of parties and equality of risk, they remained, until recently, far more committed to adversarial procedures than civil trials. Civil trials adhere more closely to the adversarial model in terms of the equal position of the litigants, but developed a more informal and flexible approach to procedures, presumably because the judge sits alone. Yet, before the enactment of the Civil Evidence Act 1995,[7] reform was moving faster in the criminal courts than the civil. The 1988 Criminal Justice Act allowed documentary hearsay to be admitted in circumstances which fell outside the then existing provisions for civil cases.[8]

The evolution of the hearsay rule is often described as historically tied to that of jury trial; although Morgan argues[9] that it is a consequence of the trial structure in an adversarial system, so that it is the adversary, rather than the jury, who is protected from hearsay evidence because of the importance of cross-examination. Damaska agrees.[10]. He cites historical instances of juries being left to "free proof", and observes that no convincing argument has yet been put forward to demonstrate that judges deal with hearsay evidence in a more rational manner than juries.[11] He argues that loyalty to

---

[5] Lord Hutchinson of Lullington, HL Deb., vol 489, col. 74, 20 Oct. 1987.

[6] Law Reform Advisory Committee for Northern Ireland, *Hearsay Evidence in Civil Proceedings*, Discussion Paper No.1 (LRAC No. 3, HMSO, Belfast, 1990), 5.38.

[7] See text to nn. 194–200 below.

[8] Although in practice many judges disregarded the technicalities of the Civil Evidence Act 1968, preferring to see the evidence and rely on their own judgment.

[9] E.M. Morgan, *Some Problems of Proof Under the Anglo-Saxon System of Litigation* (University of North Carolina, New York, 1956).

[10] M.R. Damaska, *Evidence Law Adrift* (Yale University Press, New Haven, Conn., 1997), 24–31.

[11] Cf. P. Miene, R. Park and E. Borgida, "Juror Decision-making and the Evaluation of the Hearsay Rule" (1992) 76 *Minn. L Rev.* 683.

the rule against hearsay is not merely a product of the adversarial tradition of cross-examination of the opponent's witness. Damaska points out that where witnesses are directly associated with the interests of one party or another, as they are within an adversarial framework, derivative sources of information become problematic. In Continental proceedings, judges are more involved with fact-finding, and the need to subject the means of proof to this kind of testing is less compelling. Attacks on the credibility of witnesses are comparatively rare in Continental courts.[12] Baker, however, amasses an impressive body of evidence to show that, historically at any rate, the origin of the rule is clearly linked to the development of trial by jury.[13] In leading cases, judges tend to justify the exclusionary rule in terms of the effect that hearsay evidence could have on the jury. A modern judicial statement to the same effect can be found in the judgment of Lord Bridge in *Blastland*.[14]

> "The rationale of excluding [hearsay] as inadmissible, rooted as it is in the system of trial by jury, is a recognition of the great difficulty, even more acute for a jury than for a trained judicial mind, of assessing what, if any, weight can properly be given to a statement by a person whom the jury may not have seen or heard and which has not been subject to any test of reliability by cross-examination. As Lord Normand put it,[15] . . . 'The rule against admission of hearsay evidence is fundamental. It is not the best evidence and it is not delivered on oath. The truthfulness and accuracy of the person whose words are spoken to by another witness cannot be tested by cross-examination and the light which his demeanour would throw on his testimony is lost'."

Yet we find the House of Lords entirely willing to allow the jury at an inquest to be exposed to hearsay evidence. In *Devine and Breslin* v. *A.-G. for Northern Ireland*,[16] Lord Goff explained that a coroner's inquest is not an adversarial process, but an inquisition designed to ascertain the true facts. Hence the tribunal is not bound by exclusionary rules of evidence such as the rule against hearsay. Otherwise any suicide note left by the deceased would be inadmissible, which would be ludicrous.[17]

The alleged superiority of oral testimony is not universally accepted. Like historians, continental jurisdictions prefer documentary sources. A French

---

[12] Damaska, n. 10 above, 78–80. See also, J. Spencer, "Orality and the Evidence of Absent Witnesses" [1994] *Crim. LR* 628.

[13] R.W. Baker, *The Hearsay Rule* (Pitman, London, 1950).

[14] [1985] 2 All ER 1095.

[15] In *Teper* v. *R.* [1952] 2 All ER 447 at 449.

[16] [1992] 1 All ER 609, at 613.

[17] This example gives rise to an interesting question; how, if at all, is such a suicide note admissible at a trial for murder? If it is evidence of state of mind (see text to nn. 45–55 below), why does Lord Goff consider it to be hearsay? It is potentially admissible as a dying declaration (but only in limited circumstances, see text to nn. 130–150 below) or by way of the documentary exception under s.23 of the Criminal Justice Act 1988, which is subject to a judicial discretion to exclude (see text to nn. 180–185 below).

treatise speaks of "the primacy of written proof and the mistrust which is prima facie inspired by oral testimony", which is seen as highly subjective.[18] Of the tradition of orality, the Roskill Report observed:

> "Documents are treated by the law with suspicion, and their importance tends to be undervalued . . . These rules were all clearly designed for an era when most of the population could be presumed to be illiterate. While their strict application has caused few difficulties in the general run of criminal cases, they seem increasingly inappropriate and burdensome in cases of fraud and dishonesty which themselves arise from business transactions which are the subject of written records."[19]

Honoré has shown that neither kind of evidence is inherently more reliable than the other, although oral testimony has a tactical advantage. It is also necessary to establish the authenticity of documentary evidence.[20] There certainly are cases where the available documents are more reliable than oral testimony; where complicated transactions are involved, contemporaneous records must be more worthy of trust than what the persons involved may have to say in court, particularly if the events took place years before. This problem is typically dealt with by allowing the witness to use the document to "refresh his memory",[21] and if he deviates from the facts set out in his own record, the court then faces the problem that it would rather rely on the document than what he says on oath.

Hearsay evidence suffers, according to the traditions of the common law, from various weaknesses which render it less reliable than sworn testimony.[22] If the witness in court can only repeat what he heard from the individual who actually observed the event in question and therefore has direct knowledge of it, there is an obvious risk of faulty communication. Did the witness present in court clearly hear what was said or is he or she delivering a garbled version? As far as the observer is concerned, he or she may have been short-sighted, dishonest or mad, but it is difficult to tell in relation to someone not present in court and who cannot be cross-examined. In some cases, courts refer to the danger of concocted evidence.[23] The theory is that a person who knows that what he or she says out of court could be relied on might make false assertions, secure in the knowledge that testing cross-examination is not possible. Hence, the need for a rule against hearsay to insist that this person attend as a witness.

---

[18] Dalloz, *Encyclopédie de Droit Civil sv preuve*, cited by A. Honoré, "The Primacy of Oral Evidence?" in C. Tapper, (ed.), *Crime, Proof and Punishment: Essays in Memory of Sir Rupert Cross* (Butterworths, London, 1981).

[19] *Report of the Fraud Trials Committee* (HMSO, London, 1986), paras. 5.4–5.5.

[20] Honoré, n. 18 above, 191-2.

[21] A procedure recommended by Lord Pearce in *Myers* v. *DPP* [1965] AC 1001, at 1035.

[22] For full discussion, see A Choo, *Hearsay and Confrontation in Criminal Trials* (Clarendon, Oxford, 1996), 11–43.

[23] See the cases on *res gestae*, at text to nn. 130–142 below.

Some of these objections to hearsay seem fanciful in the light of some concrete instances. For example, in *Myers* v. *DPP*,[24] mundane records of car engine and chassis numbers compiled by the manufacturer were excluded although "if the workmen . . . had testified, there would have been nothing to gain from cross-examining them; it would have established what was already known; that they had no incentive to make false records, and that the chance of their having made more than the odd error was remote".[25] This kind of problem led to the introduction of the Criminal Evidence Act 1965, the beginning of a chain of attempts to devise a workable definition of admissible documentary hearsay. As will be seen below, Parliament has found it difficult to isolate the distinction between reliable and unreliable forms of documentary evidence. But in those cases where there is a genuine danger of unreliability, why should it be assumed that a jury is constitutionally unable to grasp that a particular item of evidence should simply be ascribed less weight? They are expected to recognise the varying weights of the different sections of a statement on arrest which is partly exculpatory and partly incriminating.[26]

A significant factor in our traditional devotion to the hearsay rule lies in our obsession with cross-examination. Yet it is not clear why it is impossible to get it across by other means that the absent witness may have had motives for lying or be generally unreliable. The traditional view is that cross-examination is an instrument which uncovers the truth; in *O'Loughlin and McLaughlin*[27] Kenneth Jones J refused to admit the documentary statement of an absent prosecution witness because "[t]he jury would have had no opportunity to judge the way in which [the witness] stood up to that testing process". Another view is that cross-examination merely demonstrates "the power of a skilful cross-examiner to make an honest witness appear at best confused and at worst a liar".[28] The probability is that lawyers over-estimate the unique potential of cross-examination to establish the truth.[29] Its importance in fact lies in the adversarial structure of the trial; counsel has such ability to limit what information is given in evidence-in-chief,[30] through tight control of the witness's testimony that a balanced picture can emerge only where opponents can demand elaboration or explanation where appropriate. In any case, the adversaries are not allowed to pursue the objective truth. The scope of the questions permissible in cross-examination is tied to the specific case upon which a party relies. Cross-examination is issue-related, concerned with the reality of events only if they happen to coincide with the case pleaded. And, curiously, the logic of the hearsay rule persists

[24] [1965] AC 1001.

[25] D. Birch, "The Criminal Justice Act: Documentary Evidence" [1989] *Crim. LR* 15, 18.

[26] *Storey* (1968) 52 Cr. App. R 334; *Pearce* (1979) 69 Cr App R 365; *Duncan* (1981) 73 Cr. App. R 359; *Sharp* [1988] WLR 7. See text to nn. 105–124 below.

[27] [1988] 3 All ER 431.   [28] Birch, n. 25 above, 17.   [29] See above, Ch. 1.

[30] Above, Ch. 1.

even where the maker of the statement *is* in court and available for cross-examination; although the Civil Evidence Act 1995 in some cases allows the out-of-court statements of witnesses to be adduced,[31] in criminal trials they may not serve as evidence of the facts stated unless they fall into one of the exceptions.[32] At best, therefore, such statements may be admissible to prove consistency[33] or inconsistency, with a direction to the jury that the statement may not be treated as evidence of the facts contained in it.[34] On the other hand, where an expert witness bases his conclusions on hearsay such as published research, the courts are content to permit reference to it[35] since there is at least *a* witness who may be cross-examined on its reliability or applicability. Yet this witness is not the maker of the statement, had no part in the research, and therefore has no direct knowledge of the manner of its execution.

The response of the courts to being strait-jacketed in the hearsay rule, whose ancillary collection of exceptions does not mean that what is admitted "is invariably reliable, or that what is left out is of no worth"[36] is, in some cases, to resort to bare-faced cheating to allow in evidence information which is thought to be valuable. Birch calls the device of defining the disputed evidence as non-hearsay in order to avoid losing it altogether a "hearsay-fiddle". The result is a string of incompatible decisions, an unidentifiable concept and despair among lawyers who know the rule is immune to mastery.

The "Crazy Quilt"[37]: Definition of Hearsay

A statement made other than by a person giving oral evidence in the proceedings is inadmissible as evidence of the facts stated. In practical terms, the test is whether there is someone in the witness-box giving oral testimony, on oath, speaking from personal knowledge of the fact he or she is there to prove. Any other form of statement is hearsay, whether in a document, on

---

[31] S.6, see text to nn. 196–198 below.

[32] E.g., confessions by accused persons or statements forming part of the *res gestae*.

[33] If within one of the exceptions to the general rule against admitting self-serving statements.

[34] *Golder* [1960] 3 All ER 457.

[35] *H* v. *Schering Chemicals* [1983] 1 All ER 849; *Abadom* [1983] 1 All ER 726. The requirement from these cases that the expert witness make it clear when he relies on the work of others is frequently forgotten in practice; L.R. Haward, *Forensic Psychology* (Batsford, London, 1981), 185.

[36] D. Birch, "Hearsay-logic and Hearsay-fiddles: *Blastland* Revisited" in P. Smith (ed.), *Criminal Law: Essays in Honour of J C Smith* (Butterworths, London, 1987), 24.

[37] The hearsay rule and its exceptions likened to "a crazy quilt made of patches cut from a group of paintings by cubists, futurists and surrealists": E. Morgan and J. Maguire, "Looking Backward and Forward at Evidence" (1937) 50 *Harv. LR* 909; Birch, however, prefers the analogy of the "threshing room, in which some ancient flails are left propped up against the walls, their usefulness all but over, and shiny new machinery can be seen which has so many working parts that the major interest is to see which breaks down first" (n. 36 above).

videotape, or if it is an oral statement, express or implied, which is being quoted by the person giving evidence. This does not mean that all reported speech[38] is hearsay. As long as a fact is relevant, any person with personal knowledge of that fact may give evidence of it. If it is relevant that a particular thing was said, then anyone who has personal knowledge of that (whether by virtue of having said it or having heard it) may testify to it. It may be necessary for a variety of reasons to show that a particular thing was said; the saying of it may constitute an offence.[39] The hearing of it may constitute a valid defence to a criminal charge.[40] The fact that a complaint was made to a police officer may be relevant to show there were reasonable grounds for an arrest.

The fact that something was said may be relevant to the issue of credibility; in such a case the court is not invited to rely on any fact contained in the statement. In *Mawaz Khan and Amanat Khan*[41] lies told by both defendants to the police in similar terms suggestive of conspiracy were admitted as part of the prosecution case in chief. It was held that the stories were admissible, not as evidence of their contents, but to ask the jury to "hold the assertions false and to draw inferences from their falsity".[42] Where previous consistent statements are admissible[43] to support a witness's credibility, they may be proved by the maker or any hearer. The same is true of previous inconsistent statements; the cross-examiner may not produce evidence of a previous inconsistent statement having been made unless the witness has had an opportunity to explain,[44] but if they are denied, they may be proved by the hearer or the paper on which they are written.

Implied Assertions and Evidence of State of Mind

Statements which are adduced only to show the state of mind of either the maker or the hearer fall outside the hearsay rule:

> "It is well established in English jurisprudence, in accordance with the dictates of common sense, that the words and acts of a person are admissible as evidence of his state of mind."[45]

The most well-known case on this subject is *Subramaniam v. Public Prosecutor*.[46] Threats alleged to have been uttered to the defendant were held by the Privy Council to be admissible to show their likely effect on him. This

---

[38] "He told me that".

[39] E.g., a threat to destroy or damage property (s.2 of the Criminal Damage Act 1971); a threat to kill (s.16 of the Offences Against the Person Act 1861).

[40] For instance, provocation, duress, self-defence: *Subramaniam v. Public Prosecutor* [1956] 1 WLR 965 (n. 46 below).

[41] [1967] 1 AC 454.   [42] *Ibid.*, at 462.   [43] See Ch. 3.

[44] Criminal Procedure Act 1865, ss. 4, 5; see Ch. 3.

[45] *Lloyd v. Powell Duffryn Steam Coal Co. Ltd* [1914] AC 733, *per* Lord Moulton at 751.

[46] [1956] 1 WLR 965.

was relevant because his defence was duress. The fact that the statement was made was significant to show what Subramaniam's state of mind was likely to have been, rather than to prove the truth of its contents.

Until *Blastland*,[47] there was no direct authority to show that statements could be admitted to show the state of mind of the maker of the statement, but the House of Lords has now given official sanction to the popular assumption that they can. Their Lordships considered that the question of the speaker's knowledge of the victim's death was not relevant to the issue of Blastland's guilt, however. The third party, M was alleged by a witness to have returned home at about the time of a murder shaking, covered in mud and wet from the knees down. He told her at the time, and told others later, that a young boy had been murdered. Lord Bridge agreed that if statements were admitted solely to prove a person's knowledge, that would not be hearsay. But that knowledge would have to be relevant. Here M's knowledge as such had no relevance to the issue, unless it was considered together with an inference as to the source of his knowledge (that is, his own guilt).Taken on its own, mere knowledge that a murder has been done has no relevance to the issue whether or not Blastland was guilty of the murder. To draw the inference of M's guilt from his knowledge would be to indulge in speculation, since there was a variety of possible explanations for it. Unfortunately, the issues of relevance and hearsay have become confusingly entangled in Lord Bridge's judgment. After all, the defence were not trying to prove that a young boy had been murdered—the prosecution had already established that. The witnesses to M's statements were therefore not required to prove their contents, that the boy was dead; they were not testifying to a matter of which they had no direct knowledge. The inference of guilt did not arise from the statement itself as an implied assertion, but from the circumstances. The evidence was classic circumstantial evidence, which does not directly point to guilt but gives rise to an inference of another fact which does; the real objection to the evidence here was that the House of Lords considered circumstantial evidence against another to be irrelevant to Blastland's trial.[48]

Although in some cases it might be clear that an individual's state of mind at a particular moment is a relevant fact, it is far less so where the *Subramaniam* line of cases collides with another application of the hearsay rule, the rule on implied assertions. A statement may be made in words, but also by gesture[49] or could be implied in behaviour.[50] The test for whether evidence contains an implied (hearsay) assertion begins by asking for what purpose evidence is being put forward. If the point of producing letters to a testator, as in *Wright v. Doe dec'd Tatham*,[51] is to show that their contents indicate that the writers did not consider the testator to be insane, then the court is effectively being asked to rely on an implied statement, "You are

[47] [1985] 2 All ER 1095; see Ch. 2.   [48] See Ch. 2.
[49] *Gibson* (1887) 18 QBD 537: *Teper v. R.* [1952] AC 480.
[50] *Wright v. Doe dec'd, Tatham* (1834) 1 Ad. & El. 3.   [51] *Ibid.*

perfectly sane", which runs through the correspondence.[52] Parke B stressed the absence of the oath behind such implied statements. Another view is that if conduct is not intended to be assertive of any fact, the oath would appear to be unnecessary.[53] There seems little danger of fabrication, although the danger of inaccuracy would appear as great as with other kinds of hearsay.[54] Indeed, the danger of misunderstanding or misinterpretation may be more acute than for express hearsay statements. Notwithstanding the controversy, implied assertions are subject to the exclusionary rule in the same way as express assertions of fact.[55]

It is sometimes difficult to disentangle that which merely indicates someone's state of mind from all manner of implied assertions which may simultaneously emerge from the statement. The case of *Ratten*[56] illustrates both this point and that it is far from straightforward to draw a line between conduct which is assertive of a fact and conduct which is not. Mrs Ratten died of a gunshot wound. The defendant claimed that his gun had gone off by accident while he was cleaning it. He said that he had summoned an ambulance, and that his wife had made no telephone call herself. She was dead by 1.20 p.m., when the ambulance arrived. The telephone operator's evidence was that at 1.15 p.m. a call had been made to the local exchange from the Rattens' home, and that she heard a hysterical and sobbing woman say "Get me the police please". The Privy Council inclined to the view that this evidence probably did not infringe the hearsay rule because the significance of it was that the call was made. The nature of the call and the apparent distress of the caller were inconsistent with Ratten's account of events. Thus the operator's evidence merely described Mrs Ratten's state of mind and did not infringe the rule against hearsay. A counter-argument would be that the operator need not have repeated the words uttered by the caller. These were not themselves necessary to prove either that the call was made or that the caller appeared distressed. Admitting evidence of the contents of the call allowed in an implied assertion that someone in the house (presumably Ratten himself) was doing something unlawful and frightening, and therefore the operator was effectively testifying to a fact of which she had no direct knowledge. Admitting the words spoken by the caller inevitably would do Ratten's defence a great deal of harm, which indicates that they told the court much more than the mere fact that Mrs Ratten was alarmed.[57] The matter

---

[52] Such a statement would also be inadmissible as non-expert opinion evidence.

[53] J. Weinberg, "Implied Assertions and the Scope of Hearsay Rule" (1973) 7 *MULR* 268.

[54] *Teper* v. *R.* [1952] AC 480; *Gibson* (1887) 18 QBD 539.

[55] The Law Commission favours making implied assertions admissible, but it proposes a definition of implied assertions which somewhat awkwardly relies on identifying the purpose of the person making the statement: *Evidence in Criminal Proceedings: Hearsay and Related Topics,* Law Com. 245, (HMSO, London, 1997), Cm 3670.

[56] [1972] AC 378.

[57] Although there is an argument that to describe the caller's gasping and sobbing as fear would be unconvincing unless her words were also quoted.

was not finally resolved by the Privy Council, which was content to allow the evidence in as part of the *res gestae*.[58]

More controversial is a recent case in the House of Lords, *Kearley*.[59] The police had searched the defendant's flat. They found a quantity of prohibited drugs, which was not in itself large enough to afford evidence that he was dealing. However, during the time they were there, the police intercepted ten telephone calls (and received seven visitors at the door). All the callers were looking for Kearley and asking him to supply them with drugs. None of them was produced as a witness at his trial for possession with intent to supply. The judge at first instance could not resist the natural inference of this evidence, that Kearley was engaged in drug-dealing; neither could the Court of Appeal. The evidence was said not to amount to a hearsay implied assertion, but to demonstrate the state of mind of the callers (believing Kearley to be a dealer). It was also suggested in the Court of Appeal that the evidence simply showed that the defendant possessed a "market", part of the regular paraphernalia of drug-dealers. However, this would be circumstantial evidence of very limited probative value. The majority of the House of Lords could not see what relevance the state of mind or belief of any or all of these callers would have to the issue of guilt, unless by way of implied assertions that Kearley was a dealer. The only sworn evidence which dealt with the issue of Kearley's alleged dealing effectively came from the police witness who relayed what the callers had said. That officer had no direct knowledge that the defendant was dealing. He was reliant on the implied statement each caller made, (namely "I know you, Chippie, to be a dealer") insofar as they asked him to supply drugs. The prosecution needed witnesses with direct knowledge of his dealing, and it had none. There was a risk, also, of multiple hearsay, should it emerge that the callers had no direct experience that Kearley was a dealer, but had been told by someone else that he was. If, in this case, the defendant had been heard arranging to sell drugs to one of these callers, evidence of the conversation would have been admissible. The exclusionary rule would not have been involved. The conversation would itself have been evidence of his intention to supply. Thus in *Woodhouse* v. *Hall*[60] immoral services were offered to police officers by women who were employed as masseuses at the defendant's premises. The fact that these offers were made suggested the purpose for which the premises were being used. There was no need to rely on the truth of the contents of any statement made by the women. The evidence therefore was original evidence that the conversations took place, and not hearsay.

It is frequently difficult, as in *Ratten*, to be clear about whether or not a statement is admitted to show that it was made, the relevance being that it shows the state of mind of the maker or the person who heard it, or whether its true significance lies in its contents. The danger is that an express or

---

[58] See text to nn. 130–142 below.   [59] [1992] 2 All ER 345.   [60] (1980) 72 Cr. App. R 39.

implied assertion will lie behind what is described as non-hearsay evidence. A case which can be criticised on that ground is *Wallwork*,[61] where a 5-year-old girl was regarded as too young[62] to give evidence against her father on a charge of incest. The Court of Criminal Appeal held that although the child's grandmother should not have been allowed to give evidence of the particulars of a complaint made at the time by the child to her, since there was no question of the child's consistency, there "would have been no objection to the grandmother saying 'the little girl made a complaint to me' ". But if the statement is admissible neither as evidence of the facts complained of nor the consistency of the complainant, it appears that its only function is to create prejudice.[63]

Hearsay in a Document or Real Evidence?

Photographs are treated as original evidence and not hearsay. A photograph of the murder weapon is therefore said to be logically in the same category as the weapon itself. A videotape recording made by security cameras which shows a robbery at a building society, for instance, is admissible as real evidence of what took place. In *Thomas*,[64] the road on which a chase involving the defendant and a police car took place at night was filmed on a different occasion from a car driven by the same officers. For technical reasons this had to be done in daylight, but the trial judge held that the video was admissible at the defendant's trial for reckless driving, because it enabled the officers giving evidence to describe the scene by reference to it. They would have been able to use a photograph for the same purpose. The principle was carried even further in *Taylor* v. *Chief Constable for Cheshire*.[65] A videotape which allegedly showed the accused in the act of stealing was erased in error, but police witnesses who had seen it and recognised him gave evidence describing the event and identifying him. It was held in the Divisional Court that their evidence did not involve hearsay, since a film of the crime is real evidence of it. Logically, the officers were in the same position as eye-witnesses at the scene who see a crime as it occurs. The fact that the court was not in a position to assess the quality of the tape and was reliant on the police officers to describe the clarity of the pictures went only to the weight of the evidence.

In the case of *Cook*[66] the Court of Appeal went altogether too far. A photofit picture was compiled from the description of her attacker by the victim of robbery and indecent assault. The trial judge admitted the picture

---

[61] (1958) 42 Cr. App. R 153.   [62] Now see Ch. 4.

[63] Cf. R. Cross, "Complaints of Sexual Offences" (1958) 74 *LQR* 352; A. Keane, *The Modern Law of Evidence* (Butterworths, London, 1995), 136. Nevertheless, this approach was echoed in *R.* v. *Waltham Forest Justices, ex p. B* [1989] FCR 341. Cases to the opposite effect include *Guttridge* (1840) 9 C & P 471; *Burke* (1912) 47 ILT 111.

[64] [1986] Crim. LR 682.   [65] [1986] 1 WLR 1279.   [66] [1987] 1 All ER 1049.

into evidence at the trial. The defence argued on appeal that it was inadmissible as hearsay, but the Court of Appeal disagreed, on the analogy with photographic evidence:

> "We regard the production of the sketch or photofit by a police officer making a graphic representation of a witness's memory as another form of the camera at work, albeit imperfectly and not produced contemporaneously with the material incident but soon or fairly soon afterwards. . . . Seeing that we do not regard the photofit picture as a statement at all it cannot come within the description of an earlier consistent statement".[67]

The analogy with photographic evidence, which is itself not without hearsay taint, is entirely unconvincing. The opportunites for error, suggestion and misunderstanding is almost endless. The notion that a police sketch or other realisation of a description should serve as evidence of identification not only flouts the hearsay rule but renders otiose the statutory requirements designed to make identification evidence reliable. For example in *Constantinou*[68] a photofit was made up from witness M's recollection of an armed robbery. M's subsequent identification of the defendant in a confrontation was excluded from the trial, leaving no identification evidence against him apart from the photofit. Yet the picture was admitted in evidence against him and a conviction based almost entirely on it was upheld on appeal. This case involved a side-step not only of the hearsay rule but of the requirements in the Police and Criminal Evidence Act 1984; there is little point in the legislature stipulating the conditions in which identification parades should be held, if identification can be achieved simply by presenting a photofit compiled out of court through the efforts of the eyewitness and a police officer.

The danger of distortion was regarded as significant in *Quinn and Bloom*.[69] The offence charged was keeping a disorderly house. Three striptease artistes claimed that the act which they had been performing when police officers arrived had not been obscene and offered in evidence a videotape in which they reconstructed their performances. The tape was held to be inadmissible, since it would be impossible for them precisely to duplicate all movements and gestures, especially as a snake was involved. It was conceded that during their oral testimony the witnesses could to some extent have shown by action or mime while in the witness box roughly what they had been doing. The objection to the film centred on the risk that a full-scale re-enactment could be highly misleading, because of the scope for differences from the original. Re-enactments on videotape have been allowed in other cases, however, where the film fell into a known hearsay exception, or the danger of deviation from the event was not significant. In *Li Shu-Ling* v. *R.*,[70]

---

[67] *Ibid.*, Watkins LJ at 1054.   [68] [1989] Crim. LR 571.   [69] [1962] 2 QB 245.

[70] [1988] 2 All ER 138.

the defendant had confessed to murder and agreed to participate in a filmed reconstruction of the event. It was hearsay, but fell within the admissions exception to the rule. His lack of acting ability did not affect the admissibility of the evidence, according to the Privy Council, but arguably went to weight.

Where a machine is producing a record of events in non-photographic form, that record may consist of real evidence rather than hearsay, if there is no suggestion that any person fed in information. *The Statue of Liberty*[71] provides a useful precedent on mechanically-produced evidence. Two vessels collided in the Thames. The plaintiffs were allowed to use as evidence of the position of the vessels a film from a shore radar station showing radar echoes. Sir Jocelyn Simon placed such film in the same category as photographs. If someone had been reading a barometer, to make a judgement on weather conditions, he would be able to give evidence in court of those weather conditions, relying on the reading he took from the machine. Logically, there is no difference between that and using any record made by the machine itself in response to atmospheric pressure.

The analogy with photographs in *The Statue of Liberty* has been applied to other machines which record information without human input. So some computer printouts are treated as real evidence, as in *Castle and Cross*,[72] where the printout from an intoximeter was held not to be hearsay. Earlier cases had been contradictory on the question of evidence produced by a machine,[73] which effectively operates itself and records information from direct physical stimuli. But now the preponderance of case law shows that the question is whether a printout is a human being's "statement in a document". Where the computer is merely a means of recording that statement, its output is hearsay. When the machine receives information from non-human sources, as in a case involving entirely computer-produced evidence of telephone numbers called from a particular telephone, this is real evidence.[74]

In *Shepherd*[75] the House of Lords sidestepped the difficulty which would have been involved in drawing this distinction in the instant case. The computer in question produced till rolls in a Marks and Spencers store; some of the information it recorded itself from the "magic eye" reading of the bar code on goods sold; other information was fed in by the mainframe; and further information was entered by the shop assistant. The case turned on the interpretation of section 69 of the Police and Criminal Evidence Act 1984. This provides that a statement in a document produced by a computer shall not be admissible as evidence of any fact stated therein unless it is shown:

---

[71] [1968] 1 WLR 739.   [72] [1985] 1 All ER 87.
[73] *Pettigrew* (1980) 71 Cr. App. R 39: *Burke* [1987] Crim. LR 406.
[74] *Spiby* (1990) 91 Cr. App. R 186.   [75] [1993] 1 All ER 225.

(a) that there are no reasonable grounds for believing that the statement is inaccurate because of improper use of the computer;

(b) that at all material times the computer was operating properly or if not, that any respect in which it was out of operation was not such as to affect the production of the document or the accuracy of its contents.

Earlier cases had held that the section does not apply to real evidence computer printouts because it refers to a "statement in a document".[76] To follow those decisions would have forced the House of Lords in *Shepherd* to decide whether the till rolls were real evidence or hearsay documents. Instead, they were overruled. Despite the language of section 69, there can be no doubt that the need to show that a computer is recording accurately is as great where it produces real evidence as when it produces hearsay statements.[77] Thus section 69 must be satisfied whether documentary evidence was produced by a computer or otherwise. The House of Lords decided that for this purpose the oral evidence of the store detective, who said that she had never known the machine to make a mistake, was sufficient. Many lay persons apparently are competent to make such an assessment in this computer-literate age.[78] Their Lordships might well have found it difficult to decide the issue of the nature of these particular till-rolls. If a party wishes to adduce computer-produced evidence and is unsure whether or not it is hearsay, the safest course would seem to be to cite the business records exception to the hearsay rule under section 24 of the Criminal Justice Act 1988.[79]

In some situations it appears next to impossible to formulate a coherent distinction between hearsay and real evidence. This difficulty is exacerbated by the obvious consequence of identifying evidence as hearsay; that is, that unless it falls within the terms of an exception to the rule valuable evidence may be lost. A well-known case which exemplifies the problem is *Rice*.[80] The issue here was whether a used airline ticket, handed in after a flight and bearing the names of Rice and his co-accused, could be admitted into evidence. If admissible, it would serve as circumstantial evidence of their presence on the flight. The Court of Appeal treated it as a piece of real evidence. To avoid the rigours of the hearsay rule, such evidence must not be allowed to "speak its contents", and so is not evidence of any statement such as "my bearer is X" or "I was issued to Y"; hence it is not evidence of whom

---

[76] E.g., *Spiby* (1990) 91 Cr. App. R 186.

[77] It could be argued that in fact the necessity is the greater because of the lack of human intervention.

[78] But if it is proposed to fulfil the requirements of s.69 by way of a certificate, so that there is no witness to cross-examine on the subject of the machine's reliability, that certification must be provided by an expert.

[79] See text to nn. 164–180 below.

the ticket was issued to; only that an air ticket which has been used on a flight and which has a name on it has, more likely than not, been used by a man of that name. The decision was followed in *Lydon (Sean)*[81] where a gun was found a mile from a post office which had been robbed. It may have been the one carried by one of the robbers. Near it were two pieces of paper, on which were written, "Sean Rules" and "Sean 85". The trial judge allowed the prosecution to adduce these papers in evidence. The relevance of the writing was merely to indicate a relationship with someone called Sean. The prosecution were not seeking to establish any fact in terms of its contents.

These cases sit uneasily with decisions such as *Patel* v. *Customs Comptroller*,[82] where the Privy Council refused to treat bags of coriander seed marked "Morocco" as original evidence that they had come from Morocco. To admit the evidence would be to rely on a statement as to origin by some unidentified person. Hence claims on labels as to origin or contents are hearsay statements. We find also in *Myers*[83] that a record of car engine numbers kept by the manufacturer amounts to a series of hearsay statements by workmen at the factory. In the Court of Appeal, Widgery J said that in *Rice* a foundation of evidence to show Rice was on the plane had already been laid, and, given that the carrier had a system for the retention and filing of used tickets, it seemed wholly artificial to deprive the jury of the assistance which a reference to the file of used tickets might give.[84] He argued that here the foundation for the identification of a stolen car had been laid by the evidence of its owner, and it would be artificial to exclude either party from consulting manufacturers' records "and showing whether those records do or do not confirm the identification".[85] He concluded that the admission of such evidence "does not infringe the hearsay rule because its probative value does not depend upon the credit of an unidentified person but rather on the circumstances in which the record is maintained". In the House of Lords, Lord Reid agreed that the proposition was undeniable as a matter of common sense, but the value of the evidence in its context did not alter the fact that it was hearsay.[86]

Following *Rice*, it would appear not impossible to argue that the documents in *Myers* were in fact real evidence of the symbols which appeared on a car engine rather than a statement of fact made by a person. The document would merely indicate that an engine of that number was more likely than not to have been manufactured at the time. Yet the House of Lords regarded the records as hearsay, and in *McLean*[87] the same view was taken by the Court of Appeal of a car registration number written on a piece of paper. The victim of a robbery dictated a car registration number to B, who wrote it down. The victim did not check the note, and so was not allowed to refresh his memory with it,[88] and the writer could not give

---

[80] [1963] 1 QB 85.   [81] (1986) 85 Cr. App. R 221.   [82] [1966] AC 356.
[83] [1965] AC 1001; see n. 24 above.   [84] [1965] AC 1001 at 1008.   [85] *Ibid.*   [86] At 1023.
[87] (1968) 52 Cr. App. R 80.   [88] See text to n. 179.

evidence of the number as he had no direct knowledge of it, and to allow him to testify to the number, or to use the note itself as evidence, would be hearsay.[89] There is still no statutory exception which would allow such a document to be adduced as hearsay evidence,[90] although the more flexible version of *res gestae* offered by the House of Lords in *Andrews*[91] may provide a justification for admitting such obviously valuable evidence.

The Admissibility of Confessions and Denials

An admission is admissible as evidence of the fact stated against the person who made it; in a civil case, this seems to be the case even against a party who at the time the admission was made was under pressure from threats or inducement.[92] Confessions are equally admissible in a criminal case as evidence of guilt.[93] An out-of-court confession is hearsay because it is not made on oath and, if proffered by a police officer as evidence of the defendant's guilt, that officer is effectively testifying to something of which he or she has no direct knowledge. Confessions therefore are admitted as exceptions to the rule against hearsay; but that does not mean that they can be admitted as second-hand hearsay. Where a confession is relayed through an interpreter, albeit a disinterested intermediary, the case of *Attard*[94] applies (unless there is a tape-recording of the interview). The interpreter attended a police station interview, at which it was alleged the defendant confessed. It was held that only the interpreter could give evidence of the confession as the police officer did not have direct knowledge of it.

The exception to the rule must be confined within its own terms. In civil cases, the admission should be made by a party to the litigation or someone in privity with that party.[95] In criminal cases, the exception does not extend to confessions to crimes made by persons other than the defendant.[96] Although the common law appears to regard some statements against interest as inherently more reliable than other hearsay statements, there appears to be no available exception in English common law to accommodate third-party confessions.[97] Thus it avails an accused person in a criminal case nothing that someone else has admitted to committing the crime. If, however, that person happens to be a co-defendant, the recent case of *Myers*[98] might be of assistance. The defendant, Myers, had made admissions to the police, but the prosecution did not rely on them, as various breaches of the Codes of Practice had taken place during her interview. At their joint

---

[89] Cf. *Fenlon* [1980] Crim LR 573
[90] See text to nn. 177–180 below.   [91] [1987] 1 All ER 513.
[92] *Morleys' of Bristol* v. *Minott* [1982] ICR 444.
[93] S.76(1) of the Police and Criminal Evidence Act 1984 (subject to the safeguards discussed in Ch. 6).
[94] (1958) 43 Cr. App. R 90.
[95] *British Thomson-Houston Co. Ltd* v. *British Insulated and Helsby Cables* [1924] 2 Ch. 160.
[96] *Turner* (1975) 61 Cr. App. R 78.   [97] See Birch, n. 36 above.   [98] [1997] 4 All ER 314.

trial for murdering a taxi-driver, her co-defendant was allowed to cross-examine Myers on these admissions, which were inconsistent with her testimony. The House of Lords noted that section 76(1) of the Police and Criminal Evidence Act 1984 allows a confession made by an accused person to be given in evidence, without stipulating that only the prosecution may take advantage of it. It would have been unfair to the co-defendant to deny him this evidence, whether he used it to cross-examine her or the interviewing officers. The decision might have been different if section 76(2) of the Police and Criminal Evidence Act 1984 had been breached.[99] It should be noted that the confession by Myers was not treated as evidence of the facts stated, but went to discredit her testimony in court (which placed the blame on the co-defendant).

In an American case, *Chambers*,[100] there was a confession by someone not involved with the trial which was admitted into evidence. It was said to fall within the common law exception of statements against interest, but since the declarant was neither dead nor a defendant in the case the decision amounts to an extension of the hearsay exceptions which English courts will not follow.[101] Birch appears content with the effect of this decision, which allows the nature and reliability of the third-party confession to affect its weight, not its admissibility.[102] The Court said:

> "The testimony rejected by the trial court here bore persuasive assurances of trustworthiness and thus was well within the basic rationale of the exception for declarations against interest. This testimony was also critical to Chambers' defence."

But the risk of highly unreliable confessions being adduced by defendants as evidence of their innocence is quite substantial, especially in relation to widely-publicised crimes. These are notorious for attracting an inevitable string of false confessions. For example, the Lindbergh kidnapping in the United States resulted in over 200 confessions. At present these confessions appear to present no great practical problem to the police, as the subject can usually be eliminated from the inquiry because of insufficient knowledge of details of the crime.[103] However, new problems could be created if the person who is ultimately tried for that offence is allowed to cloud the issue by producing one or more of these confessions in his defence. It is quite obvious that the adversarial trial is incapable of dealing satisfactorily with such evidence; its structure is inappropriate to assess the proper weight to be attached to a third-party confession. Discussion of the circumstances in

---

[99] See Ch. 6. Presumably then the confession would have been totally unreliable.

[100] *Chambers* v. *Mississippi* (1973) 410 US 284.

[101] *Myers* [1965] AC 1001.

[102] Birch, n. 36 above.

[103] G.H. Gudjonsson, "The Psychology of False Confessions" (1989) 57 *Medico-Legal Journal* 93; he suggests as possible motives for such confessions "a morbid desire for notoriety", feelings of guilt, and inability to distinguish fact from fantasy.

which it was made, and the apparent degree of knowledge of detail shown by the party, are collateral issues with which the adversarial trial cannot and will not concern itself. We have seen the narrowness of adversarial reasoning taken to its limit in *Blastland*.[104] A more inquisitorial procedure, however, could deal with such confessions more easily; completely untrustworthy confessions could be weeded out at an early stage, without inconvenient insistence on oral evidence on the manner in which they were given.

The rationale of *Chambers* is that what a man says against himself may fairly be presumed to be true. This assumption affects the law of evidence in relation to admissions by parties and declarations against interest by deceased persons. There is no basis in fact for the assumption; on the contrary, there is good reason to assume that a number of self-incriminating statements are highly suspect. The work of psychologists on the pressure on suspects during interrogation, together with the effect of individual personality responses, suggests that such statements should be treated with great caution.[105] Nevertheless, this dubious premise is the basis for the admissibility of confession evidence in criminal cases. The result is that the confession of the defendant in a criminal case is evidence of his guilt. Once the law adopts that position, it finds itself unable to deal coherently with statements by accused persons which do not fall neatly into the category of confessions, if, at the same time, they do not amount to previous consistent statements by the accused. Self-justifying statements made on being first accused of the crime charged are said to be admissible for the defence if consistent with the accused's present testimony,[106] but in that case they go only to credibility. They would therefore appear to have no relevance at all if the accused chooses not to give evidence. However, the practice has developed amongst prosecutors of allowing the entire statement on arrest to be read out irrespective of contents, forcing courts to deal with two problems which arise as a result. First, courts are confronted with apparently irrelevant exculpatory statements in cases where the accused does not give evidence. Secondly, there are statements which are "mixed", in that they are partly incriminating and partly exculpatory.

In *Storey*,[107] the defendant was questioned about the presence of cannabis in her flat and claimed that a man had brought it there against her will. She did not give evidence at her trial. The Court of Appeal held that her statement was admissible to prove, not the facts stated, but her reaction when first taxed with incriminating facts. In *Pearce*[108] a shop manager within a market denied theft. He was questioned several times over four days. His statements at the end of this period therefore could only with difficulty be

---

[104] See Ch. 2 and text to nn. 47–48 above.
[105] Gudjonsson, n. 103 above, and Ch. 6.
[106] R.J. Gooderson, "Previous Consistent Statements" [1968] CLJ 64.
[107] (1968) 52 Cr. App. R 334.
[108] (1979) 69 Cr. App. R 365.

regarded as evidence of his reaction when first accused, and the trial judge excluded those parts of his statement which did not constitute admissions. The Court of Appeal took the view that the excised parts were admissible as evidence of his reaction from *Storey*, and that the length of the questioning period went only to weight—the longer the time gap, the less weight should be attached to a denial. How the jury are to apply this evidence of reaction if the defendant elects not to give evidence is not explained. Phipson concludes that the only possible use of it is the illegitimate one, namely, to conclude that the denial is true.[109] However, if the out-of-court statement is the only indication of a particular defence, such as self-defence, it does not serve as evidence capable of raising that defence.[110] There will be cases where the an out-of-court denial, admitted as evidence of reaction, is detrimental to a defendant. It may reveal an unpleasant personality. Alternatively, if the terms of the denial change over the course of several interviews, this could destroy the credibility of any defence raised at the trial.

Out-of-court denials are not evidence of innocence, and there is no legal obligation on prosecutors to introduce them into evidence.[111] Many statements made to the police by suspects are more complex, however, containing a mixture of admissions and denials.[112] It clearly would be unfair for the prosecution to be able to adduce the incriminating part of a mixed statement on its own. To allow the prosecution to rely on the admission, but edit out the exculpatory element, would be grossly misleading.[113] Then the question arises as to the significance of the various parts of the statement on arrest. Technically, the admission is evidence of guilt and the denial is evidence of reaction, if the accused does not give evidence. If he or she does give evidence, the denial could amount to evidence of consistency, if he or she gives evidence to the same effect, or (for use in cross-examination) inconsistency, if he or she gives a different version in court. In *Duncan*,[114] the accused did not give evidence at his trial for murder. He had admitted the killing to police, but his statement to them contained some evidence of provocation. There were no witnesses to testify to provocation at the trial, and therefore the issue was raised, if at all, only in his out-of-court statement, which at best was hearsay and in fact was adduced by the prosecution. The Court of Appeal recognised that the whole statement on arrest is admissible and, rather than have the judge mystify the jury with an explanation of the part which is admissible as evidence of the facts stated (the admission) and that which is only evidence of reaction (the excuse), he should explain

---

[109] *Phipson on Evidence* (Sweet and Maxwell, London, 1990), para. 12.63.

[110] *Pearce* (1979) 69 Cr. App. R 365.

[111] The defence could adduce them by way of previous consistent statements to bolster the credibility of a defendant whose testimony in court is to the same effect.

[112] E.g., "Yes, I killed him, but it was self-defence".

[113] *Sharp* [1988] 1 All ER 65, at 68.

[114] (1981) 73 Cr. App. R 359.

that the jury should consider the whole of the statement, but give the admission more weight than the rest. This approach received House of Lords approval in *Sharp*.[115]

The courts have recognised in these cases the reality that prosecutors have developed the habit of reading out the reaction on arrest, whether it furthers their case or not. Cases so far have been concerned only with the significance of such statements where this has occurred,[116] and have not discussed the question whether prosecutors carry an obligation to read self-serving statements to the court. There seems no reason to impose on them a legal obligation to do this. Phipson comments[117]:

> "While it is clear that statements by defendants which do not contain admissions are commonly admitted in evidence, it is equally clear that the defendant is not entitled to require the prosecution to produce, or to produce himself, a 'carefully prepared written statement' produced to the police with a view to it being made part of the prosecution evidence."

However, some prosecutors find that failure to explain how the defendant reacted to the accusation is treated with suspicion by the court. It might suggest the prosecutor has something to hide.

From *Pearce*, an entirely exculpatory statement is not evidence of the facts stated, and therefore does not discharge the defence's evidential burden in relation to any defence apparently arising from it, for example, a claim of alibi.[118] But if the self-serving element of a *mixed* statement contains the basis of a defence, that statement, which must be read out in its entirety, does raise any defence referred to in it, so that defence must be put to the jury.[119] Such a result is inevitable, once it is settled that the jury must be directed that the self-serving part of the statement may be treated as evidence of the fact stated, even though it has less weight than the admission. Nevertheless, it is curious that an accused may, through evidence which is technically hearsay and is adduced by the other side, raise a defence of which he provides no other evidence. The House of Lords attempted to restore the balance thus: "[t]here is [no] reason why . . . where appropriate, the judge should not comment in relation to the exculpatory remarks upon the election of the accused not to give evidence".[120]

These decisions appear to indicate a certain judicial desperation. It is apparently impossible to follow in all cases the strict logic of the rigid divide between evidence which goes to credibility and that which goes to the

---

[115] [1988] 1 All ER 65.

[116] E.g., *Donaldson* (1977) 64 Cr. App. R 59.

[117] N. 109 above, para. 12.63.

[118] *Pearce* (1979) 69 Cr App R 365; *Barbery* (1976) 62 Cr. App. R 248.

[119] *Duncan* (1981) 73 Cr. App. R 359; *Hamand* (1986) 82 Cr. App. R 65.

[120] *Duncan* (1981) 73 Cr App R 359, *per* Lord Lane CJ at 365, cited with approval in *Sharp* [1988] 1 All ER 65, by Lord Havers at 67. Now see s. 34 of the Criminal Justice and Public Order Act 1994, and Ch. 5 above.

issue—a distinction entirely jettisoned here. The logical course would be to omit the exculpatory part of a mixed statement unless it amounts to a previous consistent statement by a defendant who gives evidence, because the philosophy of the law of evidence is that it has no relevance. But the result, as seen above, would be unfair and misleading. An additional difficulty is to communicate the logic of the hearsay rule to the jury; Lord MacKay argued in *Sharp*[121] that the concepts put before a jury must be capable of reasonably straightforward expression and application. The rules on hearsay as evidence of fact, and consistent statements as evidence of witness credibility, are far too complicated for that. Lord MacKay went on to quote the Lord Justice-Clerk Thompson in *Gillespie* v. *Macmillan*[122]:

> "If law were an exact science or even a department of logic. there might be something to be said [for the Crown's argument] . . . But law is a practical affair and has to approach its problems in a mundane common-sense way."

The fact that a rule designed to promote reliability and ensure that the jury are not misled can, in some contexts, have the opposite effect is recognised in this series of cases. It may be a matter of celebration that here the courts have in respect of "mixed" statements chosen the paths of common sense and fairness. But they have, in the process, been forced to abandon the normal operation of the exclusionary rule, which prevails in other contexts irrespective of common sense or fairness. And where there is more than one accused person on trial, it is more difficult to identify what is fair. In *Lobban* v. *R.*,[123] two co-defendants were implicated in murders committed during the course of a robbery. Lobban's co-accused pleaded duress, accusing Lobban of supplying the threat. It was held by the Privy Council, following *Sharpe*, that the co-defendant's mixed statement out of court was admissible, and that a trial judge has no discretion to exclude the exculpatory part of such a statement even though it is prejudicial to the other defendant. These difficulties are a reflection of the contradictions created in the law of evidence partly by the insistence on a dichotomy between credibility and the issue of guilt, and partly because of the fundamental absurdity of the hearsay rule itself.[124]

Exceptions to the Hearsay Rule

Criminal Trials

The exceptions to the rule against hearsay which developed within the common law purport to apply to those situations where evidence is considered to be in the particular circumstances sufficiently reliable to be admitted in evidence. Close examination of these exceptions might cause a sceptic to

---

[121] [1988] 1 All ER 65 at 66.　　　[122] 1957 JC 31, 40.　　　[123] [1995] 2 All ER 602.
[124] *Sharp* [1988] 1 All ER 65, *per* Lord Havers at 68.

conclude that the true rationale of the exceptions is unwillingness to deprive the court of evidence which is clearly of considerable probative value. There are various common law exceptions which avoid some of the potential embarrassments which otherwise the exclusionary rule might create. For example, a witness, technically, could not claim direct knowledge of his or her own age. But there is an exception which relates to statements in public documents.[125] A similar exception allows into evidence works of reference.[126] Admissions and confessions, admissible at common law, and now, in criminal trials, under section 76 of the Police and Criminal Evidence Act 1984, are discussed above and in Chapter 6. The remaining traditional exceptions to the rule against hearsay are remarkable for their eccentricity.

Statements by Persons now Deceased

This exception applies to two kinds of statement. One follows the well-established assumption that any admission or other statement made adverse to the interests of the person making it is likely to be true. Thus a prospective litigant's admission that the lesion on his thumb was due to natural causes was admissible against his estate. His widow subsequently to his death had brought a civil action against his former employers in respect of an alleged injury to his thumb.[127] The other common law exception relating to someone now dead concerns statements made during the course of duty. The rationale for this exception is that the statement is likely to be accurate because of the circumstances in which it was made. *Price* v. *Torrington* concerned a drayman recording deliveries on his round; there was no reason to suppose his records were inaccurate.[128] However, the common law exception for some reason concerns only records made under a duty by someone who since has died. This requirement forced the House of Lords in *Myers* v. *DPP* to exclude perfectly reliable records kept by car manufacturers because the workmen who made them were still alive,[129] although such workmen, even if they could be identified, could not realistically be expected to recall the numbers of the engines they had made.

Res Gestae

The principle of the *res gestae*[130] exception appears to be that an utterance which is spontaneous is unlikely to be deliberately misleading. If the maker of a statement has a long time to think about it in an atmosphere of calm, he

---

[125] *Sturla* v. *Freccia* (1880) 5 App. Cas. 623.

[126] *Read* v. *Bishop of Lincoln* [1892] AC 644.

[127] *Tucker* v. *Oldbury UDC* [1912] 2 KB 317.

[128] (1703) Holt KB 300.

[129] [1965] AC 1001: no relevant statutory exception existed at the time, and the House of Lords, while recognising the anomaly, refused to extend the common law exception to records created by witnesses still alive, which would be tantamount to inventing a new one: *per* Lord Morris at 1027-8.

[130] The statement is part of the "thing in issue", or the event which the trial concerns, whether it be the crime, or the making of a contract.

or she might be tempted to state untruths. For example, it might occur to the observer of a crime out of sheer malice to implicate an enemy who was innocent of it. Some judicial decisions specifically referred to the absence of motive for concoction; if there appeared to be none, the evidence was admitted despite falling outside the definition of *res gestae*.[131] But in many cases this reasoning was not employed. In the old cases, *Gibson*,[132] *Teper* v. *R.*[133] and *Bedingfield*,[134] the fact that there was no reason to assume that any motive for concoction existed did not prevent the evidence from being excluded. The courts required absolute contemporaneity between the exclamation and the event. This was considered to guarantee the absence of concoction. Yet there was room for a great deal of unreliability in other forms; the observer, being by definition in a state of agitation,[135] might not have been particularly accurate. Given the finding that stress has a negative effect on human powers of description and recall,[136] the emphasis on spontaneity here may be misplaced.

It also led the courts into the insistence on contemporaneity which led to the now discredited decision in *Bedingfield*.[137] Mrs Bedingfield was seen by witnesses entering her room. She left it again shortly afterward, her throat horribly cut, and said to one of them, "Oh dear, aunt, see what Bedingfield has done to me". She died subsequently. Cockburn CJ held that her statement was inadmissible at Bedingfield's trial for murder, because it had not been made at the same time or in the same place as the infliction of the injury, and consequently did not form part of the *res gestae*. This rigidity was doubted by the Privy Council in *Ratten*,[138] and finally jettisoned in *Andrews*.[139] In the latter case, the victim of a stabbing went to his neighbour's for help; the police and ambulance were summoned and, after a time lag of a few minutes, the police arrived and asked who had caused his injuries. The victim's reply was admitted in evidence at the trial, and that decision was upheld by the House of Lords, which explained that that absolute contemporaneity is not the only indicator of reliability. It is enough if the event was still so overwhelmingly at the forefront of the victim's mind at the time his statement was made that the danger of fabrication is minimal. A statement, in order to be deemed spontaneous, must be so closely associated with the event which excited it that it can fairly be that the mind of the declarant was still dominated by the event. The test is not contemporaneity, but rather whether the event was so unusual, startling or dramatic as to dominate the thoughts of the witness, so that his utterance was an instinctive reaction to

---

[131] *Nye and Loan* (1977) 66 Cr. App. R 252.

[132] (1887) 18 QBD 537.   [133] [1952] AC 480.   [134] (1879) 14 Cox CC 341.

[135] Another name for the *res gestae* statement is "the excited utterance".

[136] B.R. Clifford and R. Bull, *Psychology of Person Identification* (Routledge and Kegan Paul, Boston, Mass., 1987); B.L. Cutler and S.D. Penrod, *Mistaken Identification: The Eyewitness, Psychology and the Law* (Cambridge University Press, Cambridge, 1995).

[137] (1879) 14 Cox CC 341.   [138] [1972] AC 378; see text to nn. 56–57 above.

[139] [1987] 1 All ER 513.

that event, thus giving no opportunity for reasoned reflection. The House of Lords appeared untroubled by the fact that here the statement was made in answer to a question. Other objections to the reception of the evidence were that the victim appeared to have been drinking, and there was a suggestion that he had a grudge against the person named. The question of malice, it was held, is best left to the discretion of the trial judge, who must decide whether there is a risk of concoction. Factors such as drunkenness go to the weight of the evidence.

Ashworth and Pattenden[140] point out that the recent English cases on *res gestae* concern a participant in the event, so that guidance in relation to the evidence of spectators is in short supply. It might reasonably be supposed that to observe even a serious crime being committed would have less dramatic impact than finding oneself the victim of it. The time lag allowed for bystanders would be correspondingly shorter—although to estimate the length of time it would dominate the eyewitness's thoughts involves the court in nothing more than armchair psychology. But the *Andrews* extension of *res gestae* is nevertheless of potential assistance in cases which are far less serious; for example, allowing into evidence the reaction to a road traffic accident of a bystander, even if it occurred a little before or after the event. Certainly, the time allowed for victims will now be generous. In *Carnall*,[141] the victim took an hour after he was attacked to crawl for help. He then made a statement which was held nevertheless to form part of the *res gestae*. The victims of rape might equally be thought likely to be overwhelmed by the impact of the offence for a considerable time.

In *Edwards and Osakwe*,[142] the Divisional Court was confronted with the logical conclusion of the doctrine of *res gestae*, namely that the use of hearsay evidence it permits could release the prosecution from its obligation to produce the victim of the crime in court. The appellants were charged with theft of a wallet of a person unknown, initially alleged to belong to A, a named person. A did not attend the trial, hence the alteration of the charge. The only evidence remaining was that of two police officers who said that they had seen the appellants with A and seen him lunge after them, after which the wallet was found in the doorway of a shop where the appellants had been standing until the officers drove up. However, the officers had not actually witnessed them taking it, nor discarding it in the doorway. On their being stopped by the police, A again had tried to lunge at them and said, "They're the ones . . . these two mugged me of my wallet". The officers asked A if he had been assaulted, and he replied, "No, they just stole my wallet". He identified the stolen wallet as his. He was drunk. The court appeared content with the admission of A's accusation as part of the *res gestae*, even though it supplied all

---

[140] A.J. Ashworth and R. Pattenden, "Reliability, Hearsay and the Criminal Trial" (1986) 102 *LQR* 292.

[141] [1995] Crim. LR 944.   [142] [1992] Crim. LR 580.

the evidence in relation to every fact which the prosecution had to prove. Following *Andrews*, the fact that A appeared to have been drinking was a matter going only to weight, and the magistrates had been happy to accept what he said as the truth. It was observed that prosecutors should not use the doctrine of *res gestae* to avoid having to call the appropriate witness, but there was no suggestion that that had happened here. Given reasoning of this kind, it must be possible to argue that *res gestae* statements from reluctant witnesses could be used against their wishes. On that basis, some Chief Constables are considering using the *res gestae* accusations of the victims of domestic violence, even if they refuse to give evidence and would prefer the prosecution to be dropped. To this end, it is proposed arming police officers investigating reports of domestic violence with tape recorders.

Dying Declarations

The dying declarations exception applies only to homicide trials, and only to statements made by the victim explaining how he or she came by an injury which proves fatal[143]:

> "The general principle on which this species of evidence is admitted is, that they are declarations made in extremity, when the party is at the point of death, and when every hope of this world is gone; when every motive for falsehood is silenced, and the mind is induced by the most powerful considerations to speak the truth; a situation so solemn and awful is considered by law as creating an obligation equal to that which is imposed by a positive oath administered in a court of justice."[144]

Why this overwhelming pressure to tell the truth before departing this life applies only to people who are dying of murderous wounds, and allows their evidence only in prosecutions for homicide, is not clear. The reasoning here, that "no person who is immediately going into the presence of his maker will do so with a lie on his lips",[145] has led courts to the conclusion that the statement of someone who is dying can be regarded as reliable only if the declarant at the time of making it had a "settled hopeless expectation of death". In *Perry*,[146] the defendant was accused of causing a woman's death through an illegal abortion. The woman was so ill after the alleged abortion that several days later her sister asked her why the defendant had visited her. Before describing the events, the deceased had replied, "Oh Gert, I shall go. But keep this a secret. Let the worst come to the worst." It was held that this was sufficient to show that the deceased had harboured no hopes of recovery; it was not necessary to show that she thought that she would die immediately. In *Bedingfield*[147] the deceased accused

---

[143] *Woodcock* (1789) 1 Leach 500; *Mead* (1824) 2 B&C 605.
[144] *Woodcock* (1789) 1 Leach 500, *per* Eyre CB.
[145] *Osman* (1881) 15 Cox CC 1, per Lush J.
[146] (1909) 25 TLR 676.
[147] (1879) 14 Cox CC 341 (see n. 13 above).

her husband at a time when her throat was cut from ear to ear. She may well have thought her injury mortal, but because she neglected to say so, her statement was not admissible as a dying declaration. In *Morgan*,[148] the deceased spoke with his head nearly cut off, but the court refused to infer from this that he had a settled, hopeless expectation of death.

Although the language employed in these cases is archaic and the reasoning somewhat antique, modern cynicism has not prevented the exception being employed today; there have been instances relatively recently of victims who clearly would not live long enough to give evidence being asked to name the culprit in written statements in which they formally acknowledge that their medical advisors have assured them that there is no prospect whatever of recovery. It will be seen below that the provisions of the Criminal Justice Act 1988,[149] which might have been thought to supplant the dying declarations exception in relation to any statement in writing, is in practice severely limited by the operation of judicial discretion to exclude.[150]

Documentary Hearsay in Criminal Cases

After the disaster in *Myers*,[151] where the prosecution found itself deprived of probably the most reliable possible evidence of the identity of cars alleged to have been stolen, a series of statutes attempted to devise an exception to the hearsay rule which would allow reliable documents, amounting to declarations in the course of duty, to be admitted as evidence to prove their contents.[152] The first, the Criminal Evidence Act 1965, was found wanting; confined to "trade or business records", the provisions omitted reliable documentary information compiled by people in other kinds of work.[153] The next contender, section 68 of the Police and Criminal Evidence Act 1984, caused sufficient problems within the short space of four years to find itself replaced by the Criminal Justice Act 1988. This Act now provides for the admissibility of documentary hearsay in criminal cases, if it is first-hand and the maker of the statement is unavailable. It also allows ordinary business records into evidence as a matter of course. In addition, there is also provision under section 30 that experts' reports shall be admissible as evidence in criminal proceedings, whether or not the persons making them attend to give oral evidence in those proceedings, with the leave of the court. In fact the original Bill had gone beyond "even the bold recommendations of the Roskill Committee on Fraud Trials"[154] in envisaging a scheme where first hand documentary hearsay and business documents would be generally admissible whatever the circumstances of the maker of the statement.[155] But

---

[148] (1875) 14 Cox CC 337.   [149] S.23.   [150] In ss.25, 26.

[151] [1965] AC 1001, see text to nn. 24 and 83 above.

[152] See also the exception allowing videotaped interviews with child witnesses in Ch. 4.

[153] *Patel* [1981] Crim. LR 250; lists of prohibited immigrants compiled by Home Office were inadmissible.

[154] *Report of the Fraud Trials Committee*, n. 19 above.   [155] Birch, n. 25 above.

opponents in Parliament forced the inclusion of conditions similar to those in the Civil Evidence Act 1968, whereby the reason for not calling the maker of the statement must be shown, save in respect of business documents not prepared for the purposes of pending or contemplated criminal proceedings.[156] Section 23 deals with first-hand hearsay in a document and provides as follows:

> "(1) Subject—
>> (a) to subsection (4) below;
>> (b) to paragraph 1A of Schedule 2 to the Criminal Appeal Act 1968 (evidence given orally at original trial to be given orally at retrial); and
>> (c) to section 69 of the Police and Criminal Evidence Act 1984 (evidence from computer records),
> a statement made by a person in a document shall be admissible in criminal proceedings as evidence of any fact of which direct oral evidence by him would be admissible if—
>> (i) the requirements of one of the paragraphs of subsection (2) below are satisfied; or
>> (ii) the requirements of subsection (3) below are satisfied.
> (2) The requirements mentioned in subsection (1)(i) above are—
>> (a) that the person who made the statement is dead or by reason of his bodily or mental condition unfit to attend as a witness;
>> (b) that
>>> (i) the person who made the statement is outside the United Kingdom; and
>>> (ii) it is not reasonably practicable to secure his attendance; or
>> (c) that all reasonable steps have been taken to find the person who made the statement, but that he cannot be found.
> (3) The requirements mentioned in subsection (1)(ii) above are—
>> (a) that the statement was made to a police officer or some other person charged with the duty of investigating offences or charging offenders; and
>> (b) that the person who made it does not give oral evidence through fear or because he is kept out of the way.
> (4) Subsection (1) above does not render admissible a confession made by an accused person that would not be admissible under section 76 of the Police and Criminal Evidence Act 1984."[157]

The section is tied to first-hand hearsay by the words "a statement made *by a person* in a document". That person must have had direct knowledge of the event recorded by him or her in the document. However, if someone else

---

[156] S. 24(4).

[157] This is a baffling provision; there appears to be absolutely nothing in the 1988 Act which would suggest that an accused person's confession *would* be admissible by way of *this* hearsay exception rather than that under s.76 of the Police and Criminal Evidence Act 1984, with its attendant safeguards—unless of course, the accused is dead, or cannot be found, etc., which seems fanciful, to say the least.

acted as an *amanuensis* and made the physical record on behalf and at the dictation of the maker of the statement, it is first-hand hearsay. In *McGillivray*,[158] the maker indicated that the dictated record was accurate by nodding accord as it was read back. This was held to be first-hand hearsay.

The most difficult aspect of section 23 is that the party wishing to adduce the documentary evidence must show grounds within the terms of the section for not producing the maker of the statement at the trial. The most commonly cited ground at present is fear—a product of the growing problem of witness intimidation. In *R. v. Acton JJ, ex p. McCullen et al.*[159] the Divisional Court held that "fear" in section 23(3)(b) should be assessed from the point of view of the witness, and therefore did not have to be reasonable, as long as it related to the commission of the offence. However, the ground for absence must be established beyond reasonable doubt. More recently the Court of Appeal has shown itself to be anxious to remove obstacles in the way of prosecutions where there is a risk that witnesses are being deterred from giving evidence. Prosecutors are no longer obliged to explain the reason for the fear as long as they can show it exists, although in the case in which this decision was reached, *Martin*,[160] the witness, A, explained the reason for his fear to the Recorder at the trial itself. Martin was being re-tried for arson. A had been summonsed by the police, but said he had tried to keep out of the re-trial for fear for his family. He had been approached beforehand by a person whom he had previously seen outside his door. This person said nothing. In the Court of Appeal, it was stressed that many witnesses were failing to give evidence because of intimidation. The words of the section are expressed in wide form and were designed to combat an evil. A witness might well misunderstand someone's behaviour and be afraid unnecessarily, but the fear is genuine all the same, and the prosecutor could be deprived of valuable evidence. This appears to suggest that it is unnecessary to show of what the witness is afraid, as long as it is established that there is genuine fear.

The evidence employed to establish one of the section 23 grounds must be admissible evidence, the usual rules of exclusion operating even on that ancillary issue. This is the result of the House of Lords' decision in *Neill* v. *North Antrim Magistrates*[161]; two witnesses were apparently too frightened to give evidence, but the police heard this, not from them, but from their mothers. It was held that the evidence of fear, coming as it did from the police officers, was inadmissible hearsay. Evidence of state of mind is not hearsay; hence the officers could have given evidence of the fear if the witnesses had told them of it themselves. But hearing it from their mothers made it hearsay. To apply the hearsay rule to the question of the ground for non-attendance could lead to an endless regression where documents are adduced for that purpose in lieu of live witnesses whose absence would also have to be explained by oral evidence unless yet another statutory ground

---

[158] [1993] Crim. LR 530.   [159] (1990) 92 Cr. App. R 98.   [160] [1996] Crim. LR 589.
[161] [1992] 4 All ER 846.

were satisfied. Given that the reason for absence is a collateral issue, and that the statute concerned was designed to allow more hearsay evidence to be given on the issue itself, it is absurd to insist on strict proof here. How is a party to show that a witness is abroad if a postcard is inadmissible hearsay, and the relative who saw them get on a plane cannot claim direct knowledge of the plane's destination (the indicator board being a hearsay statement)? The only method realistically available would appear to be to find someone who knows the voice of the absent witness and ask them to speak to him or her on the telephone at the foreign location.

To prove fear, anyone who heard the witness express it may attest to the fact. If the witness tells the prosecutor, the custom is to ask him or her to repeat it to a police officer, so that the officer rather than the prosecutor, can give evidence of the fear. But in *R. v. Ashford Magistrates, ex p. Hilden*,[162] the magistrates observed the witness's fear themselves. Hilden sought judicial review of his committal for trial. He had been charged with assaulting and falsely imprisoning his girlfriend. She took the oath and identified herself. But when asked to explain how she came by injuries shown in photographs, her only reply was "No comment". The magistrates decided that the witness was in fear; they were assisted in coming to this conclusion by the presence in court of Hilden's grandmother, a famous and intimidating local figure, who had accompanied the witness to court. The magistrates allowed the prosecutor to rely on the witness's written statement, on the basis that she had not given evidence through fear. Their decision was upheld in the Divisional Court, which agreed that taking the oath, identifying oneself and saying "No comment" does not amount to giving evidence.[163]

Documentary evidence in the form of a witness statement either falls within the definition of first-hand hearsay under section 23 or amounts to a business document within the terms of section 24. However, any document prepared in contemplation of criminal proceedings falls within the provisions of section 24(4), and grounds for not calling the maker of the statement must be shown. The extra reliability of documents routinely prepared during the course of employment or under similar obligations has led Parliament to draft section 24 in wide terms. Multiple hearsay in a business document is acceptable, as long as the persons who pass information on do so while acting during the course of their business.[164] The original intention of the legislature had been to render any business document automatically admissible, but amendments entered in the House of Lords[165] resulted in the restrictions in section 24(4) relating to any document created with criminal proceedings or a criminal investigation in mind. Their Lordships' adverse reaction to the liberality of the original form of the Criminal Justice Bill as it

---

[162] [1992] Crim LR 879; cf. *Martin* [1996] Crim. LR 589.

[163] Cf. *Waters* [1997] Crim. LR 832.   [164] S.24(2).

[165] See D. Wolchoever, "Criminal Trials: Proof by Missing Witness" (1987) 138 *NLJ* 525, 805, 833 and (1988) 139 NLJ 202, 242, 261, 461.

went through Parliament was based largely upon dread that accused persons could be convicted on the strength of the "police officer's notebook". The amendments mean that only "neutral" business documents will be admissible irrespective of the whereabouts of the maker of the statement[166].

Section 24 reads as follows:

"(1) Subject—
    (a) to subsections (3) and (4) below;
    (b) to paragraphs 1A of Schedule 2 to the Criminal Appeal Act 1968; and
    (c) to section 69 of the Police and Criminal Evidence Act 1984,[167]
a statement in a document shall be admissible in criminal proceedings of any fact of which direct oral evidence would be admissible, if the following conditions are satisfied—
    (i) the document was created or received by a person in the course of a trade, business, profession or other occupation, or as the holder of a paid or unpaid office; and
    (ii) the information contained in the document was supplied by a person (whether or not the maker of the statement) who had, or may reasonably be supposed to have had, personal knowledge of the matters dealt with.

(2) Subsection (1) above applies whether the information contained in the document was supplied directly or indirectly, but, if it was supplied indirectly, only if each person through whom it was supplied received it—
    (a) in the course of a trade, business, profession or other occupation, or
    (b) as the holder of a paid or unpaid office.

(3) Subsection (1) above does not render admissible a confession made by an accused person that would not be admissible under section 76 of the Police and Criminal Evidence Act 1984.[168]

(4) A statement prepared otherwise than in accordance with section 29 below or an order under paragraph 6 of Schedule 13 to this Act or under section 30 or 31 for the purposes—
    (a) of pending or contemplated criminal proceedings; or
    (b) of a criminal investigation shall not be admissible by virtue of subsection (1) above unless—
    (i) the requirements of one of the paragraphs of subsection (2) of section 23 above are satisfied; or
    (ii) the requirements of subsection (3) of that section are satisfied; or
    (iii) the person who made the statement cannot reasonably be expected (having regard to the time which has elapsed since he made the statement and to all the circumstances) to have any recollection of the matters dealt with in the statement."

---

[166] Experience with the old Civil Evidence Act of 1968 demonstrated that not only is it often impossible to ascertain the whereabouts of the maker of a statement in a complex business documents, it is frequently impossible to tell from the document who that person was.

[167] The requirements of s.69 must be met in relation to all computer-produced evidence. Hearsay evidence produced by a computer must, however, fall within an exception to the rule, such as that provided by ss. 23 and 24 of the 1988 Act in order to be admitted (*Shepherd* [1993] 1 All ER 225).

[168] See n. 157 above.

It is not always necessary to provide the court with evidence that the document concerned was produced by someone acting within the course of a business. This may be obvious from the nature of the document itself.[169]

The words "received by" in paragraph (i) of subsection (1) have caused problems of interpretation. It has been suggested that their effect is to render any document which is physically passed to a professional person, a business document.[170] But if business documents are admissible because they are perceived to be in general more reliable than other forms of written hearsay, it would be absurd effectively to upgrade into that class any document which at some time is handed to someone acting in the course of their employment. Arguably, any document presented to the court would count as a business document, because by definition it would have ended up in Crown Prosecution Service hands. All posted letters are "received" by the Post Office, but they are no more reliable than before as a result of that. In *McGillivray*[171] a statement dictated from a hospital bed did not qualify as a business document just because it was dictated in the presence of a nurse and handed to a police officer.

The drafting of section 24 has met with faint praise, not least because of the problems caused by its abandonment of recognised terminology. The human source of information is usually described, in the context of the hearsay rule, as the "maker of the statement." The use of this language can plainly be seen in section 23, where grounds must be shown for not calling "the person who made the statement". That person is not the maker of the document, as can be seen from *McGillivray*.[172] Yet section 24(1)(ii) requires that the information contained in the document should have been supplied by a person (whether or not the maker of the statement) who had, or may reasonably be supposed to have had, personal knowledge of the matters dealt with. The paragraph assumes that the maker of the statement is someone other than the supplier of the information. This seems to suggest that he or she is the maker of the document. This curious departure from the normal form of expression would be unimportant, were it not for the provisions of section 24(4). This requires proof of acceptable grounds for not calling "the maker of the statement", insofar as section 24(4) requires compliance with either section 23(2) or section 23(3), or with the alternative justification in subsection (4)(iii), namely that the person "who *made the statement*"[173] cannot reasonably be expected in the circumstances to have any recollection of the matters dealt with in the statement. There seems no reason whatever for the court to inquire into the reasons for the absence of the creator of a document, if that person had no personal knowledge of the matters dealt

---

[169] *Foxley* [1995] 2 Cr. App. R 523; the purpose of s.24 would be defeated if in every case the party producing the document had to supply evidence from the creator of the document or the supplier of the information.

[170] M. Ockleton, "Documentary Hearsay in Criminal Cases" [1992] *Crim. LR* 15.

[171] [1993] Crim. LR 530.   [172] [1993] Crim. LR 530.   [173] Author's italics.

with in it. Cross-examination of this individual would be a waste of time.[174]

Although in practice it seems that the simplest way to proceed is as if the passage in brackets in subsection (1)(ii) is not there, the Court of Appeal appeared in *Carrington*[175] to approve the notion that the creator of the document was the person whose non-appearance in court was significant. The case involved various employees at a supermarket. At the checkout, a man presented a stolen Switch card. The cashier passed it through the magnetic tape reader, called supervisor B, and tried to delay the man. B also called fellow supervisor S, who saw the man, but then left for home. The man meanwhile said he had to fetch something from his car, but did not return to the checkout. S, who went to collect her car from the car park, saw a car being driven past her at a very high speed. She recognised the driver as being the same customer, and noted his description, the model of the vehicle and its registration number on the cover of a magazine. She immediately returned to the store and reported this to the operator of the internal telephone system, who buzzed B and passed on the numbers, which B wrote on her memo pad. S, meanwhile, took no steps to ensure the accuracy of the notes taken by the operator or by B, nor did she keep the magazine. She did, however, identify Carrington at the identification parade, but neither the cashier nor B did so. When B's notepad containing the car number and a description of the man was offered as hearsay evidence, both prosecution and defence agreed that the person whose absence from the witness-box required explanation was not S, but B. The consequence was that the test, whether or not she could reasonably be expected to remember the details, was entirely inappropriate, as she had never had knowledge of them herself. The person whose evidence was crucial and whom the defence might have wished to cross-examine was S. Perhaps the Court of Appeal's apparent approval of the utterly pointless discussions about what B could or could not be expected to remember represents nothing more than acceptance of a *fait accompli.*[176]

It is not a ground under section 23 for not calling a witness that he or she cannot reasonably be expected to recollect the information in the document. In *McClean,*[177] the eye-witness who saw the getaway car could not remember the number. However, section 23 could not have helped in any case; the note of the car registration number taken by the bystander at dictation was not a first hand hearsay statement, because the eye-witness did not check it.[178] If the note had been checked, the hearsay problem would normally not arise because the witness, if available, could refresh his or her memory from an "adopted" contemporaneous note.[179] If the bystander was professionally involved, the case might fall under section 24; the most obvious professional

---

[174] See Birch, n. 25 above.   [175] [1994] Crim. LR 438.

[176] However, see *Bedi* (1992) 95 Cr. App. R 21; *Field* [1992] Crim. LR 299.

[177] (1968) 52 Cr. App. R 80 (n. 87 above).

[178] *McGillivray* [1993] Crim. LR 530 (n. 171 above).

[179] *Kelsey* [1982] Crim. LR 435.

to be involved is a police officer, and therefore the grounds for non-attendance would have to be shown under section 24(4). Then the inability to
remember such a matter would be sufficient.[180] But, in general, *McLean*
documents have not been brought within the statutory framework despite
their vital relevance and probable reliability.

Documents admissible under sections 23 and 24 of the Criminal Justice
Act 1988 are subject to a judicial discretion to exclude. The "neutral" type of
statement, prepared without criminal proceedings in mind, is dealt with in
section 25. The language of the section suggests that, *prima facie*, such a
statement ought to be admitted. The court is directed to the "interests of
justice". Section 25 provides:

> "(1) If, having regard to all the circumstances,
>   (a) the Crown Court—
>   (i) on a trial on indictment
>   (ii) on an appeal from a magistrates' court; or
>   (iii) on the hearing of an application under section 6 of the Criminal
>   Justice Act 1987 (applications for dismissal of charges of fraud transferred
>   from magistrates' court to Crown Court); or
>   (b) the criminal division of the Court of Appeal; or
>   (c) a magistrates' court on a trial of an information,
>   is of opinion that in the interests of justice a statement which is admissible by
>   virtue of section 23 or 24 above nevertheless ought not to be admitted, it may
>   direct that the statement shall not be admitted.
>   (2) Without prejudice to the generality of subsection (1) above, it shall be the
>   duty of the court to have regard—
>   (a) to the nature and source of the document containing the statement and to
>   whether or not, having regard to its nature and source and to any other
>   circumstances that appear to the court to be relevant, it is likely that the
>   document is authentic;
>   (b) to the extent to which the statement appears to supply evidence which
>   would otherwise not be readily available;
>   (c) to the relevance of the evidence that it appears to supply to any issue
>   which is likely to have to be determined in the proceedings; and
>   (d) to any risk, having regard in particular whether it is likely to be possible
>   to controvert the statement if the person making it does not attend to give
>   oral evidence in the proceedings, that its admission or exclusion will result in
>   unfairness to the accused or, if there is more than one, to any of them."

The other section dealing with judicial discretion appears to create a presumption that documents prepared for the purposes of criminal proceedings should

---

[180] If the position were reversed, so that a professional asked a passer-by to write the number
down, it is not clear whether the case would fall within s.24 or not. If the maker of the statement
could be said to have "created" the document through an *amanuensis*, it would be admissible, satisfying the grounds in s.24(4)(iii). This was the argument of Kenneth Jones J in *O'Loughlin*, [1988] 3
All ER 431 above, interpreting the different language of the Police and Criminal Evidence Act 1984.

be excluded. These "prosecution-type" documents are subject to the much stronger language of section 26:

"Where a statement which is admissible in criminal proceedings by virtue of section 23 or 24 above appears to the court to have been prepared otherwise than in accordance with section 29 below or an order under paragraph 6 of Schedule 13 to this Act or under section 30 or 31 for the purposes—
  (a) of pending or contemplated criminal proceedings; or
  (b) of a criminal investigation
the statement shall not be given in evidence without the leave of the court, and the court shall not give leave unless it is of the opinion that the statement ought to be admitted in the interests of justice; and in considering whether its admission would be in the interests of justice, it shall be the duty of the court to have regard—
  (a) to the contents of the statement;
  (b) to any risk, having regard in particular whether it is likely to be possible to controvert the statement if the person making it does not attend to give oral evidence in the proceedings, that its admission or exclusion will result in unfairness to the accused or, if there is more than one, to any of them; and
  (c) to any other circumstances that appear to the court to be relevant."

In *Cole*,[181] the defence objected that, since the defendant had no other evidence by which to contravert the prosecution case, admission of the documentary hearsay forced him into the witness box to contradict the prosecution witnesses. The Court of Appeal disagreed that this undermined the defendant's right to silence; the choice whether to give evidence or not remained his. It was not unfair to admit the witness statement in question (the witness having died before the trial). It was only one of several describing the incident, and the other prosecution witnesses could be cross-examined. It was made clear in *Cole* that judges must be wary of the argument that the defence is disadvantaged by the inability to cross-examine the absent witness. That is true in every case where hearsay is admitted. The loss of the opportunity to cross-examine must be of particular significance, which it was not, in that case:

"The mere fact that the deponent will not be available for cross-examination is obviously an insufficient ground for excluding the deposition, for that is a feature common to the admission of all depositions which must have been contemplated and accepted by the legislature when it gave statutory sanction to their admission in evidence."[182]

This and other cases suggest that, in applying the discretion under section 26, judges will take account of the centrality of the evidence in question. The more important it is, the more unfair it is that the accused cannot cross-

---

[181] (1990) 90 Cr. App. R 478.
[182] *Scott* v. *R.* [1989] 2 All ER 305, *per* Lord Griffiths at 312-3; the legislation here was a Jamaican provision similar to the unamended provisions of s. 13(3) of the Criminal Justice Act 1925.

examine the source of the information. This restrictive approach to written hearsay will deprive the courts of a good deal of highly probative evidence; it seems that the more probative it is, the more the courts will be determined to exclude it:

> "The overall purpose of the provisions was to widen the powers of the court to admit documentary hearsay evidence while ensuring that the accused received a fair trial. In judging how to achieve the fairness of the trial a balance must on occasion be struck between the interests of the public in enabling the prosecution case to be properly presented and the interest of a particular defendant in not being put in a disadvantageous position, for example by the death or illness of a witness."[183]

Evidence of identification was regarded in *Setz-Dempsey*[184] as particularly problematic in this context. Although the Court of Appeal did not consider that every hearsay statement concerning identification should automatically be excluded, it did urge caution. The inability to test identification evidence by cross-examination is especially significant. However, the main consideration in every case is the quality of the evidence. But judges are unlikely to drop traditional preconceptions overnight; in *Acton JJ*,[185] Watkins LJ remarked that section 23(3)(b) "let loose one or two unruly horses which the courts would have to be vigilant to control".

Reform: The New Civil Model

The nature of trials, both civil and criminal, is moving steadily further from the adversarial model. More pre-trial disclosure inevitably reduces the importance of cross-examination. The inadequacies of the 1968 civil legislation was referred to the Law Commission, which was faced with a challenging task; the Law Reform Commission of Northern Ireland had found it impossible to devise a satisfactory solution in terms of simplicity, certainty, cost or fairness except either to abolish the rule altogether or to abolish it subject to a judicial discretion to exclude. Simple abolition had some support in the Lord Chancellor's Civil Justice Review[186] and was actually implemented in Scotland in the Civil Evidence (Scotland) Act 1988[187] despite the objection from the Scottish Law Commission to such a course. Its report stressed the value of cross-examination as an instrument for exposing unreliable evidence.[188] But the governmental objection to the

---

[183] *Cole* (1990) 90 Cr. App. R 478 *per* Ralph Gibson LJ at 485.

[184] (1994) 98 Cr. App. R 23.

[185] (1990) 92 Cr. App. R 98 (n. 159 above).

[186] *Report of the Review Body on Civil Justice* (HMSO, London, 1988), Cm 394, paras. 266–70.

[187] S. 2(1).

[188] *Evidence: Report on Corroboration, Hearsay and Related Matters in Civil Proceedings,* Scottish Law Commission No 100 (HMSO, Edinburgh, 1986), paras. 3.31–3.34.

Commission's solution, combining a notice procedure with discretion to exclude, was that it could have the effect of simply reintroducing the rule against hearsay.[189]

The English Law Commission agreed with that of Northern Ireland, and on the strength of its recommendations,[190] Parliament enacted the Civil Evidence Act 1995.[191] The objective was to retain hearsay as a distinct category of evidence, but only to the extent that parties intending to produce it should give notice.[192] Failure to do so will not led to the exclusion of the evidence altogether, only to possible sanctions in terms of adjournment or costs.[193] Section 1(1) provides:

> "In civil proceedings evidence shall not be excluded on the ground that it is hearsay."

Perhaps it is significant, given the traditional claim that it is juries which cannot cope with hearsay evidence, that the Commission considered it appropriate for the new Act to set out guidance to help judges assess the probative value of the evidence admitted under the new provisions.[194] This has been carried into effect by section 4 of the 1995 Act, which provides in subsection (2) a checklist of circumstances to which courts may pay particular regard. These include whether it would have been reasonable and practical to call the maker of the statement, whether the statement was contemporaneous with the relevant events and whether evidence comprises first-hand or multiple hearsay.

The fear that judges, if given a discretion, might revert to old exclusionary habits has not deterred the legislators from including an "obvious safeguard"[195] in section 3 of the Civil Evidence Act 1995. A party faced with hearsay evidence may, with the leave of the court, insist on calling the absent witness with a view to cross-examining him or her. The Act of 1995 retains five common law exceptions to the rule: these include published works concerning matters of public interest, public documents and reputation evidence.[196] Section 6 allows proof of previous statements by a witness; previous consistent statements are admissible to rebut suggestions of fabrication,[197] and previous inconsistent statements may be put in cross-examination

---

[189] Lord Advocate, HL Deb., vol. 489, col. 1542, 12 Nov. 1987.

[190] Law Commission, *The Hearsay Rule in Civil Proceedings*, Law Com. No 216, (HMSO, London, 1993), Cm 2321.

[191] Procedure is contained, for the High Court, in RSC, Ord. 38 r. 204 (as amended by SI 1996/3219; for the county court, in CCR, Ord. 20, rr.14–17 (as amended by S 1996/3218).

[192] S.2; it should be clear in its terms that it is a hearsay notice. It should identify the hearsay evidence to be adduced and also the person who made the statement. It must explain why it is proposed that that person will not be called as a witness.

[193] S.2(4).

[194] Law Commission, n. 190 above, 4.17–4.19.

[195] A. Keane, *The Modern Law of Evidence* (Butterworths, London, 1995) 274.

[196] S.7.

[197] The allegation does not have to be of *recent* fabrication, as in a criminal case (see Ch. 3).

following the procedure laid down in the Criminal Evidence Act 1865.[198] The Act extends to all civil courts and tribunals where the strict rules of evidence apply[199]. This removes the absurd anachronism identified in *R. v. Coventry Magistrates, ex p. Bullard*,[200] where it proved virtually impossible to prove the liability of those who had defaulted on their community charge payments, because the computer printout of amounts unpaid was inadmissible hearsay. The Civil Evidence Act 1968 did not apply to civil proceedings in magistrates' courts.

The Law Commission has recently considered the reform of the hearsay rule[201] for criminal cases. It decided that leaving the question of admissibility solely to the vagaries of judicial discretion would create too much uncertainly. Yet to allow the exercise of judicial discretion to be the only barrier to hearsay evidence has the merit of flexibility. The proof of this lies in the fact that the Commission's proposed reforms, which are coloured by a fundamental loyalty to the principle of orality, cannot cope with the vagaries of circumstance without a "safety valve". The new scheme would make preferred categories of hearsay automatically admissible, but the court would have a residual discretion to admit hearsay of any kind, including multiple hearsay, where the probative value of the evidence demands that in the interests of justice it should be admitted. There should also be a judicial discretion to exclude evidence of such limited probative value that its inclusion would result in an undue waste of time.[202]

The dependence on a residual discretion is not surprising, given that the proposed reforms largely retain traditional and statutory exceptions, albeit in revised form. The Commission has been criticised for its contradictory stance on discretion. Some commentators also stress the alleged pro-prosecution bias of judges who try criminal cases. But there is already a discretion to exclude evidence which is irrelevant; allowing judges to exclude evidence on the basis that it is not reliable, or could be adduced by other means, appears equally consistent with the established view that an experienced judge is able to distinguish evidence which will take the case no further. And if the jury can cope with a direction that a witness's previous statement is evidence only that it was said and may not be used to prove the facts contained in it, they should be able to assess the probative value of hearsay evidence with comparative ease—and at present, of course, presumably do so when hearsay evidence (such as *res gestae* or a confession) is presented by virtue of an exception to the rule. The other side is free to make any points it wishes to devalue the force of hearsay evidence. The Law Reform Advisory

---

[199] S.11; therefore not in wardship cases or coroners' inquests (see Ch. 1).

[200] (1992) 95 Cr. App. R 175.

[201] Law Commission, *Criminal Proceedings: Hearsay and Related Topics*, Law Com. No. 245, (HMSO, London, 1997), Cm 3670.

[202] The Commission notes also the possible application of s. 78 of the Police and Criminal Evidence Act 1984 if it would be unfair to allow the hearsay into evidence.

Committee for Northern Ireland saw no problem as far as civil cases are concerned:

> "The main advantage of retaining some form of judicial discretion is that it enables hearsay evidence of probative value to be included when it does not come within any of the recognized exceptions, and conversely it enables hearsay evidence to be excluded even when it comes within a recognized exception . . . Parties should be entitled to adduce evidence of high probative value but should be protected from having to meet evidence of low probative value."[203]

Inevitably, hearsay evidence will cease to be seen as unfair, and reliability of source will be more important in relation to each piece of evidence. The emphasis on cross-examination will gradually be confined to its proper place, that is, cases where the credibility or reliability of the witness is crucial. It may be that eventually, even there, relevant hearsay evidence will be allowed on the basis that characteristics such as the truthfulness, personality or powers of perception of an absent witness can be assessed by other (and perhaps more reliable) means than cross-examination. The hearsay rule inevitably goes in retreat with its arch-ally, the adversarial trial. The utter unsuitability of both in relation to cases of any complexity is clear; it is a pity that diehards fought so hard against the recommendations of the Roskill Committee and the original version of the Bill which became the Criminal Justice Act 1988. The commercial world is smaller, but more complex, because of modern technology. It is futile to scramble in the wake of such changes attempting to devise ever more sophisticated exceptions to an irredeemably archaic rule. All jurisdictions are finding that they are dealing with elaborate frauds in both the civil and criminal contexts, and these cases are characterised by mountainous quantities of documentation with which the evidential provisions of many Commonwealth countries are ill-equipped to deal. It is certain that as methods of communicating and recording information alter, and they have been transformed in the last 20 years, the old methods of proof and evidential rules will increasingly be seen to be inadequate.

[203] N. 6 above, para. 4.11.

8

Conclusion: Future Directions

"I say that adversary system is not the best system of criminal justice, and that there is a better way . . . The American system, up to the time of final verdict and appeal, puts all the emphasis on techniques, devices, mechanisms. It is the most elaborate system ever devised by a society. It is so elaborate that in some places it is breaking down. It is not working."

> Chief Justice Burger, "The special skills of advocacy: are specialized training and certification of advocates essential to our system of justice?" (1973) 42 *Fordham L Rev.* 227.

Justice and Fairness

In mock trials which compared inquisitorial and adversarial procedures, Thibaut and Walker[1] found that whether or not the adversarial approach to evidence gathering and presentation displayed an unbiased selection of facts to the court depended on the balance of evidence in the particular case. If the case was evenly balanced on each side, the bias in one party's presentation was offset by that of the other. In such cases, the same number of facts were generally gathered whichever procedure was used. But if the case was unbalanced as between the two sides, the adversarial trial produced a biased distribution of the facts. The version offered by the party who had the fewest facts in his favour tended to over-represent the proportion of evidence favourable to his case. If the actual imbalance, for example, was 25:75, the distribution of evidence would be 36:64. This research seems to suggest that inquisitorial systems are better at information gathering and representation. However, the authors also found that a person's perception of the fairness of a proceeding is not necessarily related to his success in it. The adversarial system was perceived as fairer irrespective of the outcome; this was true even of participants brought up in the Continental tradition. But the apparent fairness of the adversarial trial to the experimental group may to some extent depend on a lack of appreciation of its full implications. The research was designed to measure the efficacy of information gathering, and therefore did not

[1] J.M. Thibaut and L. Walker, *Procedural Justice and Psychological Analysis* (Wiley, New York, 1975).

involve the more abstruse exclusionary rules, part of the repertoire of "devices" deplored by Chief Justice Burger in the quotation above.[2] And that there is large-scale ignorance of the effect of adversarial reasoning on appeals is apparent from the "gasps from peers as well as Yallop[3] himself, who was sitting in the public gallery",[4] when Viscount Colville of Culross explained it in the House of Lords:

> "There may in a criminal trial be evidence which is available and is known to one or other of the parties at that time which for one reason or another they choose not to use. In those circumstances, I do not think that some years later, because somebody considers that they were mistaken in their choice of not using it, the existence of that evidence would be grounds for reopening that matter by way of public inquiry".[5]

In an adversarial trial, each party selects the issues and evidence he wishes to bring before the court; therefore the responsibility of ensuring that the case presented is the most favourable possible from his point of view is his own. Jackson argues that adversarial process is not merely a method of fact-finding but expresses "a conception of the appropriate role of government in the resolution of disputes". Preferring to reduce governmental involvement to the most non-interventionist minimum, Anglo-American systems require only the provision of a forum for the impartial resolution of disputes.[6] Inevitably, in such systems, appeals have more to do with formal compliance with procedures than the reliability of verdicts, although when the Court of Criminal Appeal was set up in 1907, it was not clear how, if at all, it was to select its priorities from these two concerns.[7] Even in the wake of reforms inspired by a Royal Commission apparently set up in reaction to a world-famous series of miscarriages of justice perpetrated in English courts over the previous 20 years, it does not seem that the court will provide an effective safety net for those at risk of wrongful conviction. It is still expected to function within a predominantly adversarial procedure: "[j]ust as the adversarial system prevails at the trial, so does it prevail in the Court of Appeal".[8] The court is limited to a power to review issues raised by appellants; it does not have full appellate function. Operating within the adversarial system, its

---

[2] (1973) 42 *Fordham LR* 227. Although the Chief Justice excluded the English trial from the allegation that the adversarial trial put a premium on skill, adroitness and trickery, he thought the system in northern European countries such as Holland and Denmark more humane: at 236.

[3] Author of *To Encourage the Others* (2 nd edn. Corgi, London, 1990), a study of the trial of Craig and Bentley in 1952.

[4] *Sunday Correspondent*, 12 Aug. 1990.

[5] HL Debs., vol 106, col. 324, 14 June 1990.

[6] J. Jackson, "Evidence: Legal Perspective" in R. Bull and D. Carson (eds.), *Handbook of Psychology in Legal Contexts* (Wiley, Chichester, 1995).

[7] R. Nobles, D. Schiff and N. Shaldon, "The Inevitability of Crisis in Criminal Appeals" (1993) 21 *International Journal of the Sociology of Law* 1.

[8] *McIlkenny and others* [1992] 2 All ER 417, 426.

reasoning since its inception inevitably has been dominated by the "day in court" and the principle of the primacy of the jury. "We are not here to re-try cases which have been heard by a jury".[9]

Most appeals are allowed on the basis of error by the trial judge.[10] Without that, the appellant faces an uphill struggle:

> "[This was] a case in which every issue was before the jury and . . . the jury was properly instructed . . . this Court will be very reluctant to intervene. It has been said over and over again through the years that this Court must recognise the advantage which a jury has in seeing and hearing the witnesses, and if all the material was before the jury and the summing-up was impeccable, this Court should not lightly interfere."[11]

This judgment goes on to say that the court could take account of a "lurking doubt" which might not be based strictly on the evidence, but on a "general feel of the case". For all that, in the 20 years that followed it, the "lurking doubt" test had been applied to quash convictions in only few cases—only in six, according to JUSTICE. the radical lawyers' group.[12] Substandard work by defence lawyers is not generally accepted as a ground for appeal. It must be "flagrantly incompetent advocacy",[13] and so incorrect verdicts based on less obvious errors cannot be challenged.[14] Malleson's study showed that out of nine cases in which lawyer error was given as the ground for appeal, in none leave to appeal was given.[15] Thus litigants are heavily dependent on the ability of their lawyers to present their case in the best possible light. Inevitably, this means those members of society who can most easily afford lawyers who know how to operate the system will be better served than others in this respect. Until very recently, the court took a strict approach to the question whether the defence could have availed itself of evidence, now presented as fresh evidence, at the time.

The emphasis on procedural issues prevented for years a proper review of

---

[9] *McNair* (1909) 2 Cr. App. R 2.

[10] K. Malleson, *Review of the Appellate Process*, RCCJ Research Study no 17 (HMSO, London, 1993).

[11] *Cooper* (1956) 53 Cr. App. R 82, *per* Widgery LJ at 85–6.

[12] *Miscarriages of Justice: The Defendant's Eye View* JUSTICE, June 1993: but further instances were discovered in the study carried out on behalf of the Royal Commission: Malleson, n. 10 above. "Lurking doubt" may also lie, unacknowledged, at the heart of other successful appeals. (*Report of the Royal Commission on Criminal Justice*, chaired by Lord Runciman (HMSO, London, 1993), Cm 2263, 173).

[13] *Ensor* [1989] 1 WLR 497.

[14] N. 12 above, 174. Although the Report criticises the narrow approach to lawyer error, its recommendations fail specifically to address the problem. The Court of Appeal's hard line is echoed by the Scottish High Court of Justiciary: it is insufficient to show that the defence had reasonable excuse for failure to lead evidence at trial. It must be shown that the evidence was unavailable and that it could not reasonably have been made available: *Eliot* v. *HM Advocate, The Times* 16 May 1995).

[15] N. 10 above.

the now notorious "miscarriage of justice" cases. At the 1988 appeal by the Birmingham Six, the court concentrated less on the flaws in the prosecution's original expert evidence than on the question whether, in the light of the scientific evidence now available, the jury's verdict could be upheld. This meant that the defence was expected to produce explanations for the prosecution expert's test results even though his incompetence had been established.[16] In cases like this, it has been argued, it is difficult for the court to hold on to its constitutional deference to the jury without being made to appear irrational, for it actually is in a better position (by dint of fresh evidence or new light thrown on the old evidence) than the jury was to determine guilt or innocence.[17] The Court of Appeal justified its decision finally to quash the convictions of the Birmingham Six in *McIlkenny and others*[18] by treating the doubts entertained by some experts about the reliability of the forensic evidence at the trial as new wisdom, or "fresh evidence". The Runciman Commission recommended widening the grounds of appeal, but in fact the rules on fresh evidence for some reason were narrowed, replacing the duty to hear some categories of fresh evidence with a discretion whether to do so.[19] It was recommended in addition that the test for overturning convictions should be relaxed. But it is unclear whether the new wording in the Criminal Appeal Act 1995, which apparently telescopes all the old criteria into the single test of "unsafe", is wider, narrower or the same as the previous one.[20] Also, it is now doubtful whether victims of police malpractice will be able to appeal successfully, where the verdict appears nevertheless to be "safe" on the facts.[21]

None of these legislative changes encourages the view that the Court of Appeal will approach cases like the Birmingham Six in a different way. Yet an explosion of criticism and distrust of the court followed the campaigns to release them, the Guildford Four[22] and the Maguire Seven,[23] all of whom had had appeals dismissed or leave to appeal refused before their convictions were finally overturned after many years in prison. Public disillusion with the system of criminal justice was confirmed and entrenched when these cases were followed by other successful appeals from Judith Ward,[24] the Tottenham Three,[25] and others. It became increasingly obvious that the criminal trial was generally expected to do more than provide a neutral

---

[16] Nobles, Schiff and Shaldon, n. 7 above.   [17] *Ibid.*   [18] [1992] 2 All ER 417.

[19] J. Spencer, "The Criminal Appeal Act 1995" (1995) 9 *Archbold News* 3; Chalkely, *The Times*, 19 Jan. 1998.

[20] Criminal Appeal Act 1995, s.2, replacing Criminal Appeal Act 1968, s.2, which used the phrase "unsafe or unsatisfactory" but also allowed appeals on the basis of error of law or material irregularity in the conduct of the trial. See Spencer, n. 19 above.

[21] J.C. Smith, "Criminal Appeals and the Criminal Cases Review Commission" [1995] *NLJ* 533.

[22] *Richardson, Conlon, Armstrong and Hill*, *The Times*, 20 Oct. 1989.

[23] *Maguire and Others* (1991) 94 Cr. App. R 133.

[24] *Ward* [1993] 2 All ER 577.

[25] *Silcott, Braithwaite and Raghip*, *The Times*, 19 Dec. 1991.

forum for litigants, and that the Court of Appeal, operating principally as a procedural check, in fact is ill-equipped to protect victims of miscarriage of justice: "[w]e have no power to conduct an open-ended investigation into an alleged miscarriage of justice, even if we were equipped to do so. Our function is to hear criminal appeals, neither more nor less."[26] The statute confines the court to a regulatory function and its resources are limited. Spencer has pointed out that review of miscarriage of justice allegations are time-consuming: "[i]f the Court of Appeal got seriously involved doing them no one would get their appeal against sentence heard."[27] The court consist of three or four panels hearing all the appeals against sentence (which must be dealt with promptly) and against conviction from the Crown Courts of England and Wales. "One high profile case such as the Carl Bridgewater murder case which occupies a court for a number of weeks can seriously disrupt the timetable."[28] The Home Affairs Select Committee of the House of Commons concluded in 1986 that the Court of Appeal was an inappropriate body to conduct what are essentially not appeals but inquiries.[29]

The Royal Commission on Criminal Justice, chaired by Lord Runciman, was set up in response to the widespread disquiet. Inevitably, the Commission would have to consider the extent to which, if at all, the adversarial system itself had contributed to the disastrously erroneous judgments made in these cases. Few could argue, in the light of recent history, that an exclusively adversarial approach to criminal appeals was defensible. But there was a dilemma facing reformers; if trials were to remain predominantly adversarial, then the Court of Appeal had to retain its regulatory function. The retention of a predominantly adversarial culture meant that it would be pointless to reconstitute the court with non-judges, according to Richard Buxton of the Law Commission, since judges are familiar with the structure of a criminal trial and the assumptions under which it is conducted. However, the regulatory function is of little assistance in a case of the nature of the Birmingham Six. In such cases, he argued, the court should be assisted by an independent examiner who could review the case and make recommendations. "Not only would this provide an investigative function that an appellate court presently lacks, but the inquisitorial rather than purely adjudicatory function such an examiner would perform might well be more suited than the formal process of adversary evidence to elucidating the complex histories of contradictory scientific evidence and police misconduct that have burdened some recent appeals."[30] The Royal Commission's approach was less radical. It proposed that there should be a review authority

---

[26] *McIlkenny* [1992] 2 All ER 417 at 424.

[27] Spencer, n. 19 above.

[28] K. Malleson, "Miscarriages of Justice and the Accessibility of the Court of Appeal" [1991] *Crim. LR* 323.

[29] P. Thornton, "Miscarriages of Justice: A Lost Opportunity" [1993] *Crim. LR* 926.

[30] R. Buxton, "Miscarriages of Justice and the Court of Appeal" (1993) 109 *LQR* 66, 77.

which would be independent of the Court of Appeal, but would refer cases to it as the Home Office had previously had power to do. This authority would be able to direct investigations, order lines of inquiry and, in the manner of the Police Complaints Authority, require that the investigation be carried out by a police force other than that which investigated the original offence.[31]

However, it is not yet clear whether the Criminal Cases Review Commission, created in response to this recommendation, will have a major impact upon the appeal system or the inability of an adversarial system to embark on the complete re-appraisal of the facts of a case necessary to deal with alleged miscarriages of justice. With its staff of 60, it is better resourced than C3, the Home Office department which used to handle applications for referral to the court.[32] It is estimated that the Commission will have to consider an estimated 1,500 cases a year[33]—far more than the Home Office workload of about 700.[34] Although it has the power to conduct investigations itself, it is most likely to rely heavily on police assistance; under the 1995 Act, the Commission has broad powers to instruct police officers to investigate, and to demand production of documents from public bodies.[35] In fact, Malleson suggests, it is likely that this process will produce more information than defence lawyers may now obtain under the Criminal Procedure and Investigations Act 1996.[36] A criticism of C3 was that it developed a policy of second-guessing the Court of Appeal because of reluctance to refer cases which would be rejected. Thus the court's own culture and agenda were reinforced by the Home Office Department. Whether the new Commission will, in the same vein, follow a path which is anticipatory rather than proactive remains to be seen. It may not refer any but exceptional cases unless it believes that there is a real possibility that the conviction will be overturned because of arguments and evidence which were not raised in the proceedings which led to the conviction or any appeal.[37] Whether it would regard as exceptional a case like the Birmingham Six, where the chief difficulty was lack of resources for the defence expert witness who could, in theory at least, have carried out the tests which would have supported his dissatisfaction with the prosecution evidence, and which were carried out by the time of the second appeal, is not clear. Early statements from the Commission seem to indicate a refreshingly broad approach. It has announced that cases in which evidence was available at the time of trial but not raised by reason of error will be referred unless and until the Court of Appeal reacts adversely.[38] This inevitable concern for the judicial reaction means that unless there is a marked cultural shift within the Court of Appeal

---

[31] *Report,* n. 14 above, 186.   [32] Thornton, n. 29 above.   [33] *The Times,* 9 Apr. 1997.

[34] *Report,* n. 14 above, 181.   [35] S. 15–25.

[36] "A Broad Framework" [1997] *NLJ* 1023.

[37] Criminal Appeal Act, s.13; there can be no second appeal, therefore, without some new development.

[38] Malleson, n. 36 above.

itself, the new Commission may find itself having little impact upon the handling of miscarriages of justice. Systems of justice require public support, and so far the appeal structure has done little to inspire it; there is a danger that the perception of fairness within adversarial systems identified by Thibaut and Walker could be lost.

The operation of exclusionary rules of evidence which "run contrary to fact in many cases"[39] can also have consequences which run counter to intuitive notions of justice and common sense. The hearsay rule is itself under attack from the common sense lobby, but the commitment to orality in the criminal trial is not. Yet the difficulties faced by vulnerable witnesses suggest that preserving that commitment is costing us too dear. The New Zealand Law Commission has suggested that vulnerable witnesses, including frightened witnesses, should be able, as some child witnesses are, to give evidence through live television link or even by pre-recorded videotaped interview. Adversarial principles must give way when they prove counter-productive; many departures from strict theory have been identified in this book. The increased public awareness which a more critical media attention has generated in the past 30 years or so has accelerated the process of introducing more inquisitorial methods into the English system of civil and criminal justice. Trial structures can become more flexible yet. Procedures could be modified to reduce counsel's editorial control of examination-in-chief; witnesses could be permitted to give evidence more freely, as Scandinavian witnesses do. The importance of cross-examination would diminish where the witness was not tightly constrained in giving his account. Frankel[40] wrote, "[w]e should be prepared to inquire whether our art of examining or cross-examining, often geared to preventing excessive outpouring of facts, arts inevitably preferable to safeguarded interrogation by an informed judicial officer". Such views are anathema to the traditional British advocate, whose point of view is expressed in typical terms by Sheriff Stone: "strictly controlled questioning" has certain advantages—the witness is taken step by step and point by point through material facts, in a planned and orderly way.[41] This prevents him from rambling: "[i]f some witnesses were simply asked to say what they know about the facts in issue, the rules of evidence and the expertise of the advocate would disappear . . . [he] might state damaging facts, which there was no obligation to reveal, by law."[42]

Is the expertise of the advocate worth preserving merely for its own sake? Despite the conviction of many members of the Bar that cross-examination operates as a forensic scalpel with which to unmask the soul of the liar, the evidence is otherwise. Psychological research has shown that once a witness's confidence has been destroyed, he or she is less likely to be believed. Cross-

[39] R.J. Cohen, "Freedom of Proof" W. Twining (ed.), in *Facts in Law* (Steiner, Wiesbaden, 1983).
[40] M.E. Frankel, "The Search for Truth: An Umpireal View" (1975) 123 *U of Penn. LR* 1031, 1053.
[41] Although that depends on the level of preparedness of the advocate.
[42] M. Stone, *Proof of Fact in Criminal Trials* (W. Green and Sons, Edinburgh, 1984), 273.

examination therefore can undermine the correctness of verdicts. The convictions of the Maguire Seven might not have occurred but for the undermining effect of the cross-examination of the expert witness for the defence. Yet the witness lacked neither integrity nor expertise; he may have lacked self-confidence, or merely courtroom experience.[43] We have seen above[44] that cross-examination may not employ gratuitous insult or irrelevant character assassination. Yet we find a rape complainant asked, at the Old Bailey, "[i]sn't it true, Miss S, that your father recently died of Aids and you didn't even bother to see him before his death?"[45] There was no intervention from prosecuting counsel or judge. In 1995, the press reported that a trial had to be stopped because a juror admitted that she could not tolerate the bullying by a defence advocate of a prosecution witness. The potential risk of her being prejudiced against the defendant meant the trial would have to start again with a new jury. The trial judge expressed surprise; counsel was only doing his job, and the questioning was, in his view, perfectly proper. This treatment of participants in trials without doubt deters potential witnesses from giving evidence. The main difficulty is that cross-examination is frequently oppressive and reveals nothing. Recently, a Japanese student, too ashamed to tell her parents that she had been raped by six youths, was cross-examined in court for 12 days—counsel for each defendant being entitled to take a turn. Apart from such extreme cases, a common tactic is to grill witnesses on minute and irrelevant details surrounding every single material fact alleged, hoping that ultimately there will be a self-contradiction. If the witness loses composure as a result, the verdict may well be affected, but for all the wrong reasons. Eggleston argued that cross-examination as to credit should be confined to the witness's reliability in respect of the facts to which he has deposed.[46]

Even though our Law Commission recognises the irrelevance of many cross-examinations as to credit,[47] the only proposal currently being offered is that we retain the rule that a defendant who attacks the character of a prosecution witness is deprived of the shield which protects him from cross-examination on his criminal record. The Commission concede that this is the crudest "tit for tat". It is certainly no deterrent for a defendant who has no criminal record or who does not mind the jury hearing about it.[48] It

---

[43] Sir John May, *Return to an Address of the Honourable the House of Commons Dated 30 June 1994 for a Report of the Inquiry into the Circumstances Surrounding the Convictions arising out of the Bomb Attacks on Guildford and Woolwich in 1974: Final report* (HMSO, London, 1994); *Interim Report* (HMSO, London, 1990).

[44] Ch. 1.

[45] S. Lees, *Carnal Knowledge: Rape on Trial* (Hamish Hamilton, London, 1996).

[46] R. Eggleston, "What is Wrong with the Adversary System?" [1975] *ALJ* 428.

[47] *Evidence in Criminal Proceedings: Previous Misconduct of a Defendant*, Law Commission Consultation Paper No 141 (HMSO, London, 1996).

[48] See Ch. 5.

affords no protection whatever for defence witnesses. At present, for witnesses apart from the defendant, credibility is solely a matter for cross-examination, and so a one-sided picture is inevitable—the negative side only. It has been suggested that a witness who has been discredited in cross-examination should be able to call rehabilitative evidence.[49] The Law Commission rejects this idea on the ground that pursuit of such collateral matters would be distracting for the jury. Better for them to get a distorted picture, presumably. The Law Commissions of England and Wales and of Scotland, have had cause to consider the issue of vulnerable witnesses facing the rigours of giving evidence in the adversarial trial. They concluded that to consider any fundamental reform to its structure would be beyond their remit. They did not suggest within whose remit that issue might fall. Even child victims of serious abuse must therefore be able to withstand cross-examination. The situation may be even worse where an unrepresented defendant carries out the cross examination himself. In 1996 Margaret Bent gave evidence that for four years she had been terrorised by Dennis Chambers. He had no barrister at his trial for causing her grievous bodily harm, and cross-examined her himself, standing quite close to her and forcing her to look straight at him. Julia Mason, a rape complainant, was cross-examined by the defendant for six days. He wore at the time the clothes in which he committed the offence. Pending Parliamentary intervention, which seems likely for rape cases,[50] the Court of Appeal has made it clear that trial judges should be more proactive. In *Brown (Milton)*,[51] the Lord Chief Justice said that trial judges should, without descending into the arena or acting on behalf of the defence, ask such questions as they see fit to test the reliability of a prosecution witness. There is a clear duty to minimise the trauma suffered by the other participants in the trial. An unrepresented defendant does not necessarily have the right to dictate how the trial should be conducted.

Cross-examination is the creature of the adversarial trial or, particularly, of the primacy of the orality principle. If it is beyond the power of judges to prevent unnecessarily offensive questioning and the use of distress as a weapon, the value of orality itself is thrown into doubt. The departure from orality in the civil sphere may indicate that more disclosure of evidence inevitably undermines the orality of trials. In the criminal context, the development through the common law of greater obligations of disclosure for the prosecution was seen as essential to avoid the kind of miscarriage of justice which blighted the Guildford Four and the Maguires.[52] Although the prosecution obligation was cut back by the 1996 Criminal Procedure and Investigations Act, the defence was required to enter into the process of

---

[49] A. Zuckerman, *Principles of Criminal Evidence* (OUP, Oxford, 1989), 270.
[50] *The Times,* 19 Sept. 1997; 20 May 1998.
[51] *The Times,* 7 May 1998.
[52] Above, Ch. 1.

disclosure to a greater degree than ever before. A shift towards more efficient and informative pre-trial procedures[53] could mean the end of the dominance of orality. The hearsay rule would lose its status as the dominant exclusionary rule and scourge of the advocate; it could be seen in its true colours, as no more than a rough, common-sense guide to the relative reliability of evidence. Less emphasis on orality would also have the effect of undermining the division between evidence on the issue and evidence which goes only to credibility, since that is a function both of the hearsay rule and the need to avoid prolonged and complex oral trials. Once that distinction bites the dust, we can avoid the hypocrisy of the claim that the accused's criminal record is evidence only of his credibility on oath.

Transparency

Although adversarial theory is inconsistent with any process whereby one side effectively assists the other, no useful purpose is served by a system of trial which involves the presentation of two cases which have little or no common ground. The duties of defence disclosure embodied in the Criminal Procedure and Investigations Act 1996 were largely a response to allegations of ambush by defence lawyers. In fact, the "climactic and continuous trial"[54] can disadvantage either side if surprise dictates the result. In *Brown (Winston)*,[55] the defence were unaware that their two alibi witnesses had made statements to the police. These statements were not consistent with their evidence in court which provided the defendant with his alibi. One had said in the first instance that he had no memory of the events in question because he was drunk at the time; the other originally had made a statement implicating the defendant, but withdrew it subsequently, claiming that he was being threatened. At the trial, both witnesses were cross-examined on their earlier statements, to the destruction of Brown's alibi and the collapse of his defence. His lawyers objected on appeal to the fact that they had known nothing of the earlier statements; they said that they would not have called these witnesses if they had been informed of them. Yet the House of Lords held that since the prosecution was under no obligation to disclose information relevant to the credibility of potential defence witnesses, there was no reason to regard Brown's conviction as unsafe.

The House was less impressed with the practical problems with which a duty to disclose would have presented prosecutors than the Court of Appeal had been. The difficulty of predicting which witnesses the defence might wish to call is in any case now ameliorated by the new defence obligations of

---

[53] Pre-trial review, see text to nn. 66–92 below.
[54] Eggleston, n. 46 above.   [55] [1997] 3 All ER 769.

disclosure. The House of Lords preferred to regard it as a matter of principle that it is for the defence to establish and evaluate the credibility of its own witnesses—a traditional adversarial point of view. But in *Brown*, the drama of the moment when the defence witnesses' credibility was destroyed might well have distorted perception of the remaining evidence. The fact that those two were liars does not mean that the defendant was guilty; but once his alibi witnesses were exposed as such, it must have been difficult for the jury not to leap to the conclusion that he was. At the trial of Judith Ward, one of the problems for the defence was that it did not know of the track record of its own client for lying and making false confessions, and so it was ill-equipped to challenge her confession to placing a bomb on a coach on the M62 motorway. The House of Lords held that the prosecution should have disclosed Ward's earlier statements to the police on various occasions, because they were relevant to the credibility of that confession.[56] *Ward* was decided before the Criminal Procedure and Investigations Act 1996 stipulated that prosecutors disclose material which "might undermine the case for the prosecution". It would probably be followed today, since the undisclosed information undermined the reliability of the confession, a central plank in the case against her. The decision in *Brown* is, unfortunately, also probably unaffected by the statute; secondary disclosure, in the light of the stated defence, must be of "any prosecution material which has not previously been disclosed to the accused and which might be reasonably expected to assist the accused's defence as disclosed".[57] This would only apply to the witness statements in *Brown* if it were argued that knowledge of the statements would assist the defence of alibi insofar as suggesting that it should be abandoned.

The recent recognition within the civil jurisdiction that the practice of exchange of witness statements prior to trial should be adopted in all forms of civil litigation (even in jury trials) provides authoritative confirmation that current changes in procedure represent a developing policy to move in the inquisitorial direction. A former Master of the Rolls spoke of a "sea change over the last quarter of a century in the legislative and judicial attitude to the conduct of litigation which took the form of increased positive case management by the judiciary".[58] The proposals in Lord Woolf's Report,[59] are designed to reduce uncertainty, cost and delay in civil trials and will be implemented. What is striking about the reaction to the Report is that although there has been considerable debate about the cost-effectiveness of his proposals, there was little protest about his criticisms of the behaviour of lawyers, who stand accused of manipulating the adversarial process to use

---

[56] *Ward* [1993] 2 All ER 577.   [57] S. 7(2)(a).

[58] *Holden v Chief Constable of Lancashire, The Times,* 22 Feb. 1991.

[59] *Access to Justice: Final Report by Lord Woolf MR, to the Lord Chancellor on the Civil Justice System in England and Wales* (HMSO, London, 1996).

delay and cost as weapons against opponents.[60] This means that the debate has concentrated on practicalities, rather than whether the new style of trial is fairer to the parties or more likely to produce a just result, concepts themselves open to debate. In other words the concentration of effort from the judiciary has been to examine the economics of litigation and improve efficiency in dispatching cases through the system. The emphasis has not been to consider what style of procedure is the most desirable for the parties from the viewpoint of protecting their legal interests.

The result of these developments is fundamentally to change the essential nature of the civil trial both in form and in substance, diluting the importance of the advocate's role and the lawyer's personal expertise and ability to influence the outcome; it involves an inevitable retreat from adversarial principle. A dignified and considered evolution towards a less adversarial structure would, however, be preferable to an ill-considered sprint into the unknown. The danger with piecemeal reform is that the whole picture lacks coherence. The effect of procedural change on the presentation of evidence has already been noted[61]; evidence in civil cases has moved from the oral testimony to a statement effectively "settled" by lawyers in advance of the hearing, and presented in a coherent and comprehensive form wholly unlike the product of many examinations-in-chief and bearing little resemblance to the witness's own manner of communicating. This creates the risk that the judge's perception of the witness's credibility, should the case come to trial, will be more than ever influenced by the way the witness stands up to cross-examination. Some lawyers fear the effect on the witness of stepping straight into a hostile onslaught without first getting "the feel of the court" through a friendly interrogation by his own side. The exchange procedure as it is at present therefore distorts the natural balance of the adversarial trial. The Woolf Report has recommended that the practice of overdrafting be discarded, and that statements should be expressed in the witness's own words and style. To encourage lawyers to have faith in the witness's own mode of expression, judges should be flexible in allowing witnesses to add to the statement orally in court. Judges suggested to Lord Woolf that it helps them to assess the witness and puts the witness more at ease, if he or she may speak informally before coming under the pressure of cross-examination.[62] This concession by the Woolf Report is an implied acknowledgement that *dossier* trials and cross-examination do not mix. It is a pity that the Parliament which introduced the videotaped interview as a substitute for the evidence in chief of child witnesses did not consider the implications for them of being launched straight into cross-examination.

---

[60] M. Zander, "The Woolf Report: Forwards or Backwards for the New Lord Chancellor?" (1997) 16 *CJQ* 208.

[61] Ch. 1.

[62] N. 59 above.12.56.

The individuality of the lawyer's role thus is being replaced by the more methodical and mundane requirements of careful preparation and the production of a paperwork case—"lever-arch litigation"—as practised widely in Europe. This will inevitably undermine the position of the civil Bar and will probably have a more fundamental role in dismantling the distinction between barristers and solicitors than any more direct and specific legislative reforms ever will. Once important cases are perceived as being won or lost on paper and prior to trial, the difference between the style and role of the lawyers is eradicated where the decisive work takes place on the desktop, whether in a solicitor's office or counsel's chambers, rather than in the cauldron of the court. The overall wisdom of these radical reforms remains to be assessed, but the basic assumption that money and time will be saved have not been accepted without argument.[63] Furthermore, it may be that the emphasis on pre-trial preparation and paperwork (which is very expensive) will give an unfair advantage to the wealthier litigant. It has been argued that the traditional adversarial trial is better designed to encourage settlement in civil cases than its European counterpart, because the greater part of the cost is incurred towards the end of the process. If a party's major expenditure occurs at the earlier stages, then there is no disincentive to proceeding with the full trial. Thus in most European countries civil cases do go to trial,[64] whereas in England 95 per cent under the present system will settle.[65]

Greater disclosure and use of pre-trial review or case management by judges increases the transparency of a system which formerly encouraged parties to regard information as their own property. It may reduce the element of surprise and drama at trials. Critics have argued that the adversarial system is incompatible with such developments, and that courts will find that advocates simply disregard the new requirements. The spirit of the Woolf Report is that judges must be unforgiving in such cases, and employ the sanctions of striking out or punitive awards of costs against such lawyers. But it has been argued that judges are reluctant to penalise parties for the actions of their lawyers, as may be seen in both civil[66] and criminal courts.[67] Practising lawyers are traditionally reluctant to involve themselves heavily in pre-trial procedures, principally because the way in which the legal profession, and particularly the Bar, is organised militates against continuity in relationships between lawyer and client, and against the exchange of information within strict time limits. The Royal Commission on Criminal Justice, which recommended greater use of preparatory hearings in complex

---

[63] Zander, n. 60 above.

[64] C. Plant, "Chairman's address", Conference on *Access to Justice*, College of Law, London, June 1997.

[65] Zander disputes Lord Woolf's claim that there is a strong predilection for settling at the very last minute—at the "door of the court"—to the immense inconvenience of court personnel and witnesses: n. 60 above.

[66] *Ibid.*

[67] R. Leng, "Preparatory Hearings" [1995] *Crim. LR* 704.

criminal cases, was as unsympathetic as Lord Woolf proved to be to the argument that practitioners would be unwilling to comply, and that sanctions would be ineffective. "We recognise that if the scheme for pre-trial preparation which we propose in outline is to be effective, a significant change in the working habits of both solicitors and barristers will be called for. But we refuse to share the complacency of those who believe that the present system does not call for improvement at all or the scepticism of those who believe that although the earlier and better preparation of cases is desirable in principle, it cannot be achieved in practice".[68] Professor Zander regards this as wishful thinking: "[t]o rail at the failure of lawyers to comply with procedural time limits makes as much sense as to rail at the advance of the tide".[69] He considers the use of striking out as a sanction unfair, since it condemns the parties to start their legal action all over again or sue their lawyers in negligence. In April 1997, 130 civil appeals against striking out were pending in the Court of Appeal, and although it has been said[70] that 20,000 cases were struck out in the county courts for failure to comply with time limits,[71] the true figure will be much higher.[72]

The Royal Commission led by Lord Runciman was convinced that the greatest assistance that could be given to the finder of fact in a criminal trial was to have issues clearly defined and clarified. In general, documentary disclosure by both sides would be sufficient to ensure that all parties understood what the case was about, but in complicated cases either party should be able to require a preparatory hearing before the judge, to secure rulings on the main issues.[73] It was believed that such a hearing should be necessary in only about 6 per cent of Crown Court trials, but the Commission could see no reason why magistrates should not be able to participate in a similar procedure chaired by a justices' clerk.[74] The Criminal Procedure and Investigations Act puts these proposals into effect for Crown Court trials. For long or complex cases[75] preparatory hearings give judges considerable powers. They can demand advance disclosure of evidence in addition to disclosure already made because of the parties' general duties.[76]. The purpose is to identify the material issues before the jury, assist them in the understanding of these issues, expedite the proceedings and help the judge manage the trial. To ensure continuity of approach, it was recommended that the same judge preside over both the preparatory hearing and the full

---

[68] *Report*, n. 60 above, 102.

[69] N. 60 above.

[70] D. Greenslade, "A Fresh Approach; Uniform Rules of Court" in A. Zuckerman and R. Cranston (eds.), *Reform of Civil Procedure: Essays on Access to Justice*, (Oxford, Clarendon Press, 1995).

[71] Under CCR, Ord. 17, r.11.   [72] Zander, n. 60 above.   [73] *Ibid.*, 106.

[74] *Report*, n. 14 above, 116.

[75] Either party may apply for one, and the judge may at any time before the jury is sworn decide to hold one. In practice, the decision whether to hold one will probably be decided at the plea and directions hearing.

[76] S. 28–38 of the Criminal Procedure and Investigations Act 1996.

trial, but this may not be possible in practice. In the Crown Court Study,[77] it emerged that where pre-trial proceedings had taken place,[78] the same judge presided at the full trial in only 7 per cent of cases. The Royal Commission therefore recommended that rulings made at preparatory hearings on the admissibility of evidence or other legal matters should be binding on the judge at the trial.[79] Accordingly, under the Criminal Procedure and Investigations Act 1996, judges may make rulings of law which are binding on future judges, unless a party can show that such ruling should be varied or discharged in the interests of justice.[80] This would require proof of a material change of circumstances.

The importance of case management for all Crown Court trials was acknowledged in that Plea and Directions Hearings (PDH)[81] are now held in relation to all trials on indictment. Both sides must indicate the issues arising in the case, the number of witnesses, admitted facts and agreed evidence. The court will deal with applications in cases involving child witnesses for video-recorded evidence, live link, etc. It may adjudicate on the admissibility of evidence, which will be binding on whichever judge comes to try the case.[82] Many judges appear to take the view that this procedure is unnecessary in many cases where the defendant is on bail.[83] Also, it has been discovered that its effectiveness has been impeded by the lack of preparation of counsel; the barrister engaged for the trial might not appear at the PDH, although the practice rules say it should be the same person wherever practicable.[84] Nevertheless, the principle of case management is now to be brought to the magistrate's courts. The Crime and Disorder Bill provides that early administrative hearings may be conducted by a single justice of the peace or magistrates' clerk. At this stage the tribunal should discover whether the defendant has obtained legal aid and, if not, make arrangements for that.[85] Also, a single justice or clerk may dismiss an information for lack of evidence, vary bail conditions, request a pre-sentence report, give, vary or reduce the conditions for the conduct of the trial, including the timetable, attendance of the parties, service of documents and the manner in which evidence is to be given. The objective

---

[77] M. Zander and P. Henderson, *Crown Court Study* RCCJ Research Study No 19 (HMSO, London, 1993).

[78] The practice of holding plea and directions hearings grew up from the late 1970s, but only during the preparatory hearings held under the Criminal Justice Act 1987 in serious fraud cases were judges able to make binding rulings on evidential issues.

[79] *Report.*, n. 14 above,107.   [80] S. 31.

[81] Criminal Procedure and Investigations Act 1996, ss.39–43.   [82] S.40.

[83] *Review of Delays in the Criminal Justice System* (Home Office, London, 1997).

[84] *Practice Direction (Plea and Directions Hearings)* [1995] 1 WLR 1318.

[85] Unless the defendant decides not to be legally represented, he or she should use the duty solicitor in court that day unless other advice is obtained: *Review of Delays in the Criminal Justice System* (Home Office, London, 1997).

is to bring cases to completion more promptly and save on unnecessary witness attendance.

Having a Bench acquainted with the issues in the trial could assist the lawyers involved. For instance, there might be fewer interruptions asking the purpose and direction of a cross-examination once it has begun.[86] The Royal Commission anticipated resistance from the profession, however, to the principle of pre-trial review, and expressed considerable hostility to the argument that the reforms would not work in the light of custom and court practice. "It seems to us wholly wrong that a system apparently so wedded to delay and to the last minute preparation of cases should be encouraged and condoned."[87] Accordingly, under the Criminal Procedure and Investigations Act, judges may make rulings of law which are binding on future judges, unless a party can show that such ruling should be varied or discharged in the interests of justice.[88] This would require proof of a material change of circumstances. A change of advocate is unlikely to be so regarded.[89] The Bar and the Law Society were urged by the Runciman Commission to address the problems of lateness of instructions to counsel and the returning of briefs by counsel. Yet, when PDHs were piloted, only 21 per cent of defence and 9 per cent of prosecution barristers appeared at both the PDH and the trial—and the fee for an appearance at a PDH has now been reduced.[90] In some child abuse cases, the decision of a prosecution advocate to request and obtain an order at the PDH for the live link facility or for use of a videotaped interview in lieu of a child's evidence-in-chief was overturned by the advocate who actually conducted the case. This inevitably caused the witness considerable confusion and stress. Parliament has been forced to intervene; once the order is made, it is binding on any subsequent judge and irrespective of any change in counsel, unless it appears to be contrary to the interests of justice to uphold it, given that a material change of circumstances has been shown to have occurred.[91] The difficulty of establishing any continuity of advocate led to the recommendation that Crown Prosecution Service lawyers should have rights of audience at PDHs, and recently the Law Society's proposal that solicitors in certain circumstances should have rights of audience generally at Crown Courts has been approved.[92]

The contribution of the legal profession to the difficulties of organising pre-trial disclosure and review cannot be under-estimated. An archaic

---

[86] See J. Jackson and S. Doran, *Judge Without Jury: Diplock Courts and the Adversary System* (Clarendon, Oxford, 1995) for descriptions of the frustration of counsel at being asked for an explanation of the relevance of a particular line of cross-examination being embarked on. See also Ch. 3.

[87] *Report*, n. 14 above, 109.   [88] S. 31.

[89] A. Edwards, "The Procedural Aspect" [1997] *Crim. LR* 321.

[90] *Review of Delays in the Criminal Justice System* (Home Office, London, 1997).

[91] Criminal Investigations and Procedure Act 1996, s.62(2).

[92] 26 Feb. 1997, by the Lord Chancellor and four senior designated judges.

system of instructing counsel[93] undermines all notions of introducing order and clarity into the criminal process. It also means that criminal defendants, however funded, receive a very poor service much of the time. Few of them see a qualified lawyer in or outside the police station; unsurprisingly, most end up pleading guilty in front of the magistrates. At the Crown Court, where it is necessary to engage counsel, the majority of criminal defendants at contested trials are actually represented in court by a barrister other than the person who originally agreed to act. This is because of the phenomenon of the "return brief"; another barrister substitutes for the one who initially received the instructions, but who has become unavailable, usually because of the unpredictability of court listings which obliges that barrister to be in court elsewhere. It emerged in the Crown Court Study that in a quarter of Crown Court cases, counsel appearing for either side received the brief after 4.00 p.m. the day before the trial. Yet 90 per cent of barristers informed the researchers that they had enough time to prepare their cases. The Crown Prosecution Service suffers as many return briefs as defence solicitors—yet the number of judge-directed acquittals always seems to be used as a criticism of the Service rather than of a system which routinely deprives it of the advocate of choice and most familiar with the case. The chaos of the court lists, which generates this uncertainty, is mainly explained by the "cracked trial"; this is a trial listed as one which will be contested, but which suddenly collapses as the defendant changes his or her plea to guilty at the very last minute. Other cases therefore have to be brought up the list, causing the lawyers involved to find themselves double-booked and having to drop everything else. Of the trials listed as Not Guilty pleas, so that court time has been allocated for the evidence to be heard, half will crack on the day.[94] The Royal Commission's suggestion that the reason for this is the fickle nature of criminal defendants has been doubted[95]; plea bargains are usually involved, and it is statistically more likely than not that the defendant has never previously discussed the case with any barrister, and thus has not heard counsel's opinion on the prospects for acquittal. Given that counsel for both sides are quite likely to less than familiar with the case, the tendency to look for a deal is not surprising. A vicious circle has been established. Counsel may, because of unpreparedness, have an interest in advising a plea of guilty, which causes the trial to crack. The lists are consequently thrown into disarray, sending more advocates scurrying off to deal

[93] Solicitors for either side select a barrister and dispatch the brief to the appropriate Chambers, although in some cases the brief is unnamed and the barristers' clerk for a particular Chambers decides to whom it should be offered. If the selected barrister is unavailable, the clerk is likely to suggest an alternative member of those Chambers. The brief will be delivered when the solicitor regards it as ready, which may mean that it arrives very close to the date of trial.

[94] N. 77 above.

[95] M. McConville, J. Hodgson, A. Pavlovic and L. Bridges, *Standing Accused* (Oxford, Clarendon, 1993).

with cases they thought were safely down the list, leaving their other clients to search for alternative representation at the last minute.

Co-operation or Confrontation?

One of the major barriers to co-operation between defence and prosecution in criminal cases is the principle that each of the two rival sides is the sole and rightful owner of its own evidence.[96] The police have long been perceived as an agency for the prosecution of offences, but themselves, in their submission to the Royal Commission, argued for the first time for a neutral role for their service. Woolf LJ some time ago recommended closer co-operation between the different parts of the criminal justice system,[97] but the Royal Commission favoured the retention of separate roles for the two sides, claiming that this would offer "better protection for the innocent defendant".[98] Lord Woolf will probably get his way with regard to the civil jurisdiction. His Report registers disenchantment with "trial by combat"; there should be more co-operation between the two sides to a civil dispute, and the system should be run in the interests of the litigants, not their lawyers. There is much to be said for this approach in the criminal context also. The defence is frequently massively under-resourced in comparison with the prosecution; it seems that solicitors are asking their clients to do their own investigating.[99] Meanwhile, the partisanship encouraged by the adversarial system is damaging to the police themselves. They have seen themselves, and been perceived by others, as an agency whose job is to collect evidence on behalf of the prosecution, to construct a case against someone. The effect of this attitude, particularly when shared by scientists instructed by the police, has led to appalling miscarriages of justice as we have seen.[100]

If acquittal is seen as a defeat for the police, that is bad for morale, and encourages unlawful practices. During the passage of the 1996 Criminal Procedure and Investigations Act through Parliament, the Opposition tried to persuade the government to give the police a duty to carry out investigations instigated by the suspect.[101] The Act does not go so far; section 23(1)(a) provides that the Code which is to be issued under the Act must be designed to secure that "where a criminal investigation is conducted, all reasonable steps are taken for the purpose of the investigation, and, in particular, all

---

[96] C. Pollard, "Public Safety, Accountability and the Courts" [1996] *Crim. LR* 152.

[97] Woolf H, Right Honourable Lord Justice, *Prison Disturbances April 1990: Report of an Inquiry* (HMSO, London, 1990), Cm 1456.

[98] *Report* n. 14 above, 4.

[99] McConville *et al*,. n. 95 above.

[100] Ch. 1.

[101] R. Leng, "Defence Strategies for Information Deficit: Negotiating the CPIA" (1997) 1 *E & P* 215.

reasonable lines of inquiry are pursued". The Code itself explains that reasonable lines of inquiry include "those pointing towards or away from the suspect".[102] The police themselves meanwhile continue the transition from "force" to "service". They have developed "investigative interviewing", approaching the questioning of suspects and witnesses with an open mind, rather than concentrating on an interrogation which will provoke a confession. This approach was welcomed in the Runciman Report.[103] Police investigations could move away from emphasis on prosecution and confession towards a new role as neutral information gatherers. Zuckerman has argued for greater co-operation between police and defence lawyers, so that there is a gradual, mutual and progressive exchange of information leading to more accuracy and reliability of evidence.[104] Closer co-operation and exchange of information would make the criminal justice system, through increased transparency, less remote and less sinister. It would also, according to Jackson, bring it closer to a dialectic method of proof, which avoids preconceptions and therefore constitutes a more efficient fact-finding process.[105] It is also probable that maximising the exchange of information between all interested parties at every stage would do more towards stimulating high standards of professionalism in the police than developing ever more ingenious means of regulating their behaviour.

If the police were indeed to move from one-sidedness to a more neutral, central ground within the criminal process, there can be no doubt that a key element of the adversarial character of the English system would have disappeared. It would begin to resemble the systems investigated by Leigh and Hall Williams in northern Europe.[106] The meticulous review of evidence which involves all parties, including the defence, in the Netherlands for example, means that most disputes of fact are settled at an early stage. Information requested by the defence is freely provided; there is no sign of the confrontational approach with which United Kingdom lawyers are familiar. As a consequence of the consensus likely to develop early on in each case, there are relatively few contested trials and few acquittals. Pizzi, having studied a number of Continental systems of criminal justice, concluded that the acid test of whether procedures are adversarial or inquisitorial is the way in which the police are conceptualised. In the United Kingdom and the United States, they are viewed as aligned on the side of the prosecution. Each side jealously guards its file of information, only grudgingly disclosing it

---

[102] Criminal Procedure and Investigations Act 1996 (Code of Practice)(No 2) Order 1997 (SI 1997 No 1033), para. 3.4.

[103] *Report* n. 14 above, 13.

[104] A. Zuckerman, "Bias and Suggestibility: Is There an Alternative to the Right to Silence?" in D. Morgan and G. Stephenson (eds.), *Suspicion and Silence: The Right to Silence in Criminal Investigations* (Blackstone, London, 1994).

[105] "Two Methods of Proof in Criminal Procedure" (1988) 31 *MLR* 249.

[106] L.H. Leigh and J.E. Hall Williams, *The Management of Prosecution Process in Denmark, Sweden and the Netherlands* (James Hall, Leamington Spa, 1981).

when obliged to do so. Where, in some European countries, the police are supposed to be investigators for both prosecution and defence, everyone works from the same file.[107] In Jackson's model for criminal trials,[108] an independent magistrate would be involved at a pre-trial stage to ensure full disclosure of all evidence and to compile it in a report. This would be presented in advance of the trial to the triers of fact. The witnesses would be questioned at the trial by lawyers for the prosecution and defence, but also by the triers of fact, who would have power also to summon witnesses, such as the independent magistrate if clarification of the report is required. Counsel would therefore have little opportunity to control through questioning technique the evidence given by witnesses. The result would, in his view, have the closest similarity to scientific methods of fact-finding that could realistically be achieved.

In Chapter 6 it was observed that the duty of the prosecutor and his agents to observe higher standards of conduct than is necessary in the case of the defence amounted to an implied acceptance that the parties in a criminal case are not independent in the strictly adversarial sense. But in an inquisitorial system there is a danger that the prosecutor, never wholly independent of the state, is not independent either of the court which will try the case. "The essential element of the inquisitorial system, when compared to the accusatorial, is the blurring of the distinction between the function of prosecution and that of judgment".[109] Erikson argues that in a Continental system, the members of the judiciary who conduct criminal investigations, prosecutions and judgments are colleagues in the same profession. They form a separate brotherhood which is distinct from that of the lawyers who defend the accused and never prosecute or go on to become judges. The danger, however, is that securing convictions is just as dear to them as it is to police officers; despite this risk, the apparent impartiality of Italian investigating judges, brought into investigation at an earlier stage in proceedings because of criticism of police methods of obtaining convictions in the 1950s and 1960s, meant that they were given sweeping powers which would have been politically unacceptable in a police force, and, indeed, became unacceptable in the hands of the judiciary. In England, judicial criticism of police methods is not unknown, although not an everyday occurrence. Erikson suggests that separation of powers makes it more likely than it is in an inquisitorial system. There a judge would find it difficult to suggest that a colleague had lied on oath and ought to be prosecuted. Such problems suggest that we would be unwise to institute a "career judiciary" in the Continental sense. In Scandinavia and the Netherlands, however, there appears to be virtually no distrust of or complaints against the police, prosecution or magistrates amongst defence lawyers; the early involvement of all parties in the investiga-

---

[107] W.T. Pizzi, "The American Adversary System" [1997] *NLJ* 986.
[108] J. Jackson, "Two Methods of Proof in Criminal Procedure" (1988) 31 *MLR* 249.
[109] J.D. Erikson, "Confessions in Evidence: A Look at the Inquisitorial System" [1990] *NLJ* 884.

tive process encourages a co-operative atmosphere in which evidence is tested and discussed, and therefore mutually accepted or discarded, long in advance of trial.[110] It is not clear whether the roots of this consensual approach lie in a tolerant national temperament and culture, or actually flow from the nature of the procedures themselves.

Although, as we have seen, many recent departures have diluted quite considerably the adversarial properties of our system of legal adjudication, the unpredictability of the trial on the day is still unfair to some potential litigants who are unable accurately to assess the strength of their case. Yet, paradoxically, it may encourage those with little merit because something may be achieved by surprise or some other tactic. And, as we have seen, a weak case may appear comparatively stronger in an adversarial contest than an inquisitorial one. There seems to be no reason in principle why we should be reluctant to consider further developments away from traditional methods. It has been shown throughout this book that in many respects neither civil nor criminal trials are pure embodiments of adversarial principles, although they deviate in different ways from the classical adversarial pattern. We have never had a pure adversary procedure, but there is reason to believe that we are moving farther from it in both the civil and the criminal context. Unfortunately, this drift is not recognised; if it were, the insistence on retention of exclusionary rules of evidence which are appropriate only within an adversarial system would inevitably diminish.

---

[110] Leigh and Hall Williams, n. 106 above.

Suggested Reading

Bennett WL and Feldman M, *Reconstructing Reality in the Courtroom* (Tavistock, London 1981)

Birch D, "Corroboration: Goodbye to all that?" [1995] Crim LR 524

Birch D, "Hearsay-logic and Hearsay-fiddles: *Blastland* Revisited" in Smith P (ed.) *Criminal Law: Essays in Honour of J C Smith* (Butterworths, London, 1987)

Birch, "Documentary Evidence" [1989] Crim LR 15

Damaska MR, *Evidence Law Adrift* (Yale University Press, New Haven, London, 1997)

Damaska MR, "Evidentiary barriers to conviction and two models of criminal procedure: a comparative study", (1973) 121 U. Penn. L.R. 506

Davies G and Noon E, *An Evaluation of the Live Link for Child Witnesses* (Home Office 1991)

Davies G, Wilson C, Mitchell L, Milsom J, *Videotaping Children's Evidence: an Evaluation* (Home Office 1995)

Eggleston R, *Evidence, Proof and Probability* (Weidenfeld and Nicolson, London, 1983)

Eggleston R "What is wrong with the adversarial system?" (1975) 49 A.L.J. 428

K Evans, *Advocacy in Court: a Beginner's Guide* (Blackstone, London, 1995)

Frankel ME "The Search for Truth: an Umpireal View", (1975) 123 U. Penn. L.R. 1031, 1035

Gudjonsson GH, *The Psychology of Interrogations, Confessions, and Testimony*, (Wiley, Chichester, 1992)

Honoré A, "The primacy of oral evidence" in Tapper C (ed.) *Crime Proof and Punishment: Essays in Memory of Sir Rupert Cross* (1981)

Irving B and Hilgendorf L, *Police Interrogation: The Pyschological Approach: Police Interrogation: A Case Study of Current Practice* Royal Commission on Criminal Procedure Research Study Nos 1 and 2 (London HMSO 1980)

Irving B and McKenzie, IK, *Police Interrogation: the Effects of the Police and Criminal Evidence Act 1984* (Police Foundation, London, 1989)

Jackson J "Two Methods of Proof in Criminal Procedure" (1988) 51 MLR 249

Jackson J and Doran S, *Judge Without Jury: Diplock Trials and the Adversary System*, (Clarendon, Oxford, 1995)

Jones"The evidence of a three year old child" [1987] Crim LR 677

Keane A, *The Modern Law of Evidence* (Butterworths London 1995)

Koehler JJ, "Probabilities in the Courtroom: an Evaluation of the Objectives and Policies" in Kagehiro DK and Laufer WS, (eds) *Handbook of Psychology and Law* (New York; Springer-Verlag1992)

Köhnken G "The evaluation of statement credibility: social judgment and expert diagnostic approaches", in eds JR Spencer, R Nicholson, R Flin and R Bull *Children's Evidence in Legal Proceedings* (Spencer, Faculty of Law, University of Cambridge, 1990)

Leng R, *The Right to Silence in Police Interrogations: a Study of some of the issues underlying the debate*, (Royal Commission on Criminal Justice Research Study 10

McBarnett D, *Conviction* (Macmillan. London, 1983),

Murray K, *Live Television Link: an Evaluation of its use by Child Witnesses in Scottish Criminal Trials* (Scottish Office Central Research Unit 1995)

Saks MJ and Hastie R, *Social Psychology in Court* (Van Nostrand Reinhold, New York,1978)

Spencer J and Flin R, *The Evidence of Children: the Law and the Psychology* , (Blackstone, London, 1993)

Stone M, *Proof of Fact in Criminal Trials* (W Green and Sons, Edinburgh, 1984)

Tapper C, *Cross on Evidence* (Butterworths, London, 1995),

Temkin J, *Rape and the Legal Process* (Sweet & Maxwell, London, 1987)

Thayer JB, *Preliminary Treatise on Evidence at the Common Law* (Sweet and Maxwell, London, 1893)

Thompson JJ, "Probabilities as relevant facts" in (ed Thompson JJ) *Rights, Restitution and Risk*, (Harvard University Press, Cambridge, Mass. 1986)

Wigmore JH, *Evidence* 3rd edn (Little, Brown & Co., Boston, 1940) 924, 2061

Williams G, *The Proof of Guilt*, (Stevens, London, 1968)

Zander M and Henderson P , *Crown Court Study*, Royal Commission on Criminal Justice Research Study 19, (HMSO, London, 1993)

Zuckerman A, *Principles of Criminal Evidence* (Oxford University Press, Oxford, 1989)

Zuckerman A, "Relevance in legal proceedings" in (ed W Twining) *Facts in Law* (Steiner, Wiesbaden, 1983)

Zuckerman A, "Similar fact evidence - the unobservable rule" (1987) 103 L.Q.R.187

Index

Index of Authors